For Jane,

With many thanks
for the extended loan of
your *Hortus Third* while
I updated the botanical
nomenclature in this
book. Ginger

THE ONCE
AND FUTURE
GARDENER

GARDEN WRITING
FROM THE GOLDEN AGE
OF MAGAZINES:
1900 – 1940

The
ONCE&FUTURE
GARDENER

EDITED AND WITH AN INTRODUCTION BY

VIRGINIA TUTTLE CLAYTON

DAVID R. GODINE · PUBLISHER
Boston, Massachusetts

First published in 2000 by
DAVID R. GODINE, PUBLISHER
Box 450
Jaffrey, New Hampshire 03452
website: www.godine.com

Library of Congress Cataloging-in-Publication Data
The once and future gardener: garden writing fron the golden age of
magazines, 1900–1940 / edited by Virginia Tuttle Clayton. -- 1st ed.
p. cm.
ISBN 1-56792-102-7 (hardcover)
1. Gardening. 2. Gardens. I. Clayton, Virginia Tuttle, 1946– .
SB455.3.053 1999
635.9--dc21 99-25661
CIP

First hardcover printing, 2000

This book was printed on acid-free paper
Printed in the United States of America

Designed by Dede Cummings

Contents

For Jim, Kerry, Amy, and Katherine:
the next generation of gardeners.
Long may they dig.

PREFACE

ꙮꙮꙮꙮꙮ

🌱 ONE EVENING about a decade ago I discovered to my surprise that gardening articles written for early twentieth-century American magazines make excellent reading today. Researching depictions of "old-fashioned" gardens in works of art from around the turn of the century, I had come to the Library of Congress in hopes of unearthing historical data about these gardens in popular journals of that period.[1] I was delighted to find many more articles than I had expected, articles on all kinds of gardening subjects. It is with considerable embarrassment that I must now admit that I was surprised at how interesting they were, but on that day it was an exciting revelation. I was soon completely distracted from the research project that had brought me to the library. Instead, I was reading articles that appealed to me as a gardener. I wanted to study these articles carefully because they offered so much useful information. I also appreciated how beautifully the articles were written, and most of all, I was amazed that nearly one hundred years ago their authors were thoroughly conversant in what I had mistakenly assumed were strictly late-twentieth-century gardening enthusiasms and concerns.

I was sure there would be other American gardeners who were unaware of this trove of superb writings and who would find these articles as intriguing and edifying as I did. Thus began the long process of finding, studying, and choosing among them: trying to make as systematic and comprehensive a search as possible through early magazines that might have garden articles, identifying the ones that looked most promising, and later agonizing over which among the many hundreds of candidates would collectively make the best anthology.

The project, although time consuming, has been very rewarding. Not only have I garnered excellent gardening skills and design principles, but after immersing myself in these articles for a while I began to detect recurring themes and ideas, to see that there was far more of value than just fine gardening instructions. I realized that the articles were teaching me something of historical significance about how gardening was part of a new, national culture in early twentieth-century America. And so what I intended to be a purely practical gardener's project has, in the end, brought me back to the history of American gardens and art — where I began ten years ago with that fateful visit to the Library of Congress — but with an entirely new and broader perspective.

After reading thousands of articles on popular gardening I now recognize how much it was raised to an art form and how very closely it was integrated with American culture in the first four decades of this century. Perhaps most important, these articles have shown me that the aesthetic ideals of deeply committed amateur gardeners — not just professional designers — are an integral and exciting part of American garden history. For the first time the kind of practical, amateur gardening recorded in popular magazines and the more scholarly history of landscape architecture and art, have begun to seem truly connected and mutually illuminating.

While this anthology may provide insights for readers interested in the history of American gardens, I am confident it will also appeal to gardeners who simply enjoy reading fine articles on their favorite pastime and might also like to become acquainted with their avocational ancestors. They will learn what the very serious gardeners of the early twentieth century knew about our shared interest and, with decades of hindsight, see how the horticultural and design preferences of their forebears formed a coherent response to the social, political, and cultural environment of their day.

In the introduction I discuss magazines and the tremendous impact they had on American gardens, particularly those of middle-class, amateur gardeners whose expertise, contributions, and opinions have rarely been examined by garden historians. I have tried to select articles for the anthology that not only represented some of the more popular approaches to ornamental gardening during this period, but would most likely be of benefit to gardeners today. I divided the book by topic into seven chapters; some of the articles might have been as suitable for one chapter as another. Capsule biographies of the authors — those, at least, whose lives and accomplishments have been recorded for posterity — precede each article, along with notes on the article's most salient points. Nearly all the authors whose articles I chose were unknown to me when I made the selection. It was only after I had decided to include an article that I began to search for information about its writer. This biographical research, although neither extensive nor exhaustive, will, I hope, provide some interesting insights into how gardening and garden writing fit into a broader cultural context. Discovering that these authors belonged to a specific, definable group of middle-class Americans made a great difference in my own understanding of what societal and artistic forces were at work in their writing.

I confronted two special challenges. The first was the extensive revision that has been brought to bear on horticultural nomenclature since these articles were first written. Often the botanical names have changed, and in these cases I have inserted the new names in brackets; where only common plant names were originally used, I have added botanical names in brackets. I have done this only the first time each plant's name appeared in the article. Apart from correcting a few typographical errors, I have otherwise left the texts exactly as they were, even though there are some inconsistencies from one article to the next in spelling, punctuation, and the use of capitalization and italics in plant names. My primary source for updating the plants' names was the *Index of Garden Plants*, based on *The New Royal Horticultural Society Dictionary of Gardening*; I also consulted *Hortus Third* and *Wyman's Gardening Encyclopedia*.[2]

The second and most vexing problem was the inadequacy of the techniques available for reproducing the articles' halftone illustrations. Practically none of the original photographs from which the halftones in the magazines were printed survive, and even with the aid of digital enhancement the quality of reproductions made from the halftones is somewhat disappointing. Nevertheless, because they were such an important part of the articles, I have included as many of the pictures as possible. I can only hope for forgiving readers who will make the necessary allowances for their occasional lack of sharp definition and who will understand why some had to be omitted.

At the conclusion of this project it is a pleasure to express my gratitude to those who have helped me along the way. I am grateful that *House Beautiful*, *House and Garden*, and *Atlantic Monthly* allowed me to reproduce materials still under copyright. Many of my colleagues at the National Gallery have offered their support and assistance. Donna Mann and Ulricke Mills read parts of the text and offered valuable suggestions. Lee Ewing, James Locke, and Dean Beasom helped with photography. Diane Russell, Frances Smyth, Mary Yakush, Gregory Jecmen, Jane Collins, Connie McCabe, Julia Thompson, and Gertrude Olivetti shared their expertise and offered encouragement. Marca Woodhams at the Horticulture Branch Library of the Smithsonian Institution, Susan Fugate at the Special Collections Department of the National Agricultural Library, and Annie Thacher at the Dumbarton Oaks Garden Library, have been extremely generous and helpful many times over. David Godine has been both patient and encouraging throughout, Dede Cummings designed the book with great style and judgment, and Marlowe Bergendoff made excellent editorial suggestions. No one, however, contributes more to one's ability to sustain work on a project like this than one's family. My husband, Michael Clayton, and my parents, Mr. and Mrs. Robert Tuttle, have been, as always, my unfailing allies.

ENDNOTES_____

1. The research was for my article, "Reminiscence and Revival: The Old-Fashioned Garden, 1890–1910," *Antiques* 137 (April 1990): 894–905.

2. *Index of Garden Plants*, ed. Mark Griffiths (Portland, Oregon, 1994), derived from *The New Royal Horticultural Society Dictionary of Gardening*, 4 vols., ed. in chief Anthony Huxley, ed. Mark Griffiths (London, 1992), *Hortus Third: A Concise Dictionary of Plants Cultivated in the United States and Canada*, initially compiled by Liberty Hyde Bailey and Ethel Zoe Bailey, revised and expanded by the staff of the Liberty Hyde Bailey Hortorium, a unit of the New York State College of Agriculture and Life Sciences, a statutory college of the State University at Cornell (New York, 1976); *Wyman's Gardening Encyclopedia*, revised and expanded edition by Donald Wyman (New York, 1977). In some cases I was unable to find the old plant names in modern compendia; these names I simply left without updating.

Introduction

MAGAZINES PUBLISHED between the turn of the century and World War II preserve an important heritage of American garden writing and provide a remarkable record of our largely forgotten past achievements as a nation of amateur gardeners. This flourishing era of garden writing began just as broad-circulation magazines were becoming our first national medium of mass communication. From the 1890s through the 1930s these periodicals reached millions of American households and were the leading force in establishing a dominant popular culture extending through all social classes and geographical regions of the United States.[1] Their many fine garden articles helped both to stimulate and direct the creative efforts of America's gardeners, whose outstanding skills and devotion to their art we should now regard as a source of pride and inspiration.

These articles are also fascinating because they reveal that American tastes and ideals in gardening were sometimes allied with broader cultural agendas. Like every other art form, gardens can often express the ideologies their creators formulate to interpret, impose order on, and control human experience. The decision to garden in a specific style, and even the selection of particular types of plants, can be tantamount to a public statement, conscious or not, of the gardener's position on the most compelling issues of the day. As the articles in this anthology will show, naturalistic "wild gardens," gardens planned to recreate the more relaxed aura of simpler, bygone days, and gardens meant to be quintessentially "American" all convey strong messages about their makers and their times.

Motivated by the conviction that their hobby was both an elixir to ease the trauma of modern life and an opportunity to express their social and cultural enlightenment, Americans from the turn of the century to the Second World War gardened with extraordinary intensity. They zealously promoted the notion that gardening, like photography, was a highly democratic form of aesthetic self-expression, one that dedicated, gifted amateurs — perhaps even more than professionals — could elevate to new levels of artistic refinement.[2] Since magazines were the forum in which these devoted amateur gardeners articulated and shared their ideas, and since professionals relied on them to communicate with amateurs, gardening articles from the early twentieth century were typically endowed with rich content and a wonderfully appealing style.

This anthology ends with World War II because that momentous event signaled an important turning point in the history of American gardening and garden writing. While World War I and the Great Depression also affected American gardens, these changes were most apparent in the estate gardens of the upper classes; significant transformation in the gardening styles of most middle-class Americans occurred only after the Second World War. Even then garden journalism did not undergo instant and dramatic revision. Some of the same writers, their ideas about gardening basically unaltered, continued to contribute articles to magazines. But ultimately gardening tastes were influenced by the fundamental reorganization of domestic life and housing in the decades following the war. The lifestyle of Americans changed radically, as did their ideas about their country's position, politically and culturally, relative to the rest of the world. Television became the prevailing medium in American homes in the second half of the century, but gardening did not gain very much presence in the medium until quite recently. Magazines remained a more important source of garden information during the latter half of the century, but their articles, so clearly charting the new directions in American gardening, merit representation in an anthology of their own.

And now at the turn of the twenty-first century a new technology, the Internet, is increasing almost beyond comprehension our ability to disseminate information, exchange ideas, and generally promote communication among gardeners — even more than mass-circulation magazines did one hundred years ago, at the turn of the twentieth century. The onset of this remarkable new age of communication, still so unfathomable to some of us, makes a study of gardening and the revolution in communications that occurred at the last turn of the century seem particularly worthy and timely.

The Literature of Amateur Gardening

Around 1900 an attractive new crop of gardening and shelter magazines began to offer beautifully illustrated articles. Other types of journals, including literary, arts, and women's magazines, also started to publish fine garden essays in unprecedented numbers. A high level of horticultural and design expertise was the norm among their authors, who included some of the leading landscape architects and designers of the time as well as some of the best-known garden writers. But magazines also published articles by avid hobbyists who gardened with tremendous energy and commitment. They wrote eloquently and knowledgeably, often expressing their ideas in a charmingly personal and humorous style, and they were wonderfully generous in sharing information that remains remarkably pertinent today. For early twentieth-century readers these articles had an increased visual impact and sense of immediacy because many were photographically illustrated by the newly developed technique of halftone printing. These were among the first articles to have photographic illustrations, and this added graphic component afforded their audience a new and stimulating reading experience.

Since magazines were, starting in the 1890s, the first national medium of mass communication, they wielded significant influence over the country's gardening tastes and practices and Americans' perception of themselves as a nation of cultivators of the soil. There may have been a surge of interest in gardening in the early twentieth century, as many people at the time believed, or perhaps magazines had simply succeeded in creating the illusion of one. Even if it was not true that more Americans than ever before had taken up gardening, a fact that would be very difficult to establish with certainty today, those who did went about it with greater publicity and, to the disdain of some contemporaries, a keener eye to fashion and a heightened sense of aesthetics. Anyone who had access to magazines, which was just about everyone, could keep current with the latest gardening canons of taste and feel motivated to measure up to, and even help elevate, national standards.

The articles in this anthology were written for the benefit of Americans who did their own gardening — personally designing, planting, and caring for their beloved "bowers of bliss." One writer frankly limited the audience he intended to address:

> This article is not for the people who leave their gardens to the care of the hired man . . . And, moreover, the owner must belong to that demented clan, who go out before breakfast to see the new peony buds, and who come in from [the] office by way of the garden to see what the sun has opened during the day.[3]

Much of what these amateurs knew was learned, or could have been learned, from magazines. Either for professionals with a comfortable living and a relatively large garden, or for urban workers with small backyards in the city, popular magazines were truly the information medium of the gardening middle class.

The period covered in this anthology corresponds to what has been characterized as the "country place era" in America, when the great fortunes acquired during the expansion of industrialism following the Civil War led to the construction of splendid mansions surrounded by gardens of equal grandeur.⁴ Writers considering the landscape architecture of this period have almost exclusively described and analyzed these grand gardens, designed by distinguished landscape architects and installed and maintained at considerable expense. The gardens of middle-class Americans have been relatively neglected, probably in part because even fewer of these modest efforts have survived than estate gardens.⁵ Photographs, plans, and written documents may record crucial evidence about the now-vanished gardens of the wealthy, but far fewer written records systematically preserve the appearance of the lost, homemade gardens of the greater middle class. Illustrated magazine articles that addressed amateur gardeners — and were often written by them and accompanied by their own photographs — go a long way toward filling this gap. These articles add significantly to our otherwise incomplete knowledge of an important period in American gardening. They offer revealing descriptions of what was considered desirable in a garden and explanations of why that was so. Highly articulate records of their contemporary culture, they prove that to truly understand the garden history of this era, one must recognize the humble achievements along with the magnificent as complementary, interconnecting parts of a horticultural whole.

These articles also confirm that late-twentieth-century developments in garden design and plant selection are not as original and "of our time" as many of us have believed. Our most contemporary designs and inventive use of plants, such as the supposedly new "natural garden" with its bold incorporation of "previously despised" natives, are not new at all; they are simply enjoying a new cycle of popularity, probably motivated by a recurrence of similar cultural circumstances. Two or three generations ago American gardeners advocated many of the same styles that we now sometimes incorrectly assume were recently created and promoted the very same plants we think we are the first to rescue from horticultural oblivion. Our gardening forebears were skillful and intelligent gardeners, and it is wasteful indeed to neglect what their experience can teach us. Our current community of like-minded gardeners finds a surprising number of kindred spirits in the generations of our grandparents and great-grandparents. To learn from them through their written legacy can be an inspiring experience.

Unfortunately this network of written garden communication that reached millions of American households in the early twentieth century is even less accessible to most of us today than are copies of vintage garden books. Publishers have recently reissued a number of the best early books, and original editions are sometimes still available in used book shops. But old magazines, particularly in complete sets, are much harder to find. Not only are they are more fragile than books, they were generally considered disposable. Few readers made the effort to accumulate and carefully preserve successive issues over time. Even in public libraries it is not always easy to find early issues of journals that are primary sources for garden articles. Where a large collection of periodicals is available, gardening articles appear in so many monthly issues of so many different magazines — from *The Atlantic Monthly* to *The Ladies' Home Journal* — that considerable time and patience are required to locate and read through a representative sample. This anthology attempts to rectify the situation by making available a selected portion of an important yet relatively hard-to-locate body of writings, and by providing a bibliography of articles for further reading. These efforts, however, can hardly begin to suggest the vast riches still unreclaimed in magazines from the first half of the twentieth century.

A History of Magazines and Gardening

There seems to be a special affinity between magazines and gardening. Even today, magazines more fully cover our nation's most popular pastime than any other mass medium — although the Internet seems to be quickly gaining ground. The partnership of magazines and gardening is long-standing. It began around 1800 in England as working people enjoyed increased prosperity and purchased homes in the suburbs that they were eager to embellish with gardens. Demand for information on gardening grew, and publishers were able to meet that need thanks to the invention of new, less expensive printing methods. One of the most important of the early nineteenth-century horticultural journals in England was John Claudius Loudon's *Gardener's Magazine*. Loudon took his role as instructor very seriously, acknowledging an imperative "to correct or improve the conduct or condition of gardeners or others connected with gardening."[6] *Gardener's Magazine* had a tremendous impact on how gardeners practiced their art, set the style for subsequent magazines of this type, and inspired a host of imitators and competitors.

In the United States, agricultural journals that included articles on gardening were already fairly inexpensive and in relatively wide circulation by the early nineteenth century.[7] *The Horticulturist*, edited by Andrew Jackson Downing (1815–1852), elevated horticultural journalism in the United States to a new level, in many ways emulating Loudon's prestigious magazine.[8] Downing was editor from the magazine's start in 1846, and he set himself the noble task of reforming and upgrading the standards of American gardening. For him, there was a direct correlation between the quality of landscape design and the very quality of life, but his most enduring legacy was, as observed by Neil Harris, "his identification of aesthetic reform with a set of ethical and social ideas."[9] This reformist attitude, based on the premise that human character could be perfected through contact with natural beauty, was to persist in garden magazines well into the twentieth century. Sparsely illustrated with wood engravings of plants, vignettes of gardens, and other related subjects, *The Horticulturist* achieved a circulation of 2,000 with its earliest issues, which was quite impressive for the time.[10] After Downing's accidental death in 1852, *The Horticulturist* was sold by its publisher and subsequently merged with a series of other gardening journals to become part of the complex genealogy of later American gardening magazines.[11]

By the 1890s dramatic technological advances in printing and photography brought about a true revolution in communications. The invention of the rotary press, linotype typesetting, and halftone reproduction, along with congressional legislation granting reduced mailing rates for certain printed materials, greatly reduced the cost of printing, illustrating, and circulating magazines.[12] American businesses, attracted by the enormous national audience these publications were reaching, began to buy more advertising space for their products, bringing in additional revenue.[13] Publishers were able to offer magazines at much reduced prices: only ten or even five cents instead of thirty-five, which had been the price of the most successful and influential magazines of the earlier nineteenth century. The drop in price further allowed magazines to reach a vast new group of readers. Although the editors of the new mass-circulation magazines imitated to a certain extent the earlier, "genteel" magazines, they also began to adjust the content and tone of their journals to suit what they perceived to be the taste of their modern subscribers. The articles were shorter and written with greater stylistic vitality, and they covered a wider range of subjects of general as well as more current interest.

Photographic illustrations made the magazines even more lively and appealing. The halftone method of reproducing photographs dramatically changed the appearance and attraction of magazines around the turn of the century. This method was the product of a series of inventions that culminated in a means by which a single run through the press could simultaneously print photographs and text on the same page.[14] Immediately prior to the development of the halftone, the process most frequently used to reproduce imagery in magazines was wood engraving, which was quite expensive. The handwork required for each wood-engraved illustration cost as much as $300, while mechanically produced halftones cost only about $20.[15] By using halftones, editors were able to increase the number of pictures and integrate them with the text, making these journals visually much more exciting. Earlier horticultural articles illustrated with wood engravings not only had fewer pictures, but these were usually limited to botanical depictions of plants or very simply rendered images of gardens. It did not take long for magazine editors to recognize the new possibilities offered by photography. Lush views of gardens began to appear in many — although by no means all — articles, adding greatly to both the communication of information and the sensuous appeal of the written descriptions they accompanied.[16]

A number of different sources were available to supply magazines with

photographic illustrations. Sometimes an author produced both the manu-
script and photographs for an article, especially when that author was
writing about his or her own garden. But when, more typically, an author
submitted a text without illustrations, an editor might either commission a
professional photographer to produce appropriate pictures or purchase
suitable images from a photographer's existing inventory of pictures. Commercial photographers continually expanded their picture files, amassing an
assortment of highly appealing garden views for a market that demanded a
constant and ready supply. It was not unusual for an editor to use pictures
from the files of more than one photographer in a single article; nor was it
unusual for the same picture to appear in more than one article over a period
of time, since a photographer might sell the right to reproduce it to several
different clients — not only editors of magazines but also book publishers
and producers of seed and nursery catalogues. Although it was usually the
article that was selected first, initiating a search for proper illustrations,
occasionally it was the photographs that inspired the article. When a
professional photographer offered an editor an especially fine set of garden
pictures, the editor might either commission an author to write an article to
accompany them or use them as a "photographic essay" with descriptive cap-
tions. Standards for attribution were not consistent, and often there was no
credit line identifying the photographer.

The invention of a full-color halftone process made it economically possible
to print color imagery on magazine covers, and gardens were a favored subject
on the covers of some of the magazines represented here. Rather than color
photographs made directly of gardens, these cover images were often photographic reproductions of artists' depictions of gardens. Anna Peck, student of
American Impressionist painters John Twachtman and Willard Metcalf,
painted the garden scene reproduced for the cover of *The New Country Life* in
March 1918 (plate 4). Another charming illustration of a garden, this one by
Matilda Browne, member of a colony of American Impressionists working in
Old Lyme, Connecticut, appeared on the March 1924 cover of the same maga-
zine (plate 2).[17] These garden scenes are remarkably similar to those depicted
by late nineteenth- and early twentieth-century English watercolorists, artists
whose work was exhibited in this country, reproduced in articles in popular
American magazines, and displayed on magazine covers. In June 1909, for
example, the most widely circulated magazine in the United States, *The Ladies'
Home Journal*, reproduced on its cover a watercolor of an English garden by
British artist Lilian Stannard (plate 3).

An even more important impact on the design of American magazine
covers came from nineteenth-century European advertising posters, following
a stylistic progression from the Art Nouveau that typified commercial illustration in the first two decades of the twentieth century, to the Art Deco
popular in the 1920s and 1930s.[18] By the 1890s highly appealing advertising

posters had become common not only in Europe but New York, and by the turn of the century commercial illustrators in the United States were imitating posters when designing magazine covers — which in turn functioned as advertisements for the magazines they adorned.

Skillfully employing the compelling visual language of commercial design to represent idealized garden scenes, frequently English in style, these cover images became flawless icons of a collective American dream garden. Magazine editors knew that potential purchasers would find these garden fantasies irresistible, that a wonderful garden illustration on the cover would entice customers to buy a copy. These covers could be studied today not only as visual records of popular garden styles and features but as pictorializations of the abstract qualities — the "atmosphere" — that early twentieth-century Americans most wanted in a garden. Charming cottage gardens, quaint gates, paths, and walled gardens, sundials and dovecotes, sweet vignettes of spring planting, and the gardener pausing to watch brilliant autumn leaves gently drifting toward the dahlia bed; these idyllic scenes are what editors knew would sell their magazines (plates 1-21).

Photographic illustrations, lower prices, and faster-paced writing that addressed timelier subject matter all helped increase the popularity of magazines. The years 1885 to 1905 launched approximately 7,500 new magazines in the United States, although only about half of them lasted very long.[19] Survivors among the new magazines included some that were more expensive and that sought a more specific than general readership. The ones represented here often fall into this category. The prosperity and cultural clout of these more costly and specialized titles were in part the result of the popularity and power that the entire medium derived from the remarkable success of the inexpensive, broad-circulation periodicals. Magazines were now all the rage. Americans in great numbers and from all stations in life and regions of the country had begun to look to them as a primary source of information about whatever topics most interested them.

The Authors and the Influence of the Arts and Crafts Movement

A wide range of middle-class Americans read the magazines represented in this anthology, but it was primarily educated professionals at the middle to upper strata of the middle class who wrote the articles. These authors worked for a living and, although they were for the most part financially comfortable and secure, they were not rich. Biographical research on the authors whose articles are included in this volume shows that they were employed as academics, architects, clergymen, sociologists, artists, photographers, writers, editors, dieticians, and librarians, as well as landscape architects and designers. During the first two decades of the century many of them were political Progressives and supported such causes as women's suffrage, the creation of national parks, and beautification of cities. What these Progressives had in common was a desire to reform the abuses of America's new urban-industrial society and to create a more humane environment in the United States — primarily through education and, only to a lesser degree, through governmental intervention. Authors who wrote in the twenties and thirties maintained many of the idealistic notions that originated in the decades before the First World War.[20]

The authors of these articles were part of the professional middle class, a group that achieved cultural leadership in the United States by the turn of the century, replacing the "genteel elite" that had maintained command throughout most of the 1800s. As Kathleen Pyne has observed, middle-class intellectuals were "the movers and shakers within the dominant class . . . who controlled the social and educational institutions responsible for shaping discourse and reproducing social hierarchies."[21] Among their fellow citizens they were the most immediately involved in and affected by developments in the arts and culture. Prompted by the moralistic, reforming spirit of these current movements, they felt an obligation to educate and uplift those as yet unacquainted with these refining influences; with magazines as a powerful pulpit, their ideas subsequently infiltrated the rest of American society.

The gardening taste of this newly empowered middle class was formed primarily by the Arts and Crafts movement begun in England under the inspiration of William Morris and, ultimately, John Ruskin and the Aesthetic movement.[22] To accommodate American ideologies and conditions, the Arts and Crafts movement changed in some respects when it crossed the Atlantic, primarily becoming less politically radical, but its mission remained essentially the same. As part of a program of righting social wrongs, it sought both to democratize art and to elevate the aesthetic standards of homes — and even the conduct of daily life and labor — by endowing them with a simple, tasteful beauty. A new appreciation for unadorned elegance would replace the opulence and excess, as well as the shoddy, machine-made products, that had characterized the Victorian era.

This aesthetic applied to gardening as well as other creative pursuits; it focused on eliminating the garishly colored, intricately patterned flower beds, and the overblown hybrid plants gardeners had favored earlier in the nineteenth century. Arts and Crafts garden designers, first in Britain and later in America, preferred flower gardens with harmonious and subtle color schemes consisting of mainly herbaceous plants. They also promoted the kind of close connection between house and garden that they traced to the seventeenth-century, formal gardens of England and America and hoped to make modern gardens a part of routine family life. They particularly endorsed the use of indigenous plants and local construction materials.[23] If there was a single, predominant theme in articles written by Americans inspired by the Arts and

Crafts movement, it was the desire to make American gardens "livable" —
welcoming and comfortable outdoor spaces filled with thriving plants,
designed for constant, private use by their owners. Although the movement
as a whole lasted only until the First World War, the principles it introduced
endured for decades, and recurred in gardening articles of the 1920s and
1930s. Every serious American gardener and garden writer seems, for example, to have known something about the work of British Arts and Crafts
designers Gertrude Jekyll and William Robinson, whose profound impact on
American gardens in the first forty years of the twentieth century is evident in
the articles collected in this anthology.

Apart from a new set of general gardening principles, which were quite
revolutionary in their day, the Arts and Crafts movement also popularized
particular types of gardens. The most important for amateur American
gardeners were the "old-fashioned" and the "wild" gardens, although the basic
design principles of the great formal gardens of the Arts and Crafts era were
also applied to the smaller gardens of the middle classes. There are separate
chapters in this anthology devoted to each of the three catagories.

Throughout these articles readers will note passing references to old-
fashioned gardens and flowers. Since at least the early 1850s Victorian poetry
and Pre-Raphaelite painting had romantically celebrated traditional English
flowers and gardens, and the Arts and Crafts movement in Britain actively
promoted their revival.[24] In 1859 William Morris, leader of the movement,
made what is likely the first new "old-fashioned" garden for his home in Kent,
the well-known and highly influential Red House, fittingly sited in an ancient
orchard of old, gnarled fruit trees. Morris and his Red House had such authority over the taste of what Wendy Hitchmough calls "the artistic middle class"
of England that the old-fashioned garden quickly became an indispensable
"fashion accessory" for these earnest aesthetes.[25]

Since old-fashioned gardens were cherished by both cultural leaders and
the stylish middle class of Britain and were often depicted in trans-Atlantic
publications, it is not surprising that a rhapsodic affection for them soon
spread to the United States.[26] By the 1870s American middle-class, amateur
gardeners had also begun to relish old gardens and flowers and to deliberately, self-consciously make new gardens with references to the old. Here, as in
Britain, an old-fashioned garden became a highly fashionable accoutrement for
the artistic, amateur gardener. Americans naturally emulated old American
gardens — although the British cottage garden also served as a model — and
garden writers in the United States often described old-fashioned gardens as a
distinctly American type. However, it is important to remember that the
enthusiastic attitude toward gardens of bygone days and the almost
worshipful desire to reproduce them — especially their quaint flowers and
homey, relaxed "atmosphere" — were imported with the British Arts and
Crafts movement and were not American innovations.

In early twentieth-century America, where the colonial revival was in full swing, old-fashioned gardens were sometimes identified with formal colonial gardens.[27] As in Britain, however, they were most often ambiguous in their historical reference. Old-fashioned gardens, also called "grandmothers' gardens," were not associated with a specific, commonly agreed-upon moment from the past. This is demonstrated by the fact that the author of one "grandmother's garden" article in this anthology was old enough *to be* the grandparent — or even great-grandparent — of the author of another such article.[28] It was the wholesome and congenial "atmosphere" of an old garden overflowing with flowers that many Americans hoped to recreate, not a clearly defined period style.[29] Magazine articles gave wide circulation to the conviction that American gardeners had once been content with fewer varieties and simpler flowers and that their gardens were quiet, modest havens of peace, much loved and habitually used by their owners in the course of daily life. Garden writers repeatedly issued fervent pleas for an American garden style that would be simple, unpretentious, and livable: a garden like "grandmother's" that would serve as an intimate gathering place for family and friends, protected from the discord of the outside world.

Naturalistic "wild" gardens, designed to emulate an idealized concept of nature, were the second major garden type made fashionable among middle-class gardeners by the Arts and Crafts movement. The idea of the wild garden, like that of the old-fashioned garden, originated in Great Britain, and perhaps ultimately in the "picturesque" gardens of the eighteenth and early nineteenth centuries. Some American authors saw the work of Frederick Law Olmsted as an important precedent for this style in the United States. But it was William Robinson's 1870 book, *The Wild Garden*, that most helped to acquaint gardeners in the United States with its basic precepts: naturalizing large quantities of plants and making informal gardens that looked more like wild nature than carefully cultivated spaces. Robinson's book gave some encouragement to the use of native plants but mainly insisted that even exotic plants could be naturalized in wild gardens. A popular desire for these gardens easily took root on this side of the Atlantic, and by the turn of the century it flourished mightily in the hearts of amateur gardeners and garden writers. Here, however, the wild garden soon grew to be a more insistently nationalistic artifact than it had been in Great Britain.

The powerful current of cultural nationalism that gathered strength from before the turn of the century through the 1930s elicited a collective yearning in the United States for a uniquely American art and culture, as well as an American garden style. Despite its origin in Britain, the concept of the wild garden seemed to offer an appropriate format for the development of a distinctly American garden. Perceived as such, it evolved to suit American needs. Specifically, native plants and an appreciation of the natural, American landscape became essential elements in designing the wild garden in the

United States.[30] Many Americans believed they could best achieve the goal of an American garden style by using native plants, and magazines offered an abundant supply of articles about them. Among the large congregation of American native plant enthusiasts, many contended that gardeners also needed to arrange these indigenous plants in a manner that would imitate "the spirit of American nature at her best."

An article written for *Country Life in America* by Nellie Doubleday in 1908 explained why the natural garden was suitable as the quintessential American type. In agreement with other writers of her time, Doubleday subscribed to the notion that Americans were mainly of Anglo-Saxon descent and therefore heir to the affinity for nature that nineteenth-century romantic theory held to be an essential part of the Anglo-Saxon character. Our preference for gardens of native plants, designed to evoke the native landscape, and the suitability of this kind of garden as our national style, were thus the legacy of our British origins. Doubleday stated that the natural garden "accords with our racial temperament, therefore it is destined to become the dominant style of gardening here for the same reason that the English language prevails on this continent."[31]

Americans' fascination with British gardens sometimes affected their notion of how to design an American wild garden of native plants. A frequently chosen alternate plan to following the look of the native landscape in making the definitively American garden was to emulate English garden design — especially that of cottage gardens — and simply substitute our robust, native plants for those used abroad. As one article in this anthology concludes: "It is through American plants that we shall be able to get that intangible charm of English planting . . . We shall have as a result a truly American garden."[32]

Judging from the magazine articles they wrote, the gardening middle class of America appears to have considered the wild garden and the old-fashioned garden their special domain, and many seem to have believed that a taste for these gardens proved their aesthetic superiority over the rich.[33] The "foolish rich" might spend fortunes on their grandiose Italian gardens, but these were commonly considered an affront to American nature and tradition, as well as to the finer taste of sophisticated amateur gardeners. Naturalistic wild gardens might even be weedy — sometimes so much the better. To allow handsome weeds to grow in one's garden and to be capable of appreciating their more subtle charms could be, for some gardeners, a mark of distinction, a sign of high sympathy with nature — something they were sure the insensitive rich could never comprehend.[34] Similarly, old-fashioned gardens seem to have designated their owners as part of a moral elite, preservers of traditional values against the increasing onslaught of both the vulgar new rich and the recent waves of immigrants from eastern and southern Europe.

The Country Life movement that flourished during the early decades of the twentieth century expressed a popular confidence that nature offered much-needed solace to anxious, modern souls — an idea that had roots in the previous century and had manifested itself in Frederick Law Olmsted's landscape designs for public parks. The publicity surrounding the Country Life movement further encouraged a back-to-nature mentality among recently urbanized, post-industrial Americans.[35] This outdoors sentiment was in part revealed as a growing enthusiasm for gardening, particularly gardening that aspired to create naturalistic enclaves imitating wild nature. Romantically recalling earlier generations of Americans who had lived in closer association with the wilderness, early twentieth-century garden writers frequently cited Henry David Thoreau as an authority in their articles, although the communion with nature they prescribed was more for modern, therapeutic purposes — to mend fraying nerves and fragile health — than for the transcendental elevation of the spirit.[36] Articles encouraged gardeners to create an environment conducive to such salutary experience within the private confines of their domestic realms, to "bring nature to their doorstep," with native plants and with naturalistic wild gardens.

The perceived need for such a restorative environment was endemic in America during the first four decades of the twentieth century.[37] According to garden writings of the day, an intimate, "livable" garden designed with old-fashioned charm and simplicity, or one that incorporated native plants to emulate the effects of the natural American landscape, would provide the type of soothing domestic space that could counteract the ill effects of contemporary, frenzied life and restore unnerved Americans to a wholesome, contented state of mind and body. In fact any garden would serve — although simple, old-fashioned and wild gardens, with their favored associations, might prove especially effective. Furthermore, physically performing the garden work oneself would be the surest possible remedy for the malaise of modern stress and would convey the greatest possible joy to the gardener. A 1911 article in *The Craftsman* magazine concluded, in complete agreement with current popular opinion, that "we are an overwrought people, too eager about everything except peace and contentment," and it proposed gardens as a cure to this affliction: "In the garden the silence teaches the restless spirit peace, and Nature broods over man and heals the wounds of the busy world . . . And so here in America of all things we need gardens."[38]

The Magazines

The garden articles brought together in this book originally appeared in conjunction with writings on politics, natural history, literature, art criticism, and the domestic sciences of the day — as well as numerous related garden articles and some pertinent editorial pieces. Before reading them here, excerpted from their original contexts, it is worth considering the magazines from which they derived: where, when, and by whom these journals were published and edited, what kinds of articles they typically included, and what their circulation figures and their social and artistic agendas were.

The *Atlantic Monthly* and *Scribner's Magazine* were two of the leading magazines of the nineteenth-century "genteel" tradition, representing a type of journal characterized as being aloof, "leisurely in habit, literary in tone, retrospective rather than timely . . . a serene observer of the passing scene"[39] — the very antithesis of the aggressive, new magazine of the turn of the century. The *Atlantic* began publication in 1857, closely associated with Boston's intellectual upper class, and has generally been recognized as America's foremost literary magazine.[40] Ellery Sedgwick was editor from 1909 to 1938, through most of the period covered in this anthology, and he helped bring the *Atlantic* more up to date.[41] He had previously been employed by *McClure's*,[42] one of the archetypal "modern" magazines, and he modified the content of the *Atlantic* by including more articles about current events, politics, and science. The circulation of the *Atlantic* was 14,000 in 1899 and 25,000 in 1907; by 1921 Sedgwick had succeeded in raising it to 100,000 and by 1930 to 130,000. [43]

There were some fine writings on both nature and gardening in the *Atlantic*, in addition to literature and other subjects. Bradford Torrey, for example, who edited Thoreau's *Journal* in 1906, was a frequent contributor, as was the widely revered nature writer John Burroughs. Candace Wheeler, a significant figure in the Arts and Crafts movement in America, published her important three-part article "Content in a Garden" in the *Atlantic* in 1900.[44] This article expressed the awe of nature and the belief in the therapeutic powers of gardens that dominated much of American garden writing during the succeeding decades. In it she recounted:

> When I began to dig and plant, I little knew the joy which would grow out of the soil, and descend from the skies, and gather from far-off places and times to gladden my soul; but to-day, as I walk therein, or sit in the spicy shadow of its pair of fir trees, and think what it has done for me, I feel that untroubled happiness begins and ends within it; that it is truly the Land of Content. [45]

Some of the most delightful articles in the *Atlantic*, however, were the short pieces that appeared in the Contributors' Club, a department begun in 1877 by editor William Dean Howells, and it is from this regular column that the *Atlantic* articles in this anthology were gathered.[46] The club was a great success and lasted until 1942 when the combination of the Great Depression and the Second World War reportedly made its humorous resources run dry. Howells had reserved this part of the magazine for "writers who have minds upon any ethical or aesthetic subject briefly to free them . . . , and while [*Atlantic*] will not wittingly suffer a personal spite to be wreaked, [it] will especially welcome the expression of intellectual grudges of every sort."[47] There was, it seems, no shortage of grudges that in one way or another involved gardening. These articles were printed anonymously to protect the writers' freedom of expression.

Scribner's Monthly began publication in New York in 1870, became *Century Magazine* in 1881, then started independently again as *Scribner's Magazine* in 1887, with Edward Livermore Burlingame serving as editor until 1914.[48] It ceased publication in 1939. Two advantages that *Scribner's* had over the *Atlantic* were its lower cost — twenty-five rather than thirty-five cents — and the fact that it was illustrated. By 1891 its circulation reached 110,000; in 1910 it peaked at 215,000, but by 1924 it fell back to 70,000.[49] Like the *Atlantic, Scribner's* was less interested in how-to garden articles than those with a more literary or philosophical approach.

One article that typified *Scribner's* taste in garden writing was "The American Garden," by George Washington Cable, reporting on an amateur garden competition held in Northampton, Massachusetts, in 1903.[50] Cable was a successful writer, born in New Orleans in 1844. His 1904 article summarized the ideas of the intellectual, upper-middle class regarding the importance of improving the gardening practices of all Americans, including working people, and asserted that the goal of these improvements would be the development of a national American garden style. Cable, like many of his peers, firmly believed that the gardeners of the greater middle class would, if given some aesthetic guidance, succeed in developing "what we have not yet quite evolved, the American garden." This national garden style would proudly epitomize our citizens' best traits: "our strong individuality and self-assurance, our sense of unguarded security, our affability and unexclusiveness." This article illustrates the missionary zeal with which some of the most influential magazines of the early twentieth century were presenting the art of gardening as essential to the nation's future.

Scribner's also occasionally published articles on gardening in its Point of View section, the counterpart of the *Atlantic's* Contributors' Club. Again, it is the shorter, wittier pieces from this part of the magazine that are the most amusing to read today. Garden humor has not changed substantially over the intervening decades.

The Independent and *The Outlook* both began as weekly, religious periodicals, *The Independent* in 1848 and *The Outlook* in 1870, and both were published in New York.[51] They were politically progressive and became more secular in the course of time. Designed to appeal to a family readership, they offered a number of different departments to cover a variety of interests; both, for example, had a section devoted to farming and gardening. Both also included literature — *The Independent* publishing poems by Celia Thaxter, well known today for her garden on Appledore Island off the coast of Maine, and her book about that garden[52] — and articles on news and current events written by leading, progressive statesmen of the day. In both there were also important writings on nature and on art criticism that considered ideas influencing contemporary landscape painting.[53] As in the *Atlantic* and *Scribner's*, the proximity of these articles put gardening into a context that strengthened its association with progressive politics, natural history, and current literature and art. Circulation of *The Independent* was up to 60,000 by 1916, the year it absorbed *Harper's Weekly.*[54] *The Outlook's* figures were 30,000 in 1894 and 100,000 in 1902.[55] The two magazines declined in circulation in the 1920s and tried to regain strength by merging in 1928 as *The Outlook and Independent.* The last issue was published in 1932. Like those in *Atlantic* and *Scribner's*, their garden articles were more likely to present thoughtful opinions about popular approaches to gardening, or reflections about how developments in gardening mirrored the progress of society, than to offer horticultural advice. *Outlook's* editorial column, The Spectator, presented wonderfully appealing and sometimes humorous pieces on gardening, like those of *Atlantic's* Contributors' Club and *Scribner's* The Point of View.

Among the many magazines that frequently published articles on gardening, *The Ladies' Home Journal* had the widest distribution.[56] Despite its gender-specific title, it was read by both men and women; during the First World War, in fact, it was the third most popular magazine among American soldiers.[57] In 1889 Edward Bok became editor and the circulation stood at 440,000.[58] By 1903 it reached the one million mark, and by 1919 it climbed to two million.[59] As editor of *The Ladies' Home Journal* Bok was one of the most influential individuals in the country, particularly, though not exclusively, in the domestic realm. From the start his mission was to reform American life by improving homes and gardens. He noted the satisfaction he felt with having left his mark in his autobiography, strangely writing of himself in the third person:

> Bok had begun with the exterior of the small American house and made an impression upon it; he had brought the love of flowers into the hearts of thousands of small householders who had never thought they could have an artistic garden within a small area; he had changed the lines of furniture, and he had put better art on the walls of these homes. He had conceived a full-rounded scheme, and he had carried it out.[60]

Gardening had always been one of the subjects regularly covered in *The Ladies' Home Journal.* The style of these articles was sometimes less sophisticated than that of other magazines that were aimed at a more educated, intellectual readership, but they served to carry the gardening tastes of the time and information about horticultural techniques to an enormous number of households. In an article she wrote for *The Ladies' Home Journal*, Nellie Doubleday sought to convey her message in somewhat simplified terms, but it was essentially the same message — the desirability of gardening with native plants — that she carried to her more elite audience in other magazines.[61] In *The*

Ladies' Home Journal Doubleday stressed that it was economical to use native plants, and that intelligence would be a factor in recognizing their usefulness:

> The bald ugliness of many a village schoolhouse and church, the hard lines of too many farmers' homes and poor people's cabins . . . might all be mercifully adorned without money . . . if the possibilities of free flora were understood by indifferent, because unintelligent, people . . . A wild garden . . . is the garden for the million as well as the millionaire. [62]

Woman's Home Companion was a close competitor of *The Ladies' Home Journal.*[63] It began life humbly as a mail-order monthly in the 1870s and gradually grew in stature until Gertrude Lane, editor from 1911 to 1941, made it the leading women's magazine of the 1930s with a circulation of three million.[64] During the 1930s Eleanor Roosevelt was a regular contributor and even wrote an article on gardening for the March 1935 issue. Since she did not actually have a garden of her own she wrote about what she would like to grow if she did have one. She confided that she would like to have shrubs and flowers constantly in bloom, "but looking as casual and as much like wild flowers as possible," and that "no garden would be complete which did not have some old-fashioned yellow rosebushes."[65] Grace Tabor, an outstanding garden writer, was a frequent contributor to the *Companion* during the 1930s and wrote many fine, thoughtful articles, though usually brief and less complex than those she wrote for other magazines. She also frequently made her *Companion* garden the subject of her articles.

Around the turn of the century, several new magazines endeavored to cater profitably to the increasing enthusiasm for nature and the countryside, and foremost among them was *Country Life in America* — clearly modeled after the British publication *Country Life* — a thirty-five-cent publication that began life in 1901 and survived until 1942.[66] *Country Life in America* was published by Doubleday, Page and Company, first in New York, and later Garden City, Long Island. Doubleday hired Liberty Hyde Bailey, a renowned botanist from Cornell University, as editor of *Country Life*. Bailey, who only held this post for a short time, was also chairman of Theodore Roosevelt's Country Life Commission, appointed to study means of promoting rural life in America.[67] The editor of another Doubleday publication, *The Garden Magazine*, reflecting on the first eleven years of *Country Life*, wrote in 1912:

> This first decade of the new century has seen some rather remarkable achievements and advancements in the broad realm of country life. Of course, we can't pretend that we have been the cause of it; rather, we have been one of the results. *Country Life in America* was established as the organ and mouthpiece of a new movement.[68]

Country Life considered gardening one of its principal subjects. It kept its readers informed of the latest styles and printed articles on the gardens of the wealthy; one such series was called Successful American Gardens. It by no means considered itself a magazine intended solely for the upper class, however, but always included pieces on gardening that were addressed to those who were doing the work for themselves, offering instructions on how to successfully and frugally cultivate flowers, fruit, and vegetables.[69] In 1904 it offered prizes for articles submitted by amateurs relating their personal experiences in gardening and how they had benefited from reading *Country Life*. One winner, a new homeowner, told of learning to plant annuals in his first garden by reading an article on the subject in *Country Life*.[70] Another was a woman from a mining and factory town outside Pittsburgh who wrote that she had learned some useful points for designing her garden from an article about an estate garden published in the magazine the year before.[71] The publisher's civic-minded wife, Nellie, wrote about the therapeutic benefits of gardening for the middle class in a 1910 article:

> House-bound women, office-enslaved men, tired, nervous, world-weary people, compelled at last to make Nature their soul. In the soil one must dig to discover the great elixir of playfellow, find in gardening health for the body and the life.[72]

The garden editor of *Country Life in America* was Wilhelm Miller, who also served as general editor of Doubleday's publication, *The Garden Magazine*. *The Garden Magazine* started in 1905 and was undoubtedly titled to correspond to the popular British journal, *The Garden*. The two Doubleday journals promoted each other and sometimes printed notices of what was in the other magazine that month. *The Garden Magazine* was much less expensive — ten cents an issue until 1910 when it raised its price to fifteen cents — and referred to *Country Life* as its "big sister."[73] Its presentation was less luxurious, but its articles were not substantively different from those of *Country Life*, just focused exclusively on gardening. Doubleday seems to have correctly judged that there was a sufficient population of gardeners in America with enough desire for knowledge about their favorite pastime to support both publishing ventures. Miller made *The Garden Magazine* a periodical with a cause. Enlisting Americans to do their part in improving American garden craft was his most consuming passion, and he devoted himself to it like a holy crusade.[74] Notwithstanding occasional lapses into garden evangelism, *The Garden Magazine* offered excellent articles on gardening throughout Miller's term as editor. In 1924 *The Garden Magazine* became *Garden and Home Builder*, and in 1928 it was succeeded by *American Home*.

Gardeners' Chronicle of America was another popular gardening magazine of the period whose articles are represented in this anthology. From its start in 1905 it was the "official organ" of the National Association of Gardeners. Later, from April 1934 to March 1943, it was aimed more at amateur gardeners and had a special emphasis on rock gardening. During these years it was published by the American Rock Garden Society.

Published by The United Crafts organization under the leadership of Gustave Stickley, *The Craftsman* was the periodical most closely associated with the Arts and Crafts movement in America. Stickley began publishing *The Craftsman* in Syracuse, New York, in 1901 but moved the operation to New York City in 1906. He charged twenty-five cents a copy, and the journal continued publication until 1916. Stickley and Irene Sargent, a professor at Syracuse University, wrote articles for the early issues describing the mission of the magazine. Essentially this was to teach readers "to employ only those forms and materials which make for simplicity, individuality, and dignity of effect" in their homes and gardens and by this means establish greater harmony and serenity in their lives.

Following the Arts and Crafts principle of relying as much as possible on the use of indigenous materials, *The Craftsman* printed many articles encouraging the use of native wild flowers in gardens. It addressed its articles to the reasonably affluent middle-class "dirt gardeners" who, like Hanna Rion and Walter A. Dyer — two authors whose work appears in this anthology — were thoroughly devoted to their gardens and loved nothing better than working in them, even on snowy days in December. Of all the magazines included in this anthology, this is the one that most clearly represents the romantic spirit of the Arts and Crafts movement, the desire to infuse ordinary life with art, and the recognition of a deep spirituality to be discovered in nature. *The Craftsman* featured articles about naturalist John Burroughs, mentioning in one his inspiration by the American transcendentalist, Ralph Waldo Emerson.[75]

Two other important magazines that started publication around the turn of the century were *The House Beautiful* and *House and Garden*. Unlike *The Ladies' Home Journal* and *Woman's Home Companion*, they did not include fiction or articles on fashion. They dealt only with home design, decorating, gardening, and sometimes with art and antiques. They were more expensive than the *Journal* and *Companion*, and they were aimed at the middle to upper-middle income household. Their gardening articles were exceptionally good and there are, consequently, more from them included in this anthology than from any other magazines.

The House Beautiful[76] was founded in Chicago in 1896 by Eugene Klapp and Henry Blodgett Harvey to help spread the gospel of "simplicity, beauty, and utility" as guiding principles in designing the domestic environment.[77] Klapp resigned from his position as editor in 1898 to enlist as a soldier in the Spanish-American War, although he continued to contribute articles after the war.[78] Herbert S. Stone and Company purchased the magazine less than a year after it was founded. In 1911 the magazine moved to New York, and in 1915, two years after it was purchased by the *Atlantic Monthly*, it moved again, to Boston. When it was sold to International Magazines Company — which is now Hearst Magazines — in 1934, it moved back to New York.

Virginia Robie, who became editor in 1913, replaced Stone. Robie remained editor for two years and was followed by a succession of four other women editors. Its circulation in 1930 was about 100,000.[79] *The House Beautiful* published articles by important architects and landscape architects like Charles A. Platt and O. S. Simonds, and practical gardening pieces by many authors, including Clarence Moores Weed and Ida D. Bennett.

In the issue celebrating the magazine's fiftieth anniversary in 1946, editor Elizabeth Gordon explained that the magazine's underlying philosophy had been inspired by six sermon-essays titled "The House Beautiful" written in 1895 by Unitarian minister William C. Gannett.[80] Portions of these sermons were reprinted in the anniversary issue, including one succinctly stating that "beauty is simplicity and repose," a concept that Americans would find attractive as they sought to create a restorative environment for protection from the frantic pace of modern life. Virginia Robie wrote to Gordon in 1946 that "from the first, the magazine carried on a crusade for the principles of simplicity, beauty, utility, and I am constantly cheered by your own steadfast adherence to the principles of the founders."[81] Robie also recalled proudly that "in garden themes [*The House Beautiful*] was a pioneer."[82]

House and Garden began publication in Philadelphia in 1901. It was the creation of three architects, and it remained primarily an architectural magazine until 1903 when greater emphasis was given to home decorating and gardening.[83] In 1915 the magazine was purchased by Condé Nast, under whose management circulation increased from 10,000 to 130,000 in eleven years.[84] Among the numerous significant contributors of garden articles were W. C. Egan, Rose Standish Nichols, and Robert Lemmon. Most important, Grace Tabor wrote many distinguished articles — longer and more advanced than those she would later write for *Woman's Home Companion* — and a monthly garden column.

Richardson Wright became editor of *House and Garden* in 1914 and held that position until 1950.[85] He proved an outstanding leader for the magazine and presented stimulating ideas in his many fine editorials. These editorials are especially significant because they indicate the continuation into the 1920s and 1930s of the essential ideals that inspired the founders of both *House Beautiful* and *House and Garden*. In an editorial Wright contributed to the July 1921 issue, for example, he commented that "the strength of this country lies in the strength of its individual homes. Its standards can never be higher than the standards of its homes, or its sense of beauty, or its appreciation of the things that go to make a fuller life," a notion compatible with the Arts and Crafts ideologies of the turn of the century.[86] Nine years later, showing his allegiance to old-fashioned principles, he wrote:

> Ease of living and luxury can exact bitter penalties if there are absent the
> qualities of fortitude, industry, thrift and contentment — qualities that gave

our ancestry its power. Today we delight in collecting . . . objects used by that ancestry . . . why not start reviving some of its domestic virtues?[87]

In an editorial that is included in the last chapter of this anthology, Wright promoted the virtues of simplicity and contentment.[88]

Many more magazines than this collection could possibly represent participated in the formulation and distribution of garden ideas across America in the early twentieth century. Limited space necessitated selection of a small percentage from many worthy and fascinating articles, and in the process some magazines that frequently published high-quality articles on gardening were, to my regret, completely omitted. These cover a wide range, from *Delineator, Popular Mechanics*, and *Nature Magazine* to *Century, Horticulture*, and *Lippincott's*, as well as regional journals and magazines that were intended more for a professional than an amateur readership. Among my criteria for choosing articles were an engaging content and style of writing and, inevitably, some of my own personal preferences, both as a gardener and art historian, regarding what was most important and interesting.

With so many pieces available, this book could have been put together in an almost infinite number of forms. But these alternate configurations would not have varied significantly in their message. As this anthology demonstrates, there was a distinct, collective voice that spoke through these mass-circulation writings, one that sought to improve and reform, and that helped form the garden tastes of the early twentieth century in relation to the broader cultural ideologies of the period. An awareness of these writings seems at least as significant to the history of American gardening as studies of the grand estates and the gardens of the very rich. They may, furthermore, serve to remind us that our own gardens are culturally meaningful artifacts, and that our own gardening predilections — so similar to those in vogue two or three generations ago — are equally the product of our contemporary aesthetic, political, and social convictions.

ENDNOTES

1. The most important history of American magazines is Frank Luther Mott, *A History of American Magazines* 1–5 (Cambridge, Massachusetts, 1966–1968). A more recent book that adds new insights to Mott's history of twentieth-century magazines is Matthew Schneirov, *The Dream of a New Social Order: Popular Magazines in America, 1893–1914* (New York, 1994).

2. There were interesting parallels between photography and gardening at this time. In both, amateur status was prized among those who considered themselves serious, noncommercial practitioners. Each was an everyman's art, a way for ordinary people to achieve creative self-expression. Amateurs believed that sincere communication of personal feeling, which was the ultimate artistic goal of many gardeners and photographers in the early twentieth century, could be accomplished without professional training. In both gardening and photography communion with nature was a primary source of inspiration, and the intensity and intimacy of one's response to nature was the main factor that would determine success.

3. B.Y. Morrison, "A Three-Tier Herbaceous Border," *The Garden Magazine* 21 (February 1915): 15. Landscape architect Warren Manning wrote with great feeling about the importance of the amateur home gardener in his article, "Unique Little Gardens," *Country Life in America* 19 (April 15, 1911): 443–445. Frances Duncan (see below, 44) also subscribed to this notion, writing:

    > Whoever would thoroughly enjoy sitting under his vine and under his fig tree should plant them himself. To buy a place with these already set out is not the same. To hire a man to plant them destroys the peculiar charm. When one has settled the fine earth about the roots with his own fingers, pressed down the soil and then raked smooth to obliterate the footprints and make the bed look as if the newcomer had always been there, one is on terms of intimacy with a plant that nothing afterward can shake. It is intimacy and fellowship that one craves with a beloved object, not that there be acres of it. "Planting Your Own Vine and Fig Tree," *The Garden Magazine* 15 (April 1912): 158.

4. A survey of these is presented in Mac Griswold and Eleanor Weller, *The Golden Age of American Gardens: Proud Owners, Private Estates, 1890–1940* (New York, 1991). See also Guy Lowell, *American Gardens* (Boston, 1902) and Louise Shelton, *Beautiful Gardens in America* (New York, 1915).

5. Some middle-class gardens are pictured in M. Christine Doell, *Gardens of the Gilded Age: Nineteenth-Century Gardens and Homegrounds of New York State* (Syracuse, 1986). Vernacular gardens, from ancient times to the late twentieth century, are the subject of *The Vernacular Garden*, ed. John Dixon Hunt and Joachim Wolschke-Bulmahn (Washington, D. C., 1993); an essay in that compendium with particular relevance to this study is Pierce Lewis, "The Making of Vernacular Taste: The Case of *Sunset* and *Southern Living*," 107–136. Another source of information on the gardens of middle-class Americans is May Brawley Hill, *Grandmother's Garden: The Old-Fashioned Garden, 1865–1915* (New York, 1995).

6. Ray Desmond, "Nineteenth-Century Horticultural Journalism," in *John Claudius Loudon and the Early Nineteenth Century in Great Britain*, ed. Elisabeth Blair MacDougall (Washington, D.C., 1980), 81.

7. Mott, *A History of American Magazines* 2, 88–91.

8. George B. Tatum, "The Downing Decade (1841–1852)," in *Prophet with Honor: The Career of Andrew Jackson Downing, 1815-1852*, ed. George B. Tatum and Elisabeth Blair MacDougall (Washington, D. C., 1989), 29.

9. Neil Harris, *The Artist in American Society* (Chicago, 1982), 215. On Downing's conviction that improved taste would be a force in refining American character, see also David Schuyler, *Apostle of Taste: Andrew Jackson Downing, 1815–1852* (Baltimore, 1996), especially chapters 4–6, 85–155.

10. Tatum, "The Downing Decade," 29 n. 50; Schuyler, *Apostle of Taste*, 108.

11. "Fifty Years of Horticultural Journalism," *American Gardening* 17 (January 4, 1896): 1–2.

12. This is covered in Mott, *A History of American Magazines* 4, 1–14, and Schneirov, *The Dream of a New Social Order: Popular Magazines in America, 1893–1914*, 75–102.

13. Mott, *A History of American Magazines* 4, 15–34, and Schneirov, *The Dream of a New Social Order*, 140–146.

14. The development of the halftone is recounted in William Gamble, *The Beginning of Half-Tone* (New York, 1927); more recent accounts that thoughtfully appraise its cultural impact are Edward W. Earle, *Halftone Effects: A Cultural Study of Photographs in Reproduction, 1895–1905* (Riverside, California, 1989), and John Szarkowski, *Photography Until Now* (New York, 1989), 177–200.

15. Mott, *A History of American Magazines* 4, 5.

16. The influence of photography on landscape architecture of the period was noted by Leslie Rose Close in her catalogue for a 1983 exhibition at Wave Hill, *Portrait of an Era in Landscape Architecture: The Photographs of Mattie Edwards Hewitt* (Bronx, New York, 1983). Close stated that "it is

hard to overestimate the impact of photography on landscape architecture in this century . . . As garden literature—popular, professional, and academic—was produced and consumed in unprecedented volume, during the 1910s and 1920s, photographic images of gardens reached a tremendous number and variety of people" (n.p.).

17. American Impressionist garden scenes were recently analyzed in *Visions of Home: American Impressionist Images of Suburban Leisure and Country Comforts*, ed. Lisa N. Peters and Peter M. Lukehart (Carlisle, Pennsylvania, 1997).

18. A recent account of commercial graphic art, including advertising posters and magazine covers, can be found in Michele H. Bogart, *Artists, Advertising, and the Borders of Art* (Chicago, 1995).

19. Mott, *A History of American Magazines* 4, 11.

20. On the continuation of Progressive ideas — sometimes in altered form — into the New Deal era, see Arthur S. Link and Richard L. McCormick, *Progressivism* (Arlington Heights, Illinois, 1983), 105–118 and 139–140.

21. Kathleen Pyne, *Art and the Higher Life: Painting and Evolutionary Thought in Late Nineteenth-Century America* (Austin, Texas, 1996), 5. The cultural empowerment of the educated, middle class in America is also discussed in Charles C. Alexander, *Here the Country Lies: Nationalism and the Arts in Twentieth-Century America* (Bloomington, Indiana, 1980), 28–29; T. J. Jackson Lears, *No Place of Grace: Antimodernism and the Transformation of American Culture, 1880–1920* (New York, 1981), xiv–xv; David E. Shi, *The Simple Life: Plain Living and High Thinking in American Culture* (New York, 1985), 175–176.

22. On the American acceptance of Ruskin's aesthetic principles, see Roger Stein, *John Ruskin and Aesthetic Thought in America, 1840–1900* (Cambridge, Massachusetts, 1967); Eileen Boris, *Art and Labor: Ruskin, Morris, and the Craftsman Ideal in America* (Philadelphia, 1986); Doreen Bolger Burke et al., *In Pursuit of Beauty: Americans and the Aesthetic Movement* (New York, 1986), especially the essay by Roger B. Stein, "Artifact as Ideology: The Aesthetic Movement in Its American Cultural Context," 23–51. Early magazine accounts of the Arts and Crafts movement include the foreword to the first issue of *The Craftsman*, and Whiting's "Arts and Crafts: The Guild and School of Handicraft," 285–290. Recent publications on the Arts and Crafts movement in America include: Robert Judson Clark, ed., *The Arts and Crafts Movement in America, 1876–1916* (Princeton, 1972); Wendy Kaplan et al., *"The Art that Is Life": The Arts and Crafts Movement in America, 1875–1920* (Boston, 1987); Leslie Greene Bowman, *American Arts and Crafts: Virtue in Design* (Los Angeles, 1990); Kenneth R. Trapp et al., *The Arts and Crafts Move-*

ment in California: Living the Good Life (New York, 1993).

23. On the Arts and Crafts garden see: Ottewill, *The Edwardian Garden*, 97–139; Diana Balmori, "The Arts and Crafts Garden," (New Haven, 1989) *Tiller* 1 (July–August, 1983): 18–28; Deborah Nevins' introduction to the 1984 reprint of William Robinson's *The English Flower Garden* (New York, 1984), xiii–xiv; David C. Streatfield, "The Arts and Crafts Garden in California," *The Arts and Crafts Movement in California*, 35–53; Wendy Hitchmough, *Arts and Crafts Gardens* (London, 1997).

24. According to Ottewill, "Tennyson, by using them in some of his early poems, was one of the first to make 'old-fashioned' flowers fashionable"; Ottewill also illustrates Charles Collins's painting *Convent Thoughts* of 1851, which is set in an archetypal old-fashioned garden (Ottewill, 29). American garden articles, like those in this anthology, are often filled with quotations from Victorian and Romantic poetry. This is especially the case with articles on old-fashioned and wild gardens, both of which may have had their initial inspiration from this type of poetry. John Everett Millais' 1851 painting *Ophelia*, in which the artist has depicted many old English flowers floating in the water around Ophelia, was especially admired by members of the Aesthetic and Arts and Crafts movements. As Hitchmough remarks: "Painting and poetry were closely linked in the mid-nineteenth century. Paintings often depicted specific scenes from Tennyson and the fashion for Arthurian tales in literature stimulated visual responses to the poetic evocations of romantic old English gardens," Hitchmough, *Arts and Crafts Gardens*, 43.

25. "If the Aesthete's personal wardrobe was of paramount importance, the artistic condition of his or her house and garden was only marginally less portentous as a subject for soulful introspection or audacious display. Just as the soft flowing gowns of the women in Pre-Raphaelite paintings . . . had a profound influence on the wardrobes of progressive young women, the painted gardens of Rossetti, Burne-Jones, and other Victorian artists became the inspiration for old-fashioned gardens," Hitchmough, *Arts and Crafts Gardens*, 43.

26. Important British books on old-fashioned gardens, like Eleanor Vere Boyle's *Days and Hours in a Garden*, and books with illustrations that were highly influential in popularizing the old-fashioned garden, like Kate Greenaway's *Under the Window*, were published in New York starting in the 1870s and 1880s. On the impact of Greenaway on American gardens, see below xxxiv n. 34, 56, and 59 n. 11; on her importance in spreading the popularity of the old-fashioned garden, see

Hitchmough, *Arts and Crafts Gardens*, 46–53. Earlier still, as mentioned above (n. 24), Americans were well acquainted with Victorian poetry and its allusions to old-time gardens and flowers.

27. Important garden books published by authors connected with the colonial revival include Grace Tabor, *Old-Fashioned Gardening: A History and a Reconstruction* (New York, 1913); Alice Morse Earle, *Old Time Gardens* (New York, 1901); and *Sun Dials and Roses of Yesterday* (New York, 1902), as well as Earle's article "Old Time Flower Gardens," *Scribner's Magazine* 20 (August 1896): 162–178. On colonial revival gardens from a late twentieth-century perspective, see Charles B. Hosmer, Jr., "The Colonial Revival in the Public Eye: Williamsburg and Early Garden Restoration, in *"The Colonial Revival in America*, ed. Alan Axelrod (New York, 1985), 52–70. Celia Betsky's article about domestic interiors of the colonial revival ("Inside the Past: The Interior and the Colonial Revival in American Art and Literature, 1860–1914," *The Colonial Revival in America*, ed. Alan Axelrod [New York, 1985], 241–277) shows that there were many parallels between the perception of domestic interiors and gardens.

28. Edward Payson Powell, writing in 1915 ("Grandmother's Garden," 184–187), was born in 1833; Henry Stuart Ortloff, writing in 1923 ("The Gardens of Our Grandmothers," 194–201), was born in 1896.

29. In her 1995 book, *Grandmother's Garden: The Old-Fashioned Garden, 1865–1915*, May Brawley Hill reports that she found the old-fashioned garden "an American style of gardening waiting to be discovered." Hill's book, and her article, "Grandmother's Garden," *Antiques* 142 (November 1992): 727–735, have expanded extensively on ideas and references that I first advanced in my exhibition catalogue *Gardens on Paper: Prints and Drawings, 1200–1900* (Washington, D.C., 1990), 158–161, and in my article "Reminiscence and Revival: The Old-Fashioned Garden, 1890-1910," *Antiques* 137 (April 1990): 894–905.

30. At first writers like Wilhelm Miller and H. S. Adams followed Robinson's approach and insisted that wild gardens need not employ only — or even preferably — native plants. Later Miller became one of this country's chief proponents of the use of native plants in American gardens.

31. On Doubleday, see below 208–209; Neltje Blanchan [Nellie Doubleday], "Naturalistic Gardens," *Country Life in America* 14 (September 1908): 443.

32. Mary Cunningham, "New Uses for Native Plants," 148–153.

33. There were some articles in magazines, especially *Country Life in America*, that praised certain wealthy estate owners for having wild gardens. A

few examples are J. Horace McFarland, "Dolobran—A Wild-Gardening Estate," *Country Life in America* 4 (September 1903): 338–365; Wilhelm Miller, "Wild Gardening Beside a Wooded Lake," *Country Life in America* 9 (March 1906): 548–552; [anonymous], "Nature is Head-Gardener on the Estate of Mr. T. A. Havemeyer," *The Touchstone* 2 (October 1917): 44–52.

34. There was a distinct genre of wild garden article in American magazines in which the authors prided themselves in loving and protecting the poor, humble weeds that less sensitive gardeners slaughtered. For examples of this type of garden article see Clayton, "Wild Gardening and the Popular American Magazine, 1890–1918," in *Nature and Ideology: Natural Garden Design in the Twentieth Century*, ed. Joachim Wolschke-Bulmahn (Washington, D.C., 1997), 146–147. Perhaps the belief that having weeds in your garden proved you were a more artistic sort of gardener derived in part from Americans' familiarity with some of Kate Greenaway's gardening habits and tastes. Greenaway was extremely popular in the United States, especially among followers of the Arts and Crafts movement, and her book illustrations of gardens (all very tidy) were cited as inspiration in American garden articles from the first through the fourth decades of the twentieth century (see below 59n. 11). Her biography was published in both London and New York in 1905. In a March 1896 letter to Miss Violet Dickinson that is quoted in this biography, Greenaway wrote: "I can really boast with truth that we have larger and more varied weeds in our garden than you have in yours—in fact, our garden has forgotten that it is a garden and is trying to be a field again" (M. H. Spielmann and G. S. Layard, *Kate Greenaway* [New York and London, 1905], 206). I found this letter through a reference in Hitchmough, 52–53.

35. William L. Bowers, *The Country Life Movement in America, 1900–1920* (Port Washington, New York, 1974); Shi, *The Simple Life*, 193–206.

36. From early in the nation's history Americans held nature, the wilderness, as symbolic of divinity; these ideas were important to the landscape painters of the Hudson River School and landscape gardener Andrew Jackson Downing (see Perry Miller, *Errand into the Wilderness* [Cambridge, Mass., 1956], especially 204–216). These ideas are further discussed in: Leo Marx, *The Machine in the Garden: Technology and the Pastoral Ideal in America* (New York, 1964); Roderick Nash, *Wilderness and the American Mind* (New Haven, 1967); Peter J. Schmitt, *Back to Nature: The Arcadian Myth in Urban America* (New York, 1969); Wanda M. Corn, *The Color of Mood: American Tonalism 1880–1910* (San Francisco, 1972), 1–8; Donald Worster, *Nature's Economy: A History of*

Ecological Ideas (New York, 1985), especially 3–97; Catherine L. Albanese, *Nature Religion in America: From the Algonkian Indians to the New Age* (Chicago, 1990), 80–116. Magazines that featured articles on gardening often also included articles written by or about naturalists Henry David Thoreau (1817–1862), John Muir (1838–1914), John Burroughs (1837–1921), and American transcendentalist Ralph Waldo Emerson (1803–1882). A love of nature did lead to a type of nature religion and mysticism for some landscape gardeners and landscape painters of the late nineteenth and early twentieth centuries. Frank A. Waugh, landscape architect, wrote that what we are able to see is only part of the landscape: "Within those physical forms and without them and beyond them there are corresponding spiritual parts which form a spiritual landscape just as real and even more closely related to our half-human, half-divine souls" (*The Natural Style in Landscape Gardening* [Boston, 1917], 62). This may be compared to the views of landscape painter George Inness (Nicholai Cikovsky, Jr., *George Inness* [New York, 1993], 116–117), and his student William Keith (Richard Guy Wilson, "'Divine Excellence': The Arts and Crafts Life in California," *The Arts and Crafts Movement in California: Living the Good Life* [Oakland, 1993], 28–31).

37. Gail Thain Parker, *Mind Cure in New England* (Hanover, New Hampshire, 1973); James R. Moore, *The Post-Darwinian Controversies: A Study of the Protestant Struggle to Come to Terms with Darwin in Great Britain and America, 1870–1900* (Cambridge, 1979), 153–173; Kathleen A. Pyne, "John Twachtman and the Therapeutic Landscape," *John Twachtman: Connecticut Landscapes* (Washington, D.C., 1989), 49–65. The subject is most recently and thoroughly discussed in Pyne, *Art and the Higher Life*, 17–47.

38. Anonymous, "Pergolas in American Gardens," *The Craftsman* 20 (April 1911): 33.

39. Mott, *History of American Magazines* 5, 2.

40. Mott, *History of American Magazines* 2, 493–515;.

41. For his account of the *Atlantic* during his editorship, see Ellery Sedgwick, *Atlantic Harvest: Memoirs of the Atlantic* (Boston, 1947).

42. Mott, *History of American Magazines* 4, 589–607.

43. Mott, *History of American Magazines* 2, 511 n.69, and 5, 729.

44. Wheeler's article appeared in *Atlantic Monthly* 85 (June 1900): 779–784; 86 (July 1900): 99–105; 86 (August 1900): 232–238. It was published as a book in 1901 by Houghton, Mifflin, Boston. On Wheeler, see Anthea Callen, *Women Artists of the Arts and Crafts Movement, 1870–1914* (New York, 1979), 131–133.

45. Wheeler, "Content in a Garden," (June 1900): 779.

46. On the history of the Contributors' Club, see Edward A. Weeks, Jr., foreword, vii–viii, and Philip B. Eppard and George Monteiro, introduction, *A Guide to the Atlantic Monthly Contributors' Club* (Boston, 1983), xiii–xxi. Lucie Prinz, on the *Atlantic Monthly* staff, informed my father, Robert B. Tuttle, of this extremely useful book, and he in turn referred me to it; I am grateful to them both. I relied on this book's identification of the anonymous authors of Contributors' Club articles that I included in this anthology.

47. Quoted in Eppard and Monteiro, *A Guide to the Atlantic Monthly Contributor's Club*, xiv.

48. Mott, *History of American Magazines* 3, 457–479, and 4, 717–732; Robert G. Barrier, "Scribner's Magazine," in *American Literary Magazines*, ed. Edward E. Chielens (Westport, Connecticut, 1992), 308–314.

49. Mott, *History of American Magazines* 4, 723, 725, and 729.

50. *Scribner's* 35 (May 1904): 621–629. In 1887 Cable had founded what became the Northampton People's Institution to help educate and provide aesthetic values for working people. The garden competition was also reported in *The Ladies' Home Journal*: Rose Bartlett, "How One Man Made His Town Bloom," *The Ladies' Home Journal* 27 (March 1910): 36, 80, and 82.

51. Mott, *A History of American Magazines* 2, 367–379; 3, 422–435.

52. Recently reprinted: Celia Thaxter, *An Island Garden* (Boston, 1988).

53. For example: Albanese discusses an article in *Outlook* on the relationship of man to nature and to God that concluded nature was "a middle ground between God and man" (*Nature Religion in America*, 105–106); Cikovsky refers to an art review in *Independent* by Marianna Griswold von Rensslaer — who also wrote on gardening — in which she writes about Inness's landscape paintings (*George Inness*, 95).

54. Mott, *A History of American Magazines* 2, 378.

55. Mott, *A History of American Magazines* 3, 429 and 430.

56. It began as a section of and then, in 1883, became a supplement to Cyrus Curtis's *Tribune and Farmer*, and it was edited by Mrs. Curtis. Her admirable skill in selecting its contents led to a remarkable circulation of 25,000 at the end of one year. Cyrus Curtis then sold the *Tribune and Farmer* and devoted himself to further building the readership of the now independent *Ladies' Home Journal*. Through various means, including printing stories by leading authors, he was

tremendously successful. Mott, *A History of American Magazines* 4, 536–555.

57. Mott, *A History of American Magazines* 4, 550.

58. Mott, *A History of American Magazines* 4, 539. Shi writes about Bok, the Arts and Crafts movement, and "progressive simplicity" in *The Simple Life*, 181–190.

59. Mott, *A History of American Magazines* 4, 545 and 549.

60. Edward Bok, *The Americanization of Edward Bok: The Autobiography of a Dutch Boy Fifty Years After* (New York, 1921), 249.

61. Doubleday (1865–1918), who wrote under the pseudonym Neltje Blanchan, was the wife of publisher Frank Doubleday. She contributed articles to the Doubleday periodicals, *Country Life in America* and *Garden Magazine*, and to many other magazines. She also wrote a number of successful books on gardening, birds, and wild flowers. See below, 208–209.

62. Neltje Blanchan [Nellie Doubleday], "A Garden Any One May Have," *The Ladies' Home Journal* 25 (April 1908): 44.

63. Mott, *A History of American Magazines* 4, 763–772.

64. Mott, *A History of American Magazines* 4, 770.

65. Eleanor Roosevelt, "Mrs. Roosevelt's Page: Gardens," *Woman's Home Companion* 62 (March 1935): 4.

66. On the British *Country Life*, see *Gardens in Edwardian England* (Woodbridge, Suffolk, England, 1985), a reprint of the 1905 *Country Life* publication, *Country Gardens Old and New*; John Cornforth, *The Search for a Style: Country Life and Architecture, 1897–1935* (London, 1988); Brent Elliott, *The Country House Garden: From the Archives of Country Life, 1897–1939* (London, 1995); Judith Tankard, "Gardening with *Country Life*," *Hortus* 30 (summer 1994); Judith Tankard, "The Influence of British Garden Literature on American Garden Design," *Influences on American Garden Design: 1895 to 1940*, Masters of Garden Design 4 (New York, 1994), 23–24.

67. Robert E. Grese, "Liberty Hyde Bailey," in *Pioneers of American Landscape Design* ed. Charles A. Birnbaum (Washington, D. C., 1993), 9–13; William L. Bowers, *The Country Life Movement in America, 1900–1920* (Port Washington, N.Y., 1974), 45–61; Mott, *A History of American Magazines* 4, 338.

68. The Talk of the Town, *The Garden Magazine* 15 (April 1912): 152.

69. During the 1930s the magazine's content did begin to focus much more on the gardens and lifestyles of the wealthiest Americans.

70. *Country Life in America* 5 (March 1904): 410.

71. *Country Life in America* 5 (March 1904): 415.

72. Neltje Blanchan [Nellie Doubleday], "The Joy of Gardening," *Country Life in America* 17 (March 1910): 544.

73. *The Garden Magazine* 11 (March 1910): 64.

74. Two articles from *Garden Magazine* whose titles epitomize Miller's competitive attitude toward improving American gardening: "How We Can Beat the World at Wild Gardening" (November 1908), written by Thomas Mc Adam, a frequent contributor, and Miller's "What America Can Teach England About Shrubs" (see below, 47–55). On Miller, see below, 47.

75. For example, an unsigned article: "A Day with John Burroughs at Riverby and Slabsides, On the Hudson," *Craftsman* 8 (1905): 565–583.

76. The name of the magazine changed to simply *House Beautiful* in 1925.

77. See, for example, Mrs. Henry Wade Rogers, "The Simplification of Life," *The House Beautiful* 12 s(June 1902): 3–6, and (July 1902): 80–84.

78. An article by Klapp, written in 1897, is included in this anthology, 56–59.

79. Mott, *A History of American Magazines* 5, 162.

80. *House Beautiful* 88 (December 1946): 151.

81. "How We Did It in the Old Days," *The House Beautiful* 88 (December 1946): 153, 243–250.

82. Robie, "How We Did It," 244.

83. Richardson Wright, "How House and Garden Began," *House and Garden* 50 (July 1920): 69.

84. Wright, "How House and Garden Began," 69–70.

85. For biographical information about Wright, see below 275.

86. Richardson Wright, "We Buy Ourselves a Birthday Cake," *House and Garden* 40 (July 1921): 24.

87. Richardson Wright, "We Return to Our Beginnings and Discover Grandmothers," *House and Garden* 58 (July 1930): 46.

88. See below, 275–277.

THE ONCE
AND FUTURE
GARDENER

Chapter One

A YEAR IN THE GARDEN

A YEAR IN THE GARDEN

T HE ARTICLES gathered in this chapter follow the calendar of the gardening year, beginning in early spring and culminating with the onset of winter. They describe how the seasons and the changing weather influence the garden's performance and dictate what work is necessary; the close relationship between gardening and the forces of nature is a recurrent theme. The first author writes about spring in the Berkshires, when gardening tasks seem endless yet are wonderfully fulfilling, and how gardening brings him into "closer touch with the awakening earth." The second author, one of the great gardeners and garden writers of the early century, critically evaluates her garden in its midsummer glory. We next learn how to avoid the worst effects of summer drought, how a gardener savors the pleasures of a summer rainstorm, and then about reviewing this year's efforts and planning next fall's garden at the end of the growing season. The garden story narrated in the final article takes place in winter, when work continues despite the snow — to the gardener's great delight.

Spring in the Garden

WALTER PRICHARD EATON, a successful writer, critic, and professor of drama, had a profound reverence for the natural world and was an eloquent spokesman for American gardening. Born in Malden, Massachusetts, in 1878, he spent much of his life in the Berkshire Mountains of Massachusetts. When he wrote this article in 1913 he was living and gardening in Stockbridge; two photographs of his garden there appeared in a 1917 issue of *Country Life in America*.[1] The illustration on the title page for Chapter One of this book is from "Spring in the Garden"; it shows Eaton hard at work in his manure pile. In addition to plays and essays like "Spring in the Garden," he wrote travel books, poetry, natural history, and books for young people, including a series of Boy Scout stories. In 1902 Eaton became drama critic for *The New York Tribune*, then held the same position at *The New York Sun* from 1907 to 1908, and at *American Magazine* from 1910 to 1920.[2] He taught play writing at Yale from 1933 to 1947, lectured at the Columbia University School of Journalism, and gave frequent talks on gardening, colonial architecture, and drama. Modern scholarship has recognized him as a cultural nationalist committed to the cause of fostering an American tradition of play writing; he supported the little-theater circuit and amateur efforts in drama, from which he believed this native tradition would some day evolve.[3] Eaton retired to Chapel Hill, North Carolina, where he died in 1957. Two of his best garden books were *Everybody's Garden* (1932) and *Wild Gardens of New England* (1936). Another article by Eaton can be found in the third chapter of this anthology.

No DAFFODILS [*Narcissus*] "take the winds of March with beauty" in our Berkshire gardens. What daffodils we have in that month of alternate slush and blizzard bloom in pots, indoors. But one sign of spring the gardens hold no less plain to read, even if some people may not regard it as so poetic — over across the late snow, close to the hotbed frames, a great pile of fresh stable manure is steaming like a miniature volcano. To the true gardener, that sight is thrilling, nay, lyric! I have always found that the measure of a man's (and more especially a woman's) garden love was to be found in his (or her) attitude toward the manure pile. For that reason I put the manure pile in the first paragraph of my praise of gardens in the spring.

That yellowish-brown, steaming volcano above the slushy snow of March promises so much! I will not offend sensitive garden owners who hire others to do their dirty work, by singing the joy of turning it over with a fork, once, twice, perhaps three times, till it is "working" evenly all through. Yet there is such joy, accentuated on the second day by the fact that the thermometer has taken a sudden jump upwards, the snow is melting fast, and in the shrubs and evergreen hedge the song sparrows are singing, and the robins. Last year, I remember, I paused with the steaming pile half turned, first to roll up my sleeves and feel the warm sun on my arms — most delicious of early spring sensations — and then to listen to the love call of a chickadee, over and over the three notes, one long and two short a whole tone lower. I answered him, he replied, and we played our little game for two or three minutes, till he came close and detected the fraud. Then a bluebird flashed through the orchard, a jay screamed, as I bent to my toil again. Beside me were the hotbed frames, the glasses newly washed, the winter bedding of leaves removed, and behind them last year's contents rotted into rich loam. Another day or two, and they would be prepared for seeding — if I only could bring myself to work hard enough until then!

How much hope goes into a hotbed in late March, or early April! How much warmth the friendly manure down under the soil sends up by night to

From the meadow comes the ceaseless, shrill chorus of the frogs, beating in waves upon the ear and making the air yet more warm and fragrant, the promise of spring more magical.

In the sheltered lowlands where the ground has frozen deep the snow still lingers in worn, dirt-stained patches, though the first spring flowers are in bloom.

germinate the seeds, though the weather go back to winter outside — as it invariably does in our mountains! Last year, for example, we had snow on the ninth of April, and again on the twenty-third and twenty-ninth, while the year before, on the ninth, six inches fell. In the lowland regions gardening is easier, perhaps, but yet there is a certain joy in this fickle spring weather of ours, the joy of going out in the morning across a white garden and sweeping the snow from the hotbed mats, lifting the moist, steaming glass, and catching from within, strong against your face, the pungent warmth and aroma of the heated soil and the delicate fragrance of young seedlings. How fast the seeds come — some of them! Others come so slowly that the amateur gardener is in despair, and angrily decides to try a new seed house next year. The vegetable frames are sown in rows — celery, tomatoes, cauliflowers, lettuce, radishes, peppers, coming up in tiny green ribbons, the radishes racing ahead. The flower frames, however, are sown in squares, each about a foot across, and each labeled and marked off with a thin strip of wood. These are the early plantings of the annuals, for we cannot sow out-of-doors till the first or even the second week in May in our climate. Sometimes, indeed, we do not dare to sow even in the frames till well into April. The asters are usually up first, racing the weeds. The little squares make, in a week or so, a green checkerboard, each promising its quota of color to the garden, and very soon the early cosmos, thinned to the strongest plants, has shot up like a miniature forest, towering over the lowlier seedlings, sometimes bumping its head against the glass before it can be transplanted to the open ground in May. But most prolific, most promising, and most bothersome, are the squares labeled "antirrhinum," coral red, salmon pink, white, dark maroon, and so on; tiny seeds scattered on the ground and sprinkled with a little sand, they come up by the hundred, and each seedling has to go into a pot before it goes into the ground.

There is work for an April day! I sit on a board by the hotbed, cross-legged like a Turk, while the sun is warm on my neck and I feel my arms tanning, and removing a mass of the seedlings on a flat mason's trowel, I lift each strong plant between thumb and finger, its long, delicate white root dangling like a needle, and pot it in a small paper pot. When two score pots are ready, I set them in a coldframe, sprinkle them, stretch the kink out of my back, listen to the wood thrush a moment (he came on the fourteenth and is evidently planning to nest in our pines), and then return to my job. Patience is required to pot four or five hundred snapdragons [*Antirrhinum majus*]: but patience is required, after all, in most things that are rightly performed. I think as I work of the glory around my sundial in July, I arrange and rearrange the colors in my mind — and presently the job is done!

But the steaming manure pile is not the only sign of spring, nor the hotbeds the only things to be attended to. If they only were, how much easier gardening would be — and how much less exciting! There is always work to be done in the orchard, for instance, some pruning and scraping. I always go into the orchard on the first really warm, spring-like March day, with a common hoe, and scrape a little, not so much for the good of the trees as the good of my soul. There is a curious, faintly putrid smell to old or bruised apple wood, which is stirred by my scraping, and that smell sweeps over me a wave of memories, memories of childhood in a great, yellow house that stood back from the road almost in its orchard, and boasted a cupola with panes of colored glass which made the familiar landscape strange; memories of youth in that same house, too, dim memories "of sweet, forgotten, wistful things." My early spring afternoons in the orchard are very precious to me now, and when the weather permits I always try to burn the rubbish and dead prunings on Good Friday, the incense of the apple wood floating across the brown garden like a prayer, the precious ashes sinking down to enrich the soil.

The bees, too, are always a welcome sign of the returning season, hardly less than the birds, though the advent of the white-throated sparrow (who delayed till April twenty-first last year) is always a great event. He is first heard most often before breakfast, in an apple tree close to the sleeping porch, his flute-like triplets sweetly penetrating my dreams and bringing me gladly out of bed — something he alone can do, by the way, and not even he after the first morning! But the bees come long before. The earliest record that I have is March thirty-first, but there must be dates before that which I have neglected to put down. Some house plant, a hyacinth possibly, is used as bait, and when the ground is thawing out beneath a warm spring sun we put the plant on the southern veranda and watch. Day after day nothing happens, then suddenly, some noon, it has scarcely been set on the ground when its blossoms stir, and it is murmurous with bees. Then we know that spring indeed has come, and we begin to rake the lawns, wherever the frost is out, wheeling great crate loads of leaves and rubbish upon the garden, and filling our neighbors' houses with pungent smoke!

There is a certain spot between the thumb and first finger which neither ax nor golf club nor saw handle seems to callous. The spring raking finds it out, and gleefully starts to raise a blister. My hands are perpetually those of a day laborer, yet I expect that blister every spring. Indeed, I am rather disappointed now if I don't get it. I feel as if I weren't doing my share of work. The work is worth the blister. I know of few sensations more delightful than that of seeing the lawn emerging green and clean beneath your rake, the damp mould bearing itself under the shrubbery, the paths, freshly edged, nicely scarrowed with tooth marks; then of feeling the tug of the barrow handles in your shoulder sockets; and finally, as the sun is sending long shadows over the ground, of standing beside the rubbish pile with your rake as a poker and hearing the red flames crackle and roar through the heap, while great puffs of beautiful brown smoke go rolling away across the garden and the warmth is good to your tired body. Clearing up is such a delight, indeed, that I cannot comprehend why I so intensely disliked to do it when I was half my present age. Perhaps it was because at that time clearing up was put to me in the light of a duty, not a pleasure!

There is, alas, too often a tempering of sadness in the joy of taking the covers off the garden. One removes them, especially after an open winter like this season of 1912-1913, with much the same anxious excitement that one opens a long-delayed letter from a dear friend who has been in danger. What signs of life will the peonies [*Paeonia*] show under their four inches of rotted manure, and the Japanese irises [*Iris ensata*] by the pool, and the beds of Darwins [*Tulipa*], so confidently relied upon to ring the sundial in late May and early June, before the succeeding annuals are ready? How will the hollyhocks [*Alcea rosea*], so stately in midsummer all down the garden wall, have withstood the alternate thaws and freezes which characterized our abominable January and February? Then there are those two long rows of foxgloves [*Digitalis purpurea*] and Canterbury bells [*Campanula medium*], across the rear of the vegetable garden, where they were set in the fall to make strong plants before being put in their permanent places — or rather their season's places, for these lovely flowers are perversely biennials, and at least seven times every spring I vow I will never bother with them again, and then make an even larger sowing when their stately stalks and sky blue bells are abloom in summer! Tenderly you lift the pine boughs from them on a balmy April day (it was not until almost mid-April last year), when snow still lingers, perhaps, in dirty patches on the north side of the evergreens. Will they show frozen, flabby, withered leaves, or will their centers be bright with new promise? It is a moment to try the soul of the gardener, and no joy is quite like that of finding them all alive, nor any sorrow like that of finding them dead. At first I used to give up gardening forever when the perennials and biennials were winter killed, just as a beginner at golf gives up the game forever each time he makes a vile score. Then I began to compromise on a garden of annuals. Now I have learned philosophy — and also better methods of winter protection. Likewise, I have learned that a good many of the perennials which were stone dead when the covers were removed have a trick of coming to life under the kiss of May, and struggling up to some sort of bloom, even if heroically spindly like lean soldiers after a hard campaign. The hollyhocks, especially, have a way of seeding themselves undetected, and presenting you in spring with a whole unsuspected family of children, some of whom wander far from the parent stem and suddenly begin to shoot up in the most unexpected places. An exquisite yellow hollyhock last summer sprouted unnoted beneath our dining-room window, and we were not aware of it till one July morning when it poked up above the sill. A few days later, when we came down to breakfast, there it was abloom, nodding in at the open window!

Another spring excitement in the garden is the pea planting, both the sweet pea [*Lathyrus odoratus*] and what our country folk sometimes call "eatin' pea." No rivalry is so keen as that between pea growers. My neighbors and I struggle for supremacy in sweet peas at the flower show in July, and great glory goes to him who gets the first mess of green peas on his table. We have tried sweet pea sowing in the fall, and it does not work. So now I prepare a trench in October, partially fill it with manure, and cover it with leaves, which I remove at the first hint of warm weather in March. The earth piles on either side thaw out quickly, and I get an early sowing, putting in as many varieties as I can afford (my wife says twice as many as I can afford), jealously guarding the secret of their number. The vegetable peas are planted later, usually about the first or second day of April, as soon as the top soil of the garden can be worked with a fork, and long before the plowing. We put in first a row of Daniel O'Rourke's, not because they are good for much, but because they will beat any other variety we have discovered by two days at least. Then we put in a row of a better standard early variety. How we watch those rows for the first sprouts! How we coddle and cultivate them! How eagerly we inspect our neighbors' rows, trying to appear nonchalant! And doubtless how silly this sounds to anyone who is not a gardener! Last summer we got our first mess of peas on June twenty-first, and after eating a handful we rushed to the telephone, and were about to ring, when somebody called us. "Hello," we said into the receiver. A voice on the other end of the wire, curiously choked and munchy, cried, "We are eating our first peas! My mouth's full of 'em now!"

"That's nothing," we answered, "we've got our first mouthful all swallowed."

"Well, anyhow," said our disappointed neighbor, "I called up first! Goodby."
How is that for a neck-and-neck finish at the tape?

As April waxes into May, the garden beds are a perpetual adventure in the expected, each morning bringing some new revelation of old friends come back, and as you dig deep and prepare the beds for the annuals, or spade manure around the perennials, or set your last year's plantings of hollyhocks, larkspur [*Delphinium*], foxgloves and campanulas into their places, you move tenderly amid the aspiring red stalks of the peonies, the Jason's crop of green iris spears, the leaves of tulips and narcissus and daffodils, the fresh green of tiny Sweet William [*Dianthus barbatus*] plants clustered round the mother plant like a brood of chicks around the hen. You must be at setting them into the borders, too, or putting the surplus into flats and then telephoning your less fortunate friends. One of the joys of a garden is in giving away your extra plants and seedlings.

One morning the asparagus bed, already brown again after the April showers have driven the salt into the ground, is pricked with short tips. That is a luscious sight! Inch by inch they push up, and thick and fast they come at last, and more and more and more. My diary shows me that we ate our first bunch last year on May ninth. On that day, also, I learn from the same source, the daffodils were out, the Darwin tulips were budding, and we spent the afternoon burning caterpillars' nests in the orchard — one spring crop which is never welcome, and never winter-killed! At this date, too, we are hard at work spraying, and sowing the annuals out-of-doors in the seed beds, and planting corn (the potatoes are all in by now), immediately following the plowing, which was delayed till the first of May by a belated snowstorm. Winter with us is like a clumsy person who tries over and over to make his exit from a room but does not know how to accomplish it. It is a busy time, for no sooner are the annuals planted, and the vegetables, than some of the seedlings from the hotbeds have to be set out (such as early cosmos), and the perennial beds already have begun to bloom, and require cultivation and admiration, and the flowers in the wild garden — hepaticas and trilliums and bloodroot [*Sanguinaria*] and violets [*Violas*] — are crying to be noticed, and, confound it all, here is the lawn getting rank under the influence of its spring dressing, and demands to be mowed! Yes, and we forgot to get the mower sharpened before we put it away in the fall.

"May fifteenth" — it is my diary for 1911 — "apple blossoms showing pink, and the rhubarb leaves peeping over the tops of their barrels this morning, like Ali Baba and the forty thieves."

Well, well, straight, juicy red stalks and the length of a barrel, fit for a pie and the market! It is our second commercial product, the asparagus slightly preceding it. The garden is getting into shape now, indeed; the wheel-hoe is traveling up and down the green rows; the hotbed glasses are entirely removed by day; and the early cauliflower plants are put into the open ground at the first promise of a shower. The annuals are up in the seed beds; the pool has been cleaned and filled, the gold fish are once more swimming in it, the Cape Cod water lily [*Nymphaea*], brought from its winter quarters in the dark cellar, has begun to make a leaf, and we have begun to hope that maybe this year it will also make a blossom, for we are nothing in mid-May if not optimistic.

The earlier Darwins are already in bloom. The German irises follow rapidly. June comes, and we work amid the splendors of the Japanese irises and the flameline of Oriental poppies [*Papaver orientale*], setting the annuals into their beds, from the tender, droopy schyzanthus [*Schizanthus pinnatus*] plants to the various asters and the now sturdy snapdragons. The color scheme had been carefully planned last winter, and is as cheerfully disregarded now, as some new inspiration strikes us, such as a border of purple asters against salvia, with white dahlias behind — a strip of daring fall color which would delight the soul of Gari Melchers, which delighted me — and which my wife said was horrible.[4]

So spring comes and goes in the garden, busy and beautiful, ceaseless work and ceaseless wonder. But there is a moment in its passage, as yet unmentioned, which I have kept for the close because to me it is the subtle climax of the resurrection season. It comes in April for us, sometimes earlier, sometimes later. The twenty-seventh was the date last year. The time is evening, always evening, just after supper, when a frail memory of sunset still lingers in the west and the air is warm. I go out hatless upon the veranda, thinking of other things, and suddenly I am aware of the song of the frogs! There are laughing voices in the street, the tinkle of a far-off piano, the pleasant sounds of village life come outdoors with the return of spring; and buoying up, permeating these other sounds comes the ceaseless, shrill chorus of the frogs, seemingly from out of the air and distance, beating in waves on the ear. Why this first frog chorus so thrills me I cannot explain, nor what dim memories it wakes. But the peace of it steals over all my senses, and I walk down into the dusk and seclusion of my garden, amid the sweet odors of new earth and growing things, where the song comes up to me from the distant meadow making the garden close sweeter still, the air yet more warm and fragrant, the promise of spring more magical. The garden then is very intimate and dear, it brings me into closer touch with the awakening earth about me, and all the years I dwelt a prisoner in cities are but as the shadow of a dream.

House and Garden 23 (APRIL 1913): 267–269, 324–326.

ENDNOTES

1. The photographs were published with a letter he wrote Henry H. Saylor, editor of *Country Life in America* 33 (November 1917): 62.

2. *Who Was Who Among North American Authors, 1921–1939* 1, ed. Alberta Lawrence (Detroit, 1976), 464; *Who Was Who Among English and European Authors, 1931–1949* 1, eds. Edward Martell, L. G. Pine, and Alberta Lawrence (Detroit, 1978), 453; *New York Times* (obituary), February 27, 1957, 27:4.

3. Charles C. Alexander, *Here the Country Lies* (Bloomington, Indiana, 1980), 147–148.

4. Gari Melchers (1860–1932) was an American painter who spent much of his career prior to World War I in Europe. He returned to the United States in 1914, settled in Fredericksburg, Virginia, and made a splendid garden that is maintained today as part of the Gari Melchers Estate and Memorial Gallery. His paintings were often very intensely colored.

My Garden in Midsummer

Louisa Yeomans King was one of the foremost American garden writers of the first half of the twentieth century and an important participant in the garden club movement.[5] Born in Washington, New Jersey, in 1863, she published her first article in *The Garden Magazine* in 1910 and continued writing into the 1940s. She died in 1948. Mrs. King accumulated a vast knowledge of horticulture while working in her garden at Orchard House in Alma, Michigan, where she lived from 1904 until 1927 when she moved to South Hartford, New York. There she established a new garden, but it is her garden at Orchard House that she describes in this article and in many of her other writings. She published nine books on gardening and numerous magazine articles. From 1922 to 1925 she had a monthly gardening column in *The House Beautiful*. She was a friend and admirer of Gertrude Jekyll, who in turn highly esteemed Mrs. King.[6] This short article conducts us on a tour of her garden in its midsummer glory, as the master gardener casts a critical eye on her handiwork; in some places she makes decisions about how to improve it, and in others she simply revels in the recognition of how wonderful certain plants or combinations of plants are.

It has suddenly burst upon my inner vision that the pale and bright pink climbing ramblers [*Rosa*] have no place together in my perennial garden, unless used as they sometimes are most happily, tumbling over walls in great masses, near equally sumptuous masses of pale blue delphiniums, with few or no other flowers.

The thing which brings me to the aforesaid unpleasant conclusion is the present appearance of one of the gates of our garden. It is a dull green wooden gate, with an upper arch and a solid door. The frame of the gate is of trellis, and today this trellis is completely smothered by, to the left, Excelsa, and to the right, Lady Gay. Masses of these little round roses are blooming as the gentle cow gave milk in the nursery rhyme, with all their might. Below this arch of roses lies the little formal garden, with many things in bloom, delphiniums dark and light, lilies, Shasta daisies [*Leucanthemum x superbum*], violet salvias and petunias, phloxes coming and also gypsophila and a few pale pink ramblers. The expanse of color on the gate posts is out of place. It gives the look of the cover of a seed catalogue of about 1890. No, this is no place for my ramblers, fine though they are in themselves.

I walk to the upper garden from this lower, turn to the left, where at each end of a short walk of brick hedged with clipped spirea Van Houtteii [*Spiraea x vanhouttei*] there are two of the same well designed arches, such as I have mentioned. These are wreathed in pink ramblers, Lady Gay and Paradise; beyond this walk is not only smooth turf, but a fine growth of dwarf mountain pine [*Pinus mugo*] — and it is here that the little rose comes into its own. It is seen only near and against green — or as one looks at it from another angle, perhaps against the blue sky itself — where ramblers like fruit blossoms are always seen at their loveliest. But the teaching here is that the rambler rose calls for a background of green and of smooth dark green if possible, clipped arborvitae [*Thuja occidentalis*], clipped spruce [*Picea*] or other rich-hued non-deciduous tree or hedge. In England it is, of course, the yew [*Taxus*] that encircles the loveliest rose gardens; it is against that wall of green that the ropes and festoons of gay pink roses swing and smile.

"It is delightful," says Lady Eden in "A Garden in Venice," "to pick one's strawberries and cut one's tea roses from the same bed."[7] This delight is not reserved for Italy but is our own experience in Michigan. Eighteen fine bushes of rose Los Angeles skirt our four rows of that luscious strawberry, John H. Cook, than which, incidentally, a finer berry never grew to the proportions of a youthful tomato, or reddened to the color of one. The combination of the gathering and plucking of seeds, flowers and fruit is irresistible.

The Lilies

To look on lilies in the garden's green spaces, and as one looks to hear the sound of falling water, is an ecstacy in midsummer which is new, for these are not ordinary lilies. These are not the lovely *candidum*, or the gracefully hanging Nankeen lily [*Lilium x testaceum*], though both are in bloom now in my garden in scattered groups. No, this is that glory of a lily, whose noble adjective is *Regale*, and I have it this year in profusion. I do not even envy the charming writer of "A Garden in Venice" as she describes her Madonna lilies [*Lilium candidum*], often with eight to twenty flowers on one stalk and the stalk five feet high. These virgin lilies have their own pure pale beauty none will deny. The Nankeen lily has a quaint charm of form, habit and color too; so has *L.henryi*, a vivid and graceful flower; so has *L. elegans* [*Lilium maculatum*], that fiery upstanding bloom; but *Regale* surpasses them all. That glowing trumpet, that slender rosy bud, those rich white pointed petals, and to crown all, that incomparable fragrance — not heavy like *L. auratum's*, but

With the setting of the sun the incomparable fragrance of Lilium Regale, fresh and delicate as that of heliotrope, pervades the garden. Thus crowning the glowing trumpets and white pointed petals of the blossoms, it makes Regale the finest of the lilies.

as fresh and delicate as that of heliotrope [*Heliotropium*]. So soon as the sun drops in the West, before even twilight has come on, this matchless perfume rises on the evening air in the "dewey light", and all the garden seems of an unearthly sweetness. I like these lilies planted above low subjects at the opposite ends of narrow beds; while in bloom they serve as accents, their slightly bending stems and handsome flowers clear cut then against greensward. The play of light and shade upon such flowers is one of the most lovely minor sights to be seen in July. Occasionally four flowers open on the top of one stem — more often two or three. I am so lucky as to have about one hundred *L. Regale* in bloom this year; and never have I seen these squares of green turf so admirably flanked by perfect flowers as at this moment.

The elegance and charm of a little new Rambler Ghiselaine de Feligonde are beyond putting into words. The flame colored bud opens well in water and the variety of tones of color is remarkable in a cluster of say six roses, a few half open buds and two or three small ones still tight, but showing color. Three of the open flowers are pale sulphur yellow with outer petals spread well back. The newly opened roses have an enchanting pale copper hue which sets this rose apart; and the half opened buds show the deep colored center where petals are still folded, the outer ones of the light copper again. The foliage is of a medium light green, leaves more slender perhaps than on the average rambler, flowers averaging eight and ten to the cluster.

Against low clipped privet, delphiniums taller than ever before, raise their blue spires. In places Annchen Mueller or Ellen Poulsen dwarf ramblers send forth sprays of glowing pink blooms, these melting into the pale rose-colored masses of Canterbury Bells [*Campanula medium*] beside them, the two most excellent near each other. As for heucheras (the only color blot on my garden this season, but so lovely, flaming delicately about the darkest red Sweet Williams [*Dianthus barbatus*], that I simply have to leave them in the garden beds), they have flowered in a manner truly impressive. I must conclude that they too love space and air. There has seemed to be no check at all from a recent replanting; in fact, everything we moved has prospered under the process. Even the one precious plant of *Delphinium Moerheimi* which we divided into four, with some hesitation, is sending up three white flowered stems. Phlox Arendsii in its varying soft colors of pinkish lavender and of white, is now, July first, in full bloom, and back of its rounded groups are whitening the buds of the Madonna lily held high on their tall stems. Shasta daisies are opening below, budding sea holly [*Eryngium maritimum*] and some of those luscious violet petunias, known as Karlsruhe Balcony, are opening in secluded spots as if to prove their August and September worth. Delphinium blight, which seemed to hover seriously over this garden last year, has been gotten well in hand now, thanks to the lime and tobacco treatment recommended by Miss McGregor of Springfield, Ohio.

Dwarf Ramblers

It is seldom that I find myself with two opinions about a flower; but two I hold concerning the dwarf crimson rambler rose. That harsh crimson, almost as difficult to place as the over-bright hue of *Azalea amoena* [*Rhododendron x obtusum* 'Amoenum'] in spring, and so painful to contemplate as its clusters take on the purplish hue which foretells their end — that same crimson when set near the violet *Salvia virgata nemorosa*, becomes a crowning beauty on the garden's brow. No finer perennial plant for late June in our latitude can there be than this purple salvia. Entirely hardy, its inflorescence a multitude of upright spikes of small violet flowers, it has the effect of violet velvet in certain lights. Its glory however reaches a great height when the dwarf crimson rambler neighbors it. These plants, like happy lovers, seem made for each other. The rose and the salvia coincide in time of bloom. There is an agreeable contrast in the form of leaf and flower masses and no sumptuous velvet cloak of a Venetian Doge could show a prouder splendor of color than is brought forth by this coupling of flower groups above green turf. I therefore recommend to owners of dwarf crimson ramblers the securing of this superb perennial salvia to give meaning and beauty to what is otherwise a troublesome possession in plants.

House and Garden 39 (MAY 1921): 67 and 72.

ENDNOTES

5. Virginia Lopez Begg wrote on King for *Pioneers of American Landscape Design: An Annotated Bibliography*, ed. Charles Birnbaum and Lisa Crowder (Washington, D.C., 1993), 74–76.

6. Jekyll wrote the preface for King's book *The Well-Considered Garden*, and King dedicated her *Chronicles of the Garden* to Jekyll (Deborah Nevins, "The Triumph of Flora: Women and the American Landscape, 1890–1935," *Antiques* 27 [April 1985]: 909). On the friendship of Jekyll and King, see also: David Ottewill *Edwardian Gardens* (New Haven, 1989), 65; Betty Massingham, *A Century of Gardeners* (London, 1982), 139–149.

7. Caroline Eden was Gertrude Jekyll's elder sister. King refers here to a passage in Frederic Eden's book, *A Garden in Venice* (London, 1903); the book describes the English garden that the Edens made beginning in the 1880s at their home on the Giudecca in Venice. For a description and a photograph of the garden, see: Ottewill, *Edwardian Gardens*, 145.

How to Meet Drought in the Garden

BORN IN DAYTON, OHIO, in 1864, Helen Rickey Albee studied art in New York, concentrating on textile design. In 1894 she married writer and poet John Albee. He was a friend of Celia Thaxter (a poet best known today for her 1894 book, *An Island Garden*) and had attended Thaxter's famous summer salon for artists, writers, and musicians on Appledore Island.[8] The Albees moved to New Hampshire the year they married and purchased a summer home at Pequaket, near Tamworth and Madison, where they maintained a residence for the next forty-five years. Helen Albee died in Pequaket in 1939.[9] She described her country life and the evolution of her garden in three books: *Mountain Playmates* (1900), *Hardy Plants for Cottage Gardens* (1910), and *A Kingdom of Two: A True Romance of Country Life* (1913). Although "How to Meet Drought in the Garden" was not illustrated, *Hardy Plants* includes splendid photographs Albee herself made of her garden. Another of her books, *The Gleam* (1911), provides some insight into Albee's intense spirituality. She contributed excellent garden articles to *The Garden Magazine* and *The Ladies' Home Journal.* In 1897 Albee established an important Arts and Crafts industry in Pequaket, employing the rug-making skills of her new country neighbors in an organized, artistic enterprise that benefited from the improved designs and dyes that she was able to provide. Like Walter Prichard Eaton, Albee believed that it was from among such amateur groups that a "spontaneous, national expression" would develop in American culture. She named her venture the Abnakee Industry and told its story in *Abnakee Rugs: A Manual Describing the Abnakee Industry* (1903); two Abnakee rugs survive today in the collection of the Museum of New Hampshire History. By the time she wrote "How to Meet Drought in the Garden" in 1911, Albee had mastered her garden craft through long, hard experience and was ready to offer some straightforward, no-nonsense advice on the subject. Her recommendations are well worth the modern reader's consideration.

ALL AMATEUR GARDENERS of any experience will agree that drought is the most serious thing that the American garden has to contend with. We have many pests and diseases of plants, which are kept under control by insecticides and care; but a long drought, such as we have had in recent successive summers, is the cruelest disaster that occurs in the floral world.

My garden situated on a hilltop where the native soil is a poor, gravelly, yellow loam, presented a difficult problem, which was rendered still more trying because the few rains that fall in summer follow the watercourses in our mountain district, and frequently the heavy showers that fall to the south and north never reach us. Yet as this garden sustains droughts extending from six weeks to four months with no serious results the methods by which they are met may be of value to others.

Until I gave up the practice of making scattered beds on the lawn by digging over the soil and fertilizing it my efforts at gardening were total failures. At some period each summer a drought would descend that ruined everything. At the end of the season I would discover strange, anomalous growths a few inches high, with tiny wizened flowers that took imagination to identify as poppies [Papaver], asters, cosmos or morning-glories [Ipomea purpurea]. Some radical change was necessary, and it was a question whether I should not be forced to give up flowers altogether, for even shrubs languished.

I decided to make one more effort and to concentrate my plants within a given area, where the beds were dug out from a foot to two feet deep and refilled with a mixture made by dumping separate cartloads of the top loam from the vegetable garden, black muck from the woods, leaf-mould, rotted turf, sharp sand and manure, and hoeing from each of these into a central pile, where the various ingredients were thoroughly blended. This rich compost has repaid all the labor expended, for when a bed is thus prepared it does not need overhauling from time to time, and the soil is just as good now, after a lapse of eight years, as it was at first. As plants increase rapidly they require frequent lifting and division, and when they are reset I dig in new earth, highly enriched, which keeps the soil mellow and fertile. In a deep, rich loam seedling perennials will root themselves from one to two feet deep, and, in consequence, are not in the least affected by any ordinary dry weather. I make no attempt to water these beds unless the drought extends beyond ten weeks. It is where the good soil is shallow and rests upon a hard subsoil that plants root near the surface and feel drought quickly.

Some of the Advantages of Close Planting

In close planting, the second condition of my success, experience has led me to disagree with many good authorities who recommend much space about annuals and perennials. If you have a preference for isolated bushy plants surrounded by bare ground you will not care for my advice. Yet as we all have a common aim to get abundant blossom from healthy plants with the least possible effort my way of achieving that result is entitled to consideration. I found that it was the sun and not the plants that exhausted the moisture; and that if the ground was kept well covered, so that the sun could not penetrate to the roots the earth kept moist much longer. Close planting secures not only a moist soil but also bountiful masses of bloom that present a very different appearance from beds where plants stand baldly and stiffly apart with much bare ground about them. Some people carry this so far that they are able to take a walk about every plant, but their flower-beds look like miniature orchards, not parts of a garden.

So long as the soil is kept rich and mellow plants may be set from three inches to a foot apart, the only rule being not to let them overlap and suffocate each other. One way to prevent this in a perennial bed is to plant it with many varieties that come at various seasons. The early spring flowers will have plenty of room to spread themselves while the later ones are making their first slow growth. When past their bloom cut back the early ones to allow others to develop, and continue this cutting throughout the season. Each of them has thus abundant room for a given period, after which it makes way for others. Cutting plants back forces the vitality into the roots, and by this method a choice variety increases rapidly and can be divided yearly. I have now whole beds of plants which are the offspring of single specimens.

When plants have large or overlapping leaves near the root I strip off some so that they may not overshadow others too much; also that they may not cover the ground too closely, else one may lose the value of the much-needed passing shower. By keeping the ground well stirred and mellow every drop of water counts. In consequence of this method of planting my beds appear to be completely full of flowers at all seasons, though the character of bloom may change from week to week without gaps. Where the beds are cut back into a bank, and the front edge faced with a stone wall from a foot to eighteen inches high, the tangle is so thick that it overflows the boundaries; seedlings have lodged between the stones and at the foot of the wall, and the beds are clothed both inside and outside with the most vigorous growth throughout the season.

In planting beds after this method great care should be exercised not to set small, delicate plants close to those with a spreading, rapacious habit. For example, the chrysanthemum maximum and its first cousin, the Shasta daisy [*Leucanthemum x superbum*], which look harmless as seedlings, in three years' time become clumps two feet in diameter, bearing a hundred huge, daisy-formed, white flowers; also the speedwell (*Veronica*) is a mild-looking neighbor with attractive, bright blue flowers, until it gets well established, after which I have had a single plant grow four feet high in a clump two feet across and make such a close network of thousands of fibrous rootlets that it exhausted the soil for a large area. A very desirable variety of bellflower (*Campanula rapunculoides*) with many racemes of bright blue flowers will do the same thing: all these should be placed at the back of a bed where they will cast a deep shadow upon those in front, and thus shelter them from the sun during a portion of the day.

When Watering Is Necessary, Do It Thoroughly

A third way to meet drought is by proper watering. It is useless to sprinkle plants with the watering-can except as a pleasant refreshment to the foliage. Do not try it even with seedlings. Encourage deep rooting by forcing young plants to run their rootlets down for moisture early in the season. So long as the top of the ground is kept moist the rootlets will run near the surface. When you find you must water in order to save things do it thoroughly. Take a small area each day, dig it over and drench it completely, not by dashing water on it from a bucket, but if you have no hose and running water use a small dipper or old saucepan, and soak the ground about the roots to a great depth; then cover with a mulch of grass clippings, straw, hay, leaves, brush or anything convenient. In watering shrubs dig out the soil on one side down to the very tip of the roots, and then pour on several bucketfuls and replace the soil and mulch. Two such drenchings will carry a shrub through the worst seasons. Water especially the tender or choice things, those which were newly set that season and are still hardly well established, plants which cannot afford a setback, also those about to bloom — for the blossom is a supreme effort of a plant and exhausts its vitality. If you are doubtful of saving it cut it within a few inches of the ground and do not let it bloom at all. I tried this one year when I had just fallen upon a remedy for larkspur [*Delphinium*] blight that had long afflicted me, and the plants were just recovering a normal state when a bad drought overtook them. I sacrificed all my blooms by cutting them almost to the ground which not only saved the plants, but also gave me a late crop of bloom in the autumn, which was doubly appreciated because it was so unexpected. Since then I have tried this method with a number of midsummer varieties and I find that plants will readjust themselves when heavy rains do come, and bloom as if nothing had happened.

After Watering It Is Often Well to Apply a Mulch

Do not let plants go to seed in very dry weather; the seed will be worthless, and I have known hardy perennials to shrivel up and die, just as an annual does when its bloom is over. This is particularly true of sweet-william [*Dianthus barbatus*], which under favorable conditions sends out a quantity of young growths for the next year's bloom. Do not run the risk of losing anything you prize; cut it back to a few inches so as to conserve the energy at the root as much as possible. By watering a small area every evening and mulching as you go along you can carry plants forward two weeks without a second application of water. If the weather looks threatening I often remove the mulch so as to get every drop of water if it rains, and then replace the mulch before the sun gets too high the next day.

An English woman once wrote how she mulched her choicest plants by laying flat stones over the roots after a thorough watering, shifting them about from time to time to protect those most in need. I was inclined to smile upon her idea as a bit of feminine brooding until I discovered one summer, when we were suffering from the longest drought for years, that in a dry, baked walk a cardinal flower [*Lobelia cardinalis*] burst suddenly into bloom. In its native state a cardinal flower seeks the rich, black soil of shaded watercourses or swamps; it is a semi-aquatic plant; yet here it was in the hottest exposure and poorest soil of the whole garden, not merely living, but blooming happily. The secret of it was that a seed had happened to fall near a small stone that made part of a low step in the walk, and the tiny plant had run its root back under it by sure instinct; on lifting the stone I found the soil cool and damp in the midst of parched surroundings, and my English authority was justified! Since then when I set out young shrubs I cover the ground with small, loose stones as a mulch for the first season.

So eager are plants for a shelter to their roots that I find the most vigorous growths lodged in all sorts of nooks and crannies, at the margins of walks and beds outlined with flat field stones, and at the edges of steps and stone walls. Wherever my hoe spares the stray seedling later a sturdy plant appears. Following this observation I have made free use of stone walls as a shelter on the south and west sides of beds, using the small flat boulders — so abundant in New England. Sometimes these walls are built up directly from the ground two feet high; sometimes I have cut back into a bank, have faced the cutting with a low wall, and have thrown the earth over the wall so as to make a terraced bed back from it. This disposal of stones and earth affords a great variety of conditions in even a small area — full sun, partial shade in the morning or afternoon, and full shade on the roots of plants that are set next to the walls.

Few Plants Desire Full Sun All Day

My experience, which has involved the growing of seven hundred varieties of shrubs, perennials and annuals, convinces me that few plants desire full sun all day. They do best where it does not extend beyond six to ten hours. I recall a bed of the annual phlox (*Phlox drummondii*) which was planted on the top of one of my terrace beds. A portion of it was shaded by white birches [*Betula papyrifera*] after two o'clock in the afternoon, and that portion of the bed bore much stronger plants, with larger blossoms, than the other part that had sun almost all day. Where plants cannot enjoy the shadow of a wall, trees or buildings a part of the day, I set the tall perennials toward the sun, shorter growths in front and low plants at the edge, planting thickly so that each shelters the next one, and I keep the earth constantly enriched with plenty of sand, wood-ashes and leaf-mould, all of which retain the moisture. Few things thrive under trees, not only because of the shade, but also because the drip washes the roots, and a tree will, furthermore, exhaust the soil for yards about it by making laps up and down in the mellow earth.

As most people choose an eminence for a house, from which the ground falls away in such a manner that a garden cannot be laid out on the usual level, one may cut back into the higher ground and construct a terraced garden, making it face the east, southeast, or southwest if possible, and the terrace walls will give the desired protection a portion of each day. Where one cannot get stones to face the cuttings, short, round piles not over a foot long may be run back into the bank, upon which others from four to six feet long may be placed horizontally to serve as a facing or retaining wall to the cutting. Here plants can enjoy the sun on their heads and yet keep their roots cool; for such a bed never dries out as does one in the open. Sometimes under the shadow of a wall the earth is so continually moist that it becomes sour, and to avoid mildew or blight one must stir in lime or sulphur.

Not only in times of drought are these walls useful, but they are even more so in winter as snow drifts deeply under them, and the low, spring suns are long in reaching them, which prevents that dread disaster of early spring, alternate thawing and freezing. The deep snow is a perfect mulch and protection, too, even where the thermometer goes to thirty degrees below zero. I grow many things as hardy perennials that are quoted as tender: montbretias [*Crocosmia*], gaura, tritoma [*Kniphofia*], forget-me-not [*Myosotis*], Paris daisy [*Argyranthemum frutescens*]; and many that winter-kill easily, such as white larkspur, foxgloves [*Digitalis*], Oriental poppies [*Papaver orientale*] and hollyhocks [*Alcea rosea*]. I lose nothing from this cause.

The Ladies' Home Journal 28 (July 1911): 34.

ENDNOTES

8. John Albee wrote about Thaxter, who died the year he married Helen Albee, in "Memories of Celia Thaxter," *New England Magazine* n.s. 24 (April 1901): 166–172. I am grateful to Hilary Anderson at the Museum of New Hampshire History for helping me locate Pequaket and for sharing materials on Helen Albee from the museum's files. These materials included a hand-transcribed copy of Albee's obituary from the *North Conway Reporter*, October 26, 1939, 2. On Albee, see also *Woman's Who's Who of America*, ed. John William Leonard (Detroit, 1976), 40.

9. May Brawley Hill discusses her in the context of old-fashioned gardening in *Grandmother's Garden* (New York, 1995), 140–141. One could not describe Albee as primarily an old-fashioned gardener, however.

The Humble Annals of a Backyard: The Rain

THIS SHORT ESSAY is a wonderfully evocative description of the pleasure a gardener experiences watching a summer rainstorm. It is one article from a series by Walter A. Dyer that was later compiled as a book: *The Humble Annals of a Back Yard* (1916). As this title implies, the author's middle-class status — his identity as a plain, dirt gardener with a yard, not an estate — was an important motif in his writing. Dyer was born in Roslindale, Massachusetts, in 1878. In addition to his work on gardens, he also wrote about dogs and American antiques. He served as editor of *Wall Paper News* in New York from 1901 to 1905. From 1905 to 1914 he was first on the editorial staff and later managing editor of *Country Life in America*, whose offices moved from Manhattan to Garden City, Long Island, in 1910. In 1914 Dyer left his job at *Country Life* and moved to Pelham, Massachusetts, where he pursued an independent literary career. The articles that later made up *The Humble Annals* chronicle his experiences living and gardening in Long Island. The narrative begins when he and his wife move to this suburban home from their city apartment and ends when they leave to settle at Rock Walls Farm in Pelham, where he died in 1943.[10] The last article in this anthology, "Morning Chapel," is also by Dyer.

THE LADY OF THE HOUSE does not like thunder-storms, high winds or rainy days, and we seem to have a good many of all three in spite of our annual drought. I don't mind those things so much myself, though I hate to see branches blown from the trees, and I am not free from the depressing effects of a long rainy spell.

But there is a kind of rainy day that I like. It comes after a dry spell, when we have had plenty of sunshine and the garden is parched with thirst. I recall one such recently.

The sun went down in a golden haze, and in the morning we awoke to hear the steady rattle of the rain on the piazza roof. Out in the backyard the garden is drinking eagerly, and already the corn has taken on new life; it seems to have grown an inch. The grass and the lilac [*Syringa*] leaves are washed a clean, glistening green; the dahlia buds nod heavily in the dripping from the ailanthus tree above them. One of my tomato vines lies prostrate, perhaps from a too copious imbibing of the life-giving fluid.

Then I turn to the front of the house, for there is the impression I like to receive. A lone pedestrian hurries up the street, his umbrella held at an angle against the slanting spears of rain. Across the street and a little way down a covered grocer's wagon stops and a man in rubber coat and boots jumps out and dashes around the house with a basket. The horse stands and nods exactly as the dahlia buds do.

The rain comes down so steadily as to produce the effect of a fog, half blotting out the landscape and changing the aspect of familiar objects. All the sharp angles are softened a little, and the motion of the rain gives the scene a look of unreality as though it were a moving picture. All the colors are changed. There is no blue overhead, only a dull, slaty gray that casts its tone over all the landscape. Green, red, white, yellow, all are grayed as with the broad wash of an artist's brush. Only the brown of the tree trunks appear to stand out darker and more vividly. Our street seems turned into a Japanese print.

The grocer's man comes hurrying out and leaps into his wagon. The horse starts off at a smart trot and the street is deserted. I peer through the rain at the houses opposite, but detect no sign of the coming of the Prince to kiss it awake again.

I alone of all the village seem to be alive and stirring. I am shut into a little world all my own. I experience all the joy of solitude and none of its pain. The witchery of the rain makes me as lonely as a mountain in the clouds and I surrender to the enchantment.

The Craftsman 26 (JULY 1914): 389.

ENDNOTES

10. *Who Was Who Among North American Authors, 1921–1939* 1, 460; *Who Was Who in America, 1943–1950* 2 (Chicago, 1950), 167; *American Authors and Books, 1640 to the Present Day*, ed. William Jeremiah Burke and Will D. Howe, revised Irving Weiss and Anne Weiss (New York, 1972) 184; *New York Times* (obituary) June 21, 1943, 17:6.

∽ Mrs. Jay Clark, Jr.
The Last Garden of Fall

HELEN B. (MORRIS) CLARK was garden editor and writer for the *Worcester Sunday Telegram* in Worcester, Massachusetts, for more than twenty years. During the late 1920s and 1930s she also wrote on gardening for *House Beautiful*. Articles on travel were another of her specialities, and during the Second World War she contributed to the *Telegram* descriptions of European cities mentioned in the newspaper's war reports. Her husband, Jay Clark, Jr., an attorney in Worcester, was captain of the United States trapshooting team in the 1920 Olympics and an early enthusiast of automobile racing. According to an account written at her death in 1945, Helen Clark "loved the outdoors and her knowledge of flowers came from a life time spent close to the soil. And most of her spare moments from early Spring to late Fall were spent in her garden."[11] It will be apparent to any gardener that "The Last Garden of Fall" is based on Clark's extensive, personal experience. Like other garden authors of the first half of the twentieth century, she cites Henry David Thoreau as an authority on the workings of nature. She warns against trying to change the natural order of things, specifically the sequence in which plants bloom: if you want to make a fall garden, she admonishes, remember Thoreau's precept that "the greatest charm of the growing thing was an unswerving faithfulness to the almanac."

AUTUMN PICTURES are not made now. Existing ones are the result of last spring's work. Yet I can work myself up into far greater energy of action if I actually see the effect I am trying to duplicate, and have the time to take thought to its planning. So while plants for these last blooms will not be at hand for many months, now is the time to look around at gardens that are pleasing and study what makes them so.

Contrary to the general assumption, the autumn garden is never one of left-overs; never one of annuals scurrying to get in under the wire before the flag is dropped, or of late perennials showing how generous they can be with a second gift of bloom. No matter how valuable and pleasing the remontant

Roses and lavish Phlox may be, they cannot be depended upon as autumn flowers. To be certain of beauty at any particular moment, the wise course is to rely on the plants of that period. Modern wizardry has played hob with seasonableness as Nature intended it, and she tries to point out to those who will see that it is a mistake to juggle her products in a way that was never intended. We force and rush, and push and transplant, and hybridize and use up materials meant to appear in freshness later, in order to have Asters and Gladiolus and Dahlias in July, and have even been known to sink pots of Lilies from the greenhouse among the spring Tulips! Thoreau knew the value of his precept when he said that the greatest charm of the growing thing was an unswerving faithfulness to the almanac. There is no trouble about having autumn flowers as long as the frost holds off, for plenty of plants mature naturally late in the fall, and many of them are able to endure the first cold waves that are so liable to sweep down in many vicinities almost before the end of the calendar summer.

Equally important is the location in which to make your late fall showing. If the garden is a small unified plot, thought will be limited to screening and protection. But where the area is larger, if possible pick a slope for the autumn display. Air drainage plays a vital part in the matter, as cooling air descends and rolls down from any height into a lower plane and settles there. The autumn garden might not be permanently injured by the quick passage of frosty currents, when it would be destroyed if they lingered any length of time. Hill tops, seemingly quite at variance with any idea of protection in their open situation, are warmer spots than snugger corners. Water sends protection over nearby growths by evaporating mists which frosts do not readily penetrate. Ponds or pools are therefore strategic points. The ideal autumn garden faces south and is screened from the northwest winds by walls or hedges, shrubs or glass. The nearer these conditions are approximated the better the outlook in the month of October. There is one procedure quite possible for the small area, although more frequently indulged in by gardeners lavish in cash and labor. Put in position at the edge and rear of the border permanent ground fixtures to hold small poles — on the order of the familiar clothes reel base. At the hint of frost snap in the poles and tie a canvas covering over them, tent-wise. I have seen such an arrangement keep a garden in Massachusetts in perfect condition until the end of October, with splendid richness of coloring.

The plants for the autumn garden are found in every division from bulbs to vines. Start with a foundation collection of gray-leaved types, over which neither heat nor cold have any control, and which remain good-looking until they sleep for the winter. By these I mean Rue [*Ruta graveolens*], the blue-green herb of bushy tendencies that likes lime, and various Artemisias: A. abrotanum, Southernwood, tallish and wandlike, *A. albula* [*A. ludoviciana var. albula*], Silver King, shorter and shimmery, *A. frigida*, which glistens like the frost it scorns, *A. pontica*, Roman Wormwood with finely cut foliage, pale gray. Add to these Woundwort, *Stachys lanata* [*Stachys byzantina*]; *Salvia argentea*, white plush if the flower stalk is cut down, and Lavender Cotton, *Santolina* [*Santolina chamaecyparissus*]. Plant these as generously as space allows. They will form a groundwork of satisfaction. The only annual to be considered is Cosmos, and where experience has proved that the late varieties do not bloom even under favorable conditions before frost, use only the early ones. They are not as beautiful, but better than nothing. Plant them rather late, directly in the ground, about the end of May in northern gardens. When they are a foot high, give them a drastic top cutting, and they will swing into the procession as true fall members. As I have seen the new yellow varieties they are twiggy tall things, best suited for the back of a border, or grown in the cutting garden for indoor decoration. The color is good and they are dependable.

In the perennial class start with Aconitum, not from any alphabetical hint, but for the good blues which range from light to dark of the late Monkshood. *A. autumnale* [*Aconitum napellus* ssp. *neomontanum*], *A. wilsonii* [*Aconitum carmichaelii*] and *A. fischerii* [*Aconitum carmichaelii*] send up early in the spring heavy green tufts of foliage that are assets throughout the summer. Glistening blue is Sea Holly, *Eryngium* [*Eryngium maritimum*], continuous in attraction with bloom and thistle-headed globes; Mistflower, Thoroughwort [*Conoclinium coelestinum*], resembles Ageratum with fuzzy light blue masses. The use of yellow will be determined by the size of the garden, as the Heleniums, Helianthus and Heliopsis, all miniature editions of the Sunflower, are mostly rank in growth and ill-suited to any but the widest spaces. Those best fitting ordinary schemes are *Helianthus mollis*, ashy Sunflower with downy foliage and single pale yellow flowers, and Wolley Dod, a taller one, but of compact growth, with deep golden blossoms.

White is also plentiful — fine, starry Boltonia [*Boltonia asteroides*]; short, heavier Shasta Daisy [*Leucanthemum x superbum*]; the late Snakeroot, *Cimicifuga simplex*, not *C. racemosa*, more often seen; the Japanese Anemones [*Anemone x hybrida*], accounted difficult, but wrongly so if their desires are taken into consideration. They need a heavy, rather rich soil, some shade, soil pack protection in winter, and care in the spring not to break the appearing shoots, late risers as they are. Put danger signals at each clump now, red-tipped sticks for spring warning. The single ones cannot be improved upon, except pale pink Queen Charlotte, and she is only semi-double. Alba is still the beauty of the family. Where there is a multiplicity of petals the effect of rumpled tissue is unpleasing.

All these perennials would make a garden, but the glory of the autumn is found by a free use of hardy Asters, the Michaelmas Daisies, scorned by us in the wild original state, but welcomed after an English sojourn of hybridization and grooming. From the nine inches of pink Countess of Dudley to the six feet of the blue Tartaricus there is an Aster for every use. The gradations of shades read like a color chart: blue, lavender, violet, pink, white, yellow. There is no best. I like Sam Benham for a tall white, Nancy for a low flesh pink, Novae-Anglicae because its brilliant purple sheets the fields of New York State and the garden equally in splendor, October Dawn has good mauve tints, and Ericoides and Cordifolius are domesticated wildings that mind neither shade nor trees, in blue and white. You may choose blindfolded from the lists and pick winners every time. The simplest and loveliest autumn garden can be made with the gray foundation plants, Asters and such buff Dahlias and Gladiolus as Mrs. Saunders and Schwaben. Chrysanthemums for northern gardens are an exciting gamble, unless the site is favorable or artificial protection provided. The new Koreans are the most dependable, with all colors represented but blue. Or if a venture is made in other types, choose from sections marked September flowering. Chrysathemums have the lure of the uncertain, but for similar effects Asters are surer. Dahlias and Gladiolus are a subject apart. They belong more in the collector's realm than in the uses of the average gardener, although for white accents among less spectacular plants such Dahlias as Ida Perkins, Jean Kerr or White King are fine.

Autumn flowering shrubs do not provide a long list, but the quality is good and colors varied. Althaea, Rose of Sharon, Hibiscus [*Hibiscus syriacus*], all one and the same, has many uses, as individual specimens, hedges, standards, in red, rose or white; Callicarpa, Beautyberry — not to be confused with Kolkwitzia, Beautybush — has first tiny pink white flowers, then purple berries; Elsholtzia, the Mint shrub, comes in two colors, *E. stauntonii*, blue, and *E. farquharii*, pink. *Euonymus alata's* leaves are conspicuous in transparent carmine, and Caryopteris, while given under perennials, is woody and tall enough to be utilized for low shrub needs with blue, pink or white misty flower spikes. For a fine foliage effect to mingle with heavier forms, get bush clover, sometimes listed as Lespedeza or again as Desmodium. It dies down each fall but never fails to reappear in the spring with wandlike branches and rose sprays of bloom. A possibility for semi-southern gardens is the evergreen Abelia [*Abelia x grandiflora*], and the north sometimes sees it in favorable nooks.

There are enough vines to clothe any wall or lattice on the premises, and they are among the finest of the whole year. *Clematis virginiana* may flower in the late summer, but the maze of feathery seed masses prolongs its beauty for many days; Bittersweet, *Celastrus orbiculatus*, is the oriental form which fruits more profusely; *Ampelopsis tricolor* [*Parthenocissus*] has brilliant peacock blue berries staying long after the leaves have blown away. The best variety of Virginia creeper is *Ampelopsis engelmannii* [*Parthenocissus quinquefolia* var. *engelmannii*], which is a great clinger, decoration enough of itself for any spot, breath-taking in crimson color as a background for a mass of lavender and purple Asters. The annual vines *Cobaea scandens*, Cup and Saucer twiner, white Moon flower [*Ipomoea alba*] and various Morning Glories [*Ipomoea purpurea*] are true autumn bloomers, and with a sheet at hand to throw over them on frosty night will stay in flower quite as late as anyone wishes to see them.

The rock garden does not need to possess its usual sad appearance of the season's end, if there are judicious plantings of the evergreens such as low Junipers [*Juniperus*] and Thymes [*Thymus*], and room taken from the spring display to tuck in varieties which will not flower naturally until late. No leftovers for this spot. Get *Silene schafta, Sedum sieboldi* [*Sedum acre*], *Polygonum vacciniifolium* — in other words, Catchfly, Stonecrop and Fleeceflower. Add to these the Erodiums, Heronsbill, as many as can be located. Plant blue *Plumbago larpentae* [*Ceratostigma plumbaginoides*] and Cupflower, Nierembergia, to ramble over the rocks, and there will be no need to long for the lavish freshness of spring. Three bulbs claim attention, autumn Crocus, Colchicum and Sternbergia, sometimes the fall Daffodil. These should all be planted not later than August. The first two will flower the same year; the last when it gets good and ready! See the article on Colchicums in *House Beautiful*, August, 1935. In Louise Beebe Wilder's "Adventures in a Suburban Garden," the second chapter (the first being "Winter Notes") is "Spring Planning for Autumn Beauty," and a like emphasis on the subject is the only way to end the season on a high note instead of a diminuendo.

House Beautiful 78 (October 1936): 50–51, 128–129.

ENDNOTES

11. Theresa Davitt, librarian at the Worcester Historical Society, kindly sent me a copy of Helen Clark's obituary from the *Worcester Gazette*, March 7, 1945, and a copy of Jay Clark, Jr.'s obituary from the *Telegram*, February 7, 1948.

At Season's End in the Companion Garden

GRACE TABOR was born in Cuba, New York, around 1873 and lived into the 1950s, residing in the vicinity of New York City. She was one of the best garden writers of this period and shared her expertise in horticulture with an enormous audience through the many magazine articles and books she wrote. Her knowledge of plants and her talent for design were nourished by an education at the Arnold Arboretum at Harvard, the Art Students League in both Buffalo and New York City, and the New York School of Applied Art and Design for Women.[12] *The Garden Magazine, Country Life in America, Woman's Home Companion,* and *House and Garden* all published her articles. She wrote ten garden books, including one on old-fashioned gardens,[13] and articles on wild gardening that exemplified the application of careful thought to a popular topic.[14] This short piece, which records her autumn reflections in her *Woman's Home Companion* garden, presents her sensible thinking about gardens and her ability to communicate an impressive quantity of information in a minimum of space. Like Mrs. Jay Clark, Jr., she counsels against trying to defy nature: if you are not rich enough to hire help for the special treatment that violation of natural law in the garden requires, the increased burden on you will take all the joy out of gardening. Her preference for old-fashioned flowers is indicated in this article, as well as the practical reasons for that preference. The late-twentieth-century notion of minimizing the size of one's lawn in favor of a meadow garden is presaged in this short but thoughtful essay.

LOOKING BACK on what has been, in our *Companion* garden, a desperately unfavorable growing season because of lack of rain, I am impressed with two things about garden-making as it concerns especially the average home-owner who is his own gardener. The first is the mistake he makes in trying ever to garden against nature. Or, to put it a little differently, in trying to grow plants (ornamental or edible, it makes no difference which)

Cedars thrive on our garden hillside, also the hardiest butterfly bush.

that do not fit in with the conditions of soil and climate prevailing in his garden.

Large gardens may afford the labor and coddling of every specimen which unfavorable seasons will necessitate. But in the small garden all the fun of gardening is worn threadbare and turned indeed into hard labor, when each day's plant requirements make demands on time — if not on energy — which encroach upon other duties. Or other pleasures.

Let us then bravely throw out every plant that is a misfit and by discovering the plants that will fit, confine our planting to just these. Nearly all the so-called old-fashioned flowers are adaptable to almost any soil. In old gardens they grew with rampant strength. No one ever sprayed them or dusted them; rarely did anyone dig around their roots; not oftener than once in a blue moon did anyone give them a drink. Yet they carried on — and thus became old-fashioned flowers.

The second item that I want to talk about here has to do with some of the conventional demands which we make upon our garden space. For it is the desire to have what other gardens have which leads to so much needless effort.

There is the lawn, for example — one of the most exacting features imaginable, and yet the one thing that is expected of every tiny plot. Why? A small area perhaps before the doorstep, not large enough to weary with its incessant clamor for the lawnmower; a definite demarkation of one kind or another, separating this from the rest; and beyond this an uncut larger space where clover [*Trifolium*] and goldenrod [*Solidago*] and wild asters mingle in naturalistic fashion.

In the *Companion* garden we are more and more working along these lines because it seems to us important to demonstrate the effects possible with minimum effort as well as minimum cost. Our small slope with its copse and thicket treatment, for example, begins to justify itself already with the increase in bird life noticeable, as well as the beginnings of shadowy vistas that are so refreshing.

Letters from *Companion* readers almost daily include questions on what to do with a sand or a clay or a stony soil in order to grow the usual trees and shrubs and flowers thereon. If these questions could be modified to requests for plant lists suitable to the natural soil in each particular garden — whether it is sand or clay or stony gravel — fewer disappointments would then wait upon each gardener's efforts.

Woman's Home Companion 49 (November 1932): 53.

ENDNOTES

12. Virginia Lopez Begg, "Grace Tabor," *Pioneers in American Landscape Design* (1993), 119–120.

13. Grace Tabor, *Old-Fashioned Gardening: A History and a Reconstruction* (New York, 1913).

14. For example, Grace Tabor, "Wild Flowers in the Garden" *House and Garden* 24 (July 1913): 29–31, 52–54.

✍ HANNA RION
December Gardening

HANNA RION'S garden in the Catskill Mountains at Port Ewen, New York, was the subject of her books *The Garden in the Wilderness* (1909) and *Let's Make a Flower Garden* (1912), as well as several magazine articles, including "December Gardening." A somewhat expanded version of this article subsequently formed a chapter in the latter book. Photographs of the garden were not part of this article in *The Craftsman* but did appear in both of the books. Rion was born in Winnsboro, South Carolina, in 1875 and died in Bermuda when she was forty-eight years old. Her mother, Mary Catherine Rion, was an outstanding gardener and author of *The Southern Ladies' Florist* (1860) — an eminently useful, "hands-on" guide to gardening in the south. Hanna Rion not only wrote books and magazine articles on gardening but was an accomplished watercolorist and the author of a book promoting drugs for painless childbirth, a major feminist issue of the day: *The Truth About Twilight Sleep* (1915)[15]. Her first marriage was to her former art teacher, Frank VerBeck (William Francis VerBeck), who wrote and illustrated books for children. They collaborated on *VerBeck's Book of Bears* (1906). In 1912 they left New York for Warwick East in Hamilton, Bermuda. She must have sent amusing letters and photographs from Bermuda to *House and Garden.* Three times in 1912 that magazine's monthly column, The Office Lounge, included pictures of her along with accounts of her work hybridizing poppies in her new Bermuda garden.[16] She had a lively, witty style of writing and seems to have really enjoyed gardening — and sometimes quarreling with her sister, her "garden partner" — even in winter, which she knew her "city moth" friends would never understand. Social chores like answering letters were of greatly diminished importance in the face of gardening duties. This is a genre of garden writing at which Rion excelled: a cheerful account of a day's hard work and of the tremendous emotional fulfillment she derived from it. There is an equally endearing article by Rion about roses in Chapter Two.

THE FRIEND WHO HAD SPENT some time with us during the summer when the garden was in its poppied, rosy heyday wrote to me when December snows arrived: "Now that winter is here I suppose your friends may expect to hear from you once in a while, as you will certainly be forced willy nilly to lay down your rake and hoe."

It was the second of December when I smiled quizzically over this letter and wondered if this city moth would believe me if I told her I looked forward to one of my busiest months in the garden — that there would not be a day's cessation of the labor and joy in the out-of-doors.

This is a blessed provision of necessity, for with the first brittle taste of December and the crisping of energy, the very frost in the nostrils whets the muscles to toil and with every breath of the ever-chilling air there is the message to hurry, to achieve, before the ice-bound days of January are upon us.

So on the second of December I tossed aside the gray artificially scented letter, and sallied forth with my garden partner, arms laden with our precious horde of freshly arrived Japanese lilies [*Lilium japonicum*], making our way toward the Peony Kingdom. Then from the cellar was fetched the big box of sand which we had carefully stored away one warm scarlet-splashed autumn day, in expectation of this exciting December morning.

The few inches of snow were lifted with a spade and the earth proved to be frozen only a little over an inch. Holes twelve inches deep were dug, then the good old wheelbarrow was squeaked upon the scene laden with a rich compost of old manure and decayed sod and weeds. The holes were given two inches of compost in the bottom, then a heaping trowel of sand was thrown in to make a bed for the great luscious, burr, artichoke-like Auratum bulbs to lie in, with a counterpane of the same sand to cover them. We then filled the hole with the mingled compost and original soil.

Leaves which we had also prudently saved in gunny sacks for this purpose, were then piled over the hole, while over them moderately fresh manure was laid for the triple purpose of holding the leaves in place, warmth and spring fertilization.

My garden partner and I always have great difficulty to avoid coming to blows over the subject of depth in planting. Haven't you met the variety of gardener who would, if left to himself, always plant everything in the center of the earth's axis if he could dig that deep? Well, then you know what I have to contend with and what spirited discussions and stilted dignity occur before a compromise is reached.

The larger Auratum bulbs should be planted ten inches deep; the Speciosum Melpomene and smaller lily bulbs about six inches.

All told we planted twenty-six lilies among the peonies [*Paeonia*]; the latter will give the bulbs shade about the stalks in summer, conserving the moisture, while the foliage of the peonies will make exquisite leafy vases for the bouquets of lilies to rise from.

With tired backs but gleeful hearts we trudged toward the house, and on the way I stopped and brushed the snow off a border, finding a quantity of very fresh sweet alyssum [*Lobularia maritima*] smiling happily under their glittering cover. Across the path in a nook under the white lilac [*Syringa*] were several clumps of brave purple stocks [*Matthiola*] looking like monster double violets.

The next few days were spent distributing manure about the raspberries [*Rubus*] and blackberries [*Rubus*], mulching strawberries [*Fragaria*] and rhubarb [*Rheum*]. The hardy chrysanthemums were reluctantly cut down, for they still displayed touches of yellow, red, pink and white in the center within the brownish edges of the frosted outer petals. The stalks were cut close to the new growth already courageously making haste for the next season. The plants were then mulched with leaves and manure.

Between the labors we sat on the garden bench under the pines where the chickadees came and "sassed" us while a red-headed woodpecker drummed on the tree trunk above our heads.

The green Dutch and white Italian benches are always left out all winter in our garden, for why should we not enjoy a peaceful comfortable hour in the out-of-doors when it is in its most beautiful white winter stage?

Each morning after breakfast we steal out to find if Bre'r Rabbit has been to visit us during the night. I always feel a little thrill when I see the pathetic hunted tracks of the poor things. I wish there were some way in which one could convey a general invitation to all their race to make winter quarters in the safe refuge of our garden where many borders of Scotch pinks [*Dianthus plumarius*] will feed them generously. Here we find half-frozen apples from which a rabbit made a midnight supper, and there he has nibbled the Brussels sprouts.

This reminds me of that most profitable of all winter vegetables — Brussels sprouts. It seems so delightfully paradoxical to go out in a December snow and pick quarts of these tight little green rosettes, which are only made more delectable by the very cold that is death to most other members of their vegetable family. Last year we gathered sprouts far into January.

For our lunch we now dig into the frosty ground and pull forth appetizing parsnips, while for salad there is the chicory. By cutting down the chicory leaves in the fall, banking slightly as for celery, then placing rather fresh manure over them to quite a depth, it is possible to have fresh salad far into the winter from one's own garden.

The idle hotbed had been filled in the late fall with the celery not put into the deep earth trench. Just before Christmas we took off the great covering of corn shocks and snow from the top and on opening the sashes found not a trace of frost inside; the celery leaves were as green and white as though they had been flourishing out under a summer sun. We selected the most perfectly developed ones, filling many crates which we stored in the cellar for our own use during the next two months. One particularly fine crate we sent to friends in the city, to add to their Christmas cheer. On the 24th the Christmas tree was cut — always with a qualm, for it seems so cruel to end its life in the woods for such a brief gay existence indoors.

We had saved enough sand from the lily planting to use for the Christmas tree. The trunk was placed in a tub or bucket and the sand filled in about it, making the firmest and neatest arrangement possible and the simplest.

For the Christmas table decoration there is nothing prettier than cyclamen. No other flower will stand the hardships of indoor winter life as well as the cyclamen. It needs but little sun and will continue to bloom under the most vacillating conditions of heat and cold, light and darkness. It only seems fair though that between meals it should be given a chance at some bright window to enjoy a more natural existence.

The Craftsman 19 (DECEMBER 1910): 306–307.

ENDNOTES

15. Rion also once served as a nurse in the maternity ward of a hospital. Her book is cited as one of the numerous writings by early twentieth-century feminists promoting Twilight Sleep in Donald Caton's recent book, *What a Blessing She Had Chloroform: The Medical and Social Response to the Pain of Childbirth from 1800 to the Present* (New Haven, 1999), 140n. 11. On Rion, see *Who Was Who in America, 1897-1942* 1 (Chicago, 1943), 1036; Chris Pettys, *Dictionary of Women Artists* (Boston, 1982), 599; *New York Times* (obituary) May 6, 1924, 21:5. Her frequently changing whereabouts are recorded in successive volumes of *American Art Annual*, ed. Florence Levy (New York, 1903–1924/25). Rion is mentioned in May Brawley Hill, *Grandmother's Garden: The Old-Fashioned Garden, 1865–1915* (New York, 1995), 138–139, as a proponent of the old-fashioned garden. While Rion may have admired quaint aspects of old-fashioned gardens, it would be incorrect to remember her as having gardened exclusively or even primarily in such a manner.

16. *House and Garden* 21, (April 1912): 7; *House and Garden* 21 (May 1912): 7; *House and Garden* 22 (September 1912): 127. In 1921 her marriage to VerBeck ended and she married Alpheus Baker Hervey, a clergyman and author of books on botany and wildflowers.

Chapter Two

GARDENING WITH TREES, SHRUBS, AND ROSES

These writings on trees and shrubs offer some worthy ideas on how to combine woody plants for the most desirable landscape effects. They describe the importance of trees in the general scheme of the garden and recommend some particular trees and shrubs as the most attractive specimens. Several authors promote native shrubs and trees, and one encourages us to challenge the accepted fashion for undivided neighborhood lawns by planting hedges around our gardens. The final three articles provide instructions on simplifying the care of roses, making the year's choices for new additions to a rose garden, and rescuing overgrown, old-fashioned roses that are languishing on abandoned properties.

ꙮ F. F. ROCKWELL
Trees and Shrubs for Blended Borders

AN EDITORIAL NOTE that accompanied this article marveled that
Frederick Frye Rockwell had, by 1934, written fifteen garden
books and contributed articles to *House and Garden* for twenty-four
years. The editor speculated that the reason Rockwell had so little
gray hair was that his subject was always the rejuvenating one of
gardening. In fact, Rockwell was to live yet another forty-two years,
write ten more books and many more articles, serve as garden editor of the Sunday *New York Times* for nine years, edit several additional magazines, help found the Men's Garden Club of New York,
and meanwhile garden at his home in Nyack, New York.[1] In this
article Rockwell attempts to educate amateur gardeners about
more interesting ways to plant trees and shrubs. His thesis: that
simply looking at, and learning from nature would solve many
landscaping problems, that a careful inspection of natural roadsides
and hedgerows would prove to gardeners that trees and shrubs are
most attractive when planted together. Rockwell analyzes why this
is the case and makes suggestions regarding which trees are most
suitable for such planting combinations. Photographs of gardens
designed by landscape architect Marian Cruger Coffin (1876–1956)
illustrate this article and add considerably to its impact. Coffin, who
studied landscape architecture at the Massachusetts Institute of
Technology, was one of the most successful women in this profession during the first half of the twentieth century. She designed
many important estate gardens, including that of Henry F. du Pont
at Winterthur in Delaware.[2]

IT IS PARTLY the nurseryman's fault, but more largely the owners',
that so many moderate sized places are planted almost exclusively with
shrubs. The nurseryman naturally would quite as soon sell several shrubs
as one tree. If the owner, himself not having a sufficient knowledge of
plant materials and design and failing to engage the services of someone

who does, ends up with a shrubbery planting perhaps adequate in extent but wholly lacking in individuality and character, it is both unfair and profitless in consequence to heave verbal bad eggs at the nurseryman.

The root of the trouble lies in the fact that we have got into the habit of thinking of almost all trees as "specimen" subjects. Unless a place is of very generous proportions, only a few individual trees, so placed and spaced as to have nothing else near them, can be accommodated. In this as in so many other garden problems we will do well to take a look at Mother Nature's notebook, and see how she handles them.

The development of the informal type of planting small and moderate sized places — a distinctly American contribution to landscape architecture — has resulted in a more general employment of shrub borders than ever before. This is a step in the right direction, but many such borders are woefully lacking in interest because, notwithstanding variations in color, the plant habits and mass effects of materials used are too uniform, resulting in a sense of monotony and flatness.

This can easily be corrected by the planting of trees along with the shrubs in the enclosing or background border. An observing glance at any bit of woodsy growth will reveal the fact that Nature draws no line of distinction in the use of trees and shrubs. The humble hedgerow in a farm field or along any road — which has not been so "improved" as to be devoid of all beauty — will furnish a lesson in pleasant landscaping that most of us may profitably take to heart. And the attractiveness of such a bit of natural plant arrangement lies largely in the way trees of various sizes are combined with lower, more shrubby forms in a continuous mixed line of loveliness.

If one pauses to analyze a little it is at once evident why trees improve the planting. They increase by at least a hundred percent the variations in composition possible with shrubs alone: they add character and a certain sense of dignity which shrubs alone can never give; they bring in an entire new range of texture values; and, most important of all, they are the source of those shifting light and shadows, and provide that almost indefinable suggestion of "ceiling," without which no garden close quite achieves its purpose.

With these general considerations in mind, one may well resolve to add trees generously to the shrubbery border, whether it be a new one in the planning, or an old one which somehow or other has never given quite the effect anticipated. Next comes the problem of how to select the trees which will give most satisfaction under the conditions which have to be met.

To begin with, it may be well to define what is meant by a "tree" in the sense in which we are using the word here. While we think of "trees" as being taller than "shrubs," height alone is not a sufficient mark of differentiation; it is more a matter of the norm of growth — the tendency to form a single stem or trunk, with branches spreading therefrom, as against the many-stemmed habit of shrubs.

In Henry Galpin's Garden, New Haven.

Trees of a wide range in size and in form may advantageously be employed in the shrub border. It will help greatly in the process of determining what to plant if they are considered in three general groups: tall trees which will far overtop the shrubs, and give shade and a sense of canopy above; trees, tall or small, used for striking contrast in foliage or texture effect; and small trees which will blend with the shrubs, but add variety, interest and character.

As it is this latter group which will be most freely used, especially on grounds of limited dimensions, they may well be discussed first.

Most of these small trees are flowering kinds, but in the shrub border their value is by no means limited to their floral beauty, which should really be a secondary consideration in selecting them for the purpose under discussion.

Of the dozen or more kinds of small trees which are particularly desirable for use in close planting with shrubs, three are of peculiar value because of their more or less horizontal branch growth. These are the Dogwoods [*Cornus*], the Hawthorns [*Crataegus*], and the common Sassafras [*Sassafras albidum*] — a tree, by the way, altogether too little appreciated by landscapers and too much neglected by nurserymen, the golden globes of its unfolding leafbuds and flowers in early spring, and its splendid coloring in early autumn entitling it to a much more important place in our planting lists.

The ornamental fruit trees — Crabs [*Malus*], Cherries [*Prunus*] and Prunes [*Prunus*] — which, though one may desire them it is often difficult to find space for as specimens about the grounds, may be used freely in a continuous boundary planting. The varieties are too numerous to take up in detail here, but they offer a wide selection in height and shape, as well as in color.

Three small trees of unusual flower charm are the Golden Chain (*Laburnum vulgare*) [*L. anagyroides*]; the Silver Bell or Lily-of-the-Valley Tree (*Halesia tetraptera*); and the Smoke Tree (*Rhus cotinus*) [*Cotinus Coggygria*]. These stand out conspicuously as points of accent, and should be located where their beauty will be fully seen — say well to the front of the border on a swelling curve. The Golden Chain, incidentally, will appreciate the protective shelter of surrounding shrubs, as it is sometimes winter injured in exposed positions.

Three other good things for points of accent, during early spring, early summer and early fall, are the Redbuds (*Cercis canadensis* and *C. chinensis*); the Japanese Tree Lilac (*Syringa japonica*) [*S. reticulata*]; and Althea (*Hibiscus syriacus*). The Chinese Redbud, little known, is considerably more showy than our native species, and of a deeper color. The Japanese Lilac, blooming much later than the vulgaris varieties, merits a place no matter how many of the latter one may have; and it is of real tree form. And the Althea, available in several shades, gives a welcome touch of color long after almost all of the other shrubs and flowering trees have become merely masses of foliage. The Redbuds, Japanese Lilac and the Altheas may be placed at the back of the border.

The all too little known but charmingly attractive and distinctive Starry Magnolia and the graceful Tamarisk [*Tamarix*] are tall shrubs which assume tree-like form as they get older, or can easily be grown, by pruning, to a main stem or two. The former, *Magnolia stellata*, is to my mind infinitely more beautiful than the coarse flowered varieties so generally grown; and its pure white, ribbon petaled, delightfully informal fragrant blooms are always among the first to greet returning Spring. The feathery foliaged Tamarisks are a joy throughout the summer, but especially so when covered with their myriads of minute, delicate, pale rose flowers — in early spring, midsummer, or late summer according to the variety. Incidentally they are ideal for very sandy soil and for seaside conditions. Why they have been so very much neglected is difficult to understand. Both the Starry Magnolia and the Tamarisks may be placed either at the front or the back of the border.

Of the many good trees suitable for planting — usually along the back of the border — as a pleasing contrast to and background for the ordinary shrub masses, we can take space here to mention but a handful.

Were I restricted to, say four each of the deciduous and evergreen trees, easily grown and commonly available, my first choices would be as follows: Larch, Birch, Honey Locust and Mountain Ash among the former group; and Hemlock, Redcedars, White Pine and Holly [*Ilex*] among the latter.

The Larches, both the European [*Larix decidua*] and the Japanese [*L. kaempferi*], are rapid growers, even in poor soil. Being midway between the deciduous trees and the evergreens they possess an individuality all their own. They are usually among the most prized trees in any planting. The Birches are many, but for close planting with other subjects, give me every time the American White Birch (*B. populifolia*) with its white and slender limbed loveliness surpassing that of any other tree. Get a clump formation if you can — though nurserymen generally do not have sense enough to grow any of their stock that way — and give it a position where the trunks will show to the ground. If it can be silhouetted against a group of evergreens so much the better. The Honey Locust (*Gleditsia triacanthos*) is desirable for its finely cut feathery foliage, and the fact that it will grow under most adverse conditions.

The Whitney garden.

The Mountain Ash (*Sorbus aucuparia*) also has distinctive foliage and good tree form, and the clusters of orange-scarlet berries in autumn double its value.

Coming to the evergreens. I would unhesitatingly give first place to the Hemlocks. The one usually offered is the American Hemlock (*T. canadensis*), but there are several other lower growing forms. Unlike most evergreens, the Hemlocks may be kept pruned back (not sheared) to a moderate height without destroying their beauty. The various Redcedars — forms of *Juniperus virginiana* — are indispensable; for corners, forming vistas through breaks in the boundary planting, and other accent points nothing can take their place. The White Pine (*Pinus strobus*) is unsurpassed for forming a quickly grown dense background where it is desirable to block out at any point the view through deciduous shrubs in winter. Other species may be used where the blister-rust is likely to prove troublesome to the White Pine. The American Holly (*Ilex opaca*) is much less likely to brown in winter when given the shelter of other trees and shrubs. No other tree is quite so cheerful in midwinter, but to make sure of the characteristic scarlet berries, both male and female trees must be planted, the latter in the more important positions. Give Hollies acid soil, preferably quite sandy.

Even on the very small place, some overhead shade is desirable. Usually at least a few tall trees may be grown, even if there is not room to space them singly about the grounds, by placing them at the back of the boundary planting.

Among the taller trees which carry their tops well aloft as they mature, and permit the growing of shrubs and other trees in fairly close proximity, are the Elm [*Ulmus americana*], Tulip-tree [*Lirodendron tulipfera*], European Plane [*Platanus x acerfolia*] and Ginkgo [*Ginkgo biloba*]. The lower branches of all these may be kept cut off as the trees develop. Two other trees very effective in a mixed planting, but shading the ground too closely for much else to be grown in their immediate vicinity, and therefore better adapted to use where space is not at a premium, are the Horsechestnut [*Aesculus hippocastanum*] and the Willow [*Salix*].

House and Garden 65 (MARCH 1934): 36–37, 88.

Courtesy *House and Garden*. Copyright © 1934
(renewed 1962) by the Condé Nast Publications, Inc.

ENDNOTES

1. This information derives from his obituary in the *New York Times*, reprinted in *New York Times Biographical Service*, vol. 7 no. 1 (January 1976), 586.

2. Catherine R. Brown, *Women and the Land: A Biographical Survey of Women Who Have Contributed to the Development of Landscape Architecture in the United States: preliminary working paper* (Built Environment Studies, Morgan State University, Baltimore, 1979), n.p. On Coffin, see also Judith Tankard, "Women Pioneers in Landscape Design," *Radcliffe Quarterly* 79 (March 1993): 10, and Nancy Fleming, *Money, Manure and Maintenance* (Weston, Mass., 1995).

Attractions of the Dogwoods

FRANCES DUNCAN was born in Brooklyn, New York, in 1877, and her six books and many articles on gardening reached a large audience of readers during the early decades of this century.[3] She associated with some of the most influential political progressives and leading artists of her time. A well-known suffragist, she belonged to both the Woman Suffrage Party and the Woman's Political Union of New York City. Like other garden authors of this period, Duncan endorsed the notion that gardening could improve the mental and physical health of overstressed, modern Americans. Her own health must have been fairly robust as she lived to the age of ninety-five. Duncan initially learned horticulture by working and studying at Samuel Parson's Kissena Nurseries on Long Island, and later supported herself and her family as a professional garden writer. Early in her career she was garden editor and wrote a column on gardening for *The Ladies' Home Journal*, but was apparently fired by editor Edward Bok, who objected to her participation in suffrage groups. *Country Life in America*, *The Garden Magazine*, *Scribner's Magazine*, and *Atlantic Monthly* also published her articles. She often wrote on gardening for children and was active in the school garden movement. From 1925 to 1930 she was garden editor for the *Los Angeles Times*. In this short article she covers the various members of the dogwood family — including the nonnative *Cornus kousa* so popular again today — and tells how they each contribute to the appearance of the landscape throughout the year. As Virginia Lopez Begg has observed, Duncan was one of the few women at this time who wrote about trees and shrubs, rather than perennials.[4]

To HAVE ATTRACTIONS that last from January to December is a rare distinction among shrubs, but the varied repertory of the dogwoods makes it possible for them to give something exceedingly like a continuous performance. There are the red-stemmed dogwoods making warmth and color in the winter garden when even the viburnum clusters have shriveled and the last scarlet Berberis berry has dropped; there are dogwoods notable in fall for berry adornments; and in May, the carnival season for blossoming trees, the dogwoods are prominent.

In March, almost as soon as the scarlet maples [*Acer rubrum*] show their faint, airy red, the first of the dogwoods, *Cornus mas*, is abloom. The small, fluffy yellow balls of blossom, stuck like burrs to the smooth brown branches, care no more for the rough March winds than the scarlet maples or the fur-coated pussy-willows [*Salix discolor*] themselves. This *Cornus mas* is a small tree, dense and bushy in its growth, rich in foliage — for none of the dogwoods, whether tree or shrub, has any inclination to a straggling or spindling habit.

It is more than a month after *Cornus mas* blooms that the best known of the dogwoods blossoms — *Cornus florida* — and blessed is the man whose woods are full of them! About the tenth of May the trees are abloom. The white blossoms lie like snow on the level branches, making the tree a thing of beauty and a rare joy while the blossoms last. The flowers, like all those tree-blossoms which rush out before the leaves appear, are set close to the stems and with the dogwood's habit of holding its branches level, the flowers face upward, indifferent to the interest of the passer-by. It is a pity that this dog-wood is not oftener seen in its low-branched form. Growing in a forest or densely wooded place the dogwood, like any other tree, must shoot upward some distance before spreading out; but when it has the opportunity (like the beech [*Fagus*], when let alone) it throws out low branches, which give it, especially in blossom-time, a delightful effect of grace and lightness of structure. The tree, however, is usually "trimmed up" as if for street planting, a practice which robs it of its individual charm. The red-flowered variety of this dogwood (*C. florida rubra*) is charming. The blossoms when half opened make one think that the tree is thronged with scarlet butterflies just alighted on the stiff, brown branches; for dogwood "petals," not being actually petals but the involucre of the flower, have a peculiarity in opening. Two of the four petals develop first, the other two are drawn together to a dark point. This is wherein the red-flowering dogwood gets it butterfly effect. Later the flowers expand and, when fully open, look akin to wild roses. The weeping form of the common dogwood (*C. florida* 'pendula') is by no means so successful. The dogwood's vigorous character makes the drooping form one of the horticul-turist's mistakes. Genius in this case seems degeneracy.

Another tree of this type, very lovely in its spring flowering, is the Japan-ese dogwood (*C. kousa*) — Benthamia, as it used to be called — a dogwood which has that touch of ornateness, that perfection of finish characteristic of Japanese work in horticulture as elsewhere. The foliage of *Cornus kousa* is richer than that of its American fellows; instead of turning their faces to the sky, the flowers of the Japanese variety are perfectly willing to have their beauty spied and forego no such advantage; neither do the blossoms appear until they have the proper leaf-setting, but when at the end of May they do appear, creamy white, the edges of the petals daintily crimped to give added softness, they are well worth waiting for.

The shrub dogwoods are not so striking in their spring attractions as the taller-growing type. There are white blossoms on *Cornus alba*; *Cornus candidissima* [*C. racemosa*] is very lovely, and *C. amomum* makes some showing, but the autumn is their season of excellence. Then *Cornus amomum* ranks with the viburnums in its autumn brilliance. It is a tall, loose-growing shrub, with a graceful carelessness of habit. The foliage is rich and abundant, admirably suiting the large clusters of berries, white first and gradually changing to a dark, brilliant blue; later, the purple stems are beautiful in themselves. *Cornus candidissima*, another berried beauty, is of a sightly different type, not so loose in its growth as the *C. Amomum*; compact, well rounded, with a certain symmetry of outline, a dogwood in which more attention has been given to detail. In October *C. candidissima* bears abundant small clusters of ivory-colored berries as large as shot, each borne on a scarlet stem. These berries have a smooth, oily pulp and are very popular among the birds, who esteem them a special dainty. In fact, *C. candidissima* berries are snapped up quickly, as the choice bits on the hedge-row bargain counter. But even when stripped of its berries *C. candidissima* is attractive; the fine red stems that are left give the shrub a singularly delicate, spring-like effect, suggestive of the young red of the scarlet maples.

The early-flowering varieties again make an autumn showing. The yellow-flowering *Cornus mas* is rich in scarlet berries, the common dogwood shows tightly bunched clusters, and the Japanese *Cornus kousa* has fruit like large ripe strawberries.

The red-stemmed dogwoods are quite competent to give color and warmth to the winter garden, but oddly enough, *C. sanguinea* is not the reddest-twigged, being darker and duller than *C. alba* and *C. stolonifera*, the red osier dogwood; a yellow-stemmed variety of stolonifera — *C. stolonifera aurea* — gives yet another bit of brilliant winter color, vivid as the yellow-stemmed willow (*Salix vitellina*) [*S. alba* var. *vitellina*]. These red-stemmed dogwoods, vigorous like all the family, spread rapidly, throwing up suckers at a little distance from the parent shrub. There are of course other varieties, but these are the most important.

Dogwoods are not particular as to soil although they thrive on swampy ground. They form a strong, lusty family, indifferent to most insect pests, and are not half enough planted.

Country Life in America 12 (MAY 1907): 84.

ENDNOTES

3. On Duncan, see Virginia Lopez Begg, "Frances Duncan: The 'New Woman' in the Garden," *Journal of the New England Garden History Society* 2 (fall 1992): 28–35; Begg, "Frances Duncan," *Pioneers of American Landscape Design* (Washington, D. C., 1993), 45–46; *Woman's Who's Who of America, 1914–1915*, ed. John William Leonard (Detroit, 1976), 261.

4. Begg, "Frances Duncan: The 'New Woman' in the Garden," 30.

What America Can Teach England About Shrubs

BORN IN VIRGINIA in 1869 and raised in Detroit, Wilhelm Miller was encouraged by his uncle Moses Coit Tyler to study botany under Liberty Hyde Bailey at Cornell so that he might "harness a sentimental interest in nature."[5] He completed his Ph.D. in 1899 and began to serve as Bailey's associate editor for the *Cyclopedia of American Horticulture*, also contributing several entries to this significant work. Doubleday, Page and Company hired Miller to be the garden editor of *Country Life in America* in 1901, and editor of *The Garden Magazine* in 1905. He wrote many articles for these magazines, mostly in the animated, conversational mode of the following piece.

This article is one of several inspired by his 1908 trip to England, a trip he made to discover the reasons for England's superiority in gardening. Roused by the spirit of cultural nationalism that prevailed during this period, he hoped that he might encourage Americans to begin work toward surpassing England in gardening.[6] The development of an American garden style became his mission, and his extensive writings for this cause enlisted many disciples. It is not without justification that a reviewer for *Landscape Architecture* in 1916 caricatured Miller as the Billy Sunday of the gardening world. (Sunday was a former baseball player who had become a religious revival leader.) Miller recognized that magazines, with their many photographic illustrations, played a more important role than books in communicating a gardening ideal to the American public: "We have few books that have contributed much toward an American style of gardening . . . compared to the bulk of . . . magazines which give thousands of pictures of American effects. The . . . future must . . . pore over the old files of *Garden and Forest, Country Life in America, The Garden Magazine*, etc."[7]

Miller accepted a position as assistant professor of landscape architecture at the University of Illinois at Urbana-Champaign in 1912, giving up his editorial roles at *Country Life in America* and *The*

Garden Magazine in 1911. He became a close friend and follower of Jens Jensen, who advocated the naturalistic "prairie style" of landscape design for the Midwest, a style Miller hailed as a truly indigenous American style of gardening. He published his influential volume, *The Prairie Spirit in Landscape Gardening*, for the Division of Landscape Extension at the University of Illinois in 1915 and was the head of this program from 1914. It was terminated for lack of funds in 1916, and Miller lost his academic position. He never recovered from this professional setback. When he died in California in 1938 his tremendous contributions to American horticulture and landscape design had been forgotten and went unacknowledged in the periodical press he had so energetically served.

THE ONLY MATERIAL in which America has a striking climatic advantage over England is shrubbery. When my colleague, Mr. Leonard Barron, came to America, the one horticultural feature that struck him as new and strange was the burst of spring, especially the dramatic fortnight when the fruit trees are in bloom.[8] For in England spring comes so early and gradually that March is a month of unique floral charm, with its thousands of daffodils and Lenten lilies, its exquisite blue carpets of Grecian windflowers [*Anemone blanda*], and its lambent sheets of gold wrought by the winter aconite [*Eranthis hyemalis*]. But in America March is a rough and flowerless month in the North, and spring comes with a rush when the orchards bloom. England's fruit trees are mostly hidden from view behind high brick walls in private gardens. And while we know nothing about amateur fruit growing for quality, we lead the world in commercial orcharding; consequently our whole landscape is a mass of shimmering white at the poetic moment of the year, just before the trees leaf out. Now, the largest group of flowering shrubs belongs to the same family as the fruit trees, and ninety per cent. of all our shrubs join the mighty chorus that celebrates the death of our atrocious winter.

Another dramatic moment comes in October, when the American landscape has vivider foliage effects than the English. True, the biggest masses of color are supplied by the trees, but the shrubs give the finishing touch to a perfect picture. England can never enjoy such an autumn show because her cool and moist summers prolong growth, while our hot and dry ones promote maturity. England can never produce so thrilling a spring flower

An ash-leaved sorbaria from Afganistan that ought to run out of our gardens the miserable summer-blooming spireas that have stiff cones of purplish flowers.

show, because her autumn is cool and moist and therefore the shrubs cannot properly ripen their wood and make good buds.

The neglect of shrubs in English gardens will be apparent if you examine any of the sumptuously illustrated books on English gardening. The greatest collection of large photographs on this subject is called "The Gardens of England,"[9] yet I have just turned over the 272 plates thus far published without finding a single picture in which flowering shrubs play an important part! In America garden shrubs have always been a common feature, and the most precious old gardens we possess generally contain a few grand old bushes of such height and magnificence as one never sees in the ordinary mixed shrubbery.

But we need not "throw out our chest like a Russian sleigh" because of this one advantage. For it will be at least three hundred years, in my opinion, before America becomes one great garden, as England is. And our advantage in deciduous shrubs is more than counterbalanced by her advantage in evergreen shrubs, especially hybrid rhododendrons. For these gorgeous plants not only have their showy bloom, but their magnificent foliage is full of inspiration all winter, while deciduous shrubs, broadly speaking, look naked and shivery in our climate. The English winter is naturally mild, but the ubiquitous English laurel [*Prunus laurocerasus*] (which we cannot grow) makes it cheerful and beautiful, while ours is bleak and ugly. I cannot understand why horticultural writers nearly always jumble these two elements in the same article on "shrubs." For good landscape gardeners never put both in the same shrubery border. And we can have no clear thinking or good design unless we make a sharp distinction between precious and worthless material for winter since, in the North, this comprises five-eighths of the year, or from the middle of October to the middle of April. Therefore, the present article deals only with the deciduous bushes.

And now comes the third great advantage of our shrubbery, for we can beat England on red berries that last all winter and on shrubs with brightly colored bark. And just as the Canadians have made their long, steady winter an attractive season for tourists by their picturesque sports, so the fickle winter of the northern United States can be made to draw people from all parts of the world to experience the unique charm of highly colored berries and branches.

Now, then, the threefold superiority of our shrubs is apparent — the burst of flowers in spring, the vivid foliage in autumn, the brilliant berries and branches in winter. But have we developed our shrubberies along these natural lines? Not at all. On the contrary we have blindly and slavishly followed European precedents. We import all their man-made freaks and dot our lawns with them, so that they look like Joseph's coat turned inside out or the side-shows of a circus. For, every great personality among the shrubs that we ought to know and love for its own sake has its cut-leaved, weeping or purple-foliaged variety, and as to such gaudy stuff we are simply mad. It is worse than a crime to plant one's place chiefly with such truck; it is a *blunder*. I explained the reason of this last month in the article on trees.

The only one of nature's suggestions we have followed is that which culminates in the "spring garden." The most superb example of this, I suppose, is the estate of Mr. H. McK. Twombly, at Madison, N. J., where nearly every plant was chosen because of some attraction it presents between the middle of April and the first of June. Personally, I like better the year-round-home of Professor Sargent, where the spring garden is only one of many beautiful features, all well proportioned, related, and secluded. But I have no quarrel with wealthy Americans who choose to glorify spring to the utmost, so that they may walk amid a dream of beauty for the six weeks such an estate is used by the family. For private specializing on a princely scale gives us visions of new and better things that everyone may enjoy when the world gets better organized.

But for the ordinary person an exclusive specialty is all wrong. The quickest way to make America beautiful is not to have a rosarian in one house, a dahlia crank next door, and so on, but to have every place interesting the year round. The obvious reason is that the vast majority of us cannot afford more than one home at a time. And in order to make a place attractive 365 days in the year we ought to put more thought on shrubs than on any other plants. There are many reasons for this. One is that they give us brighter color in winter than evergreens and at less expense. On a great estate trees are a bigger item, because they form the framework of every home picture, while shrubs are only the trim. But city and suburban lots are so small that only a few large trees, if any, are desirable, and therefore we must always look to shrubs as the main attractions, because they are more permanent than other flowers and cheaper than evergreens.

Therefore, I believe, the instinct of the American people in making shrubbery a national institution is thoroughly sound. The American idea is to have the front yard of every small place composed of an unbroken lawn flanked by irregular borders of shrubbery. This frank, open treatment which subordinates the individual's rights to the park-like effect of the whole street, is a fit expression of a democratic people. But such publicity is abhorrent to the English, with whom privacy is the dominant passion. Therefore in England front yards in city or suburbs are surrounded by a hedge or wall, and generally contain straight rows of broadleaved evergreens, such as holly [*Ilex*], box [*Buxus*], and aucuba. The almost daily showers in England keep these noble decorative plants free from dust. In all parts of America the summer is too dry for mile after mile of streets lined with broad-leaved evergreens.

But if we have the right instinct about shrubbery, we are pitifully weak in carrying out the idea. For the ordinary mixed shrubbery is attractive only two months of the year and an eyesore for five. This is simply because the only shrubs we all know are those with showy flowers. Consequently, when ordering plants for a new shrubbery we merely write down the names of all the glorious old-time favorites such as lilacs [*Syringa vulgaris*], azalea [*Rhododendron*], mock orange [*Philadelphus*], spirea [*Spiraea*], and hydrangea, all of which are totally devoid of interest for at least five-eighths of the year, while most of them are also commonplace in foliage. The same is true of the vast majority of shrubs that are famous for their flowers. It is absolutely impossible to get artistic effects by this method. We must get rid of the pestilential old idea that shrubs are only good for flowers. The nursery-men ought to stop writing "flowering shrubs" in the catalogues instead of "deciduous shrubs." And they ought to quit booming the few shrubs that flower in July and August because we do not need excitement in hot weather; we need repose, and the most reposeful color then is green. Summer is the natural resting time for shrubbery, between spring flowers and autumn fruits, and our natural time to enjoy the texture of foliage. It is all wrong to try to make the shrubbery brilliant in midsummer with a lot of loud-mouthed purplish-magenta spireas like Anthony Waterer [*Spiraea x japonica* 'Anthony Waterer'], or "ever-blooming bores" like hydrangeas. It is bad enough to have our autumn landscape made monotonous by too many top-heavy hydrangeas in every yard, without filling the shrubbery in summer with these unnatural double flowers. A "night shift" may be proper at the glue factory, but we don't want our shrubberies to look as if they were working overtime. In other words, what we ought to have in every home shrubbery is flowers in spring; foliage in summer; colors in autumn; and berries and branches in winter.

All this we can have by planning our home grounds with reference to twelve months instead of two or three. Forget all about the old-time favorites for a minute. You need not sacrifice any of them, but try this easy plan and your eyes will be opened to a new world of beauty. It is not even necessary to know one kind of shrub from another. All I ask is that you make a list of the twelve months and have two or three attractions for each month. Now list your favorites and you will see that they help you only in two or three months. The best way to fill the big gaps is to employ a landscape gardener. If you can't afford that, go to a nursery and fill in your blanks from the shrubs themselves, instead of checking off names in an alphabetical list. If you can't do that, make up your list with the help of good classified catalogues and the list of shrubs for special purposes referred to at the end of this article.[10]

The only part of this programme that seems hard is the selection of summer or foliage effects. But here's the answer to that — Cornus and Viburnum. We've got to have lots of those bushes anyhow for autumn and winter effects. They may not be the showiest things in the world when in bloom, but for texture of foliage, play of light and shade, and individuality of bush they are hard to beat. If you want to wake right up to our "heaven-born opportunity" with shrubs, go to Boston in summer and drive through the Arnold Arboretum. For there you will see all the long-lived American and Japanese bushes that have the noblest or most graceful personality, and you will see how cheap and tawdry in comparison are such Coney Island muckers as the golden elder [*Sambucus canadenis* 'aurea'] and purple-leaved plum [*Prunus cerasifera*]. And then you will understand what the best landscape designers and nurserymen mean by such words as these: "Flowers are not the main object; they are only an incident. The principal thing is the form, texture, and density of the foliage masses and their way of carrying lights and shadows." I used to think that such talk was only "hot air" by the picayune brand of expert who exalts the technical above the human — the letter above the spirit. But it's plain, horse sense. For any particular shrub blooms only a fortnight or so; what you have to live with every day for seven months is foliage.

I am sorry to disappoint you if you were expecting me to tell you how to copy English effects with shrubbery, for there aren't any worth worrying about. Of course, I took about a bushel of notes on beautiful shrubs I saw there, but when I came back I threw them away, for they are no use to us. We have got to hew out an entirely new path. And it would be a sin and a shame for me to crow about Cornus and Viburnum and Hydrangea, simply because England can never touch us there. For, the big fact is that we are three hundred years behind England on gardening and we ought to get busy. The irregular shrubbery border is "our game," but we play it in the wrong way, and so the one thing we need most is not a list of material, but a *better way to plan a border!*

No magazine can teach the people the art of design. But here are a few rules that anyone can use with better results than the haphazard methods we commonly employ. First, draw a diagram of your home grounds to scale. Then place your trees where they will shut out unsightly things and frame pictures of beautiful objects in the distance, such as a church spire. Then indicate where big bushes are necessary to hide what you don't want to see, and leave blanks where they would cut off the good views. Then make a bold, irregular outline for your shrubbery border, leaving room in front of the tall shrubs for low ones. The rest should be unbroken lawn.

Next comes the selection of the best bushes for the chief mass effects — say twelve kinds, one for each month, and then the arrangement of these. Don't try to select all your bushes now, and don't put off arranging them until the shrubs arrive. Make twelve slips, or one for each important period — April effect, May effect, and so on. Add to each slip the ultimate height of the bush and the color of the flowers. This is the easiest way to secure "finish" and avoid color discords.

The next job is to separate the slow-growers from the quick-growers, for the former cost most and are soon crowded to death by the latter in the ordinary mixed border. The quick-growers are privet [*Ligustrum*], spirea, mock orange, hydrangea, golden bells [*Emmenanthe penduliflora*], deutzias,

Japanese crab (Pyrus floribunda) [Malus floribunda], example of the many April-flowering shrubs which bloom before the leaves and therefore show best against an evergreen background.

red-twigged dogwood [*Cornus alba*] — anything you can buy in the form of one or two year plants at $3 to $20 a hundred. This is the stuff that will attain the height of a man in three or four years. The reason you can buy it so cheaply is that it can all be easily raised from cuttings; whereas the costly shrubs have to be propagated by slow methods, such as grafting, layering, or seeds.

The quick-growers are to go in the back and the slow-growers in the front of the border. Typical slow-growers are lilacs, Japanese maple [*Acer palmatum*], white fringe [*Chionanthus virginicus*], pearl bush [*Exochorda*], Japanese redbud [*Cercis chinensis*], dwarf horse-chestnuts [*Aesculus parviflora*], and azaleas. These cost about fifty cents each or more.

Now draw the foundation line of your house and indicate all the most important windows, because we want a beautiful picture from each window and each view is to be strikingly different from every other. Nearly all the foundation line should be hidden and the ideal material for banking against a house is broad-leaved evergreens. Consider this material first, as it is the costliest of all.

Then take the view from each window in turn. Don't put your big flower show opposite the most important window, because flowers are short-lived. Put a winter effect there, and be sure it has good foliage in summer. Hold the list of effects by months in your hand and think how twelve bushes of each kind would look from each window when the plants have grown to the height of a man. Thus you will be sure of strong, simple mass effects that are good to live with, not a weak, spotty, distracting mixture.

Next indicate directly on the plan where the conifers or other evergreens are to stand. You must do this now, because your winter berries and branches will be ten times as effective if seen against an evergreen background. The same is true of forsythias and all the April flowers, since these bloom before the leaves.

Now it is safe to indicate where each tall bush is to stand. When these are full grown they will be six feet apart and for the finished picture you may not need more than six of a kind in any one group. But the right way is to order three times as many small plants as you need and set them two to four feet apart. This always seems wrong to a beginner. It looks just like a nursery-man's scheme to sell more plants. But landscape gardeners and park superintendents have no such interest and at a recent convention the senti-ment was practically unanimous in favor of the old rule, "Plant thick, thin quick." One reason is that if you plant far apart, the place looks raw the first two years. Again, it costs more for cultivation. Again, the bushes actually do not grow as fast, because they are too far apart to shelter one another from drying winds, etc. On the other hand, if you plant thickly and begin thinning the second year, you can sell the larger plants you don't need or move them to some other part of your grounds. That's the cheapest and quickest way to get the best bushes. Don't try to save three years by buying extra large bushes, except in the case of a few near the house or in the garden where immediate effect must be had. In three years small shrubs will catch up with big ones. That is not the case with trees.

The Finishing Touches

Last of all come the finishing touches. You want some edging plants that arch over to the grass, so as to make an easy transition from lawn to tall shrubbery; therefore, choose arching bushes that grow one to three feet high, like *Deutzia x lemoinei,* Japanese barberry [*Berberis thunbergii*], Thunberg's spirea [*Spiraea thunbergii*], stephanandra, and yellow-root (Xanthorrhiza). The first thing the beginner thinks of is the spice — such as purple-leaved barberry [*Berberis thunbergii 'atropurpurea'*] and variegated dogwood [*Cornus florida variegata*]. It should be the last to enter into the garden scheme.

When planting time comes interlace your big masses instead of keeping each kind in an absolutely solid mass. For instance, suppose you have twelve cranberry [*Vaccinium macrocarpon*] bushes that are to stand next to twelve common barberries. Place one or two cranberries a little inside the barberry mass and *vice versa.* Then your mass effects will be just as pure and strong as ever, but they will not seem too studied. That is the last touch that foresight can give. The crowning loveliness age alone can bring.

Garden Magazine 9 (MARCH 1909): 75–78.

ENDNOTES_____

5. He cites this advice as the inspiration for his career in horticulture in the dedication to his 1911 book, *What England Can Teach Us About Gardening.* On Miller, see Christopher Vernon, "Wilhelm (William) Tyler Miller," *Pioneers of American Landscape Design* (Washington, D. C., 1993), 86–88; Vernon, "Wilhelm Miller and *The Prairie Spirit in Landscape Gardening,*" in *Regional Garden Design in the United States,* ed. Therese O'Malley and Marc Treib (Washington, D.C., 1995), 271–275.

6. This article was later included as a chapter in *What England Can Teach Us About Gardening* (Garden City, New York, 1911). In this book he describes his initial despair at seeing how beautiful England was and believing that it would be impossible for America to equal it for a thousand years. But then he recognized that if Americans used American and Japanese plants rather than European materials, they would achieve equally brilliant effects without the wait: "We can get 90 per cent. of the English luxurance in our own lifetime by planting our longest-lived native trees and shrubs" (*What England Can Teach Us About*

Gardening, 6). Mary Cunningham makes approximately the same point in her 1925 article (see below, 148–155). Miller may be credited with introducing this plan to American gardeners with a nationalistic bent who were nonetheless in awe of English gardens.

7. *What England Can Teach Us About Gardening,* viii.

8. Leonard Barron (1868–1938) served as assistant editor of the British magazine, *Gardeners' Chronicle,* in London before moving to the United States in 1894. He was managing editor of *The Garden Magazine* from 1905 to 1911, while Miller was editor, and took Miller's place as editor from 1911 to 1928.

9. Miller is probably referring to Charles Holme, ed., *The Gardens of England in the Southern and Western Counties* and *The Gardens of England in the Midland and Eastern Counties,* which appeared as two special issues of the British magazine *The Studio* (winter 1907–1908; winter 1908–1909), each with 136 plates. A third issue in this series was published in 1911.

10. Miller listed articles on shrubs recently published by *The Garden Magazine* and *Country Life in America.*

✑ OLIVER COLEMAN [EUGENE KLAPP]
Concerning Walls and Hedges

FRANK J. SCOTT'S BOOK *The Art of Beautifying Home Grounds of Small Extent* (1870) seems to have played an important role in making fashionable in America the continuous, seemingly communal neighborhood lawn that allows no privacy within individual yards. Although in 1909 Wilhelm Miller considered this type of lawn reflective of Americans' open, frank, and democratic spirit (see above, 51), by the 1890s this arrangement had already come under aesthetic fire, and the battle continues to our day. In this article Eugene Klapp contends that the monotony of the suburbs could be substantially mitigated and beneficial privacy gained if homeowners would enclose their properties with walls or hedges — as is the custom in Europe. Klapp's reference at the end of the article to the cozy, enclosed garden scenes in illustrations by British artists Walter Crane (1845–1916) and Kate Greenaway (1846–1901) indicates that British art played a role in forming many Americans' notions of the ideal garden.[11] Klapp, an engineer from Chicago, was one of the two founders of *The House Beautiful* in 1896 and served as chief editor for the first two years of its publication. This article is from a series he wrote titled Successful Homes. The collected articles were later published as a book in 1899 and re-issued three times by 1906.

THE LINE BETWEEN selfishness and an allowable rightful insistence upon our proper rights is not always an easy one to draw. But there need be no uncertainty when it comes to a question of the privacy of the home and the never-to-be-forgotten Anglo-Saxon principle that each man's house is his castle. It is the very essence of this sturdy precept that this castle may be guarded from inquisitive eyes as well as from the impudent intrusion of each passing stranger, or the still more reprehensible prying of an officious neighbor. That the builders of our American suburbs and towns are totally lacking in any adequate conception of this idea is all too apparent. The fence, where employed to designate the boundaries of a property, fulfills its object so inadequately and serves a purpose so uncertain and imaginary in any town where the cattle have ceased to run the streets, that it seems by common consent to be passing almost into oblivion. It certainly lends no picturesque element to the landscape, and affords not the slightest trace of privacy to its owner, but simply boldly proclaims the ownership of the enclosed earth, as if to say: "I own these 60x175 feet; you may look over and covet my house, but you may not enter." There are many towns in which those who take such matters much to heart are heading crusades against the fence, and each year sees new converts to the open lawn, which soon, if not already, will dominate the landscape everywhere. There is a sameness about the uninterrupted stretch of lawn with here and there a house set down upon it which tires the eye and fails to interest the imagination. It is one of the principles of human nature that things half seen appeal most strongly to our taste and tempt us most with interest and appreciation. A fruit tree in bloom just showing over the top of a garden wall, the breath of the lilac [*Syringa vulgaris*] wafted from behind a hedge, or a short vista through a garden gate of a winding path and pink brick walls against which a row of hollyhocks [*Alcea rosea*] are stiffly blooming — each of these makes for an imaginative soul the nucleus of an exquisite picture, and leads him back many a day to catch one more look at the blooming boughs or once again to drink in the fragrance of waning lilacs. What of this can a level lawn do for a man, what can it offer to bring him back again? True, it may have been clipped since last he passed, and the sprinkler may be running with a merry whirl, throwing the water perchance away across the sidewalk, and forcing the passer by to flee into the street if he would escape a ducking. There may be flowers, to be sure, but they will be in ordered beds and far enough from the sidewalk to prevent the picking of them by the passing boy. The house is often of irreproachable architecture, but it is an unset gem; all its bad points, if such there be, glare out upon the world, and all its good points are lost in its proximity to its neighbor and the lack of picturesque surroundings. The family might as well sit upon the sidewalk, for all the privacy they secure upon the porch. The grounds are theirs, but they may not use them for the many pleasant purposes which make a country life the preference of so many. The children, when they romp without, are playing in the street. They run from house to house and lawn to lawn, and cannot be controlled in choice of playmates as their seniors wish. The fence is poor and cheap and bad, a lack of fence is unpicturesque and commonplace.

In Europe, England especially, and in a few of the older places on the Atlantic coast this problem has been solved long years ago by the wall and the hedge.

There is the wall alone, of brick or stone, and this is very good; there is the hedge alone, which answers every purpose of a wall, and finally there is the low wall with iron fence upon the top and backed by a high hedge for screen. This too is good. The wall costs money, it is true, and the hedge takes time to grow. But is not the security from constant surveillance worth almost any sum, and is not the pleasant atmosphere of an old and fragrant garden worth any time of waiting? Behind this grateful screen a man can be at home and cultivate his flowers. On a hot summer evening he can dine out of doors and leave the steaming dining room to those who have their lawns. Nor does this imply necessarily isolation or selfishness on the part of the owner. His friends will share with him the pleasure of his roses and the freedom from the sights and sounds of the city. When once within this atmosphere, the hot, distant city will seem many miles away. As to the effect of such innovations upon the general appearance of the town, can there be two questions? Are the outskirts of London and Lyons, the country towns of England and France less picturesque and interesting to visit than the parallelograms of green lawn which have in this country, under the title of suburbs, become a scornful by-word for commonplaceness? It is inexplicable why we should go on, year after year, wasting our opportunities in such a dreary manner, each living the same life, in houses with the same ground plan, upon a square of green of the same size. Let us give up the building line and the planting space, and let each one have a place different from his neighbor on the right and still different from his neighbor on the left. Let us put our house upon the street, where it will occupy perhaps the whole front of the lot; let the kitchen be in the front, the drawing room in the rear facing the garden. Wall it in and improve it as a garden and not as a yard. Or if this be too iconoclastic set the house upon that dreadful building line, with only a formal garden in front, the house showing perhaps over a five-foot hedge and between the brick posts which support a wrought iron gate. In the rear have a rambling garden with flowering shrubs and trees. Let the dining room face the garden, by all means. Nothing is more pleasant than such an outlook from a breakfast table.

Still another effect is secured by setting the house well toward the rear, leaving only sufficient room back of it for a small paved yard for kitchen and laundry uses, and using all the long sweep in front for decorative purposes.

There is in Washington a large mansion built upon the street line on a corner, behind which is a walled-in garden. From above the wall come out such songs of birds, such fragrance of flowers and such a waving and rustling of tree tops that the passer-by involuntarily stops and mentally calculates if there be no way for him to scale the wall and see what lies beyond. Baltimore has many such attractive places right within the city proper, which makes of it one of the most pleasing of all towns to live in.

There is a house in Germantown standing endwise to the street, and directly upon it. A high stone wall covered with vines is built against the corner of the house and closes in the garden, which, as well as the house, is entered by a wrought iron gate below an archway in the wall. The well known Craigie house, in Cambridge, is half hidden behind a low wall and fence, back of which a hedge grows strongly.

Walter Crane and Kate Greenaway, among other illustrators, have long appreciated the possibility of such combinations, and many of their drawings of walls and hedges with garden vistas through the gateways are so alluring as to well repay reproduction. The opportunities are unbounded and the need is crying. The advantages of such secluded gardens are so patent, the charm so irresistible and the contagion so certain that let but a few dare public disapproval and all the world must follow.

The House Beautiful 2 (JULY 1897): 42–45.

ENDNOTES

11. This was not a short-lived phenomenon. An article written nearly four decades later favorably cites an American for having designed a gate for her garden based on a Kate Greenaway illustration (Margaret Goldsmith, "Friday to Monday Garden," *House Beautiful* 75 [February 1934]: 19). Greenaway deliberately used imagery that was already old-fashioned in her time and that later generations continued to find extremely quaint and appealing (Gordon Ray, *The Illustrator and the Book in England from 1790–1914* [New York, 1976], 156–157). Ottewill describes the impact of nostalgic book illustration on garden design (*Edwardian Gardens* [New Haven, 1989], 30). For yet another article demonstrating the influence of British art on the American idea of what constituted a charming garden, see Alice M. Rathbone, "A Plea for Gay Little Gardens," *Country Life in America* 1 (December 1901): 52. Rathbone claims to have discovered the secret to creating such a garden at a recent exhibition in New England of British paintings of cottage gardens (possibly by Alfred Parsons who, Anne Helmreich kindly informed me, traveled to the United States around 1900).

∽ E. P. CAHOON
A Shrubbery Group of Wild Things

MAGAZINE ARTICLES often condemned the pillaging of wild plants from nature, but just as frequently the authors of these articles described their own plant-gathering expeditions with guilt-free satisfaction. In this article the perpetrators have just built a house in the country and have no money left in their budget for landscaping. Since it is thrifty — and hence virtuous — to use what is available for free, frugality is often the excuse for removing plants from the wild. None of the plants mentioned in this article is rare, however, so while the practice in general is pernicious, the damage in this case is surely insignificant; the scavengers are at least very careful to move the plants without damaging them. Their appreciation of native shrubs is typical of this period and the subject of many such articles on woody plants.

WHEN THE NEW HOUSE in the suburbs was fairly finished and they had moved in, not a dollar was left over; in fact, the man who came to do some extra tinkering on the cistern had to be paid, for the time being, with a promise. Under these circumstances, there was nothing of course for shrubs.

And perhaps it was just as well that it was so, for otherwise they never would have found what glories were all around them. It was summer, so of course, nothing could be planted until fall. Even then the expenditure of every cent of the family income had been planned for months to come.

That is how She came to say, "We'll dig up that Thornapple [*Crataegus*] tree we used to see when we came out to watch the house grow." It was on a stretch of wild woodland on their way to the city, and had attracted their attention in the spring by its wealth of snowy fragrant bloom.

And that set them thinking of other lovely things they had seen, and set them marking these same shrubs that they might distinguish the right ones in the fall when the bloom and foliage would be lacking, and they should come to transplant them.

In their Sunday afternoon walks they soon found a fine pink Meadow Sweet, which is really a beautiful native Spiraea (*S. salicifolia*) [*Spiraea latifolia*].

They marked it, and, at the same time, a high-bush Cranberry (*Viburnum opulus*), with a little strip of red cloth, and two months later found the birds had fancied and had carried the strip away to add a bright note to their nest-dwellings! So next time the two marked the shrubs with a bit of shingle tied on with a wire.

"We'll plant all this end of the lot with wild things," said She, "and when we can afford it we'll plant the west end of the place with nursery stock," said He; and so it was settled. In the meantime the west end of the lot was plain lawn of indifferent appearance.

They now began in earnest, and prepared the soil by working it into shape as if they were expecting a carload of things from a nursery. In the summer evenings He spaded the ground and broke up all the lumps. They outlined the plantation in a sort of irregular border such as they had seen in landscape work of neighboring places.

"Our shrubs grew in the woods; we'd better get some old decaying leaves, and some leaf-mould." So they hired a boy to scrape up and draw to the garden a load of leaf-mould, and the mistress went with him to the woods as official overseer to be sure the boy scraped and collected only the fine, soft black substance from the top of the woodland earth — the true leaf-mould.

A little sand, which the plasterer had left, was mixed with this soil for the sake of drainage, and this load of leaf-mould with a small load of fertilizer from a barnyard nearby was well mixed into it by turning with a fork and

An Elderberry bush was one of the shrubs marked for transplanting — one of the loveliest though least appreciated native shrubs.

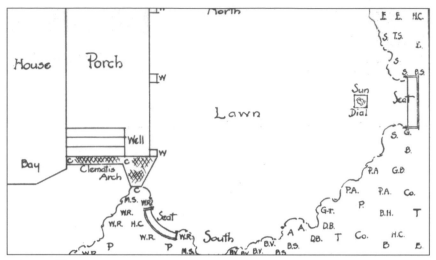

The shrubbery border as finally planted appeared as thus:

W. – Woodbine	G.B. – Gooseberry	B.S. – Bitter Sweet
D.B. – Dog Bane	H.C. – High-bush Cranberry	S. – Shrub Sumach
G. – Wild Grape	A. – Asters	T.S. – Tall Sumach
C. – Clematis	E. – Elder	T. – Thornapple (Hawthorne)
B.V. – Blue Vervain	Co. – Cornus	B.H. – Black haw
B. – White Birch	W.R. – Wild Rose	P.A. – Prickly Ash
P. – Plum	M.S. – Meadow Sweet	
B.S. – Black-eyed Susan	G.r.– Golden Rod	

The tall Sumach has not only the merit of rich fern-like summer verdure but crimson fruits in fall and winter.

spade. The ground then had to be left to warm and soften in the summer sun, with only a digging over each two or three weeks to turn the weeds under. In the fall it was in excellent condition. At the edge of a swamp down the road, not far away, they found a Black Haw (*Viburnum prunifolium*), and near it, among the Hazel [*Corylus americana*] brush, a yellow Honeysuckle vine [*Lonicera flava*] and these they likewise marked for taking up in the fall.

An Elderberry bush (*Sambucus canadensis*) was trailing its black berries from a fence corner as they passed on one of their long tramps, and that, too, was promptly marked for transplanting. Coming home they saw at a little distance a thicket of wild Plums [*Prunus hortulana*], so they went nearer to see if there were small trees among them. In addition to the plums there were three or four Cornel (*Cornus mas*) bushes that bear such beautiful blue-black berries, each on a small crimson stem.

Sumach (*Rhus Canadensis* and *Rhus cotinoides*) [*Rhus aromatica* and *Cotinus obovatus*] was easy to get, and very desirable for its vivid color in the autumn; and finally some Prickly Ash (*Xanthoxylum Americanum*) [*Fraxinus americana*] showed its scarlet seeds from the bushes along a country road, and was tagged carefully for transplanting.

Bitter Sweet (*Celastrus scandens*) and Woodbine (*Ampelopsis quinquefolia*) [*Parthenocissus quinquefolia*] were not hard to find, for the mistress knew the limestone ledge was the kind of place the first would likely have for a home, and the Woodbine (or Virginia Creeper) is likely to be found wherever a bit of woods has for a few years been left undisturbed.

A Gooseberry bush [*Ribes hirtellum*] was the find of another tramp one day, and marked for transplanting. And truly, when it was in place and sent out its clear-cut glossy leaves the next spring, it was beautiful.

The beautiful wild white Clematis (*Clematis Virginiana*) grew rampant along a pasture fence, and a Wild Grape [*Vitis*] was traced by the scent of its blossoms to the side of a spring, where a White Birch (*Betula populifolia*) proved irresistible, and in the fall almost undigable, because its roots were given to twisting themselves around the roots of everything else within reach. But its beauty, when the planting was finally made, compensated for the work.

Wild Roses, you may be sure, had their place — half a dozen of them, and marked stakes were driven where clumps of especially good perennial herbaceous plants were to be found — dainty pink, spreading Dogbane [*Apocynum androsaemifolium*], gorgeous Black-eyed Susans [*Rudbeckia hirta*] and Golden-rod [*Solidago*] of several different varieties, and seeds were gathered and planted as soon as gathered, for most of the wild flowers need parts of two seasons to get started.

When the autumn came, all these shrubs were transplanted. There is always the danger that someone else has been prompted by the tags and stakes to appropriate your discoveries, and unless you have kept some sort of a memorandum you are apt to forget some of them yourself. The consolation is that there are always more shrubs to be had at the same price. In planting, the earth around the roots of the shrubs was kept loose and damp, each plant as it was taken up had been cut back just one-half, and, in a couple of years, the east end was decked in luxurious foliage worthy of a stately park, and each shrub brought forth, not alone its natural blossoms, but a bouquet of reminiscences that, to those concerned, were fully as delightful as the flowers themselves.

House and Garden 18 (JULY 1910): 15–16, 56.

Boisfleury

JESSIE VAUGHN HARRIER wrote poetry. Several of her verses were published in *House Beautiful*, *Sunset*, and other magazines between 1919 and 1930.[12] In this article she remarks that her house and small formal garden in the San Francisco Bay area were planned by architect Julia Morgan; Morgan is best known today for having designed William Randolph Hearst's palatial residence, San Simeon.[13] A recent monograph on Morgan reports that she designed the Harrier home between 1908 and 1909.[14] Twenty-one years have therefore elapsed between the time that the site was planned and this article written. In it, Harrier says she is pleased that Morgan's design has created a "permanent and delightful relationship" between her house and its grounds, and she indicates that she has selected the plants for the garden plan that Morgan drew. Having moved to California from New England, Harrier has had to learn to adjust her plantings to suit the climate of her new home.[15] She has, however, been able to maintain the spirit of New England in the garden's design with box-edged, geometric beds. Over the years, Harrier has matured as a gardener and her taste has grown more refined. Flowering trees have become her mainstay. Her romantic preference for plants that elicit fond memories of distant places is also found in other garden writings of this period. Perhaps the most striking aspect of the article is the great enthusiasm she conveys for the beauty she has created in her garden, which she has named Boisfleury after a romantic novel written in 1897 by André Theuriet (1833-1907).

M Y FRIEND, the Garden Architect, once remarked, 'Among my women clients I find three kinds of gardeners: the first is the sort that swallows the seed catalogues whole, plants innumerable beds of annuals, and is greedy for bouquets; the second realizes certain superior qualities of dignity and permanence in perennials; and the third comprehends the infinite beauty of the branch.'

I recognize that in my San Francisco Bay garden his three types of gardener have held sway successively in my own person.

The house which gives my garden its reason for being had the extreme good fortune to be planned by Miss Julia Morgan, a distinguished architect of San Francisco. Miss Morgan drew the plan of a little formal garden, and established a permanent and delightful relationship between it and the house. From the living-room, dining-room, and sleeping chambers the occupant is always sharing in all the garden's best. No guest or caller comes to the house without savoring the perfume of the garden — even book agents and bill collectors are humanized as they gaze around from the doorstep.

In this first year or two on the bare new lot, I solaced my soul with a riot of poppies [*Papaver*], verbenas, sweet peas [*Lathyrus odoratus*], and the Geraniums and roses that bloom so willingly about San Francisco Bay.

Then came along old Riley — an ancient Irish gardener, decrepit but skillful. 'Box idges it is ye shud be havin' here!' quoth he — and with very small outlay of time and labor he made the beginning of the mossy, fragrant borders which have ever since given a year-long beauty to the picture framed by the south windows.

The box [*Buxus sempervirens*]-edged flower beds in their familiar geometric design wakened garden memories of an Eastern childhood. Old play places

The garden when Bechtel crab and wisteria are in bloom.

scented with lilac [*Syringa vulgaris*] and damask rose [*Rosa damascena*] grew vivid again. As I planned and planted, the instinct to reproduce the feeling of an Eastern garden was dominant. But gardens — like people — must take on a new type in this California setting. Here there are no snow-buried months to give the garden owner a rest, but to leave him desolate of blossom and bird for many weary weeks. Here, in the San Francisco neighborhood, a heliotrope [*Heliotropium*] under a south window calls a humming bird to sip sweetness in December. I found that a California gardener takes no vacations, and that my New England garden idea must be immediately expanded to make room for a whole new range of material and a revised calendar.

Meantime I was learning, one by one, to know the enchanting blossoming trees and shrubs, native and adopted, which will almost fill the cycle of months with perfume and color. Much planting had to be followed by much pruning and many removals — each one lamented, but necessary. Gradually the little place has grown into a name. In Theuriet's romance, his band of young Bohemians name their summer lodge from the forest that surrounds it. 'Here all the trees have flowers,' says one. 'Let us call the place "Boisfleury."'

Although my 'Bloisfleury' is New England in spirit, — with its formal pattern, its box-edged beds, its border of old-fashioned perennials, — in nature it is truly Californian. While in the East all the world lies buried deep in snowy drifts, here a scarlet single camellia bush is starting the yearly procession. It begins to bloom soon after Thanksgiving, and its red bells, with tassels of fine-spun gold for centres, are exquisite on the Christmas table. Later come the double camellias — rose, pink, and white; and when they are gone the earliest flowering-peach tree [*Prunus persica*] flings its rosy arm across the dining-room window. There are three of the deep rose-colored peach trees, and one white one that surely bears the most purely, ethereally white blossom of the flower world!

With the peaches blossom the Japanese crab apples [*Malus floribunda*], and after their bloom is shed comes the Bechtel crab [*Malus ioensis* 'plena'], shaking out its double clusters of delicate flesh-pink just outside the south living-room window. The event of the year is the April flowering of the Japanese cherry [*Prunus serrulata*] — a pink and white Princess bringing 'cherry-blossom festival' to us from the opposite shore of our great Pacific.

Trees have even more power than flowers to recall places by association. Our golden-green laburnum [*Laburnum anagyroides*] speaks of broad English lawns and sociable tea tables. The crimson wreaths of the hawthorn [*Crataegus*] bring back the thorn-grown wall of old Chester. The swaying waxen garlands of the wild Oregon syringa, with their pungent odor, seem to wave to us from forest thickets along the Columbia. The honey-sweet bloom of a pink locust revives delicious Junes that two gingham-dressed little girls spent playing within the white pickets of a New York State dooryard.

Boisfleury has lived through its share of mistakes in planning and planting.

It was a mistake to plant, in early enthusiasm, a dozen golden-flowered acacias — too many for a city square — twelve too many for a little garden! We had to commit the sacrilege of burning acacia wood for a whole winter — so rapidly did they grow, and so unmistakably was it necessary to cut them down!

Then there have been accidents — happy and unhappy! A marauding gopher killed the choicest of all the camellia group — one with flowers that looked like delicate flesh-tinted porcelain. On the other hand, the eldest and most beautiful rose-colored peach tree [*Prunus persica*] has a daughter, grown from the chance-sown pit of one of its small sour fruits, and the young tree is even lovelier than its parent and blooms in grace beside the gateway to the pergola. Toyon-berry bushes — our California Christmasberries [*Heteromeles arbutifolia*] — bought at a nursery did not thrive, but a berry falling from a discarded Christmas wreath produced a tall bush bearing fine bunches of red berries.

Bloom, color, perfume, are not the only charms of a tree garden — there is the exquisite, chaste beauty of line, the 'beauty of the branch,' of which the architect spoke, that gleams alike through slanting rain and scorching September drouth. Rarely can any bed of plants, however luxuriant, equal in a garden picture the contribution of a tree.

The beloved trees need not exclude flower beds, but they do limit their possibilities. In this San Francisco Bay climate sun is at a premium, and it is hard for any flower to get enough of it under the heavy summer foliage of trees. But again, water and labor are scarce articles too, and the patient, faithful trees render their service of beauty, making much less claim for attention than the plants.

If then, like the gardener of Bloisfleury, you must get your pleasure with a minimum of time and money, plant box edges for pattern, three slender white birches [*Betula papyrifera* or *populifera*] for grace, three dark yews [*Taxus*] for accent — and the other lovely tree creatures to fill the garden spaces with a gracious gift of year-round beauty!

House Beautiful 67 (May 1930): 621, 653–654.

ENDNOTES

12. *House Beautiful* published one of her poems two months before this article.

13. Julia Morgan was born in San Francisco in 1872. She studied engineering at Berkeley and in 1898 was the first woman admitted to the Department of Architecture at the Ecole des Beaux Arts in Paris. She established her own office in San Francisco in 1904.

14. Sara Holmes Boutelle, *Julia Morgan, Architect* (New York, 1988), 252. Boutelle lists the project as "job number 277," located at 6481 Benvenue Street, Oakland.

15. Articles in popular magazines frequently emphasized the necessity of conforming to the requirements of America's regional climates. One of the many excellent articles on gardening in California's dry climate was Charles Francis Saunders, "Awakening Self-Consciousness in the California Garden," *The Garden Magazine* 36 (December 1922): 191–194.

Learning What Roses Like: Challenging the Conventions and Simplifying Practice

THIS ARTICLE is a wide-ranging report on what the author has observed recently about roses. But these are not the random thoughts of just any rose gardener.[16] J. Horace McFarland (1859–1948), by profession a master printer and photographer, was also a leading authority on roses, the editor of the *American Rose Annual* from 1916 to 1943 and of *American Rose Magazine* from 1933 to 1942, and the author of four books on roses. His printing business, the J. Horace McFarland Company in Harrisburg, Pennsylvania, was recognized for the superb quality of its work, which included garden books and such magazines as *Country Life in America, The Garden Magazine,* and *The Photo-Miniature.*[17] Along with writing about 200 articles for *The Outlook, Atlantic Monthly, The Garden Magazine, Country Life in America, House Beautiful, House and Garden, Better Homes and Gardens, The Ladies' Home Journal,* and other magazines, he wrote books on general gardening topics and on photographing plants. His photographs appeared from time to time as illustrations in magazines. He was a close friend of William B. Howland, publisher of *The Outlook,* and of Frank and Nellie Doubleday. Doubleday's company published *The Garden Magazine* and *Country Life in America.* In addition to running his flourishing business and writing books and articles, McFarland was president of the American Civic Association from 1904 to 1924, was actively involved in the creation of national parks and the National Park Service, and achieved significant goals in the preservation of America's natural landscape.[18] He further managed to create a magnificent garden at his home, Breeze Hill, in Harrisburg. While he benefited from the advice of his friend Warren Manning, landscape architect, in the layout of the garden, he did much of the labor himself with the assistance of his son, Robert, and one garden helper. The Breeze Hill garden included many native plants as well as a rose garden.

MOST OF US garden-hoping folks have despaired at the elaborate soil preparation which is recommended, or even demanded, for rose prosperity, especially for the Hybrid-teas. The orthodox rose bed "must" be prepared two or three feet deep, and I have read of one preparation of four feet, the bottom twelve inches being of broken bricks for drainage. Then there are the "Special" beds devised by the late Frederick Efficiency Taylor, in which diagonal slices of soil and manure and what-not manage to make a three-foot-wide bed cost about two dollars the running foot. The orthodoxers also propose three-foot square-and-deep excavations for Climbing Roses, and an elaborate soil prescription to fill them.

When I began to try to have a few Roses at Breeze Hill I did my best to follow the fashion in soil fixing. True, the workman who was to trench two or three feet deep usually skimped the job, but nevertheless I did take extra trouble to see that the rose beds were extra deep, extra rich, and extra good.

After I had to transplant some Hybrid-teas that had a year in the elaborately prepared ground, I began to suspect the need for such extensive and expensive elaboration of preparations. The roots hadn't gone down into the submerged richness, and I couldn't see how they could get the good of it. Indeed, after having transplanted Hybrid-teas on multiflora, on Manetti, on Cherokee [*Rosa laevigata*], on rugosa, on their own roots, I can say that I never found one, whether it has been doing business for one year or for five, that had gotten below eighteen inches, and most of them had prospered reasonably in a foot of good ground.

In the spring of 1921 I had to transplant considerably again to condense and fill after the Easter Monday freeze of evil memory. By this time I had got ten to confidence in a foot of good soil preparation, giving my heavy shale a full third of rotted stable manure. The Roses planted in this half-orthodox soil have done well for a hot, dry year, and flowered remarkably well in the fall. What have I lost by saving time, money, and manure?

But there's more to the story. When I went over the beds last spring, I found some ten of the Hybrid-teas so nearly dead that I couldn't think of replanting them. There was a little sign of life in the roots, and as I am soft-hearted about life of any sort, I didn't dump them, but had my helper plant them in my little "nursery" in the vegetable garden, where the soil was just ordinary.

In June these "dead ones," planted thus in ordinary garden soil, without coddling, and without extra water in a dry time, had all recovered and made good tops, on which flowers of quality came and continued to come abundantly. Without spraying or dusting, these plants are free from bugs and mildew and black-spot. Even the difficult Los Angeles, one of these derelicts, has done beautifully.

What is the answer? I don't know: but my common-sense is getting busy with my memory, and telling me how Roses flourish in the rough field culture where they have been budded. No "special" beds, no three feet of preparation, no coddling at all, does the nurseryman give them, yet he gets great growth and many blooms.

Isn't it just possible that the elaborate soil preparation recommended is mostly "bunk?" Each writer has written what he read, rather than as a result of his own actual knowledge, possibly, and has passed on all this trouble and expense. I am surmising, not asserting; but, as to the necessity for elaborate and extra deep soil fixing for Roses I have moved to Missouri, and must be shown!

As to Climbing Roses. I do assert that there is no need of any cubic-yard excavation. A fairly large hole with some good soil in it will "start something" with any worth-while modern climber.

Is it not possible that many people have been scared away from rose-growing by these bogies of soil preparation, inherited from the old days when garden literature was loaded with similar and more forbidding prescriptions of soil dopes, differing for every plant? Who knows?

The Beauty of Climbing Roses

At a meeting of the Executive Committee of the American Rose Society last spring, in a discussion concerning the introduction of one of Dr. Van Fleet's new creations in Roses, several rose nurserymen were passing the word on the relatively slow sale of good Climbing Roses as compared with the Hybrid-teas. One said he had 140 varieties of Climbers, most of them good, and he insisted that others of us knew little of them.

Believing as I do in the desirability of these modern successors to the old Baltimore Belle and Prairie Queen, it occurred to me to count up the Climbers that make Breeze Hill beautiful in June. I found I had sixty-nine sorts, and as I go over them, I find myself very reluctant to give up many of them. To be sure, there are about a dozen that have not yet shown me their flowers. But that is a joy to come.

I have reached a certain state of hard-heartedness about these Climbers. If any variety fails to "make good," out it comes, to give room for another candidate. Thus have passed away Goldfinch, because it was not distinct enough, and Trier, for the same reason. Climbing American Beauty is reduced to one plant, because, though very lovely when it opens, it "holds its dead," as one friend expresses it, in retaining its faded petals. Mary Lovett froze away, and I did not renew because Silver Moon and Purity are as good, or better. I have no Crimson Rambler, and want none: Excelsa is far more satisfactory.

Several are on the suspense list: Elizabeth Ziegler may stay, or she may go. Aunt Harriet will have to prove herself a real aunt to stay in my Rose family.

Rose garden of Mrs. Edgerton Winthrop at Syosset, Long Island. The symmetric, somewhat formally patterned bed is, of course, the traditional home of the Rose and this modern adaptation has both character and charm.

The Critical Date in Planting Out

For several years I have observed that a surprising difference in eventual growth and prosperity was evident in field-grown Roses planted at varying dates in the spring. The March or early April planting has, in my experience, preceded prompt starting, satisfactory blooming, and permanent strength, while planting in late April and at any time in May at Breeze Hill has actually meant weakness of growth and bloom and sometimes a large proportion of loss.

As I write I have just been looking at certain rose beds, one of which was planted April 1st, 1920, and the other April 21st. Both were Hybrid-teas on multiflora stock, and from the same nursery. The April 1st planting did superbly that year, and the plants were established most happily; the later planting looked sick where the Roses were alive, as too many of them were not!

Possibly I have found a reason for the difference. Transplanting a home-grown Van Fleet seedling on March 12th, last year's abnormal spring following a nearly minus winter, I hit upon a condition of soil moisture which permitted the lifting of the plant with every root intact, and with earth clinging to every root fibre. I observed that the little white roothairs, which we are told are the active agents for food assimilation, were more than half-inch long, and in vigorous growth.

Now, under ordinary conditions of digging, these tender root-hairs would have been stripped off, leaving the roots bare. Is it not probable that such stripping may so weaken the root action as to check the growth of the plant? That is, the plant set after the suggested critical date is not dormant, though it may show little or no swelling of the buds — if my theory is correct. I shall at least assume its accuracy in my Rose plantings until proof that I am in error is provided.

Blooms We Enjoy in the Fall

The June bloom of Roses is a great event in any good garden. Breeze Hill has in addition to the sixty-odd varieties of hardy Climbing Roses about as many Hybrid-teas and Hybrid-perpetuals. When the full show is in process, any one flower is relatively unimportant, and one does not expect it to be lasting.

But the far fewer blooms that come in September and October are different. The superb Druschkis are regal in size, and they are good in their warm whiteness for days. The Hybrid-teas open slowly but endure long, and each one seems a real rose event.

I find that if cut as they are expanding, they will open very perfectly in the house, and there give great pleasure. For example, one late September morning I cut a great stem of Duchess of Wellington bearing three good buds, one of them showing strongly the red reflex to the outside petals characteristic of this good Rose. All opened slowly and beautifully, giving us two days of decoration in the centre of the dining table. On the third day, they were wide and flat, and suggested gigantic flowers of a semi-double ecru Japanese Anemone [*Anemone x hybrida*] rather than Roses.

Miss Cynthia Forde is another of these fall bloomers that develops slowly and beautifully, and Lady Ursula and Mme. Abel Chatenay are even better. Columbia does well, but not as well as those mentioned, nor as Ophelia. That Rose with the outrageous name, General-Superior Arnold Janssen, is as fine in the fall as is Red Radiance. (The Gude sort, not the Pierson sort, remember!) That aggravating, lovely, awkward, and captivating deep scarlet beauty with another outrageous name — Chateau de Clos Vougeot — glows in the house as its buds expand, and has the advantage of exquisite perfume.

My Hybrid-teas were rather good last fall, despite the blackspot ravages. I had every diseased leaf picked off and burned, and the plants were thoroughly dusted while wet with dew with Doctor Massey's black-spot and mildew prescription of sulphur nine parts and lead arsenate one part. This was in finely powdered form, and applied with the Corona duster. Mildew is entirely controlled, and black-spot almost so. Aphis was controlled all summer by a two-inch mulch of tobacco stems, which also keep the ground cooler than it would otherwise have been. I cherish every one of these lovely fall Roses.

The Garden Magazine 35 (MARCH 1922): 21–23.

ENDNOTES

16. McFarland wrote about himself in *Memoirs of a Rose Man* (Emmaus, Pennsylvania, 1949); Ernest Morrison has recently published an excellent, copiously detailed and documented biography of Mc Farland: *J. Horace McFarland: A Thorn for Beauty* (Harrisburg, Pennsylvania, 1995). Most of my information has been gleaned from this source.

17. His work for Doubleday Publishing ended in 1910 when Frank Doubleday built his enormous publishing and printing center in Garden City, Long Island. Mc Farland also wrote articles for *Photo-Miniature*.

18. On McFarland's work saving important sites of natural scenic beauty and establishing the National Park Service, see Morrison, *J. Horace McFarland*, 106–122, 153–162, and 173–193.

✍ [Hanna Rion]
Roses

THIS ARTICLE tells which were the favorite roses of Hanna Rion, whose writing on December gardening appears in the first chapter of this anthology. Rion names the best from different classes of roses — Hybrid Perpetuals, Hybrid Teas, Teas, and Climbers — and both old and new varieties. She also gives planting and cultivation instructions, all in her characteristically enthusiastic manner. Although this article, like "December Gardening," was not illustrated, a photograph of Rion's Dorothy Perkins rose was included in another of her articles from *Craftsman*, "The Garden of the Many Little Paths."[19]

EVER SINCE I was a little girl, I've hoped each spring some nice old uncle from India would send me fifty dollars accompanied by a gruesome threat, such as: "If you use one cent of this money for anything but roses, the first night the east wind blows a blackbird will come along and nip off your nose." But as it hasn't really happened yet, I have to pretend along the last part of April or first of May that it is about to happen and start to work to select the fifty dollars' worth.

It is so hard to advise another just which roses to get, because my list of irresistible ones grows each year, and then the rose-growers have been so generous sending me unlabeled gift roses it so happens now that some of my loveliest roses' real names are unknown to me — they've had to attain names as best they might. For instance, that delicate pinky-white climber with the great loose clusters having the odor of frankincense and myrrh, is known to us as the "horse-bitten-rose," but to you that name would not be enlightening.

Of course, we all have reminiscent reasons for wanting certain roses, and, if you are like me, you'll keep on trying Marechal Niel and Fortune's Yellow even though geography prohibits and zero browbeats you. One of my rose prides is the Cherokee [*Rosa laevigata*] which I have teased through three winters now, because of the great wild hedges I remember along the highways in the South. Each winter I lighten its protection, as I have a theory that if you can persuade a delicate rose to survive several Northern winters it grows hardier, following out Nature's old law of adaptation to condition.

Suppose we pretend together that the old uncle from India has stingily sent us only nine dollars and twenty-five cents instead of the expected fifty dollars, and make the best of it. Out of that amount we'll have to get hybrid perpetuals, hybrid teas, plain teas and climbers — and feel thankful all at the same time. The hybrid perpetuals, you know, are the perfectly hardy roses, supposed only to bloom in June, though mine bloom spasmodically through the following months until winter. After each flowering I cut the branch that has flowered almost back to the original stalk, and then it puts out new shoots which often blossom. The hybrid teas have a hybrid perpetual ancestor on one side and will stand through a Northern winter with protection. They are perpetual joys, blooming constantly until November. We'll have to have the hybrid teas even if we economize on the hybrid perpetuals.

The teas — if you live in the North — are the roses you'll keep on trying for sentimental reasons, association, or sheer bravado, because they are not hardy here. But they are the most florescent and are very beautiful, so we'll have to indulge in a few for luxury and by getting two-year-old plants we will be generously rewarded this season anyway. The climbers we'll purchase will be of the rambler and Wichuriana varieties. If we could have only one hybrid perpetual I'd beg for Gloire Lyonnaise. Its blossoms are sumptuously beautiful in form and of a golden white shade. The foliage is distinguished and it is unpopular with insects.

Soleil d'Or is the most spectacular rose — a mingling of peach, marigold and flame. Given great richness of fare the bush will grow to prodigious size. A splendid velvety reddish black rose is the Prince Camille de Rohan. With Mrs. John Laing — that exquisite pink rose, we will have a white, a pink, a red and a yellow.

If you know roses at all, and I said, "guess which hybrid tea I'll mention first," I am sure you'd say "Killarney." Well, you would be right. It's the Irish queen I'd be pining for first of all. In bud it is perfection; open, it "spreads and spreads till its heart lies bare." Even fallen, each petal is a poem — a deep pink shallop with prow of gold.

Bessie Brown is so dignified, pallid and austere she is known as Elizabeth in my garden. The Kaiserin Auguste Victoria has a Teutonic hardiness and carries her cream-white flower head high and regally.

Souvenir de President Carnot has a feminine-like blush, but a masculine vigor. The Wellesley gives us a delicious shade of pink. But here we have chosen two pinks and no red at all. How could I have forgotten that giant J. B. Clark, when he has grown nine feet in height trying to woo my Dorothy Perkins? He is the reddest, healthiest, tallest man-rose in my garden.

For yellow we will choose the Maman Cochet. Now that we have reached the plain teas I'm glad to begin with one that has proved almost as hardy with me as a hybrid tea — that is, the Coquette de Lyon, which is a lemon yellow and positively wears itself out blooming. The Souvenir de Malmaison is strictly speaking a Bourbon, but we'll let it be a tea for our purposes. It is so lovely with its shell pink tones, and we may be able to winter it, with special care.

Isabella Sprunt is another yellow rose of great florescence. It is so easy to get yellows in the teas, and yellow seems to go with frailness of constitution. But I've chosen only the ones that have proved hardiest with me, and those I can brag of having wintered a few times. For pure recklessness, let's buy the Golden Gate, simply because we can't resist its blending of pale gold and rose. Another extravagance will be the Sunset, which we will be satisfied to entertain this one summer for its topaz and ruby beauty.

Of course, we can't do without that fragile creature, the Duchesse de Brabant. Such silky texture and delicate pinkness of cheek has she.

"Citron red with amber and fawn shading," say the rose catalogues of Souvenir de Victor Hugo — nobody could resist *that*. It is all that is sung of it and more, for they do not mention its fragrance.

Here we are to climbers and I find Lynch's hybrid at the tip of my pen first. Wherever you live, you may one day see a strange rose branch looking over your fence, and I'll just tell you now, that it will my Lynch's hybrid. Not content with spreading in every direction, over all neighboring roses, I'm sure it will soon ignore garden bounds and become a wandering minstrel. I permit its branches to grow six or ten feet, then drape them over to adjacent arches or neighboring rose poles. This has happened so often that now when the Lynch's hybrid blooms there are ropes and ropes of roses swinging in every direction. It is of the Wichuriana family and blooms only in June, but it blooms all of June. Its clusters are of many perfect fairylike roses of pink, paling to white. Of the Wichurianas my next favorite is the Evergreen Gem. Its blossoms are not in clusters, but each rose comes in an *edition-de-luxe*. Of a pale yellow with apricot tones, the color of the flower is enough to recommend it. But shut your eyes and whiff its perfume, and you'll say, "ripe apple." The Evergreen Gem prefers to sprawl on the ground and delights in covering stone terraces; it can be trained up, just as a monkey can be taught man tricks, but what's the use?

Manda's Triumph (white) and Lady Gay (cherry pink) we must have. And I can't resist ending with Dorothy Perkins, but to praise her well-known charms would use up needless type. I'll only say, save all the cutting of the Dorothy you plant, so you will have at least a thousand to comfort you when you've grown old.

Now we'll count up our list and put the roses down sensibly in line so we may see both what we have and what we have spent.

Hybrid Perpetuals

Gloire Lyonnaise, larger size	$0.20
Soleil d'Or, two-year-old	.60
Prince Camille de Rohan, larger size	.20
Mrs. John Laing, larger size	.20

Hybrid Teas

Killarney, larger size	.30
Bessie Brown, larger size	.25
Kaiserin Auguste Victoria, larger size	.20
Souvenir de President Carnot, larger size	.20
Wellesley, larger size	.30
J. B. Clark, larger size	.40
Yellow Maman Cochet, larger size	.25

Teas

Coquette de Lyon, two-year-old	.35
Souvenir de Malmaison (Bourbon), two-year-old	.35
Duchesse de Brabant, two-year-old	.35
Souvenir de Victor Hugo, two-year-old	.30
Isabella Sprunt, two-year-old	.35
Golden Gate, two-year-old	.35
Sunset, two-year-old	.35

Climbers

Lynch's Hybrid ('Wichuriana), two-year-old	.10
Evergreen Gem (Wichuriana), two-year-old	.40
Manda's Triumph (Wichuriana), two-year-old	.40
Lady Gay (Rambler), two-year-old	.40
Dorothy Perkins (Rambler), two-year-old	.40

Total	$7.50

And after all we haven't used up all the nine dollars and twenty-five cents; so you may either change "larger size" to "two-year-old," or you may spend the surplus on that dream shatterer, the blue rose, which I see advertised on the back of the latest rose catalogue.

It is worth considering in connection with our expenditures, that an ordinary bunch of roses you'd buy at the florist's to send to your sweetheart might cost more than all our old miserly uncle has sent us, and the bouquet from the florist's would be withered and thrown out in a week, while here we're starting a rose garden for the grandchildren of that sweetheart to enjoy years and years from now. And so when we begin our rose garden we'll begin it right — no superficial digging and sticking in any old way of these precious plants. First we'll lay out our garden with a ball of twine tied to a stick, either informally or, improvising as we go, in some private original design which expresses us, not our neighbor. Then we will have it all dug as deep as we by strategy and beguilement can lure some man to dig. When it is all dug, then to mark out the individual holes, leaving generous space between the hybrid perpetuals because they grow to be such big fellows, and not forgetting to give Mr. J. B. Clark plenty of courting room.

The hybrid teas need less space, generally speaking, while the teas may be planted, say, about a foot apart. Save a climber to cover the arch (designed by yourself, not a store bought one) at the entrance to your rose garden, and trail the others over your paths in spots where one will have to stoop perhaps a little when passing under blossoming branches to find new beauty on the other side.

Each hole must be twenty inches deep; take all the old everyday soil out, and put a little coal ashes in the bottom for drainage. If you have a compost pile, mix compost and well-rotted cow-manure, filling half the hole with the mixture. Sprinkle this with the plain soil, then place the sacred bush in the hole, spreading the roots in the direction they naturally take. Cover the roots with more bed-soil, then press gently, gently, until the plant is firmed. Now pour in water, from which the chill has been taken, until the hole is almost full, letting it soak in gradually, then put compost and cow-manure until it is higher than the surrounding ground. Plant your feet firmly, but not disrespectfully, on the surface of the hole, packing it down around the rose-bush, which you meantime hold in upright position. As a finality, draw the bed-soil up loosely about the stem of the rose, leaving the surface quite dry so the sun may have no chance to bake or broil.

If you've done all this simple, yet seemingly complex, business properly you need never water your rose again!

When the bushes reach the blooming stage, trim back severely the branches which have flowered, always trimming so as to leave an eye *on the outside* of the branch. Don't be afraid of cutting too much. The courageous rose-surgeon is the one who gets the largest fees in flowers. If you have done enough trimming through the summer blooming months, there will be no necessity for any trimming in the fall, except always to cut out dead branches. Then, too, when you think of the cold that's coming, and the struggle the poor things will have to go through during the winter, to trim them at this perilous time would be as mean as to strike a man when he's down.

In mid-April, prune all blackened ends and weak branches. Some of your hybrid teas may look absolutely dead, but don't give them up yet. Trim the bushes down to within two inches of the ground, and shortly you will be rejoiced to see red-nosed sprouts peeping through the ground — shoots from the roots, which generally survive.

If you don't own a compost pile begin one now. Even a weed becomes valuable when pulled up and thrown on the compost. Contribute all dead blossoms, weedings, trimmings, garden rubbish, leaves, manure rakings and even some garbage and dish-water. Place the compost far enough from the house so you won't bother about the sanitary problem, and every few weeks spade a few shovelfuls of earth over the whole pile, After a year's mellowing you will have something more valuable than manure to work into your rose beds.

Dig continually with a pronged spade about your roses, being careful not to tear the roots. The soil should always be kept loose if you would be spared the bugbear of watering. Mulch with lawn clippings, spading old supply under when the fresh is ready. Spray once a week with a water made foamy by tobacco and sulphur soap. You will not vanquish the insects — no, not in this world, but even abating them is a human triumph.

About the middle of November purchase rye straw by the bundle and after tying your rose-bushes gently to a firm stake, sheathe the straw about the hybrid teas and plain teas not too tightly, tying in about three places. The hybrid perpetuals may go nude all winter.

A trip to the West Indies or Sicily about the middle of March might help you to overcome the unconquerable temptation of uncovering your roses too soon. Returning from your voyage about the second week in April, the plants could be disrobed safely, and — live happily ever after, or at least all summer.

You will realize, of course, that growing roses is not easy work. Believe me, the rose-grower can be neither a fool nor a lazy man. It's so hard to write plain, practical facts about roses. To write of them properly one would irresistibly compose a sonnet. And when you pick your first great basketful some very dewy June morning, please place them in an old blue bowl for my sake, and the sake of our Indian uncle, whom we had almost forgotten.

The Craftsman 18 (June 1910): 354–359.

ENDNOTES

19. "The Garden of the Many Little Paths," *The Craftsman* 17 (March 1910): 623. For biographical information about Rion, see above 32.

ᴇᴏ ETHELYN E. KEAYS
To the Rescue of Dowager Roses

OLD-FASHIONED ROSES were highly prized among connoisseurs in England and America during the late nineteenth and early twentieth centuries. Ethelyn Keays (1871–1961) and her sister Mabel Lyon scoured the countryside of Calvert County, Maryland, for old roses, asking owners for slips to root. Keays developed a method for successfully moving really large bushes from abandoned properties, which she describes in this article. She transplanted the old roses to her farm, Creek Side, which was near the town of Lusby, bordered by the Patuxent River and Saint Leonard's Creek.[20] She had moved to Creek Side when she was fifty-seven years old and remained there until the late 1940s. There were already old roses on the Maryland property when she arrived and in the course of her residence she added greatly to the collection. Upon leaving the farm she donated her old roses to the University of Maryland. Regrettably they have not survived. At least as recently as 1978, some roses left behind at Creek Side still managed to eke out a miserable existence among the weeds at the old site.[21] More happily, garden writer Henry Mitchell reported in his weekly column for *The Washington Post* that a fragrant multiflora rose transplanted from Keays's former property flourished in his garden.[22] Keays's book, *Old Roses*, was published in 1935. It was reissued in 1978, and the new edition includes a list of the many fine articles she wrote on old roses for the *American Rose Annual*. This journal, edited by J. Horace McFarland, published some of her earliest articles in 1932.

SO OFTEN WHEN we have been snooping in old gardens, hoping to find some interesting grandmother's Roses, we have been asked how to move an old Rose bush. Not a Rose of seven or eight years' growth, which can be taken up with a ball of earth fairly easily, but one which has been in its present place twenty-five or fifty years or even longer. Usually the need for something to be done has arisen from its having been planted near a tree which during these long years has grown to real proportions. Other times, the Rose has been so long in its location that there is evidently nothing for it to feed upon, and the poor old thing is starving to death in its old age. In neglected and abandoned gardens, the bush, root, and branch are smothered in rampant Honeysuckle [*Lonicera*], and the Rose is found carrying a terrible burden of jungle growth and fighting for life against it.

These are three of the problems we have met in acquiring some quite choice sorts. As we have made successful transplantings of ever so many dowager Roses on our place in Southern Maryland, our way of going about it may be helpful to other Rose growers.

We had to move a very old bush of a Bourbon variety, growing as well as it could on a clay hill as dry as a bone after last Summer's drought. To be safe, we waited until the foliage was off and the Rose was truly dormant. This came late in November last year. We made a trench in the form of a circle five feet in diameter and about a foot deep. This trench had to be chopped out with a grubbing hoe, the ground was baked so hard. We filled the trench with water, over and over, for many hours. At first the water stood for some time but gradually, as the soil moistened, it took up the water more readily. With trowels and hands we worked away the soil from the big roots until we could get, by feeling, the direction of the main growth. We followed out these lines with more trenches to get the water into the surrounding soil. After much time spent in soaking the root growth, we were able to open up the root habitation. A strong root went deeply down from the main center. From this we judged that the plant had been grown from a deeply-rooted cutting, probably grown under a glass jar. Another root branched out from one side and turned back toward the center, making a bow. A third went off in a line directly opposite.

Having puddled the whole root system thoroughly, we dug and pried and finally lifted the old bush, entire and dripping with mud. It took a heavy iron crow-bar to accomplish this. However, the bush came up freely but it brought along with it, in the space between the straight root and the bowlegged one, a lump of solid clay the size of a man's head which, with all our watering, was as dry as so much stone, We looked very carefully for feeding roots and, finding them largely near the head sections of the big root branches, we cut off the long woody ends with a saw, still holding in the ball of clay as something precious. Then we sank the whole root into a deep tub full of water, where it remained until that mass of dry clay gradually slid away. It was a wise precaution, for below the main trunk were many rootlets, starved by drought but still functioning, a most important part of the future feeding system.

The Rose stayed in the tub of muddy water all night. By morning, the roots were in excellent shape. We pruned the top, a duty very hard to perform, for there was not much there, barely enough to make six cuttings. We cut all broken and useless roots away. Then, we planted the worn old grandmother Rose with tender care in a bed made according to the best directions, with fine old manure bedded underneath. It was enough. This year the Rose is young on top and flourishing remarkably. It has been nicely covered with bloom throughout the Spring, has bloomed considerably during the Summer, feeling no drought but without a can of water, — only peat moss and tobacco stems. Now, in the Autumn, it is again blooming. This is the story of the rescue of a beautiful flesh-tinted Bourbon which, we think, is the true old Souvenir de la Malmaison.

Another interesting excavation, last Autumn, was the transplanting of a large China Rose [*Rosa chinensis*] which was involved with the roots of an Elm [*Ulmus americana*] tree. The Elm is three feet through at the base. The Rose was about fifteen feet from the base of the Elm. Both had been planted many years ago, and the tree had made the better go of it. Yet, there was life in the old Rose and good fighting strength, as it had shown by blooming throughout the Summer. As a problem, this was more difficult than the Malmaison. We dug our trench five feet in diameter at least, encountering tree roots six inches through. These had to be chopped, of course, but we dared not chop until we knew where the root habitation was. So we followed much the same course of careful digging and feeling and puddling. The main trunk of this Rose was, we believe, ten inches in diameter. The root system was a mesh of stout root branches, not spreading as far as Malmaison but going deeper. It proved to be necessary to soak this Rose over night, so we gave it buckets of water about eleven o'clock and left it to nature and capillary attraction. There was a great deal of clay here, too, but the masses were not so great and the slow work of the night released them. In the morning we chopped the tree roots and deepened the digging until finally, with two stout crowbars, we heaved the old "Chinee" out. Into the meshes of the roots, crossing the system, were tree roots as large as a strong man's arm. We gradually wriggled these out and trimmed the roots. The plant was so much divided in its root system, through the crossing of the tree roots, that we divided the whole plant into two, quite large enough at that. These we pruned above and planted, as we had Malmaison. They both lived to bloom, like the fine old sort that Chinas are, and as far as we can judge, they are both good for forty years to come.

The Rose with the Honeysuckle [*Lonicera*] complication we found on a slope near an abandoned negro cabin. It was a microphylla [*Rosa roxburghii*] odorata alba, a small-leaved, almost evergreen, cross of microphylla and tea, a charming old sort. During its neglected years, it had attained a spread of twenty-five or thirty feet; its main branches, two inches and more thick, rooted in at their drooping ends decades ago. This wide, thick mass had been the dumping ground for broken china, iron pots, and three-legged frying pans. With a brush cutter we made havoc of the Honeysuckle vines. Tough work, as they were very woody. The sight was a joy when we had the Rose in its fine spreading form, before us, to tackle. We had to cut some of the long branches to get into the center. Our system of trenching and watering was not possible in this instance, as there was no water. Fortunately, there was no clay. We dug the microphylla with grub hoe and spade and trowel and hands, half of the time lost to sight underneath. The Rose came up in two parts, separating naturally.

This made it much simpler to get the tough, twisting Honeysuckle roots out. Much cutting was necessary before we could get the plant into the back of the car, but such cutting gave us great promise. Once home, we immediately submerged every part in tubs of water muddied well with lumps of clay. We left all to soak for a whole day and night. During the night a skin of ice formed over the tub, but no harm was done. When we were ready to plant the microphylla, we pruned the roots with saw and clippers, and we sawed the great branches to about three feet. We planted deeply over good manure. We gave it our blessing and best wishes for the Spring. It worked.

This year those thick, old clubs have broken into strong, beautiful shoots with glistening, colorful foliage. And we have had occasional blooms of highly-fragrant, creamy white, tea-type flowers throughout the Summer. From the cuttings necessary to dress the Rose down for such a radical upheaval, we have grown more than a hundred lovely new plants. It was a rescue in a jungle, but now we know that it was worthwhile twice over to reclaim this lovely old microphylla.

Gardeners' Chronicle of America 36 (FEBRUARY 1932): 45, 57.

ENDNOTES

20. My information about Keays derives from the introduction by Leonie Bell to the 1978 edition of Keays's book, *Old Roses* (1935).

21. *Old Roses*, 6.

22. This article is included in the third and posthumous anthology of Mitchell's columns: *Henry Mitchell On Gardening*, introduction by Allen Lacy (New York, 1998), 109–110. The original publication date is not mentioned.

Chapter Three

FLOWER GARDEN DESIGN

AMERICANS LAVISHED extraordinary care on the design of flower gardens in the early twentieth century, as these articles prove. Late twentieth-century readers may marvel at the close attention their forebears gave to the fine points of composition and may benefit greatly from the efforts these ancestors made to analyze what makes a garden pleasing to the eye. The chapter includes a small sample of articles treating color in the garden, a subject that was of tremendous interest to gardeners at this time. Like other articles in this chapter, those on color expand upon and sometimes revise principles set forth by Gertrude Jekyll. The merits of annuals, biennials, and perennials are also all considered in this chapter, along with gardens meant to be enjoyed at night and the special beauty of flowers after they have died and gone to seed.

✍ ELSA REHMANN
The Distribution of Flowers in the Garden

ELSA REHMANN, born in Newark, New Jersey, in 1886, practiced landscape architecture and in the mid-1920s lectured on that subject at Vassar College.[1] She wrote magazine articles of an unfailingly high quality as well as several important books. In the earliest of her books, *The Small Place: Its Landscape Architecture* (1918), she explained that although she had enjoyed the opportunity of working on the large gardens of rich estates, she remained fascinated with the small place, "for its possibilities, which are generally overlooked, are infinite, and its limitations, which are considered as drawbacks, ought to be the very means of its making." Most of the chapters in that book had originally been published as articles in either *Garden Magazine* or *House and Garden*. Her commitment to clearly communicating good design ideas to laymen is evident in all her writings. Like articles by Grace Tabor, Rehmann's work is typically dense with carefully considered, intelligent recommendations reflecting her excellent sense of design and formidable knowledge of plants. Like many of the best flower garden designers of this period she was greatly indebted to Gertrude Jekyll. In this piece she directs our attention to the artistic placement of flowers within a garden: which should be planted in clumps, which in drifts, and which should be scattered or planted singly. The article is well worth reading with care, as it presents an immense amount of valuable information. In the romantic spirit of the Arts and Crafts movement she emphasizes that the most successful gardeners are not bound by rules but freely follow their inspired intuition. It is the garden's "mood" and "spirit" that the gardener — like the landscape painter and photographer — must express, and thereby elicit an emotional response from the viewer. Rehmann's sister, Antoinette Perrett, is the photographer responsible for the article's illustrations, one of which is on the title page of this chapter.

THE PLACING OF FLOWERS in the garden can be compared to the brushwork of a painter. It has a technique that constitutes style and expresses feeling. As in painting, too, the manner is a matter of individual choice and temperament. We may be caught in the marvel of it and yet, in trying to explain the methods by which the effects are obtained, we may lose the very essence of its magic, for those who use their technique well use it intuitively and are not bound by arbitrary rules.

In planting it would be a great deal easier if we could use plants already grown and blooming. As it is, we have to place wee plantlings. We drop a plant here, place a group there, stretch a thin line farther on and scatter other plants seemingly at random. By these spots and splashes and this pointillist method of painters, we start our garden picture. A great many people have not yet outgrown the older type of planting found in the bedding-out garden, and they still plant their flowers in solid stiff blocks and straight rows. The herbaceous border with its freer use of perennials and annuals and bulbs has given the garden this new opportunity in plant arrangement which depends upon the spontaneity with which irregular clumps and longish drifts, spots, and splashes blend the flowers together.

Certain plants like to be planted in clumps. Clumps distributed through the back of the border produce effective skylines. Hollyhocks [*Alcea rosea*] and eremurus, heleniums and buddleias and the taller perennial asters, in fact all the larger, coarser flowers, are used in this way. Occasional high spots, too, relieve a planting of comparative evenness as, for instance, when clumps of *Lilium auratum* spring up from out a mass of annual larkspurs [*Consolida*]. And sometimes tall plants like perennial asters or giant zinnias, lupines [*Lupinus perennis*] or marigolds [*Tagetes*], heleniums or cosmos, are brought well forward in the border, almost to the very edge to enliven the cross sections of borders with bold outlines.

Plants set out in clumps are most important, however, when they vitalize the borders by accents. These plants must be telling when in flower and good in foliage effectiveness at other times. Such edging plants as *Saxifraga cordifolia* [*Bergenia cordifolia*], *Iberis sempervirens*, and *Oenothera missouriensis* [*O. macrocarpa*] emphasize corners. *Limonium latifolium* with filmy flower haze, *Dicentra spectabilis* with graceful sprays of bleeding-hearts, aster St. Egwyn with rounded forms covered with myriads of little flowers make interesting accents. Dictamnus with striking racemes and ashlike foliage, *Bocconia cordata* [*Macleaya cordata*] with creamy white spires, Japanese irises [*Iris ensata*], yuccas, and lupines are telling accents. Peonies [*Paeonia*], both the single and double varieties, are especially effective for this purpose. The placing of accents should be very carefully considered. Do not have too many. Accents can hurt the garden through their very insistence; they can disturb its quiet through jerky restlessness; they can mar the design through ill-considered arrangement.

Some plants are planted singly at wide intervals through the border. Babysbreath [*Gypsophila paniculata*] and *buddleias, Baptisia tinctoria* and bleeding-hearts [*Dicentra spectabilis*], blue spiraea [*Caryopteris incana*] and Eupatorium coelestinum [*Conoclinium coelestinum*], even peonies and dahlias adapt themselves to such use. Some plants like this method, for through it they are allowed considerable room for development. It is a good method, too, when plant are choice and expensive. More often, however, it is a matter of proper proportion, for, by reason of its size or color or telling shape, one plant may be as emphatic as six or a dozen plants of other varieties planted nearby. A single *peony Kaufmannia*, an early May-flowering variety of great charm, for instance, will be telling in front of a dozen camassias or a hundred or more Darwin tulips. The effect of such spotted plants in the garden is not that of an accent, but that of an oft-recurring note of less insistence.

Quite different is the effect when the plants are scattered through the border in a way that is sometimes called 'dribbling in the plants.' It is the effect that one gets when seed is scattered ever so thinly through the border and the plants crop up here and there delicately far apart. Such planting has the spontaneity with which nature scatters her plants through the woodland. They are charmingly delicate when in bloom and yet they are never missed when out of bloom. Plants of refined and delicate form are best for this use, plants like tulips and lilies of all kinds, various snakeroots [*Cimicifuga*] and meadowrues [*Thalictrum*], *Galtonia candicans* and tuberoses, plants like columbines [*Aquilegia*], delphinium Belladonna, *Delphinium grandiflorum chinensis* [*D. grandiflorum*] and Japanese anemones [*Anemone x hybrida*]. Of annuals, I might suggest such plants as moss verbenas [*Verbena tenuisecta*] and heliotrope [*Heliotropium*], larkspurs [*Consolida*] and phlox, scabiosas and salpiglossis. *Gladiolus primulinus* [*G. dalenii*] can sometimes be used in this way with effect. Of course, all kinds of plants can be scattered through the border, even such seemingly coarse plants as zinnias can assume quite a delicacy by being scattered very lightly through the border. And all sorts of low plants, like arabis and cerastium, nepeta and pinks [*Dianthus*], veronicas and violas, like to be scattered in intermingled masses along the edge of beds or even spread in luxuriant covers over spring borders.

When, in such dribbling, plants of the same degree of delicacy are used the result is very happy. Columbines and Japanese anemones, for instance, can be intermingled with very pleasing effects. In the spring, the anemones like to shelter growing columbines; in the fall, the anemones rise high above the delicate columbine foliage. The effect is enhanced, of course, if two or three plants blossoming at the same time are intermingled in this way. I think I shall always remember the time I saw pink Japanese anemones, *Lilium speciosum* and pink snapdragons [*Antirrhinum majus*] together. The effect was very delicate and owed its special charm to the intermingling.

Then there are still other flowers that like to be planted in drifts. A drift is a thin longish line of plants. It is drawn diagonally across a straight border, or placed in a slender bow in a long bed, or arranged to repeat the garden's curves. The effect of drift planting upon the garden is distinctive. It gives continuity to the border, strength to the design and a sense of movement. The number of drifts to be used depends upon the length of the border and upon the design. The actual length of each drift depends upon the character of the plant and upon the effect desired. Twelve to eighteen plants make a sustaining drift, but sometimes six or nine plants will be quite enough. Drifts are not all of the same length, however, even when only one kind of plant is in use. The main advantage of arranging plants in drift formation is that the flowers stand out in relief away from the background. In this way, they display their sculptural beauty and their color effectiveness. Besides, a drift spreads the flowers in such a way that the sparest bloom will seem abundant. When several kinds of flowers in bloom at the same time are arranged in drifts one behind the other, the flowers rise tier upon tier in billowy masses. This arrangement emphasizes the luxuriance of the garden's bloom.

All manner of plants like to be planted in drifts. Bulbs lend themselves very happily to such arrangement. You can hardly be too lavish with them. Even in quite a small garden you can use a surprising number. I am thinking particularly of Darwin tulips. They should be scattered in much the same manner as a sower scatters grass seed with a long sweeping movement of the arm. The beginning of the line is a little broad, perhaps, the end of the line may taper out to nothing. Drifts of tulips can be repeated and repeated until literally thousands of bulbs are gathered together, drift upon drift, with color effects of surpassing beauty. With daffodils it is much the same. You cannot

A drift gives strength to the design, continuity to the border, and a sense of movement.

plant too many, whether you use them in the garden by the hundreds or whether they are removed or left to hibernate in the border.

Irises are particularly effective when they are planted in drifts. Such arrangement emphasizes the sculptural quality of the flowers and brings out the elegance of their forms. When irises are planted in clumps, the blooms are clustered and the beauty of the individual flower is lost in the display of the mass. In clumps, irises seem homely and comfortable; in drifts, they become dignified and refined. In clumps, the foliage becomes too dominant a note when the flowers are gone, while in drifts the foliage effects are delightfully subdued and can be a real contribution to the rest of the planting. Such drift methods have other advantages. Matted roots are kept together and use the minimum of floor space. Besides, when the flowers are past their blossom-time, they seem to sink away from sight and are not missed.

Many other plants, as different in character as anchusas and calendulas, as gladiolus and marigolds, as heliotrope and asters, like this arrangement of their flowers. Phloxes, too, like to be planted in drifts. No other method will display the sumptuous beauty of phlox quite as well. No other method, more-over, will keep it so well within bounds and allow you room for other flowers. Delphinium likes to be used in drifts for then the flowers assume a stately manner. Hemerocallis looks well planted in drifts, for then the sculptural beauty of the flowers is best displayed. When arranged in drifts, *Salvia farinacea* acquires airy gracefulness, foxgloves [*Digitalis*] picturesqueness, zinnias flamboyancy.

To understand the method of plant arrangement, to know which plants to arrange in drifts, which to put in clumps, which to place singly and which to scatter freely through the border is to learn the rudiments of plant distribution. There is, however, the adaptability of plants to take into consideration for they are ever variable and accommodate themselves to many uses. Without the variability, laws of plant arrangement would become lifeless and the planting of gardens a monotonous task. As it is, the adaptability of plants makes it possible to use them in such fascinating ways that they can embody the design of each garden, interpret its individual spirit and develop its own mood. The very beauty and expressiveness of a garden, the very emotional reactions it engenders depends upon the freedom of flower distribution.

To attain different effects with plants is to realize all their possibilities. Take Oriental poppies [*Papaver orientale*], for instance. I have seen them scattered singly along a shrubbery as the one vivifying effect in a green border, I seen them used in accenting clumps, but I usually plant them in drifts. I place them near the front of the border, and contrary to usual custom, parallel to the edge where the flower forms will be telling and where nothing will be able to crowd them. The main problem is to have annuals or potted plants ready to set in to their places when the foliage dries and disappears. Delphiniums show well the adaptability of plants. They can be planted in great drifts along the background of the border until they seem one continuous mass. Plants in bloom at the same time, dribbling of yellow columbines, singly placed hemerocallis, clumps of lilies will be but supplementary to them. Delphinium can be planted, too, in clumps here and there as quiet accompaniment to other flowers, to drifts of anchusas, to dribblings of *linum perenne*, to edgings of forget-me-nots [*Myosotis*]. Delphiniums can be planted as accents to terminate a drift of hemerocallis or of yellow lilies. Delphinium, especially such slender varieties as delphinium Belladonna, can be used as delicate touches. They are ever so lovely when they spring up out of fluffy annuals as they do sometimes in the early autumn. Madonna lilies [*Lilium candidum*] have the same adaptability. They may be planted as heavy bands, they may be planted in clumps, they may be sprinkled lightly. In each case they take on an individual aspect and give a special mood.

Bulbs, also, exhibit this adaptability. Take daffodils. They can be planted as a veritable carpet in a kind of allover pattern; they can be used as a thin line along the front of the border just behind the edgings; they can be used in drifts of twenty-five or fifty or a hundred. Then, it is sometimes interesting to separate these drifts by accenting clumps of a different variety. Tulips can be used in much the same way. They can be dribbled through the borders with fascinating results when one color is used or many colors. They can be planted drift upon drift in colorful assemblings, and often, especially in a small border, the drift of one color can be terminated with a clump of contrasting or vitalizing color. It is even more interesting if the drift of tulips is terminated by a clump of early-blooming iris. Hyacinths, on the other hand, seem best planted in rows where their stiff primness is emphasized and yet I have found them delightful when planted in small clumps between drifts of daffodils. Scillas, too, produce various effects. In my border, they spring up here and there in the foreground, just behind the edgings, in the most delicate way. I have seen them, however, full of elegance when hundreds of them were planted in a strong drift. Everything around them was in keeping. *Iris pallida* was clumped as accent where the drift ended; lupines raised their wonderful spires nearby; *Nepeta mussini* [*N. x faassenii*] flowered along the edges in luxuriant masses; evergreens formed a hedge in back. These examples may be enough to exhibit the fascinating adaptability of plants, and show that flowers can be used in ever-varying formations to create the garden's illusion.

House Beautiful 58 (OCTOBER 1925): 348–349, 396.
Reprinted by permission from *House Beautiful,* copyright ©
October 1925. The Hearst Corporation. All Rights Reserved.

ENDNOTES

1. Catherine R. Brown, *Women and the Land: A Biographical Survey of Women Who have Contributed to the Development of Landscape Architecture in the United States* (Baltimore, 1979), n.p.

Spire-Like Flowers

HELEN VAN PELT WILSON, a freelance garden writer and editor, was born in Collingswood, New Jersey, in 1901, graduated from Bryn Mawr College in 1923, and attended graduate classes at the University of Pennsylvania. She was a very productive author, writing books and articles on gardening and house plants into the late 1970s, and she had a special interest in African violets. Wilson also served as garden editor and consultant for several periodicals and publishing companies.[2] This article, like Rehmann's, is about arranging flowers in a garden for the most pleasing effect; also like Rehmann's essay it shows a high degree of horticultural skill and design sensibility. Wilson's mode of expression is somewhat more romantic than Rehmann's. She begins by conjuring fond memories of church spires and encourages her readers to extrapolate an important principle of design from such recollections: that if flower spires are properly placed within a border's composition, otherwise dull gardens can become works of art imbued with spiritually elevating content. This advice is then analyzed in ample and precise detail. Again, the emotional response of the viewer is to be as carefully manipulated by the gardener as it was by the contemporary landscape painter, photographer, and, as this article states, musician. Splendid photographs by Mattie Edwards Hewitt eloquently image the aesthetic principles set forth in Wilson's prose.

I N T H E M E M O R Y of each of us who loves simple, beautiful things there is treasured some picture of a little church adorned by a lovely spire. It may be the village church of home that day in and day out we have loved and watched with the sky of the changing seasons behind it and the broad green of the New England common at its feet. Perhaps the picture is but a remembered glimpse of some gracious steeple we once came upon as we turned the bend in a commonplace little Italian village to find it glorified by a "heaven-directed spire", rising in effortless beauty against a flaming sunset sky. Yet whether our memory be of home or of

House & Garden

A CONDÉ NAST PUBLICATION

ADVANCE TRADE EDITION

GARDEN FURNISHINGS NUMBER
JUNE 1931 PRICE 35 CENTS

PLATE 1. *House and Garden,* June 1931
Illustration by Pierre Brissaud

Courtesy *House and Garden.* Copyright © June 1931 (renewed 1959)
by the Condé Nast Publications, Inc.

PLATE 2. *Country Life in America*, March 1924
Illustration by Matilda Browne

PLATE 3. *The Ladies' Home Journal,*
June 1909
Illustration by Lilian Stannard

PLATE 4. *The New Country Life,* March 1918
Illustration by Anna Peck

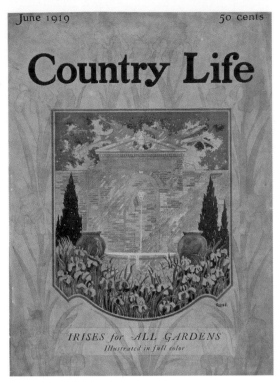

PLATE 5. *Country Life in America,* June 1919
Illustration by J. M. Rosé

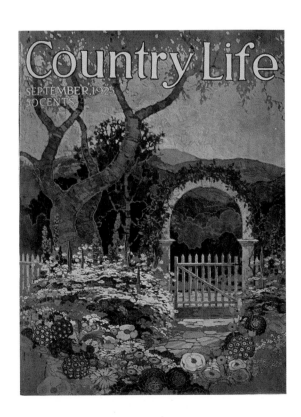

PLATE 6. *Country Life in America,*
September 1925
Illustration by Alice W. Donaldson

House & Garden

FALL PLANTING GUIDE

OCTOBER 1917

CONDÉ NAST & COMPANY *inc. Publisher*

PRICE 25 CENTS

PLATE 7. *House and Garden*, October 1917
Illustration by Charles Livingston Bull

HOUSE & GARDEN

A Condé Nast Publication

Spring Gardening Guide · March, 1933 · Price 35 cents

PLATE 8. *House and Garden*, March 1933

Illustration by Pierre Brissaud

Courtesy *House and Garden.* Copyright © March 1933 (renewed 1961) by the Condé Nast Publications, Inc.

PLATE 9. *The House Beautiful*, March 1911
Illustration by Fred Stearns

PLATE 10. *The House Beautiful*,
March 1916
Illustration by Carroll Bill

PLATE 11. *Garden Magazine and Home Builder*, May 1925
Illustration by Walt Huber

travel, we think gratefully of that church whose "silent finger points to heaven" because at one time it freed our imaginations and gave us far-reaching thoughts.

And from these memories we who are ardent gardeners draw a valuable lesson. As the church tower dignifies even the humble village, so flower spires sparingly but skillfully placed light up our gardens, drawing them from the limbo of dull "planted beds" to the realm of works of art where

> ". . . without a pang one sees
> Ranks, conditions, and degrees."

In the midst of gardens so designed we find ourselves drawing deep breaths and experiencing, in a lesser degree to be sure but still satisfactorily, that sense of exaltation invariably associated with the pleasures of architectural grandeur.

Often the garden which just misses something which is ordinary, becomes distinctive when "spire flowers" carefully chosen for each season are properly spaced in the garden sections. Too many steepled blossoms, of course, must not appear at one time or their effective quality is lost, the all-high garden being just as uninteresting as the all-low one.

For small formal gardens that measure perhaps twenty by thirty feet four sets of spires blooming at a time are plenty. These are best of one kind and are the more striking if the planting about them is somewhat open — nothing but low plants just before them and the heights of the plants beside them less than two-thirds their own stature. Crowding is sure to spoil the whole effect.

Wide and bushy side clumps make a pleasing contrast in form. If they are pushed against the spires, however, or are of the same height, they spoil the effect as would a massive warehouse built just next to our enchanting village steeple. It is important that tall temples "ascend the skies" alone, since isolation gives them added beauty.

In the long border, especially if it can be seen from a distance, several kinds of spires rhythmically spaced for each season may be used. The gardener who knows music will find that the repetition of the same flower form gives a continuity to the whole as if the same chord were struck over and over again in a prelude and, if he has a keen esthetic sense, he will try to syncopate this primary rhythm with a secondary theme of lower spire flowers. To him I recommend for careful foreground spacing, chords of Hemerocallis, Candidum Lilies, *Campanula persicifolia* or Peach-bells, the lower Aconites — *fischeri* [*Aconitum carmichaelii*] and *autumnalis* [*A. napellus neomontanum*] — and Tritomas [*Kniphofia*].

If the designer thinks in terms of etchings, he will view his garden perhaps as a linear composition, the top line of the flowers traced against the sky, appearing to be a slack chain, like those the Victorian stone posts once supported for boundary demarcations. The highest point of the chain would be the top of the spire, the lower descending to the bushy clumps just next, and the lowest to Phlox; then Platycodon heights in the center.

Large groups of spires, however, must not be placed together or the valuable pyramidal form of the individual flower will be lost. Usually a single developed plant of any of those flowers considered spire-like will suffice. A well-grown Delphinium, for example, will send up from a single crown three to a dozen blue rockets while the others of the steepled clan are almost equally vigorous.

The background of the spire should be unassuming. A flowering shrub or brilliantly berried bush will vie with the turrets of garden flowers and so rob them of their restful beauty. A plain wall of Hemlock [*Tsuga*] darkness, the quiet green of Euonymus, the soft rose red of a brick wall, the gleam of a white picket fence, or the peaceful blue of sky or sea are ideal backgrounds.

In selecting our primary spire flowers for the various seasons we must insist that each one meet certain requirements. Obviously the predominant characteristic must be height, not usually less than five feet, and the blossom should be of steepled form, preferably with the leaves growing in a low crown so that a long line of stem is visible. The plants must be moderately sturdy too, never even artistically floppy in the manner of the lovely *Salvia* azurea or the carefree hardy Asters. Their night value, for the garden sought at twilight, must also be considered.

The spires of spring will be slow to appear for it takes a long stretch of growing weather to perfect a five-foot flower spike. Perhaps for the sake of an early show it is wise to lower the standard and admit for this season a four-foot beauty — Digitalis [*D. purpurea*] Isabellina, a pale moonlit yellow. This is the loveliest of the Foxgloves, and fine for our purpose because of its definite, sturdy form. Foxgloves give strength and dignity to any border planting and "consort well with nearly every other flower, and certainly with every other color." The Giant Shirley Hybrids [*Digitalis purpurea* 'Giant Shirley'], reaching a five- to seven-foot height, are particularly fine in their wide range of color from white and shell pink to deep rose. For Isabellina a foreground planting of the hardy Pinks Dianthus allwoodii is attractive with loose masses of Chinese Delphinium [*D. grandiflorum*] at the side. Use *Anchusa myosotidiflora* [*Brunnera macrophylla*] beside the taller Foxgloves with perennial Forget-me-nots [*Myosotis scorpioides*] and coral Heuchera in front.

Summer Flowers

Summer spires are more numerous than those of spring. In June and July the lovely Astilbe Salland [*Astilbe x crispa*] reaches its peak of perfection. We see then also the Delphinium, that queen of towering flowers. The distinctive Yucca, too long disgraced by unskillful planting, shakes out its bells in June. The Foxtail Lily, Eremurus [*Eremurus himalaicus*], appears in July when "flaunts the flaring Hollyhock" as well.

Where the background is a white fence or brick wall, Hollyhocks [*Alcea rosea*] are the inevitable choice. They are most effective as Gertrude Jekyll has pointed out, if the wall is not too high and the spires shoot up "telling well against the distant tree masses above the wall."

They are particularly effective if the garden slopes down a hill and their varying heights outline the declivity. I saw them thus, both singles and doubles, in all the pink shades with Dorothy Perkins Roses strewn over the wire fence behind them and Larkspur [*Delphinium*] and Ragged Robins [*Lychnis flos-cuculi*] complementing their hues. A Mulberry [*Morus*] tree in the background emphasized the cheerful uprightness of the Hollyhocks.

Most of the Astilbes, although perfect as to form, are too low except for use as a secondary turrets. The crimson shaded Salland, however, one of the Arendsii Hybrids, grows from five to six feet tall. Mass near it for July beauty two shades of Phlox, the white Miss Lingard [*Phlox carolina* 'Miss Lingard'] and the rose Verboom, and plant *Linum perenne alba* in the foreground.

Wherever the beauty of the evening garden is considered, Delphinium, if it will grow in the locality, must be the chosen spire. The new Hollyhock, Wrexham Strain, is the best of the taller types for spires, the older Belladonna variety being useful for massing as a wave of blue particularly with yellow Daylilies [*Hemerocallis*]. Delphinium, of all spires, needs most careful staking which should be done before the wind has bent the stalks in the way they should not be inclined. With the spire Delphinium, group the long-spurred Columbine [*Aquilegia longissima*] and the yellow Evening Primrose, *Oenothera missouriensis*.

Yucca Uses

Yucca has long had the unhappy fate of growing singly and centrally in front yards of unhappy visage. Used with some relation to its surroundings it displays an unusual and individual beauty, its "tall columns like shafts of marble against the hedge trees. In the daytime the Yucca's blossoms hang in scentless, greenish white bells, but at night these bells lift up their heads and expand with great stars of light and odor — a glorious plant. Around their spires of luminous bells circle pale night moths, lured by the rich fragrance." Beside the Yucca use clumps of giant watermelon-pink Zinnias interplanted with Sea Lavender (*Statice latifolia*) [*Limonium latifolia*] and cover the ground with single, white frilled Petunias.

Eremurus himalaicus, the Foxtail Lily, is not a spire for the small garden but in the extensive border it is a handsome, though expensive plant, with white Hyacinth turrets lighted with golden anthers. Early autumn is the only time to plant it, when shallow holes should be prepared for the spreading roots. This spire of Eremurus is like a mighty wand which is very effective if only dark shrubbery is used near it. If it is to be planted in the flower border, let it be accompanied by the rose Dictamnus, purple Hesperis, and the white *Achillea ptarmica*, Boule de Neige.

For midsummer *Cimicifuga racemosa*, Snakeroot, is a lovely spire suited to a shady place. Each spike is covered with feathery white blossoms which are sweet to look at but not to smell. Let the tall white *Clematis erecta* [*C. recta*], the rosy white Veronica *spicata rosea*, and the low blue *Clematis integrifolia coerulea* stand near *Cimicifuga racemosa*.

The late Aconites also are shade loving and in that section of the border which passes under the trees they look like dark blue flames. Sparks' variety [*A. napellus* 'sparksii'] is a good deep blue but not always to be counted on for a full five feet, but *wilsonii* [*carmichaelii*], blooming later in September and October at a height of six to seven feet, must always be the spire of fall, its hooded blue the perfect foil for Anemones [*Anemone x hybrida*] and clouds of rose, lavender and white fall Asters.

Campanula pyramidalis is the steeple for the sunny autumn border. It is either blue or white with star-shaped blossoms. This Chimney Bellflower, although perennial, is not reliably hardy in many sections and is often, like most of the Foxgloves, best renewed every year. Blue and white Funkias [*Hosta*] and the tall heat-loving Betony [*Stachys officinalis*] contrast pleasantly with this Bellflower.

Besides these perennials of acknowledged spire-like form there are many Lilies which are most effective accents in the border and in the garden of any size, where two or more steeple plants may be used at a time, one at least

In every flower border there is need of variety in plant height and form, in order to escape too great a feeling of uniformity. For this reason, the spire-like blooms attain an importance quite apart from their intrinsic beauty; their presence at well selected intervals keys up the whole composition and enhances its interest. Several examples of flower spires are shown on this page.

should be a Lily. The dull apricot of the Testaceum Lilies is for the summer season. In June and July the colorful towers five feet high are particularly charming with purple Platycodon strewn at their feet and white clouds of Gypsophila Bristol Fairy [*Gypsophila panaculata* 'Bristol Fairy'] beside them.

The new white Lily, *philippinense formosanum*, which flowers in six to eight months from seed, though not at its full height, is lovely for July. Good companions for it are the golden yellow *Helianthus multiflorus florepleno* which bears in July and August Dahlia-like blossoms at a height of nearly four feet, Chinese Delphinium, and the orange Globe Flower (*Trollius europaeus*). Although *Lilium philippinense formosanum* is listed as three to four feet I know that when well fed it easily reaches six feet.

Auratum platyphyllum is the finest of the auratums and excellent for our purpose because of its sturdy eight-foot turret. It is excellent for colder states, too, and withal beautiful in its individual blossom which is white, richly spotted and banded with gold. Scatter the blue of the annual Larkspur [*Consolida*] near it and sow the canary yellow Tulip Poppy [*Papaver glaucum*] (Hunnemania Sunlight) about as a ground cover.

Select the orange-yellow Henryi for August and Sulphureum for September. All these are sturdy spires in white and yellow. The Madonna or Candidum Lilies are purposely not included because they are not tall enough for primary uses. They may be selected, however, if secondary spires are needed or chosen for mass effect particularly when Delphiniums are the plants that supply the steeples.

To the garden intimate the artistic placement of spires is an intriguing game in which he will find as he experiments at least one infallible rule — keep the width of bed or border a little greater than the tallest possible height of the spire selected. Otherwise the spires may appear precariously placed and unbalanced. If that occurs the wanderer in the garden will be subject to the same sensation felt by the too close admirer of a steeple — it will seem to be toppling down upon him.

Despite difficulties with steepled flowers, delicate and subtle effects are possible and when these are achieved the designer knows the same satisfaction as does the master builder who so skillfully draws his church up toward its faultless spire.

House and Garden 67 (MARCH 1935): 32–33, 95–96.
Courtesy *House and Garden*. Copyright © 1935 (renewed 1963)
by the Condé Nast Publications, Inc.

ENDNOTES

2. *Who's Who of American Women*, 1, 3d ed. (Chicago, 1964–1965), 111; *Foremost Women in Communications*, ed. Barbara J. Love (New York, 1970), 675. Brown, *Women and the Land*, n.p.

ꕔ LOUISE B. WILDER
A Plea for Blue in the Garden

LYNDEN B. MILLER characterized Louise Beebe Wilder as "the quintessential hands-on amateur . . . with a thorough command of her subject and the written word."[3] Born in 1878, Wilder lived until 1938 and exerted enormous influence on American gardening in the early twentieth century through her many books and articles. She had a regular column in *House and Garden* from 1925 to 1938. This article on blue gardens was written very early, twelve years before the publication of her book *Colour in My Garden* (1918) and just a few years after she began to garden at her country home, Balderbrae, near Suffern, New York. This garden was the subject of two of her important books and of magazine articles beginning in 1913. She had gardened since she was a child. In this short, unillustrated article she manages to impart all the information one really would need to design an exquisite blue garden.

BLUE FLOWERS are rare, but they are possibly more numerous than is realized by the average amateur gardener. There are many beautiful varieties, especially among the old time favorites, and their value in the garden is great; greater, to my mind, than that of any other color, except white. But they must be carefully placed and combined, or they will not do their part in the general color scheme; in fact, they will hardly show at all; for strong colors placed near them seem to absorb rather than to accentuate their blue light. An occasional flame colored poppy [*Papaver*] or lily [*Lilium*] is not harmful, and sulphur and white blossoms among the blue are lovely; but most of all they are dependent upon their own foliage and that of their neighbors to enhance their peculiar depth of charm, the green serving to blend rather than to separate the various tints. The gray leaves of the lavender [*Lavandula*] and Sage [*Salvia*] make an effective shading among their brighter sisters, and there is in this soft merging of blue and green the pleasure one always finds in quiet harmony as opposed to violent contrast.

One can grow many blue flowering plants together without fear of clashing tints, which is not true of most flowers in other colors. Delphinium, Platycodon, Aconitum and members of the Campanula family will blossom together harmoniously. A little white or sulphur used to accent the blue is always good, but they will be just as charming alone. Plant large clumps of Delphinium and Aconitum at the end of a vista and note the exquisite effect. There is a soft melting into the atmosphere of these rare blue tints which is far lovelier than the hard outlines made by red or yellow flowers at a little distance. It rightly used along the boundaries of a garden, the effect of increasing its apparent size is marked, while brighter flowers will seem to bring the boundaries nearer. This fact should not be overlooked in the planting of a small garden.

I know a small garden, literally laid against the sky, for it is built on terraces upheld by rough stone walls upon a steep south-eastern slope. The topmost terrace is crowned by a pergola, somewhat formal in design, but with rough hewn posts and beams, over which clamber Wisteria and white Clematis Paniculata [*Clematis terniflora*]. On the terrace in front, and about three feet below, grows and rejoices a blue garden, looking like a bit of the sky drawn down to earth and caught at the edges by white Pinks [*Dianthus*] and Violets [*Violas*]. It is a delight from the first shy Scilla in early Spring, — those little rising bells of the blue garden — until late autumn, when the last blue blossom nestles down to rest and awaits the next ringing of the Scilla bells.

This terrace is narrower than the others of the garden, — about eight feet wide by fifty feet long, through its width by the path and steps leading to the pergola. The ends of the terrace are somewhat shaded by trees and here have been placed strong clumps of the stately, shade-loving Monkshood [*Aconitum*], which, by planting the different varieties, can be had in bloom from June to October. Then come masses of graceful Larkspur [*Delphinium*], rearing its lovely blue spires against the gray wall and the pergola above. Old fashioned bell flowers [*Campanula*] have a place on this backmost line and white Boltonia with its myriad tiny, daisy blossoms, like mist in the sunshine. In front of these, spears of Veronica, plenty of Chinese Bell flowers [*Platycodon*] (both blue and white), and large clumps of sturdy lavender and white Phlox, blue Sage, Canterbury bells [*Campanula medium*], and sown thickly among all, silvery lavender Poppies to poke their crumpled, silken heads through wherever they can find an opening to the sun.

Across the path grow fairy blue and white Columbines [*Aquilegia*], low-growing bell flowers, Corn flowers [*Centaurea cyanus*], hardy white Pinks [*Dianthus*] and our native blue Flag [*Iris versicolor*], — called common, though so uncommonly lovely. To greet the Spring are Scillas, Snowdrops [*Galanthus nivalis*], Grape Hyacinths [*Muscari*], Wood Violets [*Viola*] and an occasional clump of yellow Daffodils [Narcissus].

There is nothing somber or dull about this blue terrace and it is ever restful.

Let some one plant for himself even a tiny blue border against a wall or in some sunny, sheltered spot. Let him go from the riotous gaiety of the rest of the garden to this quiet nook filled with soft lights and the droning of bees, and see if it does not become, in spite of himself, the best beloved and most tended part of the garden.

Plants for the Blue Garden

ACONITUM	(Monkshood or Helmet flower.) Autumnale [*napellus neomontanum*], purplish blue, September. Barbatum, cream color, July. Napellus, blue, August and September. Fischeri [*carmichaelii*], light blue, September and October.
DELPHINIUM	(Larkspur,) 2 to 5 feet. Formosum, dark blue, July to frost. Coelestinum [*elatum*] (English), light blue. x Belladonna, light blue, all summer.
CAMPANULA	(Bell flower), 4 to 5 feet. Pyramidalis. September, Carpatica, (Hare Bell), 8 inches. Rotundifolia (Blue Bells of Scotland), 1 foot, July
PLATYCODON	(Japanese Bell flower), 1 1/4 feet. Grandiflorus, blue, all summer. [*grandiflorus*] 'Album', white. [*grandiflorus*] 'Mariesii', large blue flowers.
BOLTONIA	(False Camomile), 5 feet. Asteroides, white, August.
VERONICA LONGIFOLIA	blue, 2 feet, all summer.
HARDY PHLOX	white and lilac, July and August, 2 feet.
AQUILEGIA	(Columbine), 2 feet [*caerulea*] Rocky Mountain [Colorado Columbine]
COMMON BLUE SAGE	[*Salvia*]
HARDY PINKS	[*Dianthus*], Her Majesty.
SCILLAS	
GRAPE HYACINTHS	[*Muscari*].
DAFFODILS.	
WILD VIOLETS	[*Viola*].
NATIVE IRIS	[*Iris versicolor*].
POPPIES	[*Papaver*].Carnation flowered lilac, 2 feet, from seed.
CENTAUREA CYANUS	Corn flower, 2 feet, from seed

The House Beautiful 20 (JUNE 1906): 40–41.

ENDNOTES

3. Introduction to the recently republished *Color in My Garden* (New York, 1990), xxi. On Wilder, see also Virginia Begg, in *Pioneers of American Landscape Design* (1993), 132–133.

✍ ANTOINETTE PERRETT
Modern Color in Tulip Gardens

ANTOINETTE PERRETT, a photographer and writer, was Elsa Rehmann's elder sister. She lavished praise on two of Rehmann's gardens in this article but failed to mention the family connection.[4] She and her sister collaborated on a book, *Garden-Making*, published in 1926. Born in Newark, New Jersey, in 1880, Perrett received her bachelor's degree from Vassar College in 1901. She was politically progressive and a supporter of women's suffrage. She served as architectural editor of *Good Housekeeping* and wrote on architecture, gardening, and other subjects for magazines.[5] The fine illustrations for this article attest to her expertise in photography — one appears with the chapter's table of contents, page 85. Her enthusiasm for gardening and color is truly infectious. She loves tulips for their color: "a veritable palette of the new impressionism . . . like a revelation of a new world." With nearly breathless excitement she passes along ideas to her readers as if they were her intimate friends — "there is nothing like companionship in gardening!" — sharing ideas about some luscious color combinations for azaleas and tulips. Thoroughly imbued with the Arts and Crafts romanticism of the day, she confides that to achieve really spectacular color schemes that are like stained glass windows, you need the simple heart of a medieval workman and an overpowering sense of the beauty in the new tulips' color. Perrett was positively disposed toward modernism, especially in art, and yet revered America's cultural past. In an article she wrote for *House and Garden* in 1925, "In the Pilgrim Manner," she again connected the antique and the modern in their mutual evocation of simple values: "Our age is not going back to plainness but on to an appreciation of the subtle refinements that may be inherent in the simplest things."[6]

ISN'T IT JUST the most exhilarating thing to be alive in this golden autumn, while the flower borders are still as rich and full of bloom as they can be, and to be able to bridge the thought of a flowerless winter by planning and scheming and dreaming of the spring bulbs and the tulips that are to come?

Tulips! Wonderful chalice flowers on tall stems, marvelous cups of color that they are! And how rich their history has been, how full of human adventure. Natives of the Orient, of Asia Minor, China and Japan, with a Persian name, cultivated first in reds and yellows by the Turks, brought to Vienna by an Austrian ambassador in the sixteenth century, the very rage in Holland in the time of her greatness, and now reborn in splendor in our gardens. Thirteen thousand florins were paid in the seventeenth century for a single bulb of Semper Augustus! And though the government stepped in and stopped the speculation, I'm wondering if any sum could really pay for flowers such as these.

I remember the evening I dined at Wilmington, there was a burnished helmet full of Mrs. Haskell's tulips in the centre of the table. Mrs. Haskell cultivates them with great vigor, and there they were, great petaled chalices on tall characterful stems, mahogany and bronze and purple, rich and deep beyond words and yet all a-shine and glinting as though in reflection of the armored metal that held them.

It is, however, not for their richness nor for their storied past that we love tulips. It is chiefly because, beyond all other flowers, and in Maytime especially, they are a veritable artist's palette in their myriad tones and colorings — not the snuff-colored palette of our forefathers, but a veritable palette of the new impressionism, the palette that was born in the nineteenth century, when English artists, like Constable and Bonington, first went out into the fields to paint and which has ever since been made more wonderful by painters bringing back the grays of the mist, the pearl and rose of the dawn, the lavender and blues and purples of the shadows and a host of pastel tones that are like a revelation of a new world. It is this new palette, with all its new and marvelously subtle relationships, that we can use in our tulip gardens and that gives them a significance and a new art meaning such as the world has never known before.

And how simply we can use them. In my own little front-door terrace garden, for instance, there were some Japanese azaleas [*Rhododendron*] among the box [*Buxus*] bushes at the ends of the brick terrace walls. They are low bushy shrubs with small dark green leaves that change to a rich bronzy copper in the winter time, and I could tell by the way they were thriving that they just loved it there. The only trouble was that in May they fairly broke into an all-over bloom of a sort of cerise magenta. I say trouble, but it was just like so many of our human difficulties, no trouble at all but an opportunity to develop a unique color scheme that seemed to grow right out of the garden itself, for the maroon-colored tulips, the Marconis, proved enchanting companions for the azaleas. It was, however, an altogether reciprocal relationship, for I have seen Marconis, for instance, where they seemed dark and inconspicuous, sort of background colors, but the all-over cerise magenta of the azaleas brought the Marconis right to the fore as the major and dominant bloom and made the amethyst tulips that were grouped beside them and even the lavender-blue

Dreams that are planted in long drifts across the border seem but a carrying out of the original theme. How I love this coloring — this lavender and magenta, maroon and amethyst, with just a few blush-pink tulips on either side of the Dreams to jack up, as it were, the softness of the general harmony. This jacking up, this pinging up, as an artist would call it, is very essential. Otherwise you may have an exquisite blending that leaves you strangely and mysteriously dissatisfied, like a song without an ending, like a person without personality.

This spring while I was at Wilmington for tulip time, I found that Mrs. H. G. Haskell had brilliant scarlet azaleas in front of her house and that she had scarlet tulips to match them — a rare and rich coloring all by its lonesome against the evergreens.

'Never use red tulips in your garden,' I happened to hear a woman say who has worked up a very beautiful tulip garden in soft pastel colors, and I thought it an excellent rule to follow — only rules were meant to be broken! So I am going to tell you of Mrs. Hancock's garden in Passaic, N. J. that Miss Elsa Rehmann, the landscape architect, designed. It is a small oval garden, and as you enter it, right before you, are Professor Rauwenhofs, enormous flowers on strong stems, all cardinal red with a scarlet glow inside them, a strong and exhilarating bit of color. But then the problem comes up of what to use with them and that is where you need not only a modern color sense, a knowledge and feeling for the color genius of our time, but a certain sense of restraint, a self-disciplining, which, by the way, is quite as necessary in gardens as it is in life and art in general, though we do love to think that in gardens, at least, we can run riot, though quite the reverse is true. It is as though only genius can emulate nature in running riot, as though all lesser folk only can achieve an annoying disorderliness. For a garden, like the heavenly bodies themselves, is ever so law-abiding and a lovely riot is really governed by a myriad of laws, intricately applied, whereas beginners like most of us human folk have to apply laws carefully one by one.

If you wish a garden with red tulips, then, Mrs. Hancock's is both restrained and law-abiding and yet eminently modern and arresting — for, with the cardinal Professor Rauwenhofs, there are purple tulips with small groups of the black La Tulipe Noir in back of the purple and with drifts of lavender-blue Dreams between the red.

This red and purple garden with its accents of black, and its lighter lavender-blue is a dark, rich color scheme. In contrast, just to show you the wide range of modern effects you can get with tulips, there is the lightest and airiest of color in the small dining-room garden, which Miss Rehmann again designed for Mrs. Cornelius Bliss, Jr., at Wheatley Hills, Long Island.

There is a round pool in the centre of this garden with four white azaleas — indica alba — about it, and it is these pure white flowers that are really the motif of the whole scheme. It is as though the tulips simply had taken up the suggestion and worked their magic about its virgin freshness, for about the pool there are only white tulips and clear pale yellow, with dull bronzy gold and lavender Dreams beyond the path.

Another lovely light color scheme, though not as rare and subtle, is white La Candeur tulips with blue phlox divaricata for the centre beds, and all pink from blush to the rich brilliant rose of Clara Butts for the borders. And that reminds me that La Candeur itself, all silvery white as it is when it begins to bloom, turns a soft rose white with age. La Candeur is also very lovely with the clear light blue of the tall May-flowering scillas. As for the Clara Butts, proud youthful beauties though they be and the greatest favorites, I have never seen their brilliant rose lovelier than in a little simple garden where they circled round a pool that had a sky-blue painted bottom. But even in a girlishly simple scheme such as this you must instinctively know how much color to use and how to put it in exactly the right spots. In other words, you must always remember that you have slipped your thumb into an artist's palette and, for myself, I always find that eminently difficult when I'm on my knees digging an endless number of deep little holes for the bulbs. That is why a colored plan with a pencil point for every bulb is the only thing, or how would colored pins upon a cushion do? You could pull them up and stick them in again to your heart's content until you had the bulbs distributed right! And what fascinating problems you could set for yourself! I have two such problems that have intrigued me amazingly and that I gladly pass on to you. There is nothing like companionship in gardening!

The tulip garden of Mrs. H. G. Haskell, Wilmington, Delaware

I have been speaking of azaleas and tulips, but I was especially thrilled when I heard of how Mrs. W. K. duPont had selected all her tulips to companion the Judas tree in her garden. The Judas tree — the Cercis canadensis — is an American tree that later has a thick shade of great glossy, heart-shaped leaves and that has long, common-sense-looking brown seed pods that remain on all winter, but in the spring before its leaves are out, its twigs are closely covered with a bloom of magenta pink ever so strange and Japanese and marvelously decorative. I was told what tulips Mrs. duPont selected and I was very much impressed. Curiously enough I forgot them, but the idea so appealed to me that it set my mind to working out the problem, for itself and I am passing on the problem as you may like to do likewise.

The other suggestion that inveigled my imagination was in Mrs. Charles Rumford's garden, in the old part of Wilmington, down near the Brandywine. Mrs. Rumford had what she called her stained glass bed of tulips, which has ever since made me think how lovely such a stained glass tulip garden would be outside one of our great modern studio living-rooms — a room in brown wood with a rose window in the garden! And I have been thinking how lovely it would be to have the outer beds of this garden all in early iris — although the thought of the tulips alone makes me feel that a trip to the French cathedrals will sooner or later become vital to my welfare and happiness, for think of a tulip garden, like an old rose window in a cathedral, with all the subtle tones that the ages have softened in glass turned into living bloom in your own garden. In Mrs. Rumford's bed, there were deep red tulips, rich pointed reds and scarlets, a burnished red with a yellow glow, a brown and yellow tulip, all fine-lined in its design, lavender and purple, yellow and bronze, — but naming the colors is as inadequate for such a garden as it would be in describing the charm of old cathedral glass itself. You need more than color. You need more even than its distribution in design. You need again the heart of the worker as simple as it was in those far-away ages. And you need such an overpowering sense of the new beauty in these flowers that you must simply tuck it away for the winter into the rich, good-feeling earth of your garden until in good time, with the returning spring, it will come back to rejoice you in tulip-time.

The House Beautiful 52 (OCTOBER 1922): 324–325, 374, 376.

ENDNOTES

4. Perrett provided photographs for Rehmann's article in this chapter (see above, 84 and 89), and both photographs and supplementary text for *Garden-Making* (1926). In the introduction to that book Rehmann writes of her sister: "Mrs. Perrett has a rare appreciation of garden art and of the achievements of the artists and craftsmen, of architects and landscape architects of today. It is the appreciation of one who uses the camera, not merely to reproduce her subjects, but to catch their spirit and to put her interpretation upon them" (quoted in Brown, *Women and the Land*, n.p.).

5. *Woman's Who's Who of America, 1914–1915*, ed. John William Leonard (Detroit, 1976), 640.

6. *House and Garden* 48 (December 1925): 57 and 60.

~ S. R. DUFFY

How I Learned Some Lessons from Nature

SHERMAN DUFFY lived in Illinois and from the 1910s to the 1930s wrote articles for *Garden Magazine* and *Country Life in America*. It is clear from these articles that he was an avid, middle-class gardener with a keen sense of humor. No information about him is recorded in biographical reference sources, and so it was probably only by means of these writings that he entered the realm of public recognition. In this text, which is the second half of a two-part article on color harmony, begun by Mrs. Francis King, Duffy demonstrates his concern with adapting current gardening aesthetics to the climate of mid-western America. This he accomplishes by consulting a natural landscape blossoming with wild flowers, a practice often recommended in the gardening literature of the day.

COLOR SCHEMES in print are altogether orderly, logical, and appear perfectly feasible, but when it comes to transferring them from book and paper to the soil, and reproducing these ideas in leaf and blossom — it's different. Perhaps people who know nothing about color schemes are to be envied. I was happier with my garden when I could unblushingly grow orange marigolds [*Tagetes*], purple petunias and glaring blue annual larkspurs [*Consolida*] all in a bunch and admire them.

Analyzed down to first principles, there really is nothing new in the ideas of a color scheme. The general thought is the same as the principle found in the chapter on light in elementary text books on physics — that the colors of the spectrum are arranged in perfect harmony and appear in the order — violet, indigo, blue, green, yellow, orange, red; or, more simply, blue, yellow, red.

The mistake I made was in trying to follow illustrative plans too closely without considering the fact that the writers' climates, seasons and summer sunlight were not the same as mine. The glaring summer sun softens colors and makes permissible and admirable combinations which are not even hinted by writers in more gentle climes.

I endeavored to imitate these color arrangements as closely as I could, with unfortunate results. The flowering seasons did not correspond, and that broke up the combinations of color in short order. The plans omitted plants which I had, and wanted in my border, and they didn't match up with the ones suggested; so finally I gave up trying to imitate and set about devising plans of my own.

But with all my endeavors I have some fierce-looking messes owing to my own misunderstandings of color terms and to misunderstandings of catalogue writers. The very worst was in planting Spirea Anthony Waterer [*Spiraea japonica* 'Anthony Waterer'] next to oriental poppies [*Papaver orientale*] in the belief that the spiraea was crimson and would associate with the scarlet poppies!

I understood crimson to be red, good and red, like a college color ribbon, something to arouse Taurus. Anthony Waterer spirea was described as bright crimson. That description was surely written by a color-blind man, or one deserving of that shorter but uglier word. Those spireas didn't even make a good bonfire. *Asclepias tuberosa* blooming close to a wire fence covered with perennial peas [*Lathyrus latifolius*] also proved most unhappy.

The trouble in endeavoring to attain a good color scheme is that new colors are discovered every few minutes. There are more kinds of reds and blues and yellows that don't mate up than we have imagined in our philosophy, when you get to looking them squarely in the face.

The idea of bringing a rainbow to earth and reproducing it in its changing colors in a flower border is undoubtedly an admirable one, but I can't do it. There is too much latitude in the blues and yellows and reds. Blues will combine better than anything else for me. They will make a happy family with pale yellows and then the yellows can deepen and hook up nicely with orange and scarlet; but there is a vast tribe of magentas, lilacs, lavenders, heliotropes, and that color called mauve which I haven't been able to identify twice alike in plants offered as mauve. They seem to vary from deep purple, as I understand it, to dirty white.

The only way I can get along with these subjects is to let them flock by themselves and connect by easy stages through patches of white with something else.

Working with subjects that bloom at the same time simplifies somewhat the difficulties of securing a good color scheme, for it is a simple matter to cut the blooms and spread them out and rearrange them until the colors seem well disposed and plant the border accordingly. But right there occurs another kink. The seasons of flower for most hardy perennials is comparatively short. With a good color scheme arranged for one month, what is to be done for the next and the next and so on until frost? Some plan had to be discovered that I could work out with some degree of success. It is simply impossible for me to handle more than two or three colors at a time with any degree of success and produce anything like a pleasing effect, so I have adopted the suggestion of a very plebeian model and the farther I go with it the better I like it.

A section of the railroad over which I pass every week has escaped the devastating scythe of the section hands for several seasons, and was worth looking at every day during the summer. It was some six or seven miles long and every week it presented a complete flower garden with one distinct prevailing color with just enough variation to beak up the monotony. It seemed to be a whole garden and everything seemed to belong. Every month presented some special scheme, and the entire space was covered. It needed no attention and received none. What better model could be taken?

During May the prevailing effect was shooting stars (*Dodecatheon meadia*), in pinks, deep rose and white, with variations of *Anemone Pennsylvanica* [*Anemone canadensis*] and quantities of blue-eyed grass [*Sisyrinchium angustifolium*], yellow star grass [*Xyris*], *Viola pedata*, and other low-tufted plants around and among the larger. In June the deep rose prairie phlox and the wild hyacinth or quamash [*Camassia quamash*] prevailed. July brought the gay asclepias and *Rudbeckia hirta* in spots and patches with plenty of green. In early August came myriads of spires of liatris, purple rudbeckia, the taller, long-coned rudbeckias, and golden rod [*Solidago*], with occasional clumps of physostegia. September brought banks and drifts and clouds of asters — dark blue, light blue and white, asters everywhere, with the later wild sunflowers [*Helianthus*].

If that wild strip along the railroad track without the care of a gardener could unfold one complete garden after another through the entire season, from early spring until October, and with harmonious coloring all the time, it was succeeding with a gardening principle that had eluded me. I studied that wild garden pretty thoroughly, and while the colonies of plants were fairly well defined, there being thickly settled families of them, they were scattered so well all over the space under observation as to give the effect of an entire garden. Measuring off a square foot of one of the most densely populated colonies, I took a census of its denizens and found in this small space five shooting stars, one purple rudbeckia, six spikes of phlox, three quasmash or wild hyacinth, one aster, five clumps of blue-eyed grass, two clumps of yellow star grass, and one clump of bird's-foot viola [*Viola pedata*], besides some little weeds that I didn't recognize. That seemed a tremendous lot of plant life for one square foot!

That was not a very illuminating study when applied to my border unless I copied exactly the wildlings I had enumerated, and I didn't want them. I'd go crazy trying to jam eight different kinds of plants into one foot of space, owing to the study necessary to secure combinations that would get out of each other's way, but it did appear that the whole secret was over lapping and interlacing colonies blooming at different seasons so that no space ever was wholly vacant. And the farther I go the more convinced I am that the interlacing and interweaving of colonies selected with a view to harmony of growth and coloring and seasons is the true secret of securing continuous bloom over an entire border during an entire season. However, it is out of the fryingpan into the fire for its a tougher job to mingle colonies than to plant them with definite outlines.

I compromised by overlapping the outlines of various colonies, and taking one plant right straight through the length of the border, then another and so on until I had as many as could well occupy the space, using species that would give a succession of bloom.

The most successful experiment, so successful, in fact, that I am altogether satisfied with it, I started with columbines (vulgaris, and the long-spurred hybrids). They were planted straight down the centre, a well-defined colony every now and then with individual plants and groups of two or three scattered about to give just a suspicion of an entire bed. Then larkspurs [*Delphinium*] went in. Foxgloves [*Digitalis*] were the next to be added in clumps, and individual plants. German [bearded] iris on account of its bulk and permanence was used toward the front with stokesias in front of the iris,

The lavender heads of Eug. Danzanvilliers phlox with blue sea-holly; white Fraulein G. Von Lassberg phlox to the left and Shasta daisy in front

and scattered in groups and ones and twos. Japanese anemones [*Anemone x hybrida*] and chimney bellflowers [*Campanula pyramidalis*] found places to nestle all along the length and gradually climb up as the earlier flowers were failing.

Occasionally there was a colony of some plant that did not extend over the entire scheme. This arrangement serves to break monotony and emphasize the beauty of the general scheme. I used last year the Dropmore anchusa and two or three patches of *Platycodon Mariesii* [*P. grandiflorus*] with one "picture" group composed of *Eryngium amethystinum, Echinops Ritra* and Achillea The Pearl [*Achillea ptarmica* 'The Pearl']. This combination I imitated bodily from Miss Jekyll, and it is of unusual beauty.

In planting this border I left room for groups of daffodils and tulips so that in early spring it is a bulb garden. It has been the one really worth while hardy border that I ever grew.

The prevailing colors are blue, pink and yellow in the paler shades. After considerable experimenting the columbine [*Aquilegia*] struck me as a good basis upon which to figure color schemes, for a perfect rainbow could be devised from columbines alone.

The pink and rose colors of the foxgloves, and the blue peach-leaved bellflowers [*Campanula percisifolia*] formed a fine late May and early June combination with the earlier columbines. The long-spurred columbines in scores of colors and combinations lasted well into July, while the German iris covered the transition period and as the late columbines were disappearing, the stokesias began to show flower with a finale of pink and blue again, with chimney bellflowers [*Campanula pyramidalis*] and Japanese anemones.

Another border is given over to the deep yellows and bright reds, and is still in process of evolution. With a background of hollyhocks [*Alcea rosea*] and Miss Mellish and Wolley Dod sunflowers [*Helianthus*], the main subjects are coreopsis, gaillardia, Shasta daisies [*Leucanthemum x superbum*], the new "annual sweet Williams," [*Dianthus barbatus*] and hardy pompon chrysanthemums, with clumps of asclepias, tritoma [*Kniphofia*], hemerocallis and purple rudbeckia [*Echinacea purpurea*] hybrids, the so-called "red sunflowers."

The third section of the border is devoted to oriental poppies [*Papaver orientale*] in variety and hardy asters. It is planned for two distinct effects without relation to each other. The edging is of grass pinks [*Dianthus plumarius*] and it has plantings of *Penstemon barbatus,* var. *Torreyi,* to give it character during the latter part of June before the earlier asters are in flower.

A garden, it seems to me, should be subjective rather than objective. What may appear excellent to the owner of a garden may not appear in the same light to others. That makes for individuality of gardening.

The Garden Magazine 11 (APRIL 1910): 158–159.

CAROLINE BLANCHE KING
My Moonlight Garden

CAROLINE KING (1871–1947) was a dietician, writer, and editor whose home, Arborcote, was located in Delaware County, Pennsylvania. From childhood she had experimented with both cooking and gardening, sometimes achieving unfortunate results.[7] As an adventurous young woman she accompanied her husband to Idaho, where they established a pioneer homestead among the Nez Perce Indians.[8] Later, King was Sunday editor of *The Philadelphia Press* from 1909 to 1913, on the editorial staff of *The Evening Telegraph* from 1913 to 1917, and associate editor of *The Country Gentleman* magazine from 1924 to 1942. In 1917 the surgeon general of the United States appointed King the first Army dietician, and she went to France in that capacity in 1918.[9] She purchased Arborcote after her return from France and several years after writing "My Moonlight Garden." King continued to support dietary reform for the remainder of her life; the reform of eating habits was, in fact, one important way in which educated, middle-class women sought to effect broader social improvement in the early twentieth century.[10] In addition to two cookbooks and many magazine articles on cookery she published two garden books — *Rosemary Makes a Garden* (1930) and *This Was Ever in My Dream* (1947).[11] It is not surprising that, as an accomplished cook and food critic, she was acutely sensitive to the fragrance in her night garden.

PERHAPS YOU ARE UNFAMILIAR with the bower of blossoms that is sweeter by night than in the radiance of day. For years such a garden existed only in my fancy, but gradually the imaginary groupings of plants became so real, their spell so seductive, that I resolved, at last, to make my moonlight garden an actuality.

I had observed that many of the prettiest flowers closed their petals in the evening, just when the day was most delightful; and, at the same time, I was aware that those flowers which remained open during the twilight hours gave out a fragrance more insistent than that of the daylight blossoms. Then there was a third class, which did not waken until after sunset, and these were sweetest of all.

Because they have a tendency to borrow color from surrounding plants, it is almost impossible to obtain a pure white foxglove.

After thinking the matter over throughout an entire winter I resolved to put my idea into practice. But as I felt the undertaking to partake somewhat of the nature of an experiment, I looked about for a spot in which I might group whatever flowers I pleased, regardless of the effect the aspect of the little plot might have upon the general scheme and appearance of our whole garden.

I selected a space of about twenty square feet at the extreme end of the main garden and separated from the road by an old stone wall, once a deep gray, but now faded to a pale fawn. It was just the appropriate background for the clusters of white blossoms with which I planned to adorn my moon-light garden.

After an exhaustive search through seed catalogues and florists' manuals for flowers opening only at night, and finding the choice to be somewhat limited, I decided to supplement the list with others of abundant perfume, selecting, however, only those which did not go to sleep at night. I determined, too, to use only white flowers, and preferably single-blossoming varieties. For I had noticed that in these the fragrance is usually more pronounced and delicate than in those bearing double flowers; and that white flowers are usually far sweeter than those arrayed in gorgeous tints.

Beside the old gray wall I planted white roses — the climbing Kaiserin Augusta Victoria and an old-fashioned white rose with a rich, permeating odor and creamy blossoms and a slight blush of pink at their hearts. The latter variety, I believe, is known as the Scotch white rose [*Rosa spinosissima 'Alba'*].

Moon flowers — or, as the nurserymen call them, *Ipomoea* [*I. alba*] — I planted also to develop a fine drapery for the old stone wall, from the time the roses ceased blooming until late autumn. I chose the *Noctiflora* variety for its large, silvery blossoms and its rare perfume.

In one corner of the diminutive garden I planted a syringa [*Philadelphus*], or mock orange shrub, and at the opposite corner, also against the wall, a white lilac [*Syringa*]. Neither the syringa nor the lilac blossomed the first year, but in subsequent seasons the evening breezes were laden with their delicious scent, exquisitely blended, throughout the latter weeks of May and early June.

Spiraeas and deutzias — two early spring shrubs, bearing a profusion of white blossoms — embellish the remaining corners of my novel garden, and borders of sweet alyssum [*Lobularia maritima*] and candytuft [*Iberis semper-virens*] complete the outline. Lilies of the valley [*Convallaria majalis*] reign in a moist and secluded nook next to the wall, mingling their charm with the night-scented stock [*Matthiola longipetala*] planted nearby.

The pure white stock I planted in profusion the first season and was rewarded during the warm, still nights of July and August with its soft, sweet odor wafted through the windows of my bed-chamber, though the garden was at least twenty yards from the house. I can well understand why Marie Antoinette selected this delicate flower, which the French call Julienne, as her favorite: for it is one of the most satisfying that grows. The Germans call it Night Violet, as it seems to give forth its scent only after dusk has fallen.

Nicotiana alata — or, as I prefer to call it, Star of Bethlehem — holds an important place in my moonlight garden. It is one of the flowers which refuse to bloom, save at night, and its delicate, though penetrating aroma has proven a great joy. White phlox is another lovely member of the night garden group; and the white petunia, whose scent is cloyingly sweet by day, seems to take on a subtler quality by night.

The old-fashioned country pink [*Dianthus*] — known as snow pink or star pink — is a welcome addition. Its white flowers outlined against grayish-green foliage appear almost phosphorescent under the shifting, dreamy shadows thrown upon them by that oldest of magicians, the moon.

White lilies, which open at sundown to flood the world with a wealth of ineffable sweetness, share with a few primroses [*Primula*] a conspicuous place. Of the latter I selected a variety bearing flowers of a clear, creamy white.

Tall spikes of tuberoses and Yucca lend a touch of the tropics to the aspect of the floral ensemble, standing out boldly among the smaller and less luxuriant plants. In the daytime the Yucca hangs its scentless bells as if overcome with de-spondency, but as twilight fades into night these bells expand like lighted stars and bestow upon the passerby a rich, exotic perfume savoring of the Orient.

Two restrictions limited the choice of flowers — they must be white so that they could reflect the moonlight, or they must be most fragrant only in hours after dusk. It was a novel experiment, yet wholly successful.

I found it difficult, as in subsequent seasons I enlarged my moonlight garden, to eschew all the dainty, multi-colored sweet peas [*Lathyrus odoratus*], keeping only those bearing white blossoms; but, having hardened my heart to the gay harlequins, I was amply rewarded. For the white sweet peas have an intenser scent, and their flowers, with the background of green foliage, resemble, in the moonlight, a whole school of merry white butterflies.

White pansies [*Viola x wittrockiana*] I planted also, and a few white violets [*Viola*] found a corner in which to thrive unhampered; while in the early spring the dainty white narcissus and hyacinth sweetened the air long before the other flowers dreamed of venturing forth.

Another interesting flower — although it is very little grown — I found in the *cestrum parqui* [*Cestrum nocturnum*], or night-blooming jessamine, whose small, greenish-white blossoms dispense a grateful odor throughout the dark hours. I have two of these plants in my garden, and I should advise anyone planning a similar experiment in flower culture to purchase several of them.

Another favorite is the white columbine [*Aquilegia*] — the common single variety with its flower so like a pair of doves. And the foxgloves [*Digitalis purpurea 'alba'*] also are gratifying, although it is almost impossible to get the blossoms in pure white. These exhibit a tendency to borrow colorings from adjacent flowers; and in a garden where white reigns it is possible that no varying hues would appear in them.

These, then, are the flowers which have contributed to the success of my moonlight garden. Many others there are, too, which I have not mentioned, but the list I have given is sufficiently long for the garden lover desirous of repeating my novel experiment. They will assuredly add to the pleasure of summer evenings on the porch or lawn. To appreciate the unique effect of such a garden you must see it, and inhale its fragrance. The starlike Yuccas, the white blossoms gently waving amid silvery shadows thrown by the stalks of the taller plants, the blending odors, all combine to make it a veritable garden of dreams.

Like the Persians, who gather before a blooming plant, spread their rugs and sing to the plaintive accompaniment of their lutes, we may at eventide drink in the romantic charm of our moonlit garden as we rest after the cares of a busy day.

House and Garden 28 (AUGUST 1915): 30–31, 50.

ENDNOTES_____

7. She claimed, for example, that as a mischievous young child she tried planting some grains of corn from an ancient Egyptian tomb; they had been given to her father by an archeologist. The chickens unearthed and ate the corn before her deed was discovered (Caroline B. King, *This Was Ever in My Dream* [Caldwell, Idaho, 1947], 20–21).

8. *This Was Ever in My Dream*, 21–27.

9. *New York Times* (obituary), December 4, 1947, 31:4, *Who Was Who in America* 2, 299.

10. On culinary reform, see Laura Shapiro, *Perfection Salad: Women and Cooking at the Turn of the Century* (New York, 1986).

11. *This Was Ever in My Dream* is an autobiographical, illustrated account of her garden-making at Arborcote.

Beauty After Bloom

JEAN HERSEY was another incredibly prolific garden writer. She was born in 1902 and made her home in Kennett Square, Pennsylvania. By the time she was seventy-nine, she had written a dozen books and hundreds of magazine articles, some coauthored with her husband, Robert Wilson Hersey. She was honored with the Asta award for best garden writing of the year in 1962.[12] This article is especially appealing, and it attests to her abilities as a writer and horticulturist, as well as to her heightened awareness of natural beauty. An epiphany in an autumn cornfield with milkweed growing around its edges enables her to perceive the more sublime perfection of dried seed heads. The photographs by Walter Beebe Wilder (b. 1906, Louise Beebe Wilder's son) are breathtakingly beautiful, extremely close-up views of the dried flowers: fine examples of 1930s modern photography.

WHEN I WAS NEW to the ways of plants and flowers my one aim was to fill the garden with things that bloomed from spring to frost. My next step was the discovery that the perfect garden consisted of a series of exquisite, ever-changing scenes following one another. But still I thought in terms of bloom. Life seemed altogether gorgeous the few weeks that the Wisteria dangled its pale tipsy flowers from our eaves. But I was not sorry to see these lavender blossoms with their lush scent drift to earth — earth where the first Roses of the season were beginning to unfold and occupy the center of the stage. I loved the Hollyhocks [*Alcea rosea*], too, and the Platycodon, the Phlox, and Zinnias — each in its turn. With this secondary garden enthusiasm I revelled in the arrival of every new garden star.

Then something subtle and still more lovely crept into my appreciation of gardens. I think it began one autumn when I was wandering through a cornfield in the west, where piles of ears among the raggedy shocks vied in brilliant color with the Pumpkins that grew on the coarse nubbly ground. Along the edge of this field was a profusion of Milkweed [*Asclepias syriaca*]. The graceful pointed pods burst here and there as we passed, and gentle

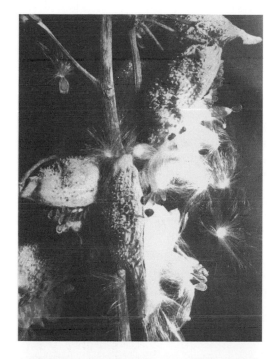

Milkweed (top left)   *Rosa Rugosa (above)*

Anemone Pulsatilla

breezes sent downy white parachutes in all directions, each with its cargo of one small brown seed. The sun glistened on these glossy wisps whirling like blowing snow. The sky was blue, the pods were gray, the Corn and Pumpkins a golden orange — and the total unforgettable.

Of that moment was born a new idea. No one could deny the charm of flowers themselves; but in always seeking blooms we had missed the beauty of this other stage of growing things. A bud may be gentle and full of promise, a flower may be vital and spectacular, but all the tenderness and drama of both are combined and intensified in the beauty of the seed pod which is their culmination. It is a beauty of form, of shape and of texture, if not of vivid color.

After this we began to consider the Dandelions [*Taraxacum*] that crept into our lawn with a hitherto unknown philosophy. We were amazed by the perfection of plan and design in these balls of fluff before they blew away. No one likes Dandelions growing in a lawn; still, finding them at this stage weakens the firmest of destructive intentions!

The flaming blooms of the Oriental Poppies [*Papaver orientale*] are no more gorgeous than the seed pods that follow. Grayish green, acorn-shaped, but larger, and with a crown of black dusted around their heads, they form on the tops of stems which are sometimes twisted and curved, sometimes straight and majestic. These stems are covered with the most delightful pale green unsophisticated prickles, like those of a baby Cucumber.

There is also charm in the small slim seeds tipped with cream color that burst from a ripe Marigold [*Tagetes*] bloom. The Columbine [*Aquilegia*] gracefully arches its adjoining pointed pods as they break apart, sending numerous offspring hither and yon. The round brown Hollyhocks [*Alcea Rosea*], compact in their pods, are neat as chocolate cookies in a tin. The small Cornflower [*Centaurea cyanus*] seeds as they leave the dry and tousled flower heads are like tiny brooms. Regal Lily [*Lilium regale*] pods keep all winter indoors. They are brown and tan and look well in bright-colored vases. The Hibiscus pods are appealingly fat and chunky, while Tulips and Iris are pointed and graceful. The orange hips of the Rugosa Rose are as lovely as the flower itself.

Even more exciting than the blooms are the large green Lotus pods in the pool. Standing tall and dignified above the water they are clearly mirrored in its depths. There each one holds its precious cargo of tiny seeds up to the sun to ripen before dropping them back into the murky depths where they start growing.

Anemone pulsatilla [*Pulsatilla vulgaris*], whose blue furry flowers inhabit spring rock gardens, also has seeds worth boasting about. They form a ball fully two inches in diameter, composed of clusters of diminutive crooked pheasant feathers — so they seem! Each feather is tipped with one small seed waiting for the breeze to waft it to its new home.

Blossoms have color, fragrance and beauty, but in these seed pods there is the promise of a million various shades, myriads of different scents, beauty galore — and I like promises!

House Beautiful 79 (AUGUST 1937): 18, 77.

ENDNOTES

12. *Contemporary Authors: A Bio-Bibliographical Guide to Current Authors and Their Works* 9–12, First Revision, eds. Clare D. Kinsman and Mary Ann Tennenhouse (Detroit, 1974), 381.

ARTHUR HAY

The Lovely Allegheny Vine:
Its Virtues and Faults

AN EPISODE in growing the native Allegheny vine (*Adlumia fungosa*), which was apparently well loved by Americans in the nineteenth and early twentieth centuries, is the subject of this story from *The Craftsman*.[13] The author and his wife learn how hard it is to establish the biennial Allegheny vine in full sun — since it prefers a shady, moist site — and they substitute hyacinth beans (*Lablab purpureus*) for it the third year. And yet, it is a charming story and presents the Allegheny vine as an interesting plant worth trying. Arthur Hay wrote for both *Craftsman* and *Country Life in America*. Like many of his progressive contemporaries he was concerned with improving the appearance and quality of life in urban environments through increased planting.[14]

WHEN WE FIRST MOVED in Jane said: "Whatever else we have, we must have maidenhair vine over the front porch."

"What's maidenhair vine?"

"Oh, it's the sweetest, most delicate thing you ever saw, with leaves like a maidenhair fern. Mrs. Morris has it and it runs on strings all over everything, and when the sun shines through it's just like lacy embroidery. It has the dearest little flowers you ever saw, too, something like lilies-of-the-valley. It dies down in the winter, but the seeds sow themselves, so new vines come up every spring."

"But what's its real name? There isn't any such thing as maidenhair vine in the florists' catalogues."

"Oh that's for you to find out. I believe some people call it 'mountain fringe,' but pretty nearly everybody I know calls it maidenhair vine."

And after a deal of trouble I did find out that what Jane wanted was Allegheny vine, *Adlumia Cirrhosa* [*Adlumia fungosa*] according to the catalogues. So we got a little package of the wee black seed, fine almost as gunpowder, sowed it in a flat in February, and in May set out a score of sturdy little plants at the foot of the porch. With supreme confidence we stretched the strings and waited patiently for the little tendrils to take hold and clamber up.

But clamber is just what the obstinate little things wouldn't do. They grew and grew and flourished their tender green tresses in every breeze, but climbing on strings was the last thing they had in mind, though we laboriously twined them up as far as they would reach. They remained as passive as Mark Twain's turnip vines. Summer ripened into fall and we resigned ourselves to having a ribbon-bed of maidenhair fern with a wind-swept lyre of white string above instead of the cool green curtain we had hoped for.

But next spring when the returning sun had set the lawn aglow with crocus, out of the heart of each sodden clump crept little green tendrils, seized upon the weather-beaten strings we had neglected to pull down and climbed. How they did climb! They climbed all night and they climbed all day. By the first of June they were at the top of the porch, waving little fingers, seeking more places to climb higher. Then they reached out here, there and everywhere, joined hands and wove a lacy net, which the ardent sun strove in vain to penetrate.

In July came the flowers — tiny little pale-pink bells, like lilies-of-the-valley as Jane said — with a faint elusive fragrance. Then the seeds in pods like tiny peas. Millions of them strewed the ground about the roots.

"What a lot we'll have next year!" we said; but to make sure we spent hours after the frost had struck our curtain down, in shelling out more.

This spring we watched closely every little green point that pushed through the ground to see it unfold the biparted leaves. "Nothing doing," as the boys say. All ragweed or wild morning glory or other useless intruders. In confidence we sowed our hoarded seed. Also "nothing doing." Not a seed germinated. From which we conclude — or as old Aesop has it, *haec fabula docet* — that Allegheny vine is a charming delicate thing, worthy of more extended use, but the reason it doesn't get it is that it is a biennial which doesn't and won't climb the first year, climbs beautifully the second, and that except under favorable conditions as to shade and moisture (which we didn't seem to have on our porch, exposed to the blazing afternoon sun) it will not reseed itself. Another time I should buy the seed from a reliable seedsman, grow it as a fern the first year and as a vine the second, setting new plants from purchased seed every year at the base of the vines.

This year we have hyacinth beans [*Lablab purpureus*] on our porch.

The Craftsman 20 (SEPTEMBER 1911): 630.

ENDNOTES_____

13. Garden writer Elizabeth Lawrence (most of whose fine writings date to the second half of the century) said that her grandmother grew the vine "in a dark, damp corner behind the laundry," and that it was difficult to establish but well worth the effort (Elizabeth Lawrence, "Biennials — An Uncertain Quantity," *Gardener's Chronicle of America* 43 [May 1939]: 150).

14. In June 1912 he wrote an article titled "Bringing Country Beauty to the City Streets" for *Craftsman*.

⍦ GRACE TABOR
Ten Annuals for This Year's Garden

WHILE THE POPULARITY of perennials bloomed magnificently in the early twentieth century, annuals still had their advocates, and Grace Tabor numbered prominently among them. In this article she states that she has resolved to try ten new annuals that year and perhaps every year thereafter. She not only explains their various merits, but passes along information on how to grow them from seed and cultivate them for the best results. Late twentieth-century seed catalogues may no longer list the same varieties, but substitutions are abundant; she does, after all, encourage a willingness to experiment.[15]

WAITING PATIENTLY in their neat packets in the seed basket to be given their chance — what should we do without annuals? For, of course, nobody ever wants actually to finish the garden; to get it all done, like the historic old town down south where not a nail has been driven since the war. Just fancy what such a garden would be like! It is too dreadful to contemplate. No indeed; variety is as desirable a condiment in gardening as in any other phase of life, even though the garden itself in its layout and general scheme is complete.

Too much variety, however, is as disconcerting as too little is dispiriting; so this year I made a resolution, when the first catalogue came in — and if it works out satisfactorily, it is going to be written down in the Book of Garden Laws. Here it is: The garden shall have ten annuals, and only ten — as unlike each other as possible, and perhaps every one shall be different from any that the garden has ever entertained before. Certainly some of them shall; and one at least must be a new variety — or as new as the season offers.

This is really a broad, elastic resolution — one that does not hamper in the least and that provides pleasurable anticipation. Here is what I am using: For the season's novelty, which has been given space enough to try it well, there is the new Shirley poppy [*Papaver rhoeas*], "Celeste" — a lovely, pallid ghost, in gray, sky-blue and lavender tones. That I am a bit skeptical of this flower only makes the anticipation the more keen. In combination with gray nothing is as lovely as purest, palest yellow; so, on the chance that the poppies may show this promised tone, they are backed with a row of the pure yellow snapdragon [*Antirrhinum majus*], Golden Queen. It will not be a bad combination even if the gray should turn out to be only a lavender.

For the rest, there is the African daisy — *Arctotis 'grandis'* [*A. venusta*] — with its great, white, starry flowers, tinted with pale bluish mauve on their backs; the pretty Clarkia in a salmon pink form for a partly shady place; quantities of double pinks [*Dianthus*] in three varieties — a pure white, a crimson and an almost black crimson that shows a white line around the edges, like rich velvet edged with ermine; California poppies [*Eschscholzia*] in yellow shades only, ranged in front of a line of double stock-flowered annual larkspur [*Consolida*]; red and white lupines [*Lupinus*] in another place that does not get the full sun; Xeranthemums in a group at one corner, and finally, a mass of verbena, a white and clear blue variety, making up the required number of ten. Enclosing the entire space where the annuals grow there is always a trim little hedge of rosemary [*Rosmarinus officinalis*], sweet-flavored and useful — a paradise for the bees. This, of course, is in its accustomed place. All walks are turf and the beds are cut down about two inches below the surface.

Of course, nothing is to be expected of the garden of annuals much before the end of June; therefore it should not be located where its barren earth will be aggressively within sight during the preceding weeks. The edging of rosemary helps to minimize the barrenness, however, and in localities where this will endure, I know of no more delightful treatment for garden beds than such a hedge, whether the walks are of grass or gravel. Common mint [*Mentha*] may be used in place of rosemary where it is not hardy, and this furnishes a pleasant and effective substitute, if trimmed well and kept within bounds.

Annuals happily will grow practically anywhere and for almost anybody, however indifferent a gardener he may be. But even annuals appreciate a good home, and will respond to good culture. Therefore it is wiser to give them a

California poppies demand nearly the care of oriental sorts and are averse to transplanting. The seeds may be sown early. Golden West is a good variety for the garden.

little more consideration than they commonly receive — to make their beds with care, and tend them according to their needs, until the plants are big enough to look out for themselves without further trouble on your part.

Each year the earth must be spaded thoroughly and worked over to a depth of eight inches or more. This insures a mellow soil for deep reaching roots, and though it seems unnecessary, perhaps, after several seasons of culture, I always feel that it is better to make no exceptions to this rule. Wet or stiff soil will need deeper work than this, especially if it is newly broken up, but a foot is deep enough for all summer flowering annuals. Vegetables and sturdier things may need greater depth, but we are concerning ourselves only with the plants which will not. Well rotted and broken up stable manure should be worked in with this spading — and finally, the surface must be raked smooth and fine.

Ordinarily I do not feel that it is worth while to start annuals indoors in pots or flats — but perhaps that is because I always have so many other things which require the space which these would take up. As a matter of fact, however, there is not enough time actually gained to make up for the extra trouble; and for the inexperienced it is far easier to sow the seed where the plants are to grow and thin them out as they come up, than to undertake to transplant them when small and tender. Some will not submit to transplanting.

The poppy is one of these; the poppy has long tap roots. It must be sowed out of doors where it is to grow. Poppy seed are very small — consequently they must be covered lightly with earth; and when the seedlings begin to prick through the ground, you will find that you have several million more plants than seemingly there is room for anywhere on earth. They are quick to germinate and the time to pluck up the superabundance of them is as soon as they are above ground, leaving enough space so that they will stand about four inches apart all over the part of the garden reserved for them. Some find it easier to sow them by mixing the seeds with some finely sifted earth, but this is a matter of choice. The one thing essential is not to drop them in clumps, but to scatter them as evenly as possible, avoiding waste. One packet of seed will sow a large space, properly broadcast. Choose a cloudy day, just after a rain if possible rather than just before one, for a rainfall will be likely to wash the seeds about distressingly and leave spots perfectly bare. Press the seed into the ground after scattering them, using a flat strip or block of wood and patting the bed with it. I usually sprinkle the ground surface with a light sifting of earth after thus pressing them down, to prevent evaporation; but such a sifting must be very light and not touched after it is applied.

The snapdragons, *Antirrhinum majus*, hybrids, are really perennials or biennials, which, like so many of their kind, are treated as annuals. They will not be ready to blossom until the middle of summer if they are not started in the house, but from midsummer on they will give constant bloom, even though sown directly out of doors. The soil for them should be light; this is, well lightened if it is clay to start with, by mixing coal ashes through it as well as manure, and perhaps some lime. This should be applied some time before sowing the seeds, however, in order to give it a chance to leach through the earth and do its work. Whether you start them indoors or out see that the plants are eight inches apart in the beds finally, and four inches back from the edge of them. The height of the variety named — "golden queen" — is about a foot and a half, this being one of the low-growing, dwarfish varieties.

African daisies will usually be in bloom on the First of July if the seeds are planted by the First of May. Wait until the ground is surely warm before putting them in though, for remember that this is a plant from a hot land. It germinates within a week — five days is the exact time usually — and the plants ought to stand a foot apart at least, as they grow to be anywhere from two to three feet high and are much branched. This will bring the foremost along a border about eight inches from the edge, to allow for the spread of the branches. *Clarkia elegans* [*C. unguiculata*], Salmon Queen, is the variety which I am using in the partial shade cast by the locust tree [*Robinia*]; and this is as easily grown as the marigold [*Tagetes*]. Plants should be ten to twelve inches apart or more; and the flowers should be cut as fast as they fade. For cut flowers indoors this is a particularly delightful species, as the blossoms will open in water after cutting, and last well.

Double pinks [*Dianthus*] are almost as lovely as carnations [*Dianthus caryophyllus*] — and they will grow in any soil providing they have full sunlight. For the white variety there is the snowball, for the red, the fireball, and for the nearly black, the mourning cloak — suggestive names which are easy to remember. Actually these are not annuals but biennials; but they are classed and treated as annuals practically everywhere. Sow them as soon as frost has departed for good, and let the plants be about five inches apart. They grow nearly a foot high, and will blossom all summer if the faded flowers are persistently cut away. It is possible to carry them through the winter with some protection, and they will boom the second season. After this, however, new plants must be raised; and ordinarily it is not thought worth while to attempt to winter the old ones.

Treat the California poppy the same as the Shirley poppy, as far as sowing is concerned, for it is also averse to transplanting. The seeds may be sown very early as it is not susceptible to cold, blooming even after frost has come in the autumn. *Eschscholzia Californica* and *Eschscholzia*, Golden West, are the two varieties which combine best with the larkspur. In addition to being delightful in flower, this plant has foliage that is distinctly ornamental. The annual larkspur [*Consolida*] will blossom in July from seeds sown late in April, which is the usual time of sowing. And there is nothing in the garden finer to my mind than the lovely blues of this plant. To be sure it comes in pinks and lilacs that are good colors, but larkspur in anything but blue is somehow not what seems right or natural, whether it is an annual or perennial. So it is in blue only that I ever make use of it — and that usually in combination with some yellow flower such as the *Eschscholzia*. It is a color harmony that never palls.

Lupines in clear rose and white in a great mass where they can have things all to themselves, are as charming as anything that can be grown. Indeed, there are few flowers that have the still and quiet stateliness of these; they always seem to be so perfectly balanced on one foot — and to be so aware of it. Preferring some shade, they are particularly adaptable to the small garden where a certain amount of it is almost inevitable. Sow them where they are to grow, for like the poppy they do not like to moved.

Xeranthemums are everlastings — and without one of these no annual garden can ever be called complete. Purple, white and rose-colored flowers in mixture is the common fashion of raising them, and indeed pure colors are not offered, the seed being sold only in mixed packets. Not very much space is needed for these, as a few will go a long way; but with the plants a foot apart, half a dozen will not take up more space than any garden can very well spare. They are really very pretty flowers apart from their everlasting qualities — which are rather more against them than for them, through the long association with unused "front parlors" which distinguishes everlastings generally.

For years verbenas have been neglected, as far as my garden is concerned, but suddenly I found myself wanting them again. Along with nearly everything else in the line of annuals, they have been improved and developed and made over into something so splendid that I am sure they do not know themselves. These are supposed to started indoors or in a hotbed; and they cannot be sown outdoors until May. So if flowers are wanted before the end of July, there is really no choice in the matter. A small flat will furnish space for a great many seedlings however, and instead of transplanting to flats or boxes of any sort, I personally would recommend little paper pots to the small grower. It is possible to make these for oneself, out of a heavy wrapping paper such as any bundle comes home in, of any desired size. And the seedlings transplanted to these are really ready for the ground without further disturbance, for the pot pulls off from the earth, which is lowered into the ground without a root being disarranged. Set them a about ten inches apart in the border, and to within five inches of the edge of it, along a walk. The straggling habit of the plants has been much overcome in the work that has been done with them; but they still are somewhat uncertain and wobbly — and need space, in case they do spread about. Their fragrance and beauty as cut flowers is one of their strongest points, and their freedom of bloom is another great advantage. But they were for so long a time such a craze that I suppose one should be somewhat careful in indulging in them now. For they are not up to the mark of a really fine garden standby in many ways.

I have spoken several times of the necessity of picking the flowers from annuals as fast as they fade. This is not only to keep the plant a more sightly object, but to stimulate further bloom. When the seed forming is thus nipped in the flower — not exactly in the bud, though figuratively so — a plant will go on producing more flowers in the effort to produce seeds, that being all it blossoms for anyway. So the removal of flowers induces more flowers, and in this way the entire season may be filled with bloom that otherwise would be over in a fortnight or a month at the most.

Planted sufficiently close for the best effect, very few beds or borders will need much care after the plants are grown — for these themselves will crowd out weeds, and keep the space about them clear. Until they are fully grown, however, it is necessary to till the soil of a flower garden quite as much as the soil of a vegetable garden. Moisture needs conserving here too — and though the annuals are hardy and will grow almost in spite of the roughest kind of treatment, they will do so much better for a little care that it is hard to believe they are the same plants. It is too much to expect to get the best results from any plants that are forced to struggle against the double handicap of weeds and dry, hard baked soil that lack of care induces.

For the sake of the garden's future, a record of this summer is to be kept — not an exhaustive one, but just a simple line or two a day, as the circumstances may demand. Some of the seed I may save, if the variety pleases; indeed it is quite possible that some really wonderful and valuable variety may be developed from the most ordinary garden, any summer. For the seed of a plant of exceptional color may lead to a find, if consistently saved, the plants of succeeding generations showing this in greater and greater intensity where only seed from the brightest or darkest flowers is saved. This is one of the "by products," so to speak, that add to the interest of the happy-go-lucky annual garden — the garden of change, of surprises, of greatest careless liberty — the one garden that, more than all the rest, is never finished because every year it is begun anew, right where it began the year before.

House and Garden 23 (April 1913): 279–281, 315–316.

ENDNOTES————————————————

15. On Tabor, see above, 29.

The Point of View: The Geranium

IN 1914 GERANIUMS (*Pelargonium x hortorum*) were apparently suffering the consequences of overuse and misuse, and no gardener of taste would have anything to do with them. This anonymous counterattack on their behalf from *Scribner's* Point of View column epitomizes the attitude of some less fashion-driven gardeners concerning their more stylish contemporaries. The geranium, this author contends, is a plant of uncommon virtue and essential to keeping the garden in continuous bloom — a real trooper when all the other flowers let you down. Indeed, it seems a model of selfless, wholesome deportment and thrives in perfect dignity despite horticulture's unwarranted contempt.

GARDENING IS A desperately aesthetic business nowadays. The refinements of it pass the refinements of esoteric philosophy. Esoteric religion is, rather, the thing with which to compare it. A superlatively discriminating sort of Calvinism holds sway over the carefully ordered beds, and forbids the intrusion of plants that are not strictly elect.

Fortunately, the qualifications are many and various, and they are subject to enlargement at any moment. A tabooed flower has frequently only to wait in patience and dignity until some swerving of taste sets the gardener to considering its possibilities. Then, if it shows itself docile to some slight suggestion of change (such as a country cousin might manifest by doing her hair in a different way), it may step at once into a position of signal favor. The rise of the dahlia is an instance of such a shifting of fortune from ignominious neglect to respected distinction. The petunia also has found itself lately re-established.

But there is one flower whose case seems hopeless, at the mention of whose name every right-minded garden-lover shrugs disdainfully; and that is the geranium. Its presence in a flower-bed is as damningly significant of crudeness and thoughtlessness of taste as a plush picture-frame on a parlor wall. Only the horticultural *bourgeoisie* allow geraniums to intrude among larkspur [*Consolida*] and foxgloves [*Digitalis*].

And yet, why? What is the matter with this ill-regarded plant? It is no more stiff in the stem than, say, valerian. It is not more mathematically symmetrical than the rose. It is tender and delicate in texture, and has a delicious fragrance which so many of its more highly favored rivals lack. It is a thoroughly well-equipped flower, and its critics find themselves hard put to it to condemn it reasonably. They have to fall back on two rather vague words which are much in use nowadays, and say that the geranium is not "interesting," it lacks "temperament."

I think, for my part, that one reason lies in its extreme good nature. It respects itself in a sort of fashion, taking all the soil and the sun and air that it needs, blooming without reserve; but it never seems to think that it has any special rights or requirements. It is not fussy about its food, it has no distinctive pest or disease — like hollyhock rust or phlox mildew — it is not particular about its neighbors; it has not even a "season," during which it monopolizes attention by its extravagant glory and after which it retires and leaves its foliage *de trop*. It seems to think that a flower's business is to bloom, and to this duty and privilege it applies itself sanely and soberly, making itself as much and as little in evidence at one time of year as another. Indoors and outdoors, in summer and winter and sunshine and storm, its brave, bright petals unfold and it bares its heart to the world. It is undisturbed in this steadfastness by the social opprobrium which rests upon it. In fact, it seems hardly aware of its own neglect. Given any chance at all, anywhere, no matter how grudgingly, it makes itself cheerfully at home and settles down to its perennial occupation. Either it does not mind being slighted, or it does not know what slighting means.

But we people of the complex world of subtle sympathies and reactions demand of one another and of our environment a sensitive response. There is no fun in disliking your neighbor unless he knows that you dislike him; and his happy-hearted flourishing under your coldly averted eye is a distinct affront. When to this unconcern is added, on his part, an obvious readiness to serve you, and on your part, an undeniable need of him, his restoration to favor is indeed desperate.

The truth of the matter is that we can none of us get along without the geranium. Or if we do, in sheer dogged perversity, we have to suffer the consequences of great, empty, crying holes in our flower-beds. We all know how it is. During May and June and part of July, our gardens exult in crowded ranks of glory upon glory. Most of our temperamental flowers catch enthusiasm from one another and have their fling all together. The result is intoxicating while it lasts, but it is followed by a disheartening midsummer slump. Suddenly the mood changes, the petals fall, the color and fragrance are gone. As dull and sober as they were erewhile brilliant and animated, our irises, peonies [*Paeonia*], roses, foxgloves, larkspur, rockets [*Hesperis matronalis*], present a monotonous sequence of barren green leaves to our disappointed eyes. The hopeful annuals are not yet more than a dubious promise; the phlox and dahlias have hardly set their buds. The whole garden suffers eclipse.

This is precisely the geranium's opportunity, and we are as cruel as we are stupid if we deny it to her. Too modest and unintrospective to select a season for herself, she might yet have one bestowed upon her — the midsummer season, which nobody else seems to want. Trust her to accept it and grace it well, not resenting its left-over nature but glad of its unequivocal call, even perhaps a little proud that she alone is able to meet it. It seems peculiarly hers when her claim to it is undisputed.

Nor need we fear that she will misinterpret and abuse her chance. Holding an even course between the extremes of expression and reticence, she understands a little of both tendencies; and she is too wise to want to interfere with the repose which must follow a period of great activity. She would only fain prevent an entire collapse, and would gently keep the garden's head above water until such time as it feels like swimming again. She can do this as no one else can, blooming brightly and quietly here and there among the discouraged plants, keeping up general appearances, saving the gardener's self-respect when passing wayfarers pause to look over his fence in quest of the color they have come to expect of him. Her very stolidity (if one wants to call it that!) is now a point in her favor. The exhausted garden needs and desires nothing emotional. It really needs (though it does not desire) to be laughed at a little; and this function the geranium can perform for it amiably, not hurting its feelings but rallying it: "Come, now! You are tired, but that does not mean that the rest of the universe is undone. Look at me. I'm as full of buds as ever. I'll save the day for you." Perfectly honest, the sturdy plant knows its own proficiency as well as its shortcomings, and does not hesitate to assume responsibility.

Ah! I confess that I like and admire the geranium. It seems to me "the real thing." And I think that the heavens must like it, too, else why should they help it to flourish so securely? Genuine flowerhood consists in glorifying God, with less thought for the means than the end, with such absorbing thought for the end that the means can almost be trusted to take care of themselves. Plants with grievances, plants with "rights," plants with chips on their shoulders, have something profoundly the matter with them. No wonder they suffer from sudden, mysterious blights. But plants with their thoughts turned away from themselves, out toward the sun and the rest of the garden, are very healthy and happy; and they can stand it if the world does not fully appreciate them. So that, after all, the geranium needs no further defence from me.

Scribner's Magazine 56 (July 1914): 130–132.

Window Gardens in New York

AN ANONYMOUS STAFF WRITER for *House Beautiful* reports the 1905 gardening news in New York: a growing number of city dwellers are decorating their windows with flower boxes, and they are going about it with more style and imagination. Still, there is room for improvement, especially regarding summer plantings which city folk tend to neglect since they leave town during the hot weather. Another news item is that New Yorkers are beginning to make gardens in their backyards, "to try a London plan of living."

THE LATE SPRING kept the floral decorations of city houses from blossoming with the brilliancy they showed a year ago at this time, but there has been the same amount of planting and preparation, and a few mild days will have their effect in reviving the beauties of last summer. Five years ago there were not many houses in New York which were decorated with window-boxes or other floral ornament when summer came. Now the number of the houses that have been so beautified is countless, says a writer in the Sun.

There is more imagination put into the grouping of flowers now, and it is recognized that there may be something besides these few varieties. One house has beautiful window-boxes of heliotrope [*Heliotropium*] and coral geraniums [*Pelargonium x hortorum*]. Another has, on three different floors, tulips in different shades of red.

Solid blocks of jonquils and pale blue hyacinths are the color-scheme of a new house in East Seventy-third Street built of pink brick.

Pansies [*Viola x wittrockiana*] and white hyacinths are a combination that at least six dwellers on upper Fifth Avenue selected, although there is very little brilliancy in the colors. Nothing is more effective, though, than the geraniums in the reddest hues, in spite of the fact that they were so common last summer. They are the hardiest of all the combinations, and do not, like the hyacinths and tulips, have to be replaced after a short time.

"I wish New Yorkers stayed in town long enough to let nasturtiums [*Tropaeolum majus*] grow," said a florist who has decorated many window-boxes this spring. "They would see then what an ideal flower for window-boxes is.

"The nasturtium is so hardy and grows so well that it would form a beautiful decoration for the houses. It would pour its blooms out of the boxes for the vines of the tall nasturtium would hang down several feet below the boxes. But it would be well into June before they reached this stage of abundant blooming, and by that time New Yorkers are away, and don't care how the exteriors of their New York town houses look.

"But the nasturtiums they will find ideal in color, and even more durable than the geraniums."

In spite of the general opinion, the gardens with the southern exposure do not prosper best. They get too much sun. Geraniums shoot up like weeds.

"If a window-box does face south and get the sun all day," a florist said, "it should be protected when the sun is hottest by a newspaper or an awning. The geraniums grow best in the houses that face north, and only the pansies and small daisies that take lots of warmth are best when they get the full sun."

This florist said that a number of New Yorkers had this year made the experiment of putting flowers into their back yards, intending to try a London plan of living. There the back yard is made a retreat during the spring and early summer, to which all the guests adjourn for tea after dinner, and in the evenings when there is a dance inside. This plan has been tried in several cases.

The House Beautiful 18 (JUNE 1905): 25

Chapter Four

~~~~~~

WILD GARDENS

THE FIRST ARTICLE in this chapter defines the wild garden and indicates that wild gardening was considered a subtle, almost mystical branch of gardening. The next makes a strong argument for developing a truly American gardening style based on the matchless natural beauty preserved along the "unimproved" roadsides of New England. Following this, another author promotes the use of native plants, hoping to foster the evolution of an American garden style that would be as "livable" as that of England. The new science of ecology is the subject of the next article, written in 1927, along with explanations of its relevance to gardening, even on a small scale. More than one of the authors in this chapter excoriates the rich, portraying them as the enemies of the natural American landscape. Gardeners are encouraged to cooperate with nature, and an amateur wild-gardener reports on his garden, its triumphs and failures, and how it has become a source of physical and spiritual strength to him, replacing — at least during the gardening season — more orthodox forms of religious worship.

ᔎ E. O. Calvene
The Wild Garden

E. O. Calvene begins this article explaining that a true wild garden is not one that is merely naturalistically planted, like those described in William Robinson's *The Wild Garden*, but one that has in it only plants native to this continent. Calvene is a romantic and regards the wild-gardener as one who needs follow no rules for arranging plants but who "must be, first of all a genius — or grow into one — hence a rule unto himself." A romantic appreciation of nature and of wild gardening prompts him to suggest that the wild-gardener requires little horticultural knowledge but instead creates garden art through a profound sympathy with plants. Wild gardening for Calvene is the most subtle form of gardening — "indeed I am almost tempted to say that it is mystic." Following this lofty start to the article Calvene proceeds to describe the more mundane attributes of the wild garden: that it must conform to its site, be screened from the outside world, be planted with species that will readily establish themselves, and have only those man-made shelters that blend inconspicuously into their setting. The illustrations on the contents page for this chapter were originally part of "The Wild Garden."

It is extremely doubtful if anyone ever made for himself a truly wild garden. Like the historic giraffe of which the farmer declared, after observing the creature long and seriously, "they ain't no such animile," wild gardens usually "ain't." For it is almost impossible, even with the purest of intentions, to prevent oneself from using plants that are distinctly not wild, and never were wild in this fair land. So let us use the term "wild garden" advisedly, and examining the question, know for a certainty when we are talking about actual wild gardens, and when about gardens in which plants are arranged to grow as if they were wild.

The true wild garden may not, in the very nature of things, harbor any plant which is not a native to this continent; and if one is to be very exact in planting, improved strains and artificial hybrids of even the common native wild flowers should not be introduced, either. The wild garden should consist of native plants, arranged according to their habit of growth under wild or natural conditions; and this is the garden which we will consider first, taking up subsequently that pseudo-wild garden wherein all sorts of things both wild and tame are planted, "wildly," so to speak, with no sort of system.

Every land is rich in wild flowers of course, for every flower is a wild flower somewhere. (Excepting those artificial hybrids before mentioned, and even these are traceable to their wild ancestors usually, without much difficulty). We are not therefore limited as to bloom in the wild garden, even though we put the strictest interpretation upon the term; and as we have every phase of physical circumstances for flowers to live under, here in America, we shall be able to meet any physical condition in selecting the plants for a particular place. Therefore why not a wild garden in the true sense, if we are to undertake one at all? Why not conform its planting as well as its arrangement to the wilderness? Let us naturalize elsewhere as many things and as many kinds of things as we choose, and have space for; but let us have the wild garden wild.

There can be no rule for arranging, nor for planting, a wild garden. Each gardener that makes such must be, first of all, a genius — or grow into one — hence a rule unto himself. And each must have the closest sympathy with and consequent understanding of, plants. This does not mean that the veriest tyro at gardening cannot succeed. Note that it is sympathy, not horticultural knowledge, that is the fundamental essential. All flowers should be approached with sympathy; but wild flowers must be, else they will elude entirely, or pine and show a broken spirit and great anguish. Hence wild gardening is of all forms of gardening the most subtle — indeed, I am almost tempted to say that it is mystic.

Yet let us understand that even this quickened perception offers no really magic success without the aid of proper material conditions. Soil and sunlight and moisture must be studied in order to learn the physical needs of every plant, and in growing wild flowers it is especially desirable to provide the exact conditions of all three under which they naturally flourish. They are like wild men or wild animals, in that civilization is likely to be too much for them; and like all wild things which are free to choose as they will, they live and thrive only where they wish to be. Skunk cabbage [*Lysichiton*] loves the muck and wet, hence in muck and wet the skunk cabbage lives; violets [*Violas*] love a sunny bank, hence on sunny banks are great violet communities. Speaking of communities, I am reminded to say, by the way, that most wild flowers have the social instinct; and that they have their particular friendships as well as their particular antipathies. Bear this in mind — and learn what they are by observing them in their natural state.

So much for the general question. Now as to the special one of making, or I should prefer to say, developing, a wild garden. The location is of course the first consideration, once the resolution to have such a garden is formed. That the possibilities and character of a place should have something to do with the forming of this resolution ought to be self-evident. Still I know that very often the wish to have a certain long-time, much-loved castle-in-Spain of a garden will lead one into really dreadful garden indiscretions and inharmonies, when the day of accomplishment at last arrives. So it is perhaps well to be reminded of the ever existent need of appropriateness.

Wild "gardens" have been known to flourish in city back yards, but they can never be more than curiosities in such an environment, even as the wild beasts of the jungles and mountains are curiosities when caged in the city Zoo. Land and space are needed for the wild garden, and varying conditions of soil and exposure and sun and shade. Yet I should say that a very satisfactory and delightful wild garden might be compassed within a place a quarter of an acre in size — which is 100 by 100 feet — and space allowed for a house besides.

On such a place, or with a wild garden in any locality for that matter, the first step towards its wildness consists in excluding from it every suggestion of the busy, everyday world. You are aiming to create not only ideal conditions for the growth of wild flowers, but also you should aim to create the illusion of wilderness. Not a peek-hole should remain after the barriers are set up, through which the outside may look in or the inside may, by accident, see out, unless some lovely bit of view exists for which allowance must be made. But even in making such allowance it is perfectly possible to exclude the outer world, to preserve inviolate the seclusion.

A boundary planting of trees and shrubbery, preferably seventy percent. evergreen, should surround in a general way the area selected for the garden, providing it is not already isolated by being in the midst of such a natural screen. This boundary is, in effect, a part of the garden, although it marks its limits. Supplementary to this comes the treatment which the natural conditions of the site may demand. If it is woodland to start with, clearing a portion entirely to provide space for such plants as require the open, will be necessary; while another part or parts will have to be left half cleared to furnish half shade. The garden site which occupies an area already cleared, on the other hand, will need forest planting to create the desired conditions. The configuration of the land will affect the work also, and the most desirable site is of course a combination of the rugged and the suave. Where such a combination does not naturally exist it is really impossible to create it, however, and we must therefore be content to a certain degree with things as they are.

And though rocks are somehow always associated in our minds with wild gardens, we must, unless we come by them as an inheritance from the land itself where the garden is to be, put the thought of them away. There are quantities of wild flowers that grow in grassy dells as well as the flowers which haunt the rocks and deep woods, and whatever we may do in the way of creating illusions of wilderness by forestation, there is absolutely no chance of any illusion when it comes to an attempt to introduce rocks where rocks are foreign.

The character of a wild garden therefore will be determined by Nature and the original character of the place, which she has supplied. It will be either woodsy; or wet — even boggy perhaps; or rocky; or possibly the combination of all three: or again it may be just a sweep of meadow with a stream bordering it, or a pond. Any one of these natural tendencies will — indeed must, govern the general scheme of it, and the flowers must be selected that will accord with that scheme.

With them selected the question of establishing them confronts us. No trouble to get them to grow, once they are established; but sometimes this problem of establishment seems to be very like the salt on the bird's tail which insures his being caught. Of course there is always a reason for failure, but very often it is so obscure and deeply hidden in the nature of the plant — what we may call so personal a reason perhaps — that it does not get itself discovered, even by a sympathetic worker, for a long, long time. A little more or a little less shade or moisture at a certain time; or shelter from the sun for just the earth above the roots while the plant itself stands erect in full sun; or a thin crevice in a rock through which long roots may reach deep into cool black earth — these are a few of the things which may affect the success of a wild flower. Is it any wonder that one must have a love for them quite different from that fancy which admires an iris or a rose, in order to take the pains and to have the infinite patience and keenness of observation necessary to note all these things?

The choicest wild flowers to me are, in the approximate order of their blossoming — and this selection is made to secure bloom all summer as well as for the beauty of the flowers themselves — hepaticas, anemones, trilliums, violets, marsh marigolds [*Caltha palustris*], cranesbill or wild geranium, the wild iris or flag [*Iris versicolor*], bunchberry [*Cornus canadensis*], wild lupine

The wild garden does not necessarily mean a garden of wood, rocks, or streams. It may combine these features or it may be a corner of a field by a river bank, such as this one, where the lupine grows.

[*Lupinus*], the lilies, hawkweed [*Hieracium*], columbine [*Aquilegia*], false Solomon's seal [*Smilacina*], cardinal flower [*Lobelia cardinalis*], bee balm or Oswego tea [*Monarda didyma*], milfoil or yarrow [*Achillea*], Joe-Pye-weed [*Eupatorium purpurea*], the wild asters, goldenrod [*Solidago*], meadowsweet [*Filipendula*], hardhack [*Spiraea tomentosa*], black snakeroot [*Cimicifuga racemosa*], gentians, the sedums, the speedwells [*Veronica*] and the meadow rue [*Thalictrum*]. Then there are ferns of many kinds and the wild orchids [*Cypripedium*]; and for trailers the partridge berry [*Mitchella repens*] and arbutus [*Epigaea repens*], while Virginia creeper [*Parthenocissus quinquefolia*], bittersweet [*Celastrus scandens*] and wild grape [*Vitis*] supply vines in abundance.

In planting and grouping, Nature's methods must of course be followed. Certain flowers grow always in colonies, while others are not so neighborly, as mentioned before. Observe the natural growth of the plants you propose using, and plant them as nearly in the relation which they like as it is possible to do. And finally, *do not* bring these things in from the woods. Certain things may grow in such plenty that there may be no harm in a few persons helping themselves, yet it is generally a pernicious practice and for that reason merits the strongest disapproval we can give it. And certain other things which are naturally shy growers are already almost exterminated from the country side. There are dealers in native wild flowers who furnish plants that will become established far more readily than the actually wild denizen of nature's own growth, and many things will be better for being raised from the seed just where they are to grow permanently.

Wild gardens may have garden shelters if they are desired, providing they are made as inconspicuous as birds' nests among the trees, but it is rare to find a structure that may actually be hidden and seem a part of the wilderness. Low, broad lines rather than much elevation, and thatch for the roof, are the two means best calculated to accomplish this end; and afterwards a literal burying in vine growth and shrubbery. Where stones or rocks are much in evidence in the garden they may be introduced into the work with good effect, if they are not laid conspicuously with mortar. All freak forms should be shunned, and the end of furnishing a retreat that shall positively be unsuspected ought to be constantly in mind in designing or building anything, be it summer house, bird house or seat, if the ideal is to be achieved.

Of the so-called wild gardens which boast all kinds of flowers and plants, growing as if they were native to the spot, there does not, after all, seem to be much to say. Such are not wild as before pointed out; they are, more properly speaking, naturalistic gardens; and they are in many cases decidedly lovely and well worth while. But where general conditions not only permit but seem to demand the wilderness, gardens of merely naturalistic tendencies do not provide the perfection of harmony which we have a right to expect in our own and other people's gardens.

House and Garden 22 (JULY 1912): 22–24, 53–54.

◆ WALTER PRICHARD EATON
The Garden Beside the Highway

THIS ARTICLE comprises some of the most important and recurrent themes of early twentieth-century American writings on the wild garden. Eaton, the archetypal nature lover, scorns modern tourists in motor cars who, he believes, will never partake of the lessons of "the American roadside gardens" that, if only recognized, would elevate their spirits and help improve our country's garden craft.[1] This nature lover, resident of the Berkshires, also despises the rich, the "captains of industry" who spoil the countryside with pretentious Italian villas and French Renaissance chateaus. And indeed, there *were* some famous Italian and French gardens in the Berkshires at the time — including Edith Wharton's home, the Mount — and Eaton may have had some of them specifically in mind.[2] He disdains efforts to reproduce Japanese gardens here, pointing out that the Japanese garden is essentially a replication of its *own* native landscape. As Eaton, a drama critic, was opposed to the nearly exclusive production of European rather than American plays in our theaters, so was he against the importation of foreign gardening traditions.[3] He delighted in the natural, native growth along country roadsides and believed that it should provide inspiration for American gardeners.[4] Like other early twentieth-century Americans who looked to nature as a paradigm of harmony and beauty, Eaton revered Thoreau and cites him three times in this article.

A MOTOR PULLED up at the cross roads this morning evidently waiting until my dog and I reached the spot. Three goggled fat women sat on the rear seat. A goggled fat man and a goggled chauffeur sat on the front. All five were covered with dust. The goggled fat man had a map spread out on his fat knee. "Pardon me," he said, running his fat finger over this map, "but can you direct us to Great Barrington? We can't quite make out the road."

I gave them the directions, and the chauffeur backed the car half-way around, cut out his muffler, and sent the machine with a leap and an explosion like a battery of Gatling guns tearing down the road. It disappeared in a cloud of dust.

"Barney," said I to my dog, "they are seeing the Berkshires."

Barney looked, wagging his tail, and then set off into the field on a wood-chuck scent. I continued my plod up the side road till presently I reached the Berkshire garden which I sought, and the perfect view of Monument Mountain. There were no motor tracks in the road here, since it leads only to a little pond and a farm or two, ending against the wooded hill. It was a clear autumn morning, crisp without chill, and fragrant as new cider. Already the pageant of the season was being staged over hill-slope and swamp. The red banners of October were flying in the woods, and with every gust of wind a little battalion of dead leaves roused into life in the road at my feet and rushed forward as upon some foe.

The spot where I paused was on a slight elevation of pasture land, commanding a wide prospect. The road was bounded by low stone walls, gray and half hidden with careless briers. A few hundred rods ahead, where the road dipped through a tamarack swamp, lay a little pond, reflecting now the autumn foliage on its banks like colors laid on a palette of black glass. To the right, across the fields, a mouse-gray farmhouse nestled in an orchard, two piles of bright red apples under the trees adding a rich and cheerful note. Immediately at my feet, on either side of the brown carpet of fallen leaves and extending to the gray stone walls, were two delicate and exquisite garden beds, sown with the careless symmetry of nature. They held little blue asters, sometimes called iron weed asters [*Vernonia*]; just that and no more, save a few feathery tufts of dead grass between the clusters of blooms. These little asters, which flower

Beside the road grow the delicate and exquisite garden beds that held the tiny blue asters which, flowering after the frost, hold a faintly faded blue of summer in their tiny petals.

after the frost, hold a faintly faded blue of summer in thin tiny petals, and spread a bit of sky along our New England roadsides more satisfying and suggestive to me than any formal border on the grandest estate.

Just behind the stone wall to the left of my roadside garden rose a single white pine [*Pinus strobus*], bifurcated near the ground as pines so often are when they stand alone, and extending wide lateral branches. One of the these branches hung over the wall like the binding line of a Japanese design, and beneath it, two miles distant across a corn field and the green-spired expanse of a young hemlock [*Tsuga*] wood, rose the solid battlement of Monument Mountain, proud with its banners of autumn, perfectly framed by the pine above and the wide garden of roadside asters below. The corn was stacked in the foreground field and orange pumpkins glowed against the brown soil. The odor of autumn was in the air, the smell of fallen leaves and garnered corn. I put my pipe in my pocket and sat down on the wall.

Presumably, by the time I had looked and sniffed my fill, my fat friends in their motor, who were "seeing the Berkshires," had passed under the crags of Monument, where the paper mills huddle, and were tearing along beside the trolley track on their way to Great Barrington and lunch. It was little enough of the true Berkshires they had seen, or ever would see — the true charm of our hills and valleys lying in these lovely pictures which everywhere abound, under the limb of a pine, down the vista of a country road, between the shaggy trunks of the sugar maples [*Acer saccharum*], or across green meadows to the silvery willows [*Salix*] and the winding river, pictures which are only to be had, however, for a little searching and experiment, and savored at leisure and in quiet. Of the roadside gardens they could know less than nothing, for these fairest jewels of old New England lie too close under their rushing wheels, and demand beside for their savoring a certain meekness and delicacy of spirit, a child-like content to roam slowly in small spaces and find beauty and happiness in the common things of the wayside. One of the greatest of American artists, and one of the gentlest and sweetest of men, has planted the roadside before his house with goldenrod [*Solidago*], though formal terraces and marble gates and all exotic blooms were at his command. I like to read a symbol of his greatness in those careless drifts of gold, and in the sturdy apple [*Malus*] trees which stand beyond them up the slope to his spacious dwelling.

Indeed, there is many a symbol to be found, and many a lesson to be read, in our American roadside gardens, alike for the elevation of our spirit and the improvement of our garden craft. One of the quaintest of misconceptions in our gardening is the too frequent attempt to reproduce a Japanese effect on an estate in Long Island or Westchester or New England. The first principle of Japanese gardening, underlying even its religious formalism, is the principle of landscape reproduction. The Japanese garden, though it be made in a pie plate, must reproduce a native landscape of Japan. The Japanese art of dwarfing trees, of course, is an outcome of necessity, to maintain the proportions of Nature.

Such flowers, even, as are found in the Japanese garden are there not for their own sakes, but because they belong to the landscape. The true Japanese garden in America, then would contain no pergolas and moon bridges and stone lanterns and wistaria. It would much more properly contain a bit of old road winding between gray walls fringed with clematis and asters into the shadow of the pine or the emerald shimmer of the birch [*Betula*] woods. Over its water feature would hang the purple of wild grapes [*Vitis*]; and water lilies [*Nymphaea*] not lotus, would nod on the ripples. The "tea house" would be a square, mouse-gray dwelling, reproduced to scale, with great central chimney and lean-to roof behind, the type which all of us associate with our fairest and most characteristic country landscapes. Against the weathered clapboards of this house the hollyhocks [*Alcea rosea*] would nod, and in spring its gray would be exquisite amid the bursting pink of the orchard.

Such would be the true Japanese garden in America. Does it exist? Our architects, at the instigation of our "captains of industry," go gleefully forth and crown a New England hilltop with an Italian villa, planting Lombardy poplars [*Populus nigra 'Italica'*] where oak [*Quercus*] and pine and maple grew, to say nothing of the stately elm [*Ulmus americana*]. They go into a tract of woods, hew out an opening and erect a French Renaissance chateau of imported marble and bay trees [*Laurus nobilis*] on the terraces, lotus in the fountain pool, and rare, exotic blooms in a thousand formal beds where marble statues stand and seem ashamed of their nakedness. To me, at least, such estates and gardens are the Twentieth Century equivalent of the French-roofed houses with a tower at one corner and great lawns sloping up broken by a huge ugly bed of canna and an iron deer, which were the acme of taste in our mid-Victorian era. Our estates cost more now, and we copy better models. We have substituted Donatello for the iron deer. But we are little nearer either an architecture or a garden craft of our own. Especially in our gardens, the New England back road still shames us in its artless use of native materials and the simplicity and grace of its effects. The old New England farmhouse against a background of orchard, pine and wooded hills, seen up an undulating road bordered with pink and gold and azure blue, still puts to shame our modern country villas amid their pseudo Italian or French or Japanese gardens — sometimes all three together, with a dash of Tudor-English thrown in. Because it is indigenous to its site and soil, it has the ultimate quality of spontaneity, and hence it is seemly and beautiful. As once we were in our literature, so we are still in our gardening — too often mere parrots. A true Japanese garden is the concentrated delicacy and fragrance of the landscape of Japan. How many American gardens catch and compose in little the charm and freshness of our native landscape? Do we think when we enter our gardens, of Nature and the peace of Nature, and its pictorial magic? or do we think of a florist's catalogue and a photograph of Italy? For me, I prefer a certain cross-road triangle of wild sunflowers [*Helianthus*] and thistles [*Cirsium*] to your formal beds of phlox that lead to a Grecian pergola behind a Tudor sundial, flanked by a Japanese pool and an Italian Renaissance stone bench.

One of the roads winds down the hill to Tyringham, through ranks of giant sugar maples that on the dullest day of autumn seem to hold the imprisoned sunlight in their golden depths, and in mid-summer frame between their shaggy trunks the level meadows far below, the roofs of the village, and the distant hills beyond. When you come to the cross-road, your ear catches the tinkle of a brook, and your dog, sniffing water, disappears into the bushes, whence you hear his greedy lapping. The spot is warm and sunny, the sound of water refreshing. In the untrimmed delta, so common when country roads intersect, the wild sunflowers grow shoulder high, and among them, forcing their heads up level with the golden blooms, hundreds of pink thistles add their delicate but daring color. Over this bank of pink and gold hovers in mid-summer a shimmer of brown, rising as you draw near, a cloud of tiny butterflies; and in it incessantly, warm as the sun itself, stirs and hums the business of the bees. There are few passers on this Berkshire by-way. The valley town lies far below, reached by other roads less steep. The gorgeous garden spreads its color for the bees and butterflies and for an occasional farmer on his way to market. It asks no care of any one, no trimming of the edges nor thinning of the roots. It is just a jewel set in the landscape by a better Architect than we, on the sleepy road to Tyringham.

Such gardens, with as limitless a variety and succession of wild blooms as any garden annual can compile for you, are still common on our American back roads. They used to be common everywhere, before the invasion of lumber men, telegraph and telephone poles, stone crushers and other servants of utility. They might be common still for a little love and care. The wanton destruction of timber on the borders of our public roads, once universal, is yielding slowly to a more enlightened sentiment. But there is no more reason why the wild flowers on the untimbered borders should be mercilessly mowed down, and the roadsides reduced to ugly stubble. One prays for a Senhouse in every American county, to resow our highways with their natural wild loveliness, to weave our roads into the landscape with a binding chord of color, to show us in time, perhaps, how we might, out of native materials, achieve a garden craft of our own.[5] So far as we know, this is an opportunity for village improvement societies, not yet grasped. Their activities mostly cease where the houses of town cease and the true landscape begins.

What formal drive on the most elaborate of estates can match for beauty the bend of the country road into the dark shadows of the hemlocks, where the banks are lush with moss, and on this richest green velvet the scarlet bunch-berries [*Cornus canadensis*] glow? Perhaps, too, a tiny thread of water runs by the road, fringed with gentians. The road is unparched and cool, the green moss cool, the color rich but sparing, the shadowing trees stately and quiet as a church. You will go far amid the gardens made by man, to match it. Nor will you easily match so humble a garden as a field of the stubborn pasture weed some New Englanders wrongly call hardhack [*Spiraea tomentosa*], when on a neglected slope it spreads its yellow blooms from the roadside to the border of the forest or the green bulwark of a mountain. Pure gold it is amid the pasture rocks, and cowpaths wind between the clumps with a quaint suggestion of a map of Boston. And can you better that shrubbery effect where the laurel [*Kalmia latifolia*] is massed against the trees, and the road bends around it as if in deference to its charm?

Few of my readers, probably, have been in Mount Washington Township in the southwest corner of Massachusetts, an upland plateau behind Mount Everett. The post office is the top of a desk in a boarding house, and boasts nine boxes. Mount Washington Township is not densely populated. But it has in prodigal profusion what many a gardener would perjure his soul to possess, established clumps of mountain laurel, eight and ten feet high and sometimes twenty feet in circumference, lining every roadside, lifting proudly over every gray stone wall, and stretching up the pastures into the mountain forest till the hill-slopes fairly riot with their wealth of pink. Mountain laurel has been occasionally transplanted with success; but usually the most careful attempts to domesticate it fail. It demands to be let alone, amid its pasture rocks and briers, the self-sufficient aristocrat of our native landscape. Some of us love it the better for this, and make annual pilgrimage to the gardens where it grows, nor find its loveliness less because it flames by gray stone walls and over rocks and briers, instead of beside formal paths and upon clipped lawns; and because beyond it we see not an Italian garden and the stone portals of a French chateau, but only green rows of corn, perhaps, and a mouse-gray barn and then the doming ridge of the Taconic Hills. We like to think that laurel is one of those things money cannot buy. We cannot have a formal garden with a marble sundial and lotus flowers on the pool. But, for a ten cent fare on the trolley to South Egremont and a five mile walk past a perpetual roadside garden and a dancing brook, we can achieve such pink glory as no nursery man ever rivaled, where the only gardeners are the cows.

The Japanese scorn roses as too "obvious," though they cultivate, somewhat paradoxically, it seems to us, the peony [*Paeonia*]. There is something a little showy about roses, however, something suggestive of feminine vanity and expense, especially when they are cultivated in formal beds and forced for large and odorous blooms. But the climbing rambler would be a sorry loss as an aid to architectural picturesqueness, and against the American wild rose, surely, no Japanese could cavil, for in its manner of growth, its delicacy and its harmony with the landscape, it is almost the most Japanese of all our flowers. It opens its heart by the wayside when the world is growing lush with green, and beside old fences hung with clematis or gray walls where the blueberries [*Vaccinium*] are coming to fruit, it masses its pink blooms, each one delicate and perfect but all together making a rich note of color against the virgin

Over the bank of pink and gold hovers in midsummer a cloud of tiny butterflies and within it stirs and hums the business of the bees. The valley lies far below.

green and white of little birches and golden summer fields. How carelessly massed the wild roses grow, yet how they seem to fall into skillfully calculated beds. They add warmth to the June day, and they add a delicate wistfulness, too, by their individual quality of petal and feminine poise, even as MacDowell has caught them in his music.[6] To one who loves Nature (oh, perilous phrase!), and flowers as part of Nature, of the landscape, of the pictorial loveliness of the world, the wild rose garden by the wayside has a charm and beauty no collection of her showier sisters behind a yew [*Taxus*] hedge, bounded by formal paths, can hope to match.

The more striking roadside shrubbery planting, such as the clumped sumac [*Rhus*], rich in autumn with its red leaves and deep, luscious red bloom spikes, has been frequently copied by gardeners, employing the same material. The fragrant trailing clematis [*Clematis terniflora*], too, running wild over wall and fence, runs no less readily to rule, though seldom in the formal garden has it the same charm in winter, when, by the wayside wall, the white relics of its blossoms are borne on delicate sprays against the snowy mystery of buried fields and shrouded hemlocks . We prize the flowers of spring, as well, and save a corner of our garden to hold the trilliums, the bluets [*Houstonia coerulea*], the anemones, the violets [*Violas*], the columbines [*Aquilegia*], which grow so carelessly just out of the wheel ruts on the borders of country roads, as if they had come down from the woods and fields to speak to the passer-by of May. Yet even with our most careful art we can hardly rival the white snowfall of hepaticas under leafless trees nor catch the careless grace of a columbine swaying its red bells on a ledge of rock above the bend of the road, a ledge where the violets climb up from the ferns and the shy anemones lurk in the grass. Nor shall our garden hold that vista round the curve, of wood and field and purple hills.

Of the humbler flowers, the roadside weeds, few are the praises sung, though Thoreau did say of mullein [*Verbascum*] that it is "so conspicuous with its architectural spire, the prototype of candelabrums." But one expects the praise of humble weeds from Thoreau. There are among the library poets no sonnets to hardhack or orange milkweed [*Asclepias tuberosa*], no odes to toadflax [*Linaria vulgaris*], no lyrics to celebrate hemp weed [*Cannabis*] or bed straw [*Galium*]. Yet each in its season praises its Maker with bloom and color along our northern roads, and adds to the artless gardens the charm of its petals and fragrance. What the farmer knows as wild carrot [*Daucus carota*] bears a dainty, flat-topped white bloom sometimes as large as a saucer, and a long bed of them will often appear like a strip of delicate embroidery along the wayside, making their more aristocratic title of Queen Anne's lace entirely applicable. In winter, too, they are still beautiful, for the blooms curl up on the tall, dry stalks and hold, after a storm, each its little cup of snow. Indeed, there is seldom the stark desolation of the formal garden in winter about the roadside garden. There is, primarily, always the line of the road and the white, encompassing, free landscape. Then there are, beside the cups of the wild carrots, the glowing berries of the bittersweet [*Celastrus scandens*], a red limb of them hung athwart the snowy world, as if New England were intent to show that it, too, can produce a Japanese screen; the lavender stalks of blackberry vines [*Rubus allegheniensis*]; the tawny stems of the willows. In autumn the asters bloom when the frost has killed the last of the flowers in the formal garden, and when all leaves are gone there is still the belated blossom of the witch hazel [*Hamamelis virginiana*], shining like thin gold where, a burning bush, it crests a bank against the western sun.

"The housewives of Nature," said Thoreau, "wish to see the rooms properly cleaned and swept before the upholsterer comes and nails down his carpet of snow. The swamp burns along its margin with the scarlet berries of the black alder [*Ilex verticillata*], or prinos; the leaves of the pitcher plant [*Sarracenia*] (which old Josselyn called Hollow-leaved Lavender) abound, and are of many colors from plain green to a rich striped yellow, or deep red."[7]

It is just here, where the road crosses a swamp and is raised a little above the surrounding level, that one sees his roadside garden stretching off and merging completely with the landscape. Above tall grasses the taller stalks of the cat-o'-nine-tails [*Typha*] lift their brown fingers; the irises gem the sedge, scattered like stars, not lined in formal rows as in a man-made garden; the brownish-red pitcher plants in bloom glimmer dully; or over against the woods, the sticky wild azalea or meadow pink [*Rhododendron*], masses its color and sends out all the long June day its incomparable perfume. Perhaps a dark swamp pool is pricked with water lilies, and tall brake or modest maiden-hair [*Adiantum pedatum*] fringes the slope at your feet. Such, in one season or another, is the roadside swamp, a garden wandering with the leisure of still water courses away into the woods or fields, as much a permanence of the landscape as the sky above your head or the far horizon line.

House and Garden 22 (OCTOBER 1912): 222–225, 248-249.

ENDNOTES

1. On Eaton, see above, 4.

2. On the grand gardens of the Berkshires, see Mac Griswold and Eleanor Weller, *The Golden Age of American Gardens: Proud Owners, Proud Estates, 1890–1940* (New York, 1991), 54–59.

3. Charles Alexander, *Here the Country Lies: Nationalism and the Arts in Twentieth-Century America* (Bloomington, Indiana, 1980), 147.

4. This was not a unique idea in 1912; there was a popular movement for roadside beautification and the concept was widely discussed in magazines. *Garden Magazine* had, for example, proposed a "Roadside Gardening Club" in July 1908, to try to protect natural roadside growth where it still existed and to reestablish it where it had been destroyed. On Jens Jensen and the "Ideal Section" of the Lincoln Highway, see Robert E. Grese, *Jens Jensen: Maker of Natural Parks and Gardens* (Baltimore, 1992), 106–110. Harriet Joor's December 1911 article "My Garden in the Snow," for *Country Life in America*, is a particularly lyrical piece about the beauty of wild road

side vegetation in winter. The invasive character of some roadside plants was also recognized; see a letter to the editor in *Garden Magazine* 8 (October 1908): 150 and 152.

5. John Maxwell Senhouse was a fictional gipsy-scholar, the protagonist in three novels by Maurice Hewlett: *Halfway House* (1908); *The Open Country* (1909); *Rest Harrow* (1910).

6. American composer Edward MacDowell (1861–1908). Eaton may be referring here to MacDowell's "Woodland Sketches" (*opus* 51).

7. Thoreau was referring to John Josselyn (fl. 1630–1675) who visited North America in 1638–1639 and lived here from 1663 to 1671. His account of the discoveries he made are recorded in his book *New England's Rarities Discovered* (London, 1672). He was especially interested in the flora of America and was the first European to describe many of our native plants (James L. Reveal, *Gentle Conquest: The Botanical Discovery of North America* [Washington, D. C., 1992], 25).

ᴥ MARY P. CUNNINGHAM
New Uses for Native Plants

MARY PARSONS CUNNINGHAM, who died in 1934, was a graduate of Vassar College and the Cambridge School, an institution that trained women for careers in landscape design. She became a member of the American Society of Landscape Architects in 1924 and worked for landscape architect Ellen Shipman. She also taught at both the Cambridge School and Lowthorpe, another school for women preparing for careers in landscape design.[8] Cunningham wrote garden articles for *House Beautiful* as well as *Country Life* and *Garden Magazine*. During the 1920s and 1930s she had monthly gardening columns in *House Beautiful*: first, Month by Month in the Garden and later, To Do This Month in the Garden. Although she was aware that the popularity of native plants in America was not new, she nonetheless begins her 1925 article by stating that the use of native plants is the most distinctive phenomenon in American gardening of the past decade.[9] She points to signs that our preference for and knowledge of native plants is growing and makes recommendations for which species to use in American gardens, including formal ones. Cunningham admires the "liveableness" of English gardens and hopes that this quality will eventually become a defining feature of gardens here. To achieve this, she explains, we must use our native plants more often; they will flourish luxuriantly and seem at home, "which is not the least part of the beauty of English planting. We shall have as a result a truly American garden." Like many advocates of wild gardens and native plants, Cunningham was also interested in old-fashioned gardens; in 1921 she wrote an article on them for *Garden Magazine*.

PERHAPS THE MOST distinctive thing in the history of planting during the last ten years is the use of our native plants. During the next ten years we shall use them even more.

Our early settlers brought over plants from their own native lands. The wild asters that crept into the neat beds were pulled out as weeds. Queen Anne's lace [*Daucus carota*], goldenrod [*Solidago*], black-eyed Susan [*Rudbeckia hirta*], the daisy [*Leucanthemum vulgare*] — all of these must have been

Brookside planting at the Arnold Arboretum, showing the possibilities of kalmia and leucothoe in such a situation

thought beautiful even then but they were not regarded as belonging to the garden proper. Nor are they now. The wild-flower garden, the rock and water gardens, the meadow and roadside plantings have given these hardy sons of the soil their innings in an appreciation and a proper place.

The wild garden did not include the native trees and shrubs until even later than the flowers. The natural and informal school of planting in England was reflected over here, but we still used Continental plants, not realizing the incongruity. Later on, at the beginning of the century, the knowledge and popularity of wild plants made this style more intelligently interpreted and even more popular.

We do not confine ourselves now to any one style, for we know that either formal, informal, or natural planting is good only when it fits into and is related to its surroundings. We can have wild gardens if both fit into the big dominant scheme without destroying its unity. A plant need not be rare or expensive to be beautiful but "what is fair must first be fit." Thus it is with styles — and thus it is with plants.

We have got safely by the period when we tried to turn deserts into swamps and make English lawns on rocky crags (although even at this writing the beautiful Bass Rocks section of Massachusetts is being uptorn in spots to make way for lawns!) The wisest of us plant our gardens as we build our homes — with some sense of relation to their surroundings. If we must have a rose garden on the moors we choose a place directly connected with the house, which is formal by nature of its being, and close it in. We do not let it compete with an ocean view or spoil the feeling of open freedom on a sweep of moorland, else why choose such a spot to live in?

Many signs of the times reflect the popularity of native plants. The wild plant show in Boston a few years ago and the hundreds, even thousands, of people who saw it is significant, and the way it was staged even more so. There were no rows of bottles with specimens and printed labels under each, but instead a blueberry bush [*Vaccinium*] growing by a stream, a single beautiful specimen; a red cardinal flower [*Lobelia cardinalis*] swayed with the fall of water; quantities of fern and ground covers and dogwood [*Cornus*] and azaleas [*Rhododendron*] massed in among tall cedars [*Juniperus virginiana*]. There were these and many others in natural settings and all chosen from the best of Nature's patterns and often improved. Nature can only give the key. We can help her to perfect the picture, for Nature's plantings are rarely perfect.

The nurseries are apparently realizing that native trees and shrubs are profitable. One of their lecturers recently remarked that "the whole North Shore is buying nothing else." Another prominent catalogue announces that "landowners are leaving the formal for the naturalistic and the cry is for a distinctly American style of treatment."

But these men give only half the story. We do not want a national garden simply because it is national — in fact, we actually lean to reproducing the English gardens, especially their planting. This is because of the liveableness of their gardens, not their nationality. Their planting is informal and intimate and luxuriant. We can get the same effect by using our own plants. We have many more deciduous trees and shrubs in this country than England has, hundreds from Japan and China from situations of climate so similar that they become or are becoming naturalized here as for instance the Japanese barberry [*Berberis thunbergii*].

The really new phase in the use of natives is their employment as the bulk of material in our cultivated areas. Natives are obviously the thing to use in wild planting. Some are also adapted to the most formal garden — witness the red cedar and flowering dogwood. Practically all are suitable for informal shrubberies not necessarily strictly wild. Some will respond remarkably to cultivation, and there is a great future in their descendants.

Among our evergreen trees the red cedar stands foremost as the tree for formal planting. It has the architectural qualities of the Italian cypress [*Cupressus sempervirens*] more than any other tree, and is most loved by the architect. Equally at home in a formal site or on a shrubby hillside, it fraternizes with blueberry, low cedar, bayberry [*Myrica pensylvanica*], and barberry, or if invited is liked as well by the more elegant laurel [*Kalmia latifolia*], rhododendron, and azalea.

The hemlock [*Tsuga*] is the second applicant for the formal garden. It is the best substitute for the yew [*Taxus*] hedge of English gardens and for us is more hardy and rapid growing provided we give it moist soil. Of our pines we should use the red [*Pinus resinosa*] more than we do — in windy places where the white [*Pinus strobus*] grows thin. Among our spruces are the Colorado [*Picea pungens*], Engelmann's [*P. engelmannii*], the red [*P. rubens*], white [*P. glauca*] — all good.

We use our broad-leaved evergreens better in formal work and cultivation than we do in wild planting. Leucothoe in a mass by the brookside shows its real beauty far more than in the commonly planted wisps around house foundations. Rhododendrons themselves are better in masses with strong

A landscape picture at the Arboretum painted wholly with native plants.

background than when shown as specimens. This is because their form is not interesting in itself. There are two supreme instances of rhododendron planting: one in the Hunnewell gardens at Wellesley where masses of deep rich green foliage show against a stronger background of dark, dignified old spruces and firs; the other is the Arnold Arboretum collection at the foot of Hemlock Hill. Rhododendrons are also good used even more naturally along edges of woods as they grow outside Scranton, with enough sun filtering through the trees to cover them with bloom.

Laurel is likewise adapted to many uses. It makes a perfect filler among the broadleaved evergreens on account of its good neutral green and non-emphatic form. The little inkberry [*Ilex glabra*] can serve a like purpose on a smaller scale in size and leaf. Laurel is not good for a specimen except perhaps in its most favored haunt on a springy hillside in full sun.

Andromeda [*Pieris*] fills choice places in garden or shrubbery or can act as a picturesque specimen to give height and strength in a rock garden. Its compact round shape, clean foliage, and refined flower all appeal to the formal planter.

There is a large class of native material especially interesting because ordinarily relegated to wild planting, yet capable of more choice use. The high-bush blueberry [*Vaccinium corymbosum*] of this group is beautiful at all seasons, in mass or alone, and like the red cedar is equal to any situation. Bayberry is another of this type yet how often do we see it used? Its shining bronze green leaves last late and then leave neat branches and gray berries. Its sturdy character makes it good in native work. If bayberry were still green at Christmas it would soon cease to exist, as holly [*Ilex*] and laurel are beginning to cease to exist. Even now it is all too popular as indoor decoration in summer. Friends of this plant will do well to pick only the side branches and not all from the same bush if we are to have it with us long.

The tree shad [*Amelanchier*] is almost in the class with flowering dogwood, though more delicate and more unusual. One of these stepping forth from a stage of red cedar can send a message to our imagination as beautiful and as delicate as a fairy's whisper, or we may have it as we often see it, in a mass rising from the swamp like mist.

The flowering dogwood, itself the leader of many cousin dogwoods, illustrates a native which in cultivation has supplied good varieties. We can now have a bright pink dogwood [*Cornus florida rubra*] within our trim garden, a pure white one in the lawn shrubbery, and a mass of white and light pink ones deep in the wood beyond.

Many combinations suggest themselves, especially of little-used natives with some of our well known shrubbery familiars. Why should we not use sweet pepper [*Clethra alnifolia*] with mock orange [*Philadelphus*] since it is willing to compromise and accept a good garden soil in place of its ericaceous home? Its leaf color and twigs and general character harmonize with mock orange and it makes a good succession of bloom.

Sumacs [*Rhus*] can never be used in any but the most informal or natural planting. We should use them more often for quick thickets and screen planting near camp houses and on rough banks. These, with groundings of aster and goldenrod, enriched perhaps by cedar, wild rose, and bayberry, make one of the loveliest fall groups of native plants.

The common high-bush chokeberry [*Aronia arbutifolia*] is a magnificent fall shrub under good conditions, especially its variety grandifolia. It is less meagre when cultivated and fairly covered with shining black fruit the size of shoe buttons, and has deep wine red fall leaves. I have seen this growing in part shade with sprays of wild clematis [*Clematis terniflora*] flowering among its branches — a lovely suggestion for indoor and outdoor flower arrangement.

Few people realize that the mountain holly [*Ilex ambigua*] grows compact and fat under cultivation in the open shrubbery, and nursery grown clumps make an immediate effect for a screen. The gray dogwood is another of the same type, with even better foliage because darker green and neutral.

There are, too, the "hyphens" — plants naturalized here for so long that we consider them natives. The common barberry [*Berberis vulgaris*] is one, and the Japanese barberry is already found escaped in many places. Sorbaria, spindle tree [*Euonymus*], briar rose [*Rosa canina*], and common privet [*Ligustrum vulgare*] may join these and be as good as natives for wild planting by virtue of their easy reproduction.

These are but a handful out of many suggestions. When we have half begun to appreciate our natives enough to try them in cultivation we shall find some of the exquisite possibilities of these plants. It is through American plants that we shall be able to get that intangible charm of English planting, for they will respond to care by luxuriance, which is not the least part of the beauty of English planting. We shall have as a result a truly American garden.

Country Life in America 47 (FEBRUARY 1925): 35–39.

ENDNOTES

8. Catherine R. Brown, *Women and the Land: A Biographical Survey of Women Who have Contributed to the Development of Landscape Architecture in the United States* (Baltimore, 1979), n.p.; *House Beautiful* 79 (December 1933): 249; Dorothy May Anderson, *Women, Design, and the Cambridge School* (Mesa, Arizona, 1980).

9. A similar article written twenty-three years earlier by Eben E. Rexford begins: "During the last few years a decided change has taken place in one phase of American gardening. The attention of the home gardeners has been called to the beauty and other good qualities of our native plants," *Lippincott's Magazine* 69 (April 1902): 483. Being revolutionary, part of a new movement, seems to have excited romantic gardeners interested in the "wild" style; consequently it was perpetually viewed as having just been introduced and as being on the defense against more traditional styles of gardening (see Virginia Tuttle Clayton, "The Wild Garden and American Popular Magazines, 1890–1920," in *Nature and Ideology*, ed. Joachim Wolske-Bulmahn [Washington, D.C., 1997], 144–147).

ᔓ Edith A. Roberts and Elsa Rehmann

Plant Ecology: The Contribution to Naturalistic Planting of This Study of Plants in Relation to Their Environment

In 1924, the Conservation Committee of the Garden Club of America published a booklet by botanists Edith A. Roberts and Margaret F. Shaw, *The Ecology of Plants Native to Dutchess County*. This booklet became the inspiration for a wider-ranging series of twelve articles by Roberts and landscape architect Elsa Rehmann, whose writings also appear in Chapters Three and Five of this anthology. The twelve articles on ecology appeared in *House Beautiful* between June 1927 and May 1928, and in 1929 they were published as a book, *American Plants for American Gardens*.[10] The following article served as the introduction to the series, explaining the concept of plant ecology and the format of the succeeding articles. It also makes clear the purpose of the series: to encourage gardeners to recreate on their properties "the very spirit of the natural landscape," whether that property is a large country estate or a smaller plot of an acre or less. These articles demonstrate the more scientific approach to natural gardening introduced in the American popular press during the 1920s, an approach still in harmony with the romantic notions of earlier decades. Roberts was born in Rollensford, New Hampshire, in 1881 and earned her Ph.D. at the University of Chicago in 1915. Henry Chandler Cowles (1869–1939), the first American to write about ecology, was Roberts's major professor and he may have inspired her to pursue this field of study.[11] Roberts taught botany at Vassar College from 1919 to 1950 and probably became acquainted with Rehmann while Rehmann was lecturing there on landscape architecture during the 1920s.[12]

WHEN WE BEGIN to observe nature, we usually first learn the names of the flowers and delight in each one for its special loveliness. Or we identify the trees by their distinctive characters. Such an interest enlivens every excursion out of doors, whether we travel along the road through the countryside by automobile or follow the courses of streams while trout-fishing, whether we skim lake and river in canoe or climb over the mountain trail. It is then that we begin to associate the individual plants with the locations where we find them. The juniper [*Juniperus*] is always a real part of the exposed hillside where it makes its picturesque groupings. The marsh marigold [*Caltha palustris*] can never be taken from the winding stream where it makes its sunlit fringe. The pitcher plant [*Sarracenia*] is incomplete without its larch [*Larix*]-surrounded boggy setting. The windswept seaside is always the background for the rugged beauty of the bayberry [*Myrica pensylvanica*]. The waterlily [*Nymphaea*] cannot exist without its reflecting pond. The asters and goldenrods [*Solidago*] make the open fields their setting. The oak [*Quercus*] woods are inseparable from pictures of hepaticas and anemones, flowering dogwoods [*Cornus florida*] and laurels [*Kalmia latifolia*], azaleas [*Rhododendron*] and maple-leaved viburnums [*Viburnum acerifolium*]. Beeches [*Fagus*], maples [*Acer*], and hemlocks [*Tsuga*] furnish the slopes with verdure. The hemlocks are often found alone in the ravines. Gray birches [*Betula populifolia*] group themselves together on the side of the hill. The northern mountains are made magnificent by the pines [*Pinus*] that are characteristic there.

What are these pictures that we have suggested but the beginning of a realization that plants are an integral part of their own landscape? As soon as we catch this close relationship of plants to the places where they grow, we are potential ecologists, whether the name is familiar to us or whether we have to look it up in the dictionary to discover that ecology is the study of plants in relation to their environment.

In the next eleven numbers of the *House Beautiful*, we are going to take up this study of plants in relation to their environment. We are going to use as examples the most characteristic landscapes of our Northeastern States. We want to name the most important plants in each scene and give the fundamentals that underlay each assembling. We want to outline the compositions that they make and suggest how they can be interpreted in grounds and gardens. We want to show what ecology has to offer to all who are doing naturalistic planting.

Each section of our country has, to be sure, its distinctive landscape. Picture the woods of Virginia with the flame azaleas [*Rhododendron calendulaceum*]. Imagine the almost untouched mountains of the Carolinas, where such precious plants as Rhododendron carolinianum grow in high altitudes.

Think of the live oaks [*Quercus virginiana*] of the South, with their sweeping mosses of semitropical Florida. Bring to mind the great coniferous forests of the Rockies. Remember the gray-green foliage in the arid places of the Southwest, or the amazing picturesqueness of cacti, yuccas, and agaves against the sands of the desert.

In your trips across the continent such outstanding situations will be sharply defined. You will, perhaps, catch only the general character from a speeding train, but even then the distinctive fitness of plants to their particular surroundings will be remarkably clear. Far journeys are not necessary, however. Your own county will lend itself to delightful research, amid all the subtleties of ecological study, with the minutest flower detail. We want to emphasize the intimate scenes of your own environment, for it is these that you can preserve and recreate for yourself.

Each section requires special study. We are choosing our examples from the Northeastern States. They show plants assembled into distinct groups through inherent congeniality. Ecology calls these groups 'plant associations.'

In the July *House Beautiful* we shall start with the group of plants that grows naturally along the seaside. We have placed it first, because it attracts special attention during this holiday season. It shows the dependence of plants upon their environment, for the vigorous beauty of this vegetation is due to the windswept situation. It is such a fundamental part of the landscape that it illustrates in a vivid way how appropriate indigenous plant material is for the settings of our houses.

The month of August is an opportune time to introduce the Aquatics, for it brings into bloom the waterlily, the pickerelweed [*Pontederia*], and the arrowhead [*Sagittaria*] that delight in the still water of the ponds.

In September the open fields make their greatest display, with great masses of flowers like the goldenrods and the asters. The warmth and light of the whole summer seem to culminate in their colorful abundance.

We have placed the Juniper Association in the October number. It makes a fascinating setting for a house. It seems especially interesting when we return from our summer holiday, for it is at the height of its effectiveness in the autumn. It is a small group, but it is self-contained and self-sufficient. It shows the dependence of plants upon the contour of the land. It points out the rigorous effects of poor soil upon their character.

The Oak Association is so rich in effects that it would suit any month. We place it in November because the foliage holds its coloring so late. In fact, the leaves of some varieties often stay on all winter long. It is especially important to consider the oak woodland, because it forms the extensive background for the other scenes.

We have left the pines for December when the winter sports take us to northern mountains. The Beech, Maple, and Hemlock Association is so delightful amid the snow that it has been reserved for January. The ever-greens of the hemlock ravines are wonderful even in the midst of February weather. And the gray birches [*Betula populifolia*] are kept for March, when they make conspicuous black and white effects amid the still leafless trees.

The month of April is a good time to introduce the Brookside Associa-tion, which is full of interest throughout the year, with all its varied luxuriance that is due to abundant moisture.

And the May number will appear as the flowers are getting ready to bloom in the bog. These plants, with their roots often actually in the water, find it as difficult to obtain the necessary water supply as if they were in an extremely dry situation. This is the result of what is called physiological drought, due to the high degree of acidity. It makes all the plants rare-looking, and the group unique.

When you take your next excursion out of doors, note how these plant associations begin to stand out. Look for them. Do not miss a single one. You will find that each one is easily identified. You can recognize it by its very name. It is called either by the name of the tree that is prominent in it, or by the situation where it is found.

After we have learned that certain associations of plants belong to certain environments, ecology draws our attention to the fact that nature is ever in transition. One plant group no sooner becomes established than its very development in all its perfection creates satisfactory surroundings for a new group. In fact, Nature arranges these transitions with consummate order. Take, for example, the way in which the birches, the pines, the oaks, and the beech, maple, and hemlock associations follow one another in a definite succession. It is the open field with its sunny exposure that is the fitting place for the germination of juniper seeds. The shade and protection of the junipers encourage the seed of the birches to take hold and develop. Birch copses, in their turn, are the nursing-places for the pines. The pine green, though too dense for its own seed, provides just the right degree of darkness for the oaks. In their maturity the oaks become the cradles for beeches, maples, and hemlocks. All three of these spring up within their own shade, but where the shade becomes deepest and where it is coolest in the ravines only hemlocks germinate.

We can take the abandoned farm as an illustration of what happens to our own home environment when Nature is left to run her own course. The once cultivated fields are being covered with junipers, or perhaps they have already reached the stage of the gray birches or even that of the pines. The woodlot, left to itself, changes from pine to oak. The rarer old, old woods that were never touched by the woodcutters are still the rich forest lands that our forefathers found when they came.

Nature is ever tending toward the most luxuriant form of vegetation which conditions permit. In ideal situations she has reached the finest development. Beech, maple, and hemlock cover vast areas in varying proportions. Where they do not exist, their establishment has been prevented by adverse conditions — such as the exposure upon the seashore, or the lack of water on the dry hillside, or the severe cold of the northern mountains. Then, Nature's course is retarded through her own fundamental causes.

It is delayed, too, by man-made interruptions. It is often held back by accident. Take the destructive force of fire. When an oak woodland, for instance, is severely burned over and no humus remains, Nature courageously starts at the very beginning again. The fireweed [*Epilobium angustifolium*] is the first to find foothold in this desolation. When oaks are cut or receive but a superficial burning, the wood takes care of itself. Young sprouts appear very shortly around the base of old trunks, while the undergrowth reestablishes itself. When pines are cut down, Nature accommodates herself to this man-imposed retrogression and goes back again to birches, so that they can provide once more the shelter for new pines. The sturdy young trees soon assert themselves. When the pine wood is well upon its way, though still in the birches' care, the stages of this re-creation become noticeable. And when some of the old trees with wind-bent crowns are left uncut on the edge of the young forest with its slender and ephemeral birches, they are not only a reminder of their former greatness but a promise of what is to come again.

The harbingers of the new association and the remnants of the old often meet. You often see groups of birches springing up amid the junipers. Groups of old pines are found remaining amid the oaks, or the young oaks show their slender trunks in the midst of a mature pine forest. The meadow rose, *Rosa blanda*, which grows so luxuriantly in the open field, delights in its association with junipers, but is no longer found amid the birch copses. The laurel, which never appears among the pines, makes one of the most beautiful contributions to the oak woods. It stays with the coming of the beech, maple, and hemlocks, but it does not blossom so freely. The yew [*Taxus*], however, does not appear at all until the full shade of the Beech, Maple, and Hemlock association is established.

The evidence of such transition is found not only in the trees and shrubs. The flowers, even, bear their own fascinating testimony by carrying their little pictures from association to association. The heart-leaved aster [*Aster cordifolius*], for instance, is found as long as there is sufficient sun — in the open field with the junipers, under the delicate shade of gray birches. The pyrolas and pipsissewas, the spotted wintergreen [*Chimaphila maculata*] and the partridgeberries [*Mitchella repens*], do not appear until sufficient shade is developed; then they carry their delightful groundcovers from pine to oak and from oak to beech, maple, and hemlock. The true solomonseals [*Polygonatum*] and bishopscaps [*Mitella*] only start in the Oak Association, and continue under the even deeper shade of the hemlock.

While each association is quite distinct in itself, it is never isolated. You have but to keep to the road to realize this. In the passage up hill and down dale, from mountain-top to river valley, you pass from one association to another. Even on a single day afoot, or during a few hours on the train, you can catch their outstanding characteristics. Or go across country. Wander deep into the wood, ascend a ridge, and then climb down the rocky side of a mountain stream. Follow a trail through the field, skirt a pond, cross and recross the meandering stream, and, if you dare, wade into the enchanted bog. In this way you can get close to flower and moss and fern, and watch for the minute details in each association. Sometimes in a single view there will be a veritable cross section of several. Take a single example: a slope where beeches, maples, and hemlocks grow between the oak-crowned ridge and the sycamore [*Platanus occidentalis*]- and elm [*Ulmus americana*]-fringed stream-side. Sometimes all the different associations are gathered together about an open field. Such a place would be a typical area for a country estate, with sweeping acreage and varied topography. The woods would make a setting for the house. The fields and meadows would be an expansive foreground. The hilltop would become a vantage point for distant views. The wood paths and the ways along sunny stream and around pond would make many little land-scapes delightful in color and picturesque detail.

Property lines may enclose a less varied scene. Even if such a setting is limited to a single association, it has opportunities. Take as an outstanding example a camp site amid the pines in the Adirondacks, where not a tree nor even a single partridgeberry-vine seems to have been destroyed, and where the building stands hidden in the sheltering forest, with a view of the lake but out of its sight. Or take the Pennsylvania mountains with their hem-locks and rhododendrons, the juniper hillsides of Connecticut, the rocky coasts of Maine and Massachusetts, the seaside of New Jersey, the dunes of Long Island, and the river banks and oak ridges throughout these sections. These are ideal settings for a winter lodge, for a summer cottage, for all-year-around homes. They should all be retained in their full beauty, with all their individual characteristics. Sometimes this is a problem entirely of preservation, and sometimes it is a matter of filling-in and completing the existing scenes.

Even a plot of an acre or less is full of possibilities. Let us take a single example. Think of a house placed upon a slope at the fringe of a woods. Ju-nipers skirt the edges in picturesque hedgerows, gray birches surround a dell, a little brook tumbles over great boulders in the hollow. Here the scars are apt to be bigger and more noticeable, but every cherished scene can be fully reestablished with delicate detail. Even a still smaller property has the opportunity of being true to its environment. Its location within a well-defined area may be the key for preserving its native and original plants. Or a single tree left standing may become a sign. Take a single white oak [*Quercus alba*], for instance, in a little property upon a ridge. It may be taken as a guide for the use of the shrubs and flowers that are appropriate to it.

This picture may have to be no bigger than a miniature, but it can have, nevertheless, delightful details and the very spirit of the natural landscape.

House Beautiful 61 (June 1927): 805, 842, 844–845

Reprinted by permission from *House Beautiful*, copyright © June 1927. The Hearst Corporation. All Rights Reserved.

ENDNOTES

10. The book is back in print (Athens, Georgia, 1996) with a foreword by Darrel G. Morrison that discusses Rehmann's and Robert's work in the context of the early ecology movement in the United States.

11. Henry Chandler Cowles, "The Ecological Relations of the Vegetation on the Sand Dunes of Lake Michigan," *Botanical Gazette* 27 (1899). For another early reference to ecology in American garden literature, see Frank A. Waugh, *The Natural Style in Landscape Gardening* (Boston, 1917), 51–52; Waugh mentions that German landscape architect Willy Lange had most clearly elucidated the principles of ecology in his book *Die Garten-Gestaltung der Neuzeit* (Leipzig, 1907). On Lange: Joachim Wolschke-Buhmahn and Gert Groening, "The Ideology of the Nature Garden: Nationalistic Trends in Garden Design in Germany During the Early Twentieth Century," *Journal of Garden History* 12 (January–March, 1992), and Joachim Wolschke-Buhlman, "The 'Wild Garden' and the 'Nature Garden.'" *Journal of Garden History* 14 (July–September, 1992).

12. *American Men and Women of Science* 5, ed. The Jacques Cattell Press (New York, 1976), 3714.

The Contributors' Club:
Nature and the Rich

VIOLA ROSEBORO' (1858–1945) was fiction editor of *McClure's Magazine* from the mid-1890s until 1906, while it was one of the most widely read magazines in the United States. She has been credited with helping to start the literary careers of some important early twentieth-century American writers, including O. Henry and Booth Tarkington.[13] Unlike many of the articles that appeared in *Atlantic's* Contributors' Club, Roseboro's anonymous essay was not meant to be at all humorous. It is a bitter expression of the class warfare that was being waged in the gardens of this period, an angry attack on the "stupid rich" who spoiled natural beauty with their ignorant and ostentatious garden building, and a sneer at the poor who "have no better taste" but are less empowered by money to be destructive. Many members of the educated middle class considered themselves the last bastion of respectability in this country and the last true defenders of American nature.[14] They were not only disgusted by the legions of new rich, they also despised the poor, especially immigrants, who they were sure had no appreciation of America's natural beauty. This article was written at a time when industrialism had created an unprecedented number of new millionaires, and when unparalleled numbers of immigrants were arriving in America.[15] Both seemed threats to the stability of the United States and caused terrible apprehension among some native-born Americans. The fair mentioned at the beginning of the article was the Columbian Exposition of 1893 in Chicago, the grounds of which were landscaped by Frederick Law Olmsted.

THE TALK OF WHAT the Fair may do, must do, for higher civilization in America has been endless, and yet I have waited for months, and waited in vain, to hear one word as to its influence on the need nearest my heart. I long to have some one, some one with such learning and authority as

I cannot pretend to, take up the theme of — how shall I word it? — natural resources in landscape gardening.

A deal of praise is being lavished on Mr. Olmsted, but no one is properly underscoring, for the benefit of the stupid rich, the best lesson in his work at the Fair, — the lesson of the lagoon on the value of cultivating and heightening, without change of character, nature's own choice effects.

Of course, when put that way, such value appears so obvious, so in harmony with the philosophy of all art, that it seems incredible that the point should need theoretical emphasis, however much we might have to learn practically.

But we have only to look at the pleasure grounds of the rich, from Newport to Oconomowoc, to see that the notion that Nature anywhere knows what she is about is quite foreign to the popular creed in gardening. Nobody could oppose the creation of lawns and flower beds; they assuredly have a right to a place in the scheme of things; but why presume that lawns, flower beds, and the like are the only possibilities for beautiful "grounds"? All too often nothing else seems possible, or at least nothing else is so easy to achieve. But when Nature has lavished herself on some rare spot; when, as on so much of our northern Atlantic coast, she has brought together a host of lovely things, roses, spiraea, iris, bay [*Myrica pensylvanica*], clethra, morning-glories [*Ipomoea purpurea*], and has put in nothing that is not lovely, why should the rich man have but one notion of his opportunities, — that, after carefully buying the most charming spot he can find, it is his duty to sweep all these exquisite growths into a bonfire, and, starting from the bare ground, create a lawn and plant evergreens? If he must do that, why, — I ask it with bitter passion, — why is he not content to choose some ugly spot for his work, one of the many places that even his crudest methods would improve? Is there any hope that Mr. Olmsted's following and heightening of Nature's own effects in parts of the lagoon will broaden the rich man's notions of the possible? If he could only once conceive that money may be spent in this way as well as another, possibly he would be reconciled to try it. But of course there is the disadvantage that the result does not tell loudly of the money spent, and in many cases that would doubtless be a fatal drawback.

In promulgating my little views conversationally I am continually overcome with surprise at the failure of sympathy in some quarters where I had confidently expected it; at the inability of various charming people to conceive of any way of assisting Nature but by making lawns and flower beds, no matter what the conditions; and as for letting her alone, a course I praise only as a lesser evil than destroying all vestiges of her best schemes, that simply strikes them as low, — as the conduct adapted to squatters, and no one else. They tell me Newport is beautiful, and are only mystified when I quote Mr. John La Farge (am sure he will not mind my sustaining myself with his name in so good a cause) as saying that the sight of Newport saddens him, because one of the most beautiful coasts in the world, a place that should have been sacredly preserved in its pristine, unique loveliness, has been — simply destroyed.[16]

But I have, by much experiment, chanced upon a way of inserting the new idea that rarely fails to give pain, — the pain that testifies to some success in inoculation. I mention it for the benefit of any other member of the Club who may be carrying on a similar crusade.

I say: "Why can't we do as the Japanese do so often, — at Nikko, for instance? There is a spot that is one of the sights of the world for beauty; it has had the most devoted care lavished upon it for hundreds of years, and yet, except in the temples and tombs, you cannot trace the hand of man. It has not been left alone, but it has been beautified with such subtle art that it looks as if it had."

I cannot say why this crude and probably inaccurate statement (for it is little enough I know about Nikko) should make an impression, but it does: it often gives my victim his first notion that maybe there is something to be said on my side; that I am not simply a "crank." So I am thinking that something might be done to save some acres of wild roses, some lily ponds, for the next generation, if the energetic, the able, and the wise would begin a propaganda in the names of the Fair and the Japanese. But success will have to come soon, or there will be nothing left to save. Every summer sees the ignorant rich descend like the locust upon all that is fairest in the land. Doubtless the poor, as a rule, have no better taste, but they have less power, and one cannot hate them for what they might do as one hates the others for what they have done.

Atlantic Monthly 73 (June 1894): 858–859.

ENDNOTES

13. *New York Times* (obituary) January 30, 1945, 19:3.

14. Celia Betsky, "Inside the Past: The Interior and the Colonial Revival in American Art and Literature," *The Colonial Revival in America*, ed. Alan Axelrod (New York, 1985), 241–277; Clayton, "The Wild Garden and American Popular Magazines, 1890–1920," 144–147.

15. In 1861 there were only a few dozen millionaires in the United States, in 1900 there were 4,000; in 1907 alone nearly 1,300,000 immigrants arrived, most from countries not well represented in the original ethnic mix of American colonists (see Clayton, "Wild Gardens and the American Popular Magazine, 1890–1920," 135).

16. John La Farge (1835–1910) was an American painter and decorative artist. Known as a highly literate artist, it not surprising that he was an acquaintance of Roseboro', with whom he also shared an admiration of Japanese art.

Planting a Slope

DURING THE 1930s, there were still articles on wild or natural gardening in popular magazines, but not as many as in the preceding decades. Perhaps the increasing fashion of rock gardens had, to some extent, replaced the passion for wild gardens. Many articles on wild flowers or naturalistic gardens were more concerned with solving a landscape problem, like planting in shade or on a slope. In this essay Tabor encourages readers to try to cooperate with nature rather than attempting to change it: recognize that lawns are difficult to maintain on a hill and study how nature gradually covers a slope with vegetation. Would the reader not rather see "a meadow effect . . . with long waving grasses and wild flowers interspersed?" She explains how to plant such a meadow garden and how to mow it to keep it a meadow, rather than allowing it to evolve into a forest.

SOME THINGS OFFER so great resistance to our gardening intentions that it is better not to struggle against them. This does not mean a weak-spirited surrender to them, but rather a compromise wherein the gardener does not lose even though he yields. Indeed in the final results he triumphs perhaps to a greater degree than would have been possible if he had his own way altogether.

I have in mind especially the problem of a slope. Whether it is an entire hillside or only part of a hillside does not really matter. Nor need it be very steep to present great difficulties, if it is considered in terms of the conventional garden site where lawn and flowers in well-ordered relation are expected to grow. The point is that a slope ought never to be so considered. Thus the first step in dealing with it is the readjustment of ourselves.

We should come to such a problem in a spirit of cooperation rather than of grim determination. Which brings us immediately to the first consideration; namely, what happens to hillsides when they are left to themselves, when they have been undisturbed from time immemorial? Vegetation

What happens to hillsides when they are left to themselves?

invariably covers them, does it not, unless they are outcroppings of solid rock? First will come the lowest plant forms, the creeping and insinuating mosses; then ground-clinging plants; next weeds and grasses; then woody things — the plants that form undergrowth when real trees have had time to grow; and last of all, the trees themselves.

Thus forest would reclothe even a small garden slope, given time and freedom so to do. Or would reclothe rather the slightly elevated level space where the slope had been, after erosion of the bare earth had leveled it down. Study any old abandoned sand bank and you will see this happening — sand and earth gradually washing down and out upon the level at the bottom, diminishing the angle of the slope and gradually permitting weeds and small trees and bushes to gain root-hold.

And so it is apparent that sloping earth cannot be left to the free action of rains and thawing ice and snow even for a single season. It must be provided with protection — coverage — at once. It is actually an emergency demanding quick action and relief, if there has been grading and consequent stripping off of vegetation.

Nor will it be enough to cover the surface of the soil. Plant roots must be woven through it as rapidly as possible to form a web that will hold it beneath as well as on the surface. And of course the steeper the slope, the greater the need of deep-rooting growth to reset the greater tearing-down energy of the elements.

A safe rule is never to attempt making a lawn intended to be mowed close with a lawn mower on a slope greater than twenty-five degrees, unless the sloping space is very limited — such a small declivity as a wide lawn some-times offers here or there. Long slopes even of this degree are certain to wash into gullies in their lower portion under heavy rainfall unless the soil is extremely dense and resistant clay. Furthermore it is hard to mow grass to the required perfection on such a slope and when it is so mowed the loss of water which drains off instead of sinking in makes brown and parched effects inevitable.

Considering all these things it is not hard to abandon preconceived ideals of lawn and to substitute for them something more in keeping with the character of the land itself: a meadow effect for example, with long waving grasses and wild flowers interspersed; perhaps a little clump of trees to cast shade and roses to form an encircling hedgerow. Doesn't this sound good to you?

Here is the procedure: First seed generously with a good mixture of meadow grasses. And be prepared to reseed and reseed until the upper por-tions of the slope are as well grassed as the lower. They will not be unless you do this reseeding, for of course the seed and sprouted seedlings too will wash down under every rain until the young grasses are well rooted.

Mix with the grass seed of your second and any subsequent seeding whatever choice of flowers you have for naturalizing — columbine [*Aquilegia*], black-eyed Susan [*Rudbeckia hirta*], butterfly weed [*Asclepias tuberosa*], yarrow [*Achillea*] and such strong growing things native or otherwise. But do not use too many kinds; nature never does.

Leave the whole thing severely alone after it is actually covered, not mowing at all until the grasses have tasseled and ripened. Then mow with a scythe, but not closely. Finally, bear with the resulting stubble which will be brown and dry like a hay meadow until the rain starts up new growth and it becomes freshly green with a second crop of grasses. By the second mowing time autumn crocuses [*Colchicum*] will be on the market, and drifts of these flung widely across the space and planted where they fall will introduce a new beauty within a few days. Later make a similar broadcast of the spring crocus, scilla and muscari bulbs for late winter and early spring.

When surface protection has thus been established, as just a single season will in this way guarantee, you may add other things as you will — things which will eventually choke out the grass, if you prefer a shrubby cover which will grow more and more woodsy as it matures and never need any care whatsoever — not even the twice-a-summer mowing. In properly acid soil a planting of heather [*Erica*] or our native laurel [*Kalmia latifolia*] is ideal. With the last-named, trees may also have a place, since laurel grows naturally in open woods as well as in full sunlight.

Never try to plant these heavier things, however, until the initial retaining web of grass roots and matted tops is woven. For trees alone, set in naked earth, are helpless against the rush of water down a slope during torrential rains. They may not be washed out altogether but their roots will be so un-covered that mere survival is all they can manage.

Woman's Home Companion 53 (SEPTEMBER 1934): 47.

Wild Gardening by a Wild Gardener

FREDERIC ALMY offers an amateur's point of view on wild gardening. A social worker with a degree in law, he was born in 1858 and lived near Buffalo, New York. At the time he wrote this article he was president of the National Conference of Social Work.[17] He wrote several books and many magazine articles on charity organizations and social work, as well as a number of nature and garden poems. This was his only prose article on gardening. His colleagues recognized him as not only an outstanding contributor to his profession but as a fine impromptu speaker, "a poet of distinction, a lover of nature and an authority on most of the things that make life worth while."[18] An archetypal Progressive, Almy was a supporter of women's suffrage and of prohibition. He died in 1935. In this article he tells us that he has created a wild garden on his property where he — a "wage slave" — works on Sundays during the summer rather than going to church: "If playing with flowers is breaking the Sabbath, my Sundays will continue to be brittle." He is not always successful with his plants, but he takes it all in good humor and finds in gardening a source of spiritual and physical strength. He spontaneously expresses himself in the language of Romantic poetry: his "heart leaps up" when he beholds a *mountain* in the sky.

THE WORLD BEGAN with a man and a woman in a garden. The trouble began when the man and the woman left the garden. As Abraham Cowley said, "God the first garden made, and the first city Cain."[19] I agree with Bacon that "God Almightie first planted a Garden. And indeed, it is the Purest of humane Pleasures. It is the Greatest Refreshment to the Spirits of Man."[20] Bacon has his very favorite plants and shrubs for each month: "For December and January you must take such Things as are Greene all Winter: Holly; Bayes; Eugh; Pine-Apple-Trees; Firre-trees." Do you recognize yew, and did you know before that pine trees used to be called pine-apple trees?

In my eighteen acres at a wild place called Jericho my failures have been as perennial as my faith. There is an old farmhouse, built in 1852, covered to the chimneys with Virginia creepers [*Parthenocissus quinquefolia*], which, like the lobster, are green living and red dying. These have succeeded, but along the low piazza a row of the single Japanese peonies [*Paeonia*] which look like a huge wild rose was to have been cascaded over with honeysuckles [*Lonicera*], thrusting in and out among the peony leaves. In the shade the honeysuckles ran more to bugs than to flowers. Nevertheless, the wild clematis, or old-man's-beard [*Clematis terniflora*], is taking hold as it should and fuming over the peony leaves in a gray cloud.

Near the house is a lily pond, the size of a room, which bears chosen water lilies [*Nymphaea*] from June until frost. The goldfish in it reappear each spring, as if the ice which covered them had never existed. It seems to me as much a death and a resurrection as with the flowers, which are as good an emblem of life after death as the butterfly.

The little pond is surrounded by a profusion of wild flowers which are all hand planted. I think the art conceals art, for visitors seldom say more than that we are fortunate in having so many wild flowers. They come in procession — hepatica, trillium, and bloodroot [*Sanguinaria*]; violets [*Violas*] and columbine [*Aquilegia*] in profusion; iris of many kinds, candlestick lilies [*Lilium pennsylvanicum*], and the tawny day or road lily [*Hemerocallis fulva*], which will grow and bloom even when an automobile runs over it; gorgeous swamp mallow [*Hibiscus moscheutos*], swamp milkweed [*Asclepias incarnata*], a quantity of joepye-weed [*Eupatorium purpurea*], splendid stalks of vervain [*Verbena*], cardinal flowers [*Lobelia cardinalis*], and at the last goldenrod [*Solidago*], aster, and Rudbeckia. Not many at one time, for it is only a small pond, but there are so many in all that it seems as if, like Box and Cox, they must rotate in the same beds.[21]

On one side of the pond scarlet tulips (*Gesnerana*) grow wild in the grass, like poppies [*Papaver*], and are cut down with the grass in June. There are also guinea-hens, or fritillaria [*Fritillarea meleagris*], with their odd checkered calico bells, and some autumn crocus [*Colchicum*]. On the other side I have worked hard over a colony of butterfly-weed [*Asclepias tuberosa*], which is the most flaming thing I know in the way of wild flowers. It is a royal color. A weed is said to be a flower in the wrong place, and I know good people who, when they talk with me, impress me as weeds. The butterfly-weed, with its brilliant orange, makes as fine a show as King Cophetua's beggar maid after her social reconstruction.[22]

When I have a large wild garden, it must have a mountain. My heart leaps up when I behold a mountain in the sky. I have never had anywhere in my life nearly half enough of mountains. Not long ago the coming down from the summit of Mount Washington, much of the time on the heights, sometimes descending in the bed of a brook, was a singing joy. To be sure it is not always comfortable to share the same bed with a brook, The cold, watery sheets sometimes make you want to say "blank-et." This is again an escape from my subject, and I will return to botany.

One of my successful floral experiments was edelweiss [*Leontopodium*], which I bloomed for three summers next to a boulder on top of the bank, but it took continual watering in summer, and was such a tyrant that the fourth summer I refused to truckle to it. This so-called boulder we thought was about the size of a bucket, but a little digging showed that it had size, and it proved to be as large as a barrel. With a four-horse team to haul it, we made a feature of it under an apple [*Malus*] tree, and a mason from the city spent half a day cutting a shallow basin in its top for a bird bath. I have seen three birds at once splashing in it until its sides were dripping.

Let no one suppose that even with flowers I am wise. I just fool with them; and for any sort of success I need plants that are fool-proof. I wish the florists' catalogues would advertise such flowers. Creeping phlox [*Phlox stolonifera*], for instance, is said to establish itself and increase rapidly in the poorest soil. I set out two dozen on a sunny knoll, and, like a careful shepherd, I watered my phlox, but, like the sheep of Bo-peep, they deserted me. Orange hawkweed, or devil's-paint-brush [*Hieracium*], is described as such a farmers' pest that where once established it can never be extirpated. It can only be burned out with fire. I got some hawkweed started, and by conveying water a quarter of a mile at frequent intervals I kept it alive two years. Then it disappeared.

There is no question that plants have character. When they will, they will, you may depend on it; and when they won't, they won't, and there's an end on't. The wild morning-glory [*Convolvus*], or bindweed, cannot be kept out of our flower-beds by any pains, and unless watched it almost strangles the larkspur [*Consolida*] and the lilies [*Lilium*]; but when I plant it where I want it, and cosset it, it refuses to grow. I have thought that it might scramble over the rough bank in front of the house, but it thinks otherwise, and you can guess which wins. I have seen bittersweet [*Celastrus scandens*] grow through our dirt cellar floor when it would not grow in a bed. Flowers must be feminine.

If a stone were set at Jericho for each plant that never came up, the place would look like a cemetery. In Kipling's elusive story called "They" a lonely woman so desires children that her big house is filled with their forms and voices, seen and heard only by her and a few who can understand. At Jericho there are few places in my walks where I do not see the ghosts of flowers that were planted but never grew.

I have said that flowers show character. It takes character to start underground in the dark; to wait six months in the dark for the first signs of spring; to insist absolutely on being a lady's-slipper [*Cypripedium*], or a Shirley poppy [*Papaver rhoeas*], or whatever you were meant to be, and nothing else; to draw food from the dark and keep at it until frost, even though no one sees. The evangelist Moody tells us that character is what a man is in the dark.[23] If character is what you are in the dark flowers have character.

I have been asked how a wage slave finds time for gardening, even if it is wild gardening. An answer which has got me into serious trouble with the good is that I think going to church in summer is breaking the Sabbath. So it is if you have no other day in summer to be outdoors and you *like* outdoors. If playing with flowers is breaking the Sabbath, my Sundays will continue to be brittle.

It renews my strength, both spiritually and physically, to touch the earth. I am like the giant Antaeus, who could not be defeated by Hercules because every time he was thrown down and touched his Mother Earth he rose twice stronger for the contact. It was only when Hercules lifted him and held him up among high things, but away from the earth, that his strength left him.

Gardening is an ancient profession. We are told in "Hamlet" that "there is no ancient gentlemen but gardeners, ditchers, and grave-makers." I am all three. I garden, I ditch, and I make graves for about half of my pets. Herod never slew more innocents than I have. And yet I always begin the long winter months with a naive faith that in the spring resurrection I shall see most, if not all, of those that I consigned to the ground in the fall. There are five hundred Spanish iris [*Iris xiphium*] (they cost thirty cents a hundred); there are one hundred Florentine tulips, or wood tulips [*Tulipa sylvestris*]; there are one hundred feathered hyacinths [*Muscari*], also called tuzzy-muzzys; and some crown imperials [*Fritillaria imperialis*], which I have tried three times with never a sign of life. When you have six months to wait, you value what you wait for, and during the long winter, when I can garden only in catalogues (an expensive operation), my thoughts turn often to what is waiting for me under the sod. And when the spring comes, and the summer, and the autumn, I shall be walking about all over the place, seeking for the first signs of old friends and looking eagerly for the strangers to see what they look like and what sort of clothes they wear. I repeat what Bacon said, that gardening "is the Purest of humane Pleasure. It is the Greatest Refreshment to the Spirits of Man."

The Outlook 116 (MAY 30, 1917): 229.

ENDNOTES

17. *Who Was Who in America, 1897–1942* 1 (Chicago, 1943), 20. In 1919 Almy was honored in a ceremony marking the twenty-fifth anniversary of his service to this organization, recounted in a professional journal for American social work: P. R. Lee, "Twenty-Five Years of It; The Social Service of Frederic Almy," *The Survey* 42 (May 24, 1919): 309–310.

18. Lee, "Twenty-Five Years of It," 310.

19. Abraham Cowley (1618–1667), *The Garden.*

20. Philosopher Francis Bacon (1561–1626) was the author of the well-known essay "Of Gardens"; Almy quotes its opening passage here.

21. Box and Cox were farcical characters in an 1867 operetta written by Sir Francis Cowley with music by Sir Arthur Sullivan. Cox worked all day and Box all night; their landlady cheated them by renting them both the same room (and bed), shrewdly calculating that they would not discover her trick because they would never be there at the same time.

22. According to a legend that is mentioned in several of Shakespeare's plays, and served as the inspiration of Alfred Lord Tennyson's "The Beggar Maid," King Cophetua was a misogynist African king who fell in love with and married a beggar maid.

23. The "evangelist Moody" whom Almy cites was Dwight Lyman Moody (1837–1899), a revivalist who preached what he called "the Old Time Gospel" in a six-month campaign during the Chicago World's Fair in 1893, and then in New York, Boston, Philadelphia, and other cities. He was a mentor to Billy Sunday (see above, 47).

Chapter Five

OLD-FASHIONED GARDENS

T HE ARTICLES in this chapter represent the old-fashioned garden more as a nostalgic trope of early twentieth-century garden writing than as an actual garden style. It was certain intangible qualities — a type of atmosphere — that gardeners sought to achieve through the use of flowers bearing quaint association, while trying to emulate their forebears' manners and attitudes of working and living in the garden. The authors suggest that life was in some ways better in past generations, that there were lessons to be learned from old gardens that could help reform modern America and restore some of the virtues of bygone days. They reveal how much gardeners longed for the kind of *charm*, *simplicity*, and *"liveableness"* that they were sure dignified the gardens of their grandparents. These imagined spaces became a peaceful dream world for Americans suffering from the quickened pace of modern, industrial life; they also served to reaffirm the gardeners' connection with their Anglo-American roots at a time when immigrants of different ethnic stock were entering the country in unprecedented numbers. The popularity of colonial revival homes inspired some gardeners to create what they believed were authentic period gardens. Lists of old-fashioned plants appear frequently in these articles; using plants that would conjure comforting associations, that would create a charming atmosphere, seems for the most part to have been more important than making historically accurate gardens.

❧ LOUISE BEEBE WILDER

Old-Fashioned Gardens That Continue to Charm

THE MOST COMMON THEME of early twentieth-century writings on the old-fashioned garden was that modern life lacked some of the finer attributes of the old, and that the inspiration of old-time gardens might help restore traditional values to American life. In this article Wilder ponders exactly what people mean when they speak of old-fashioned gardens.[1] After considering various historical possibilities, she decides that such gardens are probably illusionary, the "abode of peace," the friendly gardens we knew as children, and more the stuff of dreams than reality. On further consideration, though, she wonders if in fact there is not something more to it, if there were not some qualities possessed by old gardens that are missing in those of her day, despite the many clear advantages enjoyed by modern gardeners. Wilder believes that gardens were a more integral part of the family's daily life in earlier times, designed for leisure and comfort rather than the display of wealth. Like other authors writing on this subject, she presents an inventory of the plants thought to belong in an old-fashioned garden. Wilder understands the connection between American and British old-fashioned gardens; to define the "simple directness" of early American gardens, she quotes Reginald Blomfield writing about formal gardens in Britain.[2] Antiquarinism was rampant on both sides of the Atlantic in the late nineteenth and early twentieth centuries, and Americans often borrowed ideas and motifs from the English repertory of nostalgic design.

WHEN WE SPEAK of an "old-fashioned garden" just what, exactly, do we mean? It is one of those magic phrases that paints a picture in the mind, not one picture, indeed, but many, for the gardens of the past flowered into as many forms as men have been "diversely delighted." Utter the incantatory words and from out the mists may dimly loom a little walled inclosure close within the shadow of a grim monastery, where gentle monks tend a meager assemblage of herbs and roots. Here we find only plants of practical value, medicinal herbs and vegetables, for in those austere days gardening for beauty's sake was not followed — though beauty was there, but with other reasons than itself for being. Among the worthy "leekes" and potent "fenyl" smile gay red and white Roses, spread of Violets [*Viola*], brilliant Poppies [*Papaver*], "the great silver Lily," Primroses [*Primula*], Cowslips [*Primula veris*] — each, in those days, a "plant of virtue" prized for meat or medicine; and in the spring against the dark walls fluttered the blossoms of Cherry [*Prunus*] and Quince [*Cydonia oblonga*], Apple [*Malus*] and Pear [*Pyrus*].

Or perhaps we see a fair Tudor garden set forth with little beds in quaint patterns, "so enknotted it cannot be expressed," and

"With arbours and alleys so pleasant and so dulse
The pestilent airs with flavours to repulse."

This is a more spacious scene; the garden paths are wider and there are gracious terraces, and the parterres are embroidered with numerous "outlandish flours" lately crept in to "intice us to their delight." Here for the first time we see the Iris, not in the bewildering raiment of to-day, but meekly clad, the astonishing Tulipas from Turkey, the gorgeous Crown Imperial [*Fritillaria imperialis*] and the little Checker-lily [*Fritillaria meleagris*], Sweet Sultans [*Amberboa moschata*], Marigolds [*Tagetes*], Larkspurs, annual [*Consolida*] and perennial [*Delphinium*], Jacinths (Scilla), and Snowdrops [*Galanthus nivalis*], called Bulbous Violets, the Mock Orange [*Philadelphus*] and the Laburnum; and lowly Leek and Fennel are banished to a region of their own.

Or is the scene Victorian showing intricate beds charged with Geraniums [*Pelargonium x hortorum*] and Calceolarias in a very glare of insolence? In this garden we vainly seek the Hollyhocks [*Alcea rosea*] and Rockets [*Hesperis matronalis*], for all "such like old contraptions" are in hiding before the wrath of fashion, and sleek bedding is the order of the day.

For most of us, however, probably the old-fashioned garden is none of these, but merely some friendly garden known in childhood — a garden watched over by great trees, pervaded by loved forms, where Johnny-jump-ups [*Viola pendunculata*] played hide-and-seek among the Currant [*Ribes*] bushes; and inter-mingled Phlox and Tiger Lilies [*Lilium lancifolia*] boldly proclaimed each other's inferiority; where summer days were long and luscious fruit hung always within reach. This garden appears to us as the very abode of peace, and always old, restfully mature and settled, never by any chance as newly made and stark in the glare — though the oldest must have experienced this awkward age — and never was it subject to sudden changes of intention with subsequent disfiguring upheavals. Here, verily, God did not send us new flowers every year; we were as sure of the stout Peonies [*Paeonias*] as of the Rock of Gibraltar, the corner where the first Violets were to be found was ever the same, and the white Lilac [*Syringa vulgaris alba*] was a landmark. Of such a garden the poet sang,

> "And here on Sabbath mornings
> The goodman comes to get
> His Sunday nosegay — Moss Rose bud,
> White Pink, and Mignonette."

But whatever the picture invoked for us by the magic phrase, it is more dream stuff than reality — shadows lie in its corners and affection gilds its edges — and at the gate stands the Angel of Sentiment, waving us back when we would approach to obtain what the movie people call a "close up."

What were these old gardens like in reality? Is the spell they cast over us, even after many years, woven entirely of sentiment and time's silver cobwebs; or had they, in truth, qualities and characteristics that made them superior to the gardens of to-day? We have come a long road since monastic gardens were the only ones; a long way, even, since yesterday when our mothers exchanged roots of waxen Dahlias over the garden gate, and were satisfied with Hybrid Perpetual Roses and the old purple Flag Iris [*Iris versicolor*]. It is conceivable that in our haste to grasp all that the unwinding road disclosed, we have dropped a grace or two that we might well turn back and seek.

In many parts of the East, gardens made in the early days of our country still survive, and their charm is distinctly felt, even where neglect and decay have had their way. Many of these old gardens are what is termed formal in design, but how poorly the grandiloquent phrase indicates the simple direct-ness of their arrangement. "The characteristic of the old formal garden," writes Mr. Reginald Blomfield, "was its exceeding simplicity. The primary purpose of a garden as a place of retirement and seclusion, a place for quiet thought and leisurely enjoyment was kept steadily in view. The grass and the Yew [*Taxus*] trees were trimmed close to gain their full beauty from the sunlight. Sweet kindly flowers filled the knots and borders. Peacocks and pigeons brightened the terraces and lawns. The paths were straight and ample, the garden-house solidly built and comfortable; everything was reasonable and unaffected."

This is a pleasant picture. One can imagine the peaceful vistas along straight shadowed walks, suggestive of unhurried peregrinations from one point to another, rather than the awkward short cuts and labored windings that obtain in many gardens of to-day. Shade was of prime importance, and comfortable seats in shady places lured to work or repose in the open air. Often rows of white beehives, ranged beneath the Apple [*Malus*] or Pear [*Pyrus*] trees, gave a sense of line and intention to the riot of bloom about them, and a quaint dove-cote supplied a very creditable "architectural feature."

Such old gardens we feel were designed with reference to the daily life of the family, their convenience and enjoyment, rather than with any idea of display; and we know that much of the family life and activity took place, weather permitting, in the garden, thus impressing it with the personality and individuality that only use can bestow. Perhaps it is this "lived in" quality that we miss in modern gardens more than any other; for to-day, we do not live in our gardens — we work in them, we prowl about them inspectingly, we take our guests the rounds of them, but when it comes to sewing, or reading, meditating or entertaining guests at tea, we retire to the screened piazza, or some indoor fastness, so that the garden acquires the reserved atmosphere of the "best parlor," or the spare bedroom that seldom fulfills its destiny.

Richard Le Gallienne gave forth the discouraging opinion that a garden to be a garden must be old, "for a new garden, quite obviously, is not a garden at all."[3] But more *living* in the new garden, and planning it in the first place with a *view to living in it*, would go a long way toward putting the new garden in a class with the old, so far as atmosphere is concerned, and when it comes to the flowers themselves, there is no doubt that we are immeasurably richer and more intelligent than were the gardeners who have preceded us.

A modern garden touched with old-time grace. When the spirit of bygone days can be so rehabilitated and continued in the midst of whirring, modern suburban life — for this garden is but a score of miles from the "Big City" — it furnishes heartening assurance that beauty and not fashion guides the genuine gardener. Garden of the Misses Mulford, Hempstead, N.Y.

But let no one be of the opinion that early gardens were ill-furnished. In 1629 John Parkinson published his great "Paradisi In Sole," describing "all sorts of pleasant flowers which our English ayre will permitt to be noursed up," with sections devoted to the Kitchen Garden and the Orchard.[*] There are six hundred and twelve pages to the fine volume, and among them one may lose his way along many a fragrant by-path, astonished at the rare and lovely flowers he finds and envious of the old London Gardener's knowledge and skill. In March we find blooming in Parkinson's own garden "the double blew Hepatica and the white and the blush single, many sorts of Crocuses, double yellow Daffodils, Oriental Jacinths, the Crowne Imperiall, divers sorts of early Tulipas, some sorts of French Cowslips, both tawny, murry and blush, the early Fritillaria or checkered Daffodil, and some other sorts of early Daffodils and many sorts of Anemones." "In April," he continues, "commeth on the pride of these strangers," and enumerates forthwith such a list of treasures as will make gardeners who are satisfied with their April crop of a handful of Crocuses and Snowdrops and a few Daffodils, sit up and look to their laurels. Elsewhere in the great book he devotes one hundred and fourteen pages to the description of Tulips, "which are of so many different colours that it is almost impossible to express them." Also he describes 25 kinds of Daffodils, 22 Lilies, 31 Iris, 31 Crocuses, 8 Campanulas, 12 Fritillarias, 12 Clematis, 21 Primroses and a like profusion of Roses, Gillyflowers [*Matthiola*], and innumerable others.

Yes, undoubtedly there were plenty of flowers in the old-fashioned garden, but it is nevertheless true that we live in a world to-day where flowers are not only more numerous and various, but where the best of the old friends have been greatly improved and their sphere of usefulness much extended — here we have distinctly gained, not lost.

A few flowers cherished by an older day have disappeared and will perhaps, "no more know the dew of gardens;" others like Bouncing Bet [*Saponaria officinalis*] and the pretty blue-belled Rampion [*Campanula rapunculus*], have taken to the open road and rejoice in companions as free-thinking as themselves. The garden regrets them not. Some lovely old friends carelessly regarded by the present are worthy of being restored to favor. Notable among these are the old-fashioned Roses — York and Lancaster [*Rosa damascena cv. 'Versicolor'*], the Scotch Briers [*Rosa spinosissima*], the Province Rose, the Damask [*Rosa damascena*], Maiden's Blush, and the Persian Yellow [*Rosa foetida*], whose place is not filled even by the wonderful race of Hybrid Teas and the great variety of hardy Climbing Roses recently developed.

The little Star-of-Bethlehem [*Ornithogalum umbellatum*] is a charming flower of old gardens, now seldom seen, to which we might turn gratefully in the present shortage of bulbous plants. Double Rockets it would be pleasant to find more often and Fair Maids of France [*Saxifraga granulata*]; many fragrant herbs such as garden Valerian [*Valeriana*], Honesty [*Lunaria annua*] or White Satin, and others. It is rather sad, too, to find the stiff Japanese Spruce (*Pachysandra terminalis*) more and more asserting itself in shady places where once spread the fine dark green of the friendly little Periwinkle [*Vinca*] with its wide blue eyes so ready to gleam for us upon the first mild day in spring. Also I do not like the fat double Lilacs [*Syringa*] of to-day, and to my eye the Delphinium has a somewhat diminished grace and charm — put on flesh and lost its winsome curves — but on the whole there is little to complain of and much to rejoice in.

The Dahlia's advance from soap-like stolidity to the present exquisitely careless assemblage of petals is a triumph. Remember the terrible commotion of color that used to arise from a mixed packet of Zinnias, and consider the fine color-tones now to derived from the same source. Think upon the Iris! A whole book must needs be written to describe the wonders that have befallen this simple flower in recent times. And the Phlox, lifted from wayside indigence to its present grand estate! Who now sighs for the Sweet William [*Dianthus barbatus*] of other days when such splendid varieties as Newport Pink and Scarlet Beauty are grown? Nor has it lost, in its new guise, its "homely cottage smell," for which it has always been beloved. Consider the added ruffles of the Petunias; and the good clear colors, the exquisite tints to found in the augmented beauty of Sweet-peas [*Lathyrus odoratus*], Calendulas, Poppies [*Papaver*], Stocks [*Matthiola*], Columbines [*Aquilegia*], Michaelmas Daisies [*Aster novi-belgii*], Peonies [*Paeonia*], who must all be saying with the old lady in the nursery rhyme, "Can this be I?"

Consider, too, the great treasure that has come to us from foreign lands, to say nothing of that which lies within our own country which we are only lately coming to appreciate and to make use of. Undoubtedly it is a fine thing to be making gardens in this great twentieth century with its manifold advantages, but it is well to bear in mind that its greatest advantage lies in all that has gone before. Let us look attentively at the old gardens and try to endow our splendid new ones with the charm of their settled repose, their unaffected simplicity, their inviting livableness.

The Garden Magazine 34 (NOVEMBER 1921): 130–133.

ENDNOTES

1. On Wilder, see above, 98.

2. Blomfield promoted formal gardens in his book, *The Formal Garden in England* (London, 1892).

3. Richard Le Gallienne (1866–1947), was a poet, editor, and writer. In one of his magazine articles, "The Soul of a Garden," *House and Garden*

33 (March 1918): 19–20, he combined mystical nature religion and gardening in a manner typical of this period.

4. Parkinson (1567–1650) catalogued the plants cultivated during his lifetime in this important illustrated book.

Old-Time Charm in Gardens

REHMANN CONSIDERS how gardeners might recreate the magical charm associated with old gardens, how they might make gardens that look as if they have always been there.[5] Like Wilder, she briefly reminisces about an assortment of ancient, faraway gardens, culminating with old English cottage and cathedral gardens and colonial American gardens. She also supplies the reader with an ample list of plants "of charmed association" appropriate to the old-fashioned garden. But she cautions against trying to copy these old gardens, suggesting instead that gardeners try to adapt their spirit to the increased freedom enjoyed in the 1920s. Her observation that modern gardens are too neat, that gardeners should blur the edges a bit to make their gardens more charming, to make them appear antique, is another idea commonly found in articles about old-fashioned gardens. It is a romantic idea with a legacy extending back into the eighteenth century, when French artists were charmed by the disheveled, softened appearance of old, overgrown gardens in France and Italy.[6]

CHARM IN A GARDEN is an illusive mood, an intangible feeling, rather than an actuality. It is a condition dependent more upon the spirit of the garden than upon any of its varied elements. Charm is a sort of enchanted atmosphere that wraps itself around the garden and draws us within its spell. There is something magical about it for it may elude us, for all our endeavoring, and then again it may come quite unexpectedly without our really being conscious of it as though it were wrought of our very heartstrings.

Charm is a quality that we are wont to associate with old gardens, with gardens of bygone centuries, with gardens of far-away places, with gardens of other climes. The hanging gardens of Babylon have held us in their magic spell since their creation in the very haze of time. By Homer's description we know that the garden of Alcinous was as fair as any place Ulysses visited in his far journeying. Even now, the gardens of China and Japan are full of the witchery of strangeness.

The walled gardens of Madeira with their decorative fig-trees and their tropical vegetation, the gardens of Spain with their interwoven cypress arches,

Italian gardens with their singing waters and ilex walks hold enduring enchantment. In the paved courtyard of the Frans Hals Museum at Haarlem, one time Home for the Aged, the old-time parterre with its boxwood arabesques makes a quaint ornament for the red brick buildings.

The very mention of English cottage gardens has its delight born of tangled bloom and the fragrance of lavender [*Lavandula*]. Every cathedral town has its ever fascinating memories of gardens standing in the very embrace of the cathedrals themselves, though but little glimpses of them can be obtained through gateways. Mount Vernon casts a spell with each recurring visit and each recurring memory of its delightful surroundings. And boxwood [*Buxus*] gardens, in old and half-forgotten places of Colonial heritage, have their own witchery as if the very fragrance had penetrated their designs and made them poignant with the quaintness of days gone by. No reproductions of these gardens can bring back their enchantment. Copies become lifeless. They can become inspiring guides, however, for the shaping of new gardens so that the old spirit may be wrought in new and freer form adapted to our time and condition.

Some spots adapt themselves peculiarly to gardens. Orchards make happy settings for gardens; and fruit trees adapt themselves for backgrounds and find comfortable places inside the garden itself. It is, indeed, fortunate that their blossoming comes with that of bulbs and early flowers so that they may be associated with them in exquisite color effects.

Glades surrounded by birches [*Betula*] make fairy gardens. Sunken dells amid dogwood [*Cornus florida*], cedar [*Juniperus virginiana*]-girdled spots, tree-encircled places with interwoven sunlight and shadow make charmed gardens. A garden within walls or high hedges, a garden with hidden ways and secluded nooks for seats, a garden with a sense of mystery, a secret garden, may be wrought with witchery.

Certain familiar plants harbor charmed associations. None hold more than boxwood, for no other plant has its fragrance, none its wondrous green, none its exquisite texture. There is boxwood for every alluring garden desire. There are box-edged flower borders and alleys bordered with hedges of boxwood; there is boxwood in quaint scrolls and patterns, and boxwood in pyramidal form and in curiously clipped figures. There are boxwood bushes left all beautiful unclipped, and boxwood growing wondrously into feathery tree forms.

Lilacs [*Syringa*] are so dear to us that we question whether it is right to give them but a second place in such a list as this. They have become genial dwellers beside the farmhouse door and dignified associates of statelier buildings as well. They have become a veritable symbol of American domesticity. It is strange to think of them as foreign born. But so they are. They came to Flanders several centuries ago out of the Near East by way of Constantinople and hence across the ocean to our shore.

Snowberries [*Symphoricarpos alba*] are closely associated with our grand-mothers' gardens. Althaeas [*Hibiscus syriacus*] and snowballs [*Viburnum opulus 'roseum'*], mockoranges [*Philadelphus*] and bridalwreaths [*Spiraea prunifolia*] have many old-time qualities. Of the various vines, wisterias and honeysuckles [*Lonicera*], even more than climbing roses, have enchanting associations. Old-fashioned roses, sweet briers [*Rosa eglanteria*], moss roses [*Rosa centifolia*], China roses [*Rosa chinensis*], best of all Harison Yellow roses [*Rosa x harisonii*], have an old-time sorcery. The hybrid perpetual roses blooming with larkspur [*Consolida*] in New England doorway gardens have a charm quite their own.

And, what of the flowers that hold these allurements! Perhaps pinks [*Dianthus*] and sweet-williams [*Dianthus barbatus*] in all their motley colors are held in special favor. Then there are Canterbury-bells [*Campanula medium*] and foxgloves [*Digitalis purpurea*], bleedinghearts [*Dicentra spectabilis*] and valerian [*Valeriana*], stocks [*Matthiola*] and heliotropes [*Heliotropium*], peonies [*Paeonia*] and hollyhocks [*Alcea rosea*], zinnias and pot marigolds [*Calendula*], forget-me-nots [*Myosotis*] and violets [*Viola*], poet's narcissus and lilies-of-the-valley [*Convallaria*], and how many more!

Flowers of sweet perfume, more especially rose geranium [*Pelargonium capitatum*] and lemon verbena [*Aloysia triphylla*] breathe many an old-time memory. I have seen standard heliotrope [*Heliotropium*] rising out of beds of fragrant flowers in a tiny garden that was filled with charm.

Not only the flowers themselves count, but their very intermingling and their color. Flowers of mellow coloring, medleys of annuals, tumbling masses of chrysanthemums by old doorways are but a few suggestions that will surely wake a score of lovely pictures in your mind.

A garden ought to attain, even in its first years, some feeling of age for this alone may lend it charm. This aspect of a garden is sometimes due to making use of existing conditions. I have seen an old well with rough stone head and sweeping handle become the keynote of an old-fashioned garden. I have seen a spring house under spreading trees form a background for a garden whose coloring was as mellow as the gray stone. I have seen old arbor-vitae [*Thuja occidentalis*] hedges hold a garden in bewitching embrace.

I know a garden in a natural hollow where every curve lends itself to genial plant forms. I know a garden of concentric ovals that is full of quiet appeal, and another where old apple [*Malus*] trees upon the lawn give the encircling flower borders their grace.

This feeling of age is sometimes due to the use of old materials. Used and weathered bricks make delightful walks; broken flagging or field stones have an old and worn fascination; dry laid retaining walls soon acquire age; water-worn millstones have special allurements. Sometimes it is due to what might be called studied neglect, a learning to leave well enough alone. There may be a cherry tree [*Prunus*] in the midst of the border so that the prescribed scheme of flower arrangement gives way to a planting of ferns and funkias [*Hosta*], of meadowrues [*Thalictrum*] and columbines [*Aquilegia*], of violets and lilies-of-the-valley. Certain plants may be allowed to run wild and rampant; a lilac or a sweet-smelling hawthorn [*Crataegus*] may crowd out some precious flowers, a grapevine [*Vitis*] may trail luxuriously over a wall, a Rosa multiflora may become so rampant that it will trail into a syringa [*Philadelphus*] bush and shower it with delicate blossoms.

A bit of real untidiness may even be justified at times. Our gardens are apt to look too well swept. A rosy pool of fallen crabapple [*Malus*] petals or a snowy field of fallen plum [*Prunus*] blossoms may be welcome. Our gardens are apt to be too trim. Let the grass grow between the broken stone of the walks and let it be vernal grass so that you may crush it into fragrance under foot. Let a hundred little rock plants and trailers grow between the stones and let edging plants grow in tangled masses over the edges of the walks. For there is real charm in blurring the edges of a garden. It is these things that make a garden appear as if it had always been there.

The House Beautiful 56 (AUGUST 1924): 119.

ENDNOTES

5. For biographical information on Rehmann, see above, 86.

6. Virginia Tuttle Clayton, *Gardens on Paper: Prints and Drawings*, 1200–1900 (Washington, D.C., 1990), 127–134.

ꙮ E. P. POWELL
Grandmother's Garden

EDWARD PAYSON POWELL was a Congregationalist minister and a journalist. He was born in Clinton, New York, in 1833, graduated from Union Theological Seminary in 1858, and was ordained in 1861.[7] He joined the staff of *The Independent* and began writing editorials in 1900, maintaining this position through the glory days of that magazine. Among his books were *The Country Home* (1904) and *How to Live in the Country* (1911). Toward the end of his life he resided in Sorrento, Florida; he died there about two weeks after the publication of this article.[8] It is a wistful remembrance of the gardens of his youth — his grandmother's garden, which would probably have been made around 1800. Having reached the age of eighty-three, he is not so sure that gardening is getting better. The simplicity of the old gardens is what he longingly recalls, the flowers and the old roses. He yearns to go back in time and find peace in gardens presided over by the old grandmothers, remembering them as old-fashioned settings for family gatherings, and that it was "with flowers that they bound the folk together, and with flowers that they trained the children."

W E ARE NOT QUITE SURE that we have been making progress of a genuine sort all thru these years since gardens stopped being grandmotherly. In our own gardens things climb over each other to get a breath of air and a streak of sunshine. Grapes and passion vines twist together, and on our verandas a rose can scarcely get leave to exist. The old-fashioned garden had an old-fashioned formality about it, to be sure, but it did not have any more varieties than could be talked over by the grannies when they visited each other.

Of all plants these ladies loved best pinks [*Dianthus*] and sweet peas [*Lathyrus odoratus*]. The sweet peas were of the old style, and sweet they were. They ran over brush until they got to the trellis or clothes line, and there they built a hedge hard to beat. One might smell them thru the whole garden, the odor mingled with that of honeysuckles [*Lonicera*] just across the path. We like to take a whole lap full to school; we mean we used to like to do it, to Lucy; and she, on the sly, would give us as many kisses as one might count while the schoolma'am's back was turned. It was a good thing that floors creaked in those days, and one might know when to be on the sly. Does anybody know where we can find a bunch of the old genuine grass pinks [*Dianthus plumarius*]; I mean the roots?

Tulips and jonquils came next in favor, and with them, of course, were the golden daffodils. We always did love tulips and always will. It is a wonderful flower, because you can have so many of them. If you will but stick them into your strawberry bed, they will come up and blossom and then get out of the way before the strawberries need the sunshine and the dews. So one may have two of the finest things in the world combined. There is a dignity about this flower, and then there is a certain dignity of character in the jonquil — but we think not so much of it. The spicy flavor varies almost as much as the striping and the spotting. We love all this group, and in our northern garden never can get too many of them. An old tulip couch, where hundreds of them have been cultivated, will never wear out. The bulbs multiply for years after the ground has been turned to sod, and up comes the memory of old gardens, laughing thru the meadow grass, daffodils winking with the dandelions.

As we remember the old garden, there was abundant color in all seasons. Somewhere these dear old women had got a sunflower that was not big enough to grow for chicken feed, and they were growing them along the grape arbors. They were not so bad after all for bouquets, for a single flower was allowed to fill the whole dish. Carrot leaves were already exquisitely beautiful in those days, but I do not remember that beets had become crimson leaved, or that the vegetable garden was valued for its florescence — with one exception. If you must know what one flower of our grandmother still best holds its own it is that wonderful pickle flower, the nasturtium [*Tropaeolum majus*]. A wonderful sweet flower, teasing you with all sorts of color, and asking only the poorest soil, the "sturtion" still is worthy of highest praise.

These dear grandmothers did not know the pansy [*Viola x wittrockiana*], but they got on very well without it, so long as they had the johnnie-jump-up [*Viola pedunculatum*]. We do not know whether this little flower was the parent of the gorgeous pansy or not, but we do know that it is one of the sweetest and prettiest little letters of the alphabet. A small bunch of them would serve for a buttonhole bouquet, and they did nicely in saucers placed in our bedrooms.

There were two or three kinds of roses only, but truly we would like to see all of these brought back once more into the garden. How many of our readers remember the cinnamon rose [*Rosa cinnamomea*]? It was not large, but it had a nice color, and that real raggedness that goes with abundant flowering. The cinnamon rose stood in the corner of the fence, out of the way, and just blossomed all over.

Down here in Florida we have the Cherokee rose [*Rosa laevigata*], that grows all over the houses of the "darkies," and covers our sheds and hen houses, but it is not quite up to the cinnamon rose. Lower down, not more than two feet high, generally bordering the path to the street, and mixed in with the red and white peonies [*Paeonia*], was the Thousand-to-one rose [*Rosa centifolia*]. That means a rose that gave a thousand petals to every blossom. We never counted them, but really those roses were huge and sweet and should never have gone out of fashion. They were also called cabbage roses. We have them still, growing along with Druskies and Marechal Neils; but we have no longer, alas! either the grandmother or the mother. We wonder if they are still cultivating roses in Paradise.

A little later there came about two climbing roses: the Baltimore Belle and the Queen of the Prairies. Bless us! but how these did win the hearts of our mothers! I have a Baltimore Belle modestly covering a whole shed roof, and yielding in May such bunches of sweetness and delicacy as fascinated my forbears. The Queen of the Prairies is a bit coarser, but it is a great thing, all thru the farmyards where it can be allowed to cover a stump or climb a fence.

We could talk a good while longer about this dear old garden, where we used to lie down by the side of a brook and pick watercress; or sit on a stone and patter our feet in the water for the fish to nibble; but as we remember it we see just now only one more flower as notable as those we have named, or nearly so. It grew high upon the banks next to the house. We wonder how often some little girl or boy pulled open the gate and modestly begged for a "piny." Some said "pinny," and for that matter it did no harm, as grandmother herself always said "pinies." How proud a day it was when a magnificent double white was planted alongside the superb old crimson!

To be sure, the world has improved, and as for the new flowers there is no end of them; yet there come times when the world needs a rest, a sort of general world sleep. We would like to see all the old grandmothers back again for a spell, and in full charge of the houses and gardens. They deserve it; did they not do well enough to give them a longer lease of life? We were happy under their rule. Yes! let us go back and be at peace.

And now, as we look back, we see there was this about those old time gardens, that they were drawing-rooms for friendly intercourse; they were not reserved for flowers alone, but for folk also. Best of all was the kindly intercourse, the exchange of garden lore, and the rich delight of sharing what one most enjoyed. The world was very small in those days and the people got together in their churches and their gardens, without hearing every time about the Republic of China and the thirty thousand importations by the Department of Agriculture. It was altogether more like a single home, where one sweet soul could grandmother a whole community. Her herbs went to every sick chamber and pinches of sweet william seed made all the young mothers more cheerfully start out in life. It was with flowers that they bound the folk together, and with flowers that they trained the children.

The Independent 82 (April 26, 1915): 145.

ENDNOTES

7. A photograph of Powell relaxing in a hammock appears in another article he wrote: "Laying Out a Country Home," *House and Garden* 8 (November 1905): 194.

8. *New York Times* (obituary), May 15, 1915, 13:6; *Who Was Who in America 1897–1942* 1 (Chicago, 1943), 988.

[Elisabeth Woodbridge Morris]

The Contributors' Club: Escaped from Old Gardens

ELISABETH WOODBRIDGE MORRIS was born in Brooklyn, New York, in 1870; in 1898 she was one of the first women to receive a Ph.D. from Yale University. She taught English and history at Vassar and later wrote articles for magazines, as well as plays, essays, and books.[9] In her essays Morris made frequent reference to her ancestor, theologian Jonathan Edwards. This article, "Escaped from Old Gardens," was later included in *The Jonathan Papers* (1912), the first compilation of her natural history essays originally published in *Outlook*, *Atlantic*, and *Scribner's*. It is an evocative portrayal of sentiments that helped popularize the old-fashioned garden in the early twentieth century. More eloquently phrased than Powell's article, it is equally persuasive that old gardens are emblematic of a more "leisurely, decorous, well-considered" life, one that had "faith in an established order and an assured future." Unlike Powell, she does not claim to have actually known such gardens when they were new; like Rehmann, she prefers the shabby, softened aspect of the old, enchanted garden she has discovered. For Morris the garden, though physically real, has become in its abandonment more akin to Wilder's illusory abodes of peace, a dream world in which to escape the wearisome realities of life. At the end of the article she declares that she would herself choose to be forgotten, as the old garden has been, and to remain dreaming in it forever. Using the garden as a literary device for conjuring a solitary, visionary realm of tranquility and contentment, she has followed a tradition dating to at least the beginning of the eighteenth century; the early poetry of Alexander Pope linked gardens and dreams and may have served to influence the subsequent development of the English landscape garden. [10]

IN THE DAYS WHEN I deemed it necessary to hunt down in my well-thumbed Gray every flower of wood and field, and fit it to its Latin name, I used often to meet this phrase.[11] At first, being young, I resented it. I scorned gardens: their carefully planned and duly tended splendors were not for me.

PLATE 12. *House and Garden,* February 1916
Illustration by Ruth Eastman

PLATE 13. *House and Garden,* June 1918
Illustration by Charles Livingston Bull

PLATE 14. *House and Garden*, August 1916

Illustration by E. F. Betts Bains

PLATE 15. *The House Beautiful*, April 1917
Illustration by Norman Kennedy

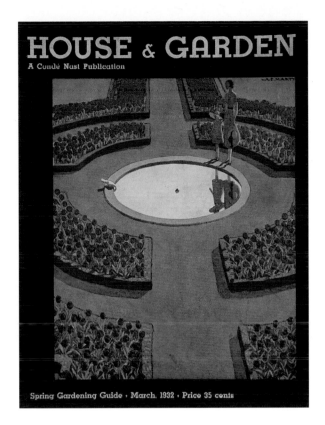

PLATE 16. *House and Garden*,
March 1932
Illustration by A. E. Marty
Courtesy *House and Garden*. Copyright ©
March 1932 (renewed 1960) by the Condé Nast
Publications, Inc.

PLATE 17. *The Garden Magazine*,
April 1924
Illustration by Carl E. Johnson

PLATE 18. *Country Life in America*, August 1926
Illustration by Frank Hazell

PLATE 19. *House Beautiful*, August 1933
Illustration by
Marjorie Hargens

Reprinted by permission from *House Beautiful*. Copyright © August 1933. The Hearst Corporation. All Rights Reserved.

PLATE 20. *House Beautiful*, May 1935

Illustration by Leon Carroll

PLATE 21. *House Beautiful*, May 1934

Illustration by Leon Carroll

Reprinted by permission from *House Beautiful*. Copyright © May 1934.
The Hearst Corporation. All Rights Reserved.

The orchid [*Cypripedium*] in the deep woods or by the edge of the lonely swamp, the rare and long-sought heather [*Erica*] in the open moorland, these it was that roused my ardor. And to find that some newly discovered flower was not a wild flower at all, but merely a garden flower "escaped"! The very word carried a hint of reprobation.

But as the years went on, the phrase gathered to itself meanings vague and subtle. I found myself welcoming it and regarding with a warmer interest the flower so described. From what old garden had it come? What associations and memories did it bring out of the past? Had the paths where it grew been obliterated by the encroachments of a ruthless civilization, or had the tide of human life drawn away from it and left it to be engulfed by the forest from which it had once been wrested, with nothing left to mark it but a gnarled old lilac [*Syringa*] tree? I have chanced upon such spots in the heart of the wood, where the lilac and the apple [*Malus*] tree and the old stoned cellar-wall are all that are left to testify to the human life that once centred there. Or had the garden from which its seed was blown only fallen into a quiet decay, deserted but not destroyed, left to bloom unchecked and untended, and fling its seeds to the summer winds that its flowers might "escape" whither they would?

Lately, I chanced upon such a garden. I was walking along a quiet roadside, almost dusky beneath the shade of close-set giant maples [*Acer*], when an unexpected fragrance breathed upon me. I lingered, wondering. It came again, in a warm wave of the August breeze. I looked up at the tangled bank beside me — surely, there was a spray of box [*Buxus*] peeping out through the tall weeds! There was a bush of it — another! Ah! it was a hedge, a box hedge! Here were the great stone steps leading up to the gate, and here the old, square-capped fence posts, once trim and white, now sunken and silver gray. The rest of the fence was lying among the grasses and goldenrod [*Solidago*], but the box still lived, dead at the top, its leafless branches matted into a hoary gray tangle, but springing up from below in crisp green sprays, lustrous and fragrant as ever, and richly suggestive of the past that produced it. For the box implies not merely human life, but human life on a certain scale, leisurely, decorous, well-considered. It implies faith in an established order and an assured future. A beautiful box hedge is not planned for immediate enjoyment, it is built up inch by inch through the years, a legacy to one's heirs.

Beside the gate posts stood what must once have been two pillars of box. As I passed between them my feet felt beneath the matted weeds of many seasons the broad stones of the old flagged walk that led up through the garden to the house. Following it, I found, not the house, but the wide stone blocks of the old doorsteps, and beyond these, a ruin — gray ashes and blackened brick, two great heaps of stone where the chimneys had been, with the stone slabs that lined the fireplaces fallen together. At one end was the deep stone cellar filled now with young beeches [*Fagus grandifolia*] as tall as the house once was. Just outside stood two cherry [*Prunus*] trees close to the old house-wall — so close that they had burned with it and now stood, black and bare and gaunt, in silent comradeship. At the other end I almost stumbled into the old well, dark and still, with a glimmer of sky at the bottom.

But I did not like the ruin, nor the black well lurking in the weeds and ashes. The garden was better, and I went back to it and followed the stone path as it turned past the end of the house and led, under another broad hedge of box now choked by lusty young maples, to the old rose-garden. Beyond were giant lilacs, and groups of waxberry [*Symphoricarpos alba*] bushes covered with the pretty white balls that children love to string; there was the old-fashioned "burning-bush," [*Euonymus atropurpurea*] already preparing its queer, angled berries for autumn splendors. And among these, still holding their own in the tangle, clumps of the tall, rose-lilac phloxes that the old people seem specially to have loved, swayed in the light breeze and filled the place with their heavy, languorous fragrance.

Truly, it is a lovely spot, my old garden, lovelier perhaps, than when it was in its golden prime, when its hedges were faultlessly trimmed and its walks were edged with neat flower borders, when their smooth flagging-stones showed never a weed, and even the little heaps of earth piled up, grain by grain, by the industrious ants, were swept away each morning by the industrious broom. Then human life centred here, now it is very far away. All the sounds of the outside world come faintly to this place and take on its quality of quiet — the lowing of cows in the pastures, the shouts of men in the fields, the deep, vibrant note of the railroad train which goes singing across distances where its rattle and roar fail to penetrate. It is very still here. Even the birds are quieter, and the crickets and the katydids less boisterous. The red squirrels move warily through the tree-tops with almost a chastened air, the black and gold butterflies flutter indolently about the heads of the phlox, a humming-bird, flashing green, hovers about some be-lated blossom-heads of the scarlet bee-balm [*Monarda didyma*], and then, as if to point the stillness, alights on an apple-twig, looking, when at rest, so very small! Only the cicada, as he rustles clumsily about with his paper wings against the flaking bark and yellowing leaves of an old apple tree, seems unmindful of the spell of silence that holds the place.

And the garden is mine now — mine because I have found it, and every one else, as I like to believe, has forgotten it. Next to it is a grove of big old trees — would they not have been cut down years ago if any one had remembered them? And on the other side is a meadow whose thick grass, waist-high, ought to have been mowed last June and gathered into some dusky, fragrant barn. But it is forgotten, like the garden, and will go leisurely to seed out there in the sun; the autumn winds will sweep it and the winter snow will mat down its dried tangle.

Forgotten — and as I lie in the long grass, drowsy with the scent of the hedge and the phlox, I seem only a memory myself. If I stay too long I shall forget to go away, and no one will remember to find me. In truth, I feel not unwilling that it should be so. Could there be a better place? "Escaped from old gardens"! Ah, foolish, foolish flowers! If I had the happiness to be born in an old garden, I would not escape. I would stay there, and dream there, forever!

Atlantic Monthly 101 (JUNE 1908): 859.

ENDNOTES

9. *New York Times* (obituary), April 3, 1964, 33:2; *Who Was Who Among North American Authors*, 1038.

10. John Dixon Hunt, *The Figure in the Landscape: Poetry, Painting, and Gardening during the Eighteenth Century* (Baltimore, 1976), 58–104.

11. Morris is referring to Asa Gray's (1810–1888) *Manual of the Botany of the Northern United States* (New York, 1859).

✍ A. CLINTON
Our Old Timey Garden

THIS STORY FURTHER reveals the range of emotional responses conjured up by old-fashioned gardens. That such gardens were prized as evidence of "a sort of ancestry" indicates that early twentieth-century Americans longed to securely connect themselves with their past, an understandable reaction to the rapid and unsettling changes of their era. Possession of old gardens, like colonial houses and antiques, came to embody a new form of social snobbery. Celia Betsky has commented on this desire for a material heritage in connection with colonial revival interiors: "The new religion was 'ancestor worship.' The domestic interior was supposed to house genealogical prestige . . . A kind of nobility of native origins evolved as the fear of foreign immigration grew."[12] And yet the couple depicted in this article seem innocent of the invidious, nativist attitudes this anxiety might generate; they experience pure delight in their newly inherited treasure.

WE HAD COME into our inheritance. Lydian said she had always desired to be an heiress, but had never expected to have her longings satisfied, even in a small way, until the inheritance was established on the firm foundation of the lawyer's word for it.

The inheritance was ours, however, for Great Aunt had been gathered to her fathers, leaving her possessions to her "next of kin," and our identity having been established, we moved in: Lydian and I.

We had found the house, its hospitable, inviting door with its trellis covered with vines, seeming to smile a welcome as we faced it on a dreary spring morning. It really reached forth a friendly hand with a "Glad to see you" sort of an air, to which our whole hearts responded.

The view from the side windows we knew at a glance would be a never-ending delight, for they overlooked a meadow that stopped only at the bank of a turbulent brook, filled full to the brim from the melting of winter's ice and snow.

Then, too, there was the barn, standing a little back, with its roof rambling off onto sheds like a prosperous, established head of a family who reaches out to gather in kin-folks. The sheds were a sort of general utility receptacles, judging from the accumulation of rakes, hoes, spades and an erect, green wheelbarrow which (with its alertness and shine) seemed to invite and expect us to readily know it to be one of the most important factors in the inheritance.

"Oh," said Lydian, "there must be a garden, for here are all the garden implements. I do hope it is a real old timey one, for there is nothing in this world that makes for real joy and self-respect like being the owner of a garden that has won for itself the recognition of establishment. It's a sort of ancestry, don't you know?"

And so we looked next for the garden! "Did we find it?"

A long drawn sigh from Lydian told me she was sure and satisfied that the garden was a real old timey one. There it was on the south side of the house and beyond the barn, two sides bordered with box [*Buxus*] and giving out the most delightful odors of misty dampness. Never can there be another perfume quite equal to that to a genuine garden lover.

Yes, the garden was old timey, and Lydian and I rambled in it and reveled in it, too, peeping under leaves and twigs, longing to see what possibilities there were in store for us, yet not daring to rudely awaken the inhabitants out of their winter naps, or to remove the coverings for fear of colds or chills. But the progressive garden folk did not need to be reminded that the awakening time had come, for soon from beds and borders came leaf and bud reaching up to the light and sunshine in response to the vernal coaxing of Mother Nature, who knows so well when to tuck her earth children away in their restful beds and when to call them forth to newness of life and renewed activity. Oh, the dear garden! sighed Lydian rapturously, as she took deep breaths of the pure odorous air, looking over the box borders into the walks beyond.

But the first impressions were as nothing compared with the later and richer experiences! Those experiences of picking our own roses or gathering our hands full of the beautiful lilies of the valley [*Convallaria*] that we might have them for a feast of delight on our own breakfast, luncheon or dinner table. And, if perchance a friendly guest sang the praises of such fine flowers, we have the pleasure of assuring him they were grown in our own garden and under our own encouragement at that. One who has tried even in a small way to grow a few asters, pansies [*Viola x wittrockiana*], or hollyhocks [*Alcea rosea*], knows the joy.

The House Beautiful 29 (MARCH 1911): 126.

ENDNOTES

12. Celia Betsky, "Inside the Past: The Interior and the Colonial Revival in American Art and Literature, 1860–1914," *The Colonial Revival in America*, ed. Alan Axelrod (New York, 1985), 265–266.

H. STUART ORTLOFF
The Gardens of Our Grandmothers

HENRY STUART ORTLOFF was a landscape architect born in Syracuse, New York, in 1896. He attended Massachusetts State College and Columbia University, later lived in Arlington, Vermont, and died in 1971.[13] Ortloff frequently contributed articles to *House and Garden* and *Country Life in America*, writing eight books, most of them coauthored by H. B. Raymond. By the 1920s the popularity of colonial-style homes had grown tremendously as result of the colonial revival, and many owners were eager to adorn them with the proper period furnishings and gardens. In Ortloff's article we find the most significant ideas associated with old-fashioned gardening in horticultural journalism of the day. There is, for example, the underlying assumption that earlier generations were endowed with virtues now fast disappearing among Americans, and that these forebears — and their gardens — should be models for contemporary citizens. There is a telling repetition of certain words and phrases that convey this idea: "simplicity"; "charm and simplicity"; "dignity"; "sweet, simple dignity"; "proud colonial ancestry." Ortloff, like other authors, advises that it is not the plant material that makes an old-fashioned garden successful, but the spirit in which it is planned, the *simplicity and feeling* with which the design is imbued. He agrees with the consensus that the gardens of our ancestors were meant to be lived in, that they promoted what today's politicians like to call "family values."

THE PRESENT-DAY DESIRE for remodeled and reconstructed old houses of good Colonial design has, in a measure, brought back to us the charm and simplicity of those earlier days when beauty and utility went hand in hand. With the demand for this type of house comes the desire for a garden which will be in keeping and in character with it, so we turn back to consider the quaint old gardens which were the joy of our grandmothers. We still admire their stateliness and simplicity, delighting in the old garden favorites which have survived the passage of time and are still able to trace their dignified ancestry to the seeds and bulbs procured under many difficulties to enhance the beauty of those first gardens in a new country.

The colonial garden was usually in close proximity to the house. There were two good reasons for this: one was that the cultivation of it depended upon the moments in the day which the busy housewife could spare from her many household tasks in order to work among her flowers and keep it trim and neat. The other was that a garden near the house was more easily utilized as an outdoor room, a place to rest a bit while doing some small household task, darning perhaps, or to have tea with a neighbor, or to keep a watchful eye from indoors when the children were out to play.

The stern religion of the very early settlers forbade gardens for pleasure, but fortunately kitchen gardens escaped this ban by their practicality. Many of the pleasing Colonial examples of gardening had birth in such a humble manner, for as the spirit of the times grew less severe these little gardens were added to, until the host of flowers far outshone the more humble vegetables.

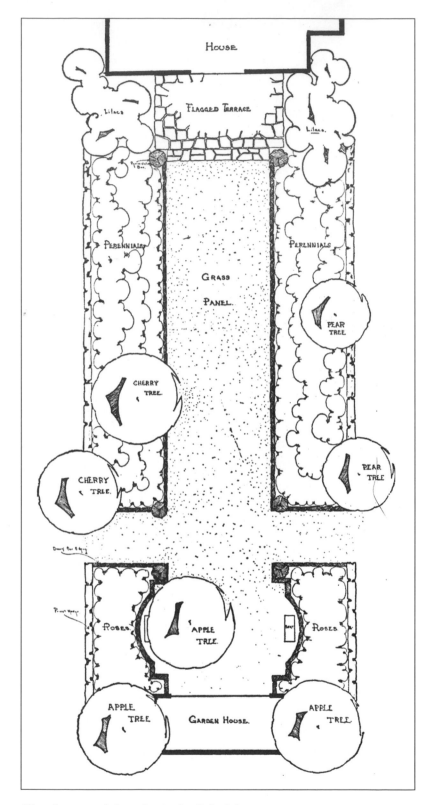

Plan for a paneled garden in the Colonial manner.

At the same time many of these quaint little gardens, which make such admirable settings for Colonial houses, had their beginnings in the stiff, formal borders which lined the still more stiff and formal approach to the front door, leading across the little fenced-in "front yard," and used only on state occasions, such as the minister's call or funerals. Time changes all things, and so these little gardens gradually lost their stiff primness and took on the quiet and kindly dignity of their mistresses, qualities which in spite of present-day fashions and appearances we still admire and strive to obtain in the present gardens of Colonial spirit.

The design of these gardens of the olden days was usually very simple, a favorite form being a broad grass path or panel, banked at either side with masses of flowering things, and terminated by a gazebo — a garden house — or by a trellis of quaint and simple design, usually in keeping with the architecture of the house, although sometimes it was built in the rustic manner and thatched. In other instances the design was more intricate, with paths more narrow and laid in accordance with a set design, usually around some central motive, such as a well-head, a sun-dial, or a large tree with a garden seat around its trunk; or perhaps the much used summerhouse was located in such a spot, where it could command a view in all directions.

These summerhouses or arbors were the parents of the popular pergola, and were usually of very simple construction, but with a kindly care of details in post, rafter, and finial which put them in a class by themselves far above the machine-made things of the present. Such houses provided ample shade for comfortable furniture, making the garden a place to live in as well as a place to be preserved. Vines crept up over and embowered them until they seemed a very part of the garden, springing like their neighbors, the flowers, from the soil.

Still another interesting characteristic of these gardens was the use of trees. True, for the most part they were fruit trees, whose chief importance was the increasing of the family larder, yet their value was even greater, for they gave abundant shade and a wealth of bloom in spring, while in winter when the snow and ice had given them regal garments, they traced fantastic shadows on the snow-covered garden walk. As a result of these utilitarian plantings, many old gardens are secure in their charm by interesting rows and groups of gnarled trees with far flung branches. These seem to have a more permanent air about them than many of the gardens we see to-day, which are apt to appear flat and uninteresting, not only because they lack the dignity and age of these old gardens, but because they do not depend upon their simplicity for their charm.

The broad panel or central path, in fact nearly all the paths, were bordered with box [*Buxus*], whose pungent odor and evergreen beauty have long made it a favorite for edgings, and in its old and rugged age it still marks the boundaries of old gardens; in many instances it has become so overgrown that is has crowded out both path and bed. Sometimes it was impossible to use box, and low-growing plants were used as substitutes. Creeping phlox [*Phlox stolonifera*], grass pinks [*Dianthus plumarius*], with their dense tufts of gray-green foliage, or even the shrubby aromatics so dear to the hearts and essential to the welfare of our ancestors, such as thyme [*Thymus*], savory [*Satureja*], lavender [*Lavandula*], hyssop [*Hyssopus*], and sage [*Salvia*], were close clipped into tiny hedges to stem the tide of bloom which otherwise might overflow and fill the pathway.

Behind these edgings ranged the old-time favorites, each with its attendant tale of interest concerning whence and how it came to be among its gay fellows, for it was the custom to exchange slips and seeds, and presents of bulbs and new plants were always esteemed. The present-day nursery which supplies our wants being almost unknown, it was difficult to obtain new and interesting things.

Around the whole garden, in order to make it more secluded and adaptable to the intimate life of the family and friends, and also to keep out stray dogs or cattle, was a fence, wall, or hedge. The fences of those days were usually of picket, in a few instances walls of masonry and brick were used, but for the most part the walls were low, four or five feet in height, and made of the rough boulders and rocks from near-by hills and far lands. These were fitted together with such skill that many of them have withstood the rigors of passing time and still stand as landmarks of garden progress, and memorials to the skill of the old time workman. Vines clambered over the walls and small plants sprung from crevices where some wind-blown seed had found a lodging and covered the bare rocks with garments of a green and gay color. Hedges were not common in the very old garden because it was rather difficult to secure adequate material for them. Privet [*Ligustrum*] was not common until much later, although it was used and grew steadily in favor, but lilacs [*Syringa*], Rose of Sharon [*Hibiscus syriacus*], and other shrubs were used more or less successfully. Box was given the place of honor in evergreen hedges, but it was only in the South that it grew luxuriantly and with sufficient rapidity to be effective; but cedars [*Juniperus virginiana*], hemlock [*Tsuga canadensis*], and arborvitae [*Thuja occidentalis*] attained prominence in the North as substitutes. Nowhere were these hedges as effective or as much in keeping with the times as the fences, which when wreathed in vines became quite gardenesque.

Inside the fence or hedge were placed the taller growing things, the snowball [*Virburnum opulus 'roseum'*], calycanthus, with its odd brown blossoms and pungent odor, purple and white lilacs, with here and there a Persian variety [*Syringa persica*], the sweet scented mock orange [*Philadelphus*], the rose of Sharon, and in many instances native shrubs from the woodlands — viburnum, clethra, sumac [*Rhus*], azaleas [*Rhododendron*], and many others. Our Colonial forebears were very early in not only appreciating native flora, but in realizing that there was demand in Europe for such oddities, and many a ship carried over a snug bundle of plants in exchange for Old World seeds and plants, and other necessaries.

These tall flowering shrubs made excellent background for the display of the perennials which were planted in front of them. It is impossible to enumerate all of the things which were planted, many of them having disappeared or been so changed by the hybridizer that they are unrecognizable, but here are many survivors which are still reigning favorites. It is, however, a mistake to seek only for the flowers our grandmothers knew, for they were very progressive ladies for their times. They searched long and

In designing old-fashioned gardens new varieties should not be excluded. It is the spirit rather than the letter — the old-time atmosphere — that we should seek to reproduce, making use of present-day improved descendants of our grandmothers' flowers.

laboriously for the best within their means in order that their gardens might be more complete and more beautiful. Because they, for instance, only knew the flaunting red "piny" [*Paeonia*] is not reason why we should not use the soft creamy whites and delicate pinks which the horticulturist has developed in this flower. You may rest assured that if these had existed a hundred or more years ago our grandmothers would have left no stone unturned to avail themselves of such wonderful treasures.

We should, therefore, in designing old-fashioned gardens, not exclude the new varieties; we should endeavor to catch the spirit in which our grandmothers gardened. One of the ways to do this is to consider plants in groups and to select from our present-day store like material so that they will blend together with the old things and not seem new and obtrusive. For instance, in the old days the back of the border was made gay with the spires of hollyhocks [*Alcea rosea*], foxgloves [*Digitalis purpurea*], garden heliotrope [*Heliotropium*] or valerian [*Valeriana*], and wonderful masses of larkspur [*Consolida*], sweet rocket [*Hesperis matronalis*], perhaps the taller growing veronica, and Canterbury bells [*Campanula medium*]. Today we might add to these the heleniums, the tall chimney flower [*Campanula pyramidalis*], the aster (that is the perennial sorts), and all the hardy chrysanthemums; such things would have been prized not only for their range of color but also for their brilliant blaze of autumn bloom.

The middle ground of these old gardens was made gay with peonies, iris, phlox, lychnis, all of which have been developed into larger and more beautifully colored flowers, still maintaining, however, their proud Colonial ancestry. Wall flowers [*Erysimum cheiri*] with their yellow, red, and brown flowers, and the sweet scented gas plant, fraxinella [*Dictamnus*], were there in numbers, and it is sad to feel that these are fast disappearing through lack of use.

Lilies were exceedingly popular; there were not as many as we have today, but it possible to include all of the hardy ones in our list, for the tall stems adorned with delicate blooms were treasures often procured from distant parts by the old sea captains, and even the native wood lilies [*Lilium philadelphicum*] were transplanted into the garden. There were large clumps of the day lily [*Hemerocallis*] in many New England gardens, and in some places it has escaped from cultivation and strayed far along the dusty roadside. Roses there were, but not in the profusion of varieties as we know them now, for there were no hybrid teas or perpetuals. The York and Lancaster roses [*Rosa damascena cv. 'versicolor'*] with their red, white, and particolored blooms, the hundred-leaved rose, Rosa centifolia, the old damask rose [*Rosa damascena*], and the cabbage rose [*Rosa centifolia*] found favor. Imagine the rapture that Los Angeles or Ophelia would have created.

The lesser plants behind the trim borders in the old gardens were such things as pansies — Johnny-jump-ups [*Viola pedunculata*] they were then called — four o'clocks [*Mirabilis jalapa*], pinks [*Dianthus*], poppies [*Papaver*], ten-week stocks [*Matthiola incana cv. 'annua'*], grass pinks, asters, candytuft [*Iberis*], and balsam [*Impatiens*], but we have hundreds more to use and fill the spaces between the large plants with myriads of bloom. Nasturtiums [*Tropaeolum majus*], heliotrope, petunias, marigolds [*Tagetes*], and all the rest would have created a mild sensation in our grandmothers' day.

Bulbs were greatly valued, but unfortunately only a few tulips, narcissus, crown imperials (*Frittilaria imperialis*), snowdrops [*Galanthus nivalis*], and grape hyacinths [*Muscari*] were known. There were no Darwins, no vast procession of daffodils, no hyacinths as we know them, yet had there been they would all have found a ready home in some trim Colonial garden, where they would have ordered out stern winter and ushered in delightful spring much earlier.

So it is not the plant material which makes a successful old-fashioned garden, but rather the spirit in which we plan and plant it. It is the simplicity and feeling which we put into the design. It is the personal, loving touch which we bestow on each growing thing which brings to mind the sweet, simple dignity of Colonial days and creates for us the proper atmosphere and setting for our home in Colonial taste.

Country Life in America 44 (JUNE 1923): 74–75.

ENDNOTES

13. *Who's Who in America* 5, (Chicago, 1973), 548.

Antique Hunting Among the Plants

PARTAKING DEEPLY in the spirit of the colonial revival, Margaret McKenny purchased a two-hundred-year-old house on the Long Island Sound in Connecticut and filled it with appropriate furnishings to restore "the atmosphere of Colonial days." Her friend Harry, a landscape architect, then assisted her in creating a suitable garden. This article, with the enthusiasm it expresses for correct period gardens, is roughly contemporary with the restoration for public exhibition of Colonial Williamsburg and its gardens, and the publication of the Garden Club of America's *Gardens of Colony and State: Gardens and Gardeners of the American Colonies and of the Republic Before 1840.*[14] McKenny, born in Olympia, Washington, was associated with the City Garden Clubs of America in New York. With Roger Tory Peterson she coauthored *A Field Guide to Wildflowers of Northeastern and North-Central North America* (1968). She also wrote *The Wild Garden* (1936) and, with Edward Loomis Davenport Seymour, *Your City Garden* (1937), as well as books on flowers, trees, "wayside fruits," and attracting birds to the garden.[15]

FOR TWO HUNDRED YEARS the little Colonial house has hunched its shoulder against the prevailing winds which sweep in from Long Island Sound in this part of Connecticut. Great elms [*Ulmus americanus*] hold back a little of the wind's force, and lilacs [*Syringa*], higher than the house itself, tie it to the little grass knoll on which it stands. Lost in a meadow of high grass, the little house seemed to call lonesomely to me as we stopped our car in the narrow fern-bordered road. I knew that moment that I wanted to own it.

Skip the business details. Suffice it to say that the house with its wide, simple mantels, its built-in cupboards, its hand-hewn rafters fastened with wooden pegs, became mine, and though the city still holds my mercenary body too much of the time, my heart is always in the country. And the house is no longer lonely, for fires on the wide hearths have kindled new hope within its walls, where simple old furniture, hooked rugs and hand-woven bedspreads have restored the atmosphere of Colonial days.

For a time I left the garden as I found it. Then Harry came to visit me, and Harry is a landscape architect. He arrived in the evening, but before breakfast he was out of doors. I followed him and we stood in front of the little house, so naively aslant against the wind.

"Fine lilacs," mused Harry, "good old New England planting."

Then his eye caught the fringe of shrubs across the front of the house like ragged lace on an old petticoat. "Spiraea Vanhouttei, a late planting, absolutely out of place."

I had rather disliked that scraggly row myself, but thought I had to accept it as part of the little house. "What do you mean, Harry, by 'late planting'? They look old enough to me."

"Why, spiraea Vanhouttei wasn't brought into this country until after 1850. You have been so careful with your period furnishings inside the house, why not keep the planting a period thing, too?"

It took but a moment to grasp the logic of Harry's idea. And thus began my apprenticeship in gardening. Not only in gardening, but in period gardening, and, oh, how hard it is to explain to the average nurseryman what that means! I put the planting into Harry's hands, as I would have turned over the furnishing of the little house to the tender mercies of an interior decorator, had I not known decorating myself, and that very night he drew a plan, showing the plants which would give my house a Colonial setting.

Now Harry is no hidebound period gardener, and, while he was quite firm about the foundation planting, he acceded very readily to my desire to have a retaining wall to support the knoll on which the house has stood for so many years. In that wall I had the joy of placing all the newly introduced alpines, which the rock-garden catalogues give such glowing accounts. But that is another story. I think Harry let me busy myself with the wall that I might not be too impatient about the main planting. He knew it would be a slow and wearisome task to get all the oldtime plants which were to frame the house itself. And, as I said, Harry was very firm about every detail of that foundation planting. No plant that was introduced into cultivation in America later than 1750 (well, there are a very few of around 1800) must show its face, and the planting must be severely simple, yet give me the color and perfume which delight my soul. And this is the way it worked out.

Of course the lilacs were left. They were, doubtless, the descendants of those planted long before the War of the Revolution. They stand at the right-hand corner as you enter the house. On the left corner, on a wobbly frame, sprawled a crimson rambler rose. Harry could hardly wait to get that flaunting parvenu out of the ground. He would have discarded it entirely, but I begged to have it planted against the silvery gray of a distant barn, and there it languishes. I am afraid that Harry gave the gardener very casual directions for its transplanting. In place of the rose now stands a mammoth old-fashioned mockorange [*Philadelphus*]. We wangled this shrub with great difficulty from a reluctant nurseryman who tried his best to sell us the newly developed double scentless hybrids. He had been in this country only a few years, had bought the mockorange with his place, and its associations meant nothing to him. So at last, grumbling that it was too large to move, he excavated it (digging is no word for his toil), and we brought it home in a truck. Harry planted it himself, digging a hole big enough to bury a horse, and every day last summer I watered it. Its shape and size suit Harry's sense of fitness absolutely, and its waxy, perfumed flowers flooded the air with the fragrance of the past, even though it had just been moved.

For prim guardians on each side of the entrance steps Harry placed box [*Buxus*] bushes. We hoped to get billowy old pioneers from a garden in the neighborhood, but had to compromise with well-balled stock from a nursery. The subtle, tangy odor of the foliage speaks of many old-world gardens, as well as of those modeled on them in early days in America. Just to the left of the box is a hawthorn, Paul's Double Scarlet [*Crataegus laevigata* 'Paul's Double Scarlet'], instead of the English white mayflower [*Crataegus monogyra*], which would have been more in keeping, but would not have given me the blaze of color which some day I shall see against the sober white Puritan wall. Then near the foundation on each side of the steps we put double-flowering pink almond [*Prunus glandulosa*], so beloved in every New England dooryard. I think Harry gave me a little leeway with the time of its introduction, but, as I said, he is not too severe, and I do so love its soft rose in spring above the early blooming bulbs in drifts of blue.

From the sentinel box on the right of the steps to the lilacs and to the mockorange on the left runs a precise little row of germander [*Teucrium*]. Harry explained to me that the cottage gardens before 1800 contained mostly herbs from which the housewife distilled the simple household remedies. He said I could make an excellent decoction for gout from this germander. Behind this border, leaving space for the drifts of spring bulbs, snowdrops [*Galanthrus nivalis*], squills [*Scilla*] and grape hyacinths [*Muscari*], rise the swordlike leaves of Florentine iris. We rescued this exquisite white iris from a corner of an abandoned farmyard. Harry delighted in its appropriateness for my planting. He had no need to expatiate on its beauty, for I have long dwelt lovingly on its delicately veined petals, and appreciated its faint perfume, even though I didn't know that it was one of the first flowers mentioned in American gardens.

On the south side of the house we made a long bed and placed here all the herbs mentioned in the records. This bed, so near the kitchen door, is a constant joy to me, for here within a step I may pick mint [*Mentha*], thyme [*Thymus*] and summer savory [*Satureja hortensis*] for my sauces and gravies, and tarragon [*Artemisia*] and chives [*Allium Schoenoprasum*] for my French dressing, as well as a few petals of pot marigold [*Calendula*] for a special soup, or a few of the golden flowers for the breakfast table. Among the close-set rows of herbs stand great clumps of the old peonies [*Paeonia*], both the red and the white. On the southeast corner we put a crabapple [*Malus*] tree, none of the new species recently imported, but the old-fashioned Siberian crab [*Malus baccata*], grafted on dwarf stock, so that it will never grow too large.

Harry's work, for one year at least, was now completed. There was one shrub I still longed to possess, the old smoketree [*Cotinus coggygria*], and I wanted all the old spicy roses. But Harry said: "Remember this is New England — use restraint." So I looked again at the shapely little crabapple tree, and sniffed my very own box. I think the box and the crabapple give me more joy than any of the rest of the planting. The box means England to me in all its ordered beauty, just as it did to those who before 1800 planted it in memory of home, and the crabapple means New England, jelly and apple butter-making in the wide old kitchen, the great kettle bubbling over the log fire, the copper saucepans winking in jolly communion on the walls, and the air heavy with the spicy fragrance which means home in the New World.

House Beautiful 75 (MAY 1934): 79, 132, 134.

ENDNOTES

14. On the restoration of the gardens at Williamsburg, see: Charles B. Hosmer, Jr., "The Colonial Revival in the Public Eye: Williamsburg and Early Garden Restoration," *The Colonial Revival in America*, ed. Alan Axelrod (New York, 1985), 52–70; M. Kent Brinkley and Gordon W. Chappell, *The Gardens of Colonial Williamsburg* (Williamsburg, 1996), especially 2–4. Alice G. B. Lockwood compiled and edited *Gardens of Colony and State* (New York, 1931–1934).

15. *Contemporary Authors: A Bio-Bibliographical Guide to Current Writers* 73–76, First Revision, ed. Frances Carol Focher (Detroit, 1978), 422; *Authors of Books for Young People* (Metuchen, New Jersey, 1990), 470.

Chapter Six

FORMAL AND ITALIAN GARDENS *and the Use of* *Architectural Features and Furnishings*

THE TRUE DOMAIN of the "Italian garden" — a term that was often synonymous with "formal garden" in popular American garden writings — was the great country estate of the very rich; middle-class garden writers often scorned or ridiculed so-called Italian gardens as pretentious and tasteless. Nevertheless, formal design principles did have an impact on amateur gardens of the early twentieth century, and they were the subject of some fine, thoughtful articles. More sophisticated writers, like Neltje Blanchan (Nellie Doubleday), acknowledged that the formal garden was first revived in England as part of the Arts and Crafts movement, citing important British authors Reginald Blomfield and John D. Sedding. In articles featuring the great estate gardens, authors often took pains to emphasize that the elements of these formal gardens were adaptable to smaller properties. The main point many writers tried to convey was the importance of relating the garden to the house and relating both to the classic use of pergolas, arches, walks, pools, sundials, and benches and carefully planned vistas.

Neltje Blanchan [Nellie Doubleday]
The Formal Garden in America

Nellie Doubleday was born in Chicago in 1865. In 1886 she married Frank Nelson Doubleday, who became manager of the new *Scribner's Magazine* in 1887 and founder of Doubleday, Page and Company a few years later. The Doubledays lived in a highly literary environment, associating with some of the foremost authors of their day. Nellie Doubleday was active in such organizations as the American Civic Association and the American Red Cross; she died in Canton, China, at the end of World War I while on a special assignment as commissioner for the Red Cross. A great nature-lover, Doubleday wrote books and articles on birds and wild flowers as well as gardens. As Beverly Seaton has noted, Doubleday's nature writings were typical of those produced by Americans involved with the conservation movement in the early twentieth century. Lively, enthusiastic texts, they sought to educate the public about our nation's "magnificent natural heritage" and to gain support for conservation efforts.[1] This essay on formal gardens in America, along with several others that first appeared in *Country Life in America*, was subsequently included in Doubleday's book, *The American Flower Garden* (1909).

In this article Doubleday analyzes the formal, Italian garden and its importance in early twentieth-century America.[2] She gives a synopsis of the controversy in England between Reginald Blomfield and William Robinson over the formal garden and the role of the architect in garden design while tracing the history of the formal garden from antiquity to the Italian Renaissance. Recognizing that many Americans are contemptuous of formal gardens, she insists this is based on a misunderstanding, that Americans wrongly associate Italian gardens with the vulgar, ostentatious copies made for the rich, rather than the original masterpieces in Italy. This article introduces themes that will appear in other articles in this chapter. First, it emphasizes that the most important lesson to be learned from the Italian garden is the integration of home and garden — visually through compositional form, and in practice through making the garden a private and accessible outdoor living space — and the merging of the garden with the surrounding landscape. Doubleday also explains the essential function of such features as

paths, pergolas, and pools, and observes that less affluent gardeners can purchase inexpensive, cement copies of Italian fountains,
sundials, and benches. Finally, the article points out that our own
beloved colonial gardens are in fact the descendants of Italian gardens, via seventeenth-century England, and that "nowhere so well
as on a small place, where the house is the dominating object in the
home picture, is the formal or architectural treatment of the
grounds so well adapted."

SINCE ORTHODOXY was ever "my doxy," it need surprise no one but the
merest tyro in gardening to learn that this, the most peaceful of the arts, has
the greater part of its devotees divided into two bitterly hostile camps. The
"spirit of sect," so heartily deplored by Turgot in matters of politics and
religion,[3] is rife even in their midst, and there would seem to be no more
likelihood of a truce between them now than in the days when the affected,
complacent Addison made admirable copy in the *Spectator*,[4] and Pope,[5] that
most artificial of jingling rhymesters, amused his generation by poking fun at
formal gardens generally, and not alone at the errors which undoubtedly
disfigured much of the "Italian" gardening in the England of his time. Pope,
while he professed to abhor hedges, pleached walks and statuary in gardens,
nevertheless went on piling up rocks and shells into grottos at Twickenham,
making cascades, bridges, miniature torrents and wild, mountainous impossi-
bilities in a pastoral landscape until he had, in much condensed, compendium
form, a sample of every kind of scenery his fertile brain could conjure, and all
within five acres.

These two literary men, Addison and Pope, with not a little help from
Walpole,[6] neither artists nor yet gardeners, who knew not what they were
undoing, must be held largely responsible for bringing about the radical
reaction in garden methods which swept away with axe, plough and grubbing
hoe most of the tree-lined avenues like cathedral aisles, the ancient evergreen
hedges, the broad terraces and box-edged parterres that had been the glory of
the old English estates, influenced by the Renaissance. The saying that nature
abhors a straight line was construed to warrant the destruction of every line
of oaks and elms, every direct road and path on English country places. People professed to travel cheerfully, in the name of reform, twice the distance in
meaningless serpentine twists and turns to reach either their entrance gate or

the kitchen garden. The planting of trees and shrubbery was supposed to be ridiculous if wild nature were not copied literally. Hence the logical step was presently taken of setting out an occasional dead tree in English parks. Devotees of the so-called natural school went so far as to refuse to clip their lawns — those wonderful velvet lawns which are the very heart of the English garden. Quite as many crimes were committed in the name of nature by the unintelligent followers of Repton and "Capability" Brown as had been done in the name of art by the formal gardeners who had reached the baroque period of decadence before Addison's day.[7]

For the novice who turns for inspiration to Robinson's "The English Flower Garden,"[8] one of the most delightfully infectious books on gardening ever written, is to be taught that the formal garden is most unlovely and absurd. Robinson is an enthusiastic horticulturist who simply cannot see the architectural point of view. On the other hand, let the novice take up Blomfield's "The Formal Garden,"[9] or Sedding's exquisitely written "Garden Craft,"[10] and he will get the notion that the naturalistic method of making a garden or treating a landscape is unworthy to be called an art at all.

"The question is a very simple one," says Blomfield, who is Robinson's special bête noire. "Is the garden to be considered in relation to the house, and as an integral part of a design which depends for its success on the combined effect of house and garden; or is the house to be ignored in dealing with the garden as a part of nature? The latter is the position of the landscape gardener in real fact. There is some affectation in his treatises of recognising the relationship between the two, but his actual practice shows that this admission is only borrowed from the formal school to save appearances, and is out of court in a method which systematically dispenses with any kind of system whatever."

And so the battle of words comes down to the present day in England, from whence our training in garden tactics has been largely derived. Not until quite lately have we any garden literature of our own, and even now England continues to supply most of the text books. To the dispassionate observer it is quite plain that ammunition for both sides of the conflict has been gathered, not from the best examples of the formal or the naturalistic school of gardening, but from the poorest examples of the other's work that the partisan devotees of each could find.

Where did the formal garden originate? Wherein lies the magic that draws men to it in every age?

Maspero, in his "Dawn of Civilisation,"[11] tells of an Egyptian nobleman who lived over four thousand years before Christ, whose splendid fruit, vegetable and flower garden, formally laid out, was described upon his tomb. When various forms of art spread from Egypt to other lands, no doubt the art of gardening was widely copied. Even the sea-roving Phoenicians had fine gardens, and we feel sure that the famous hanging gardens of Babylon, from the very nature of their site, could have been nothing but formal. Greek gardens, which, like the Egyptian, were a combination of the utilitarian and the decorative, were laid out with cold precision, purely in keeping with the classic severity of the architecture they surrounded. They must have been too severely formal to be enjoyed and lived in as the Romans enjoyed and lived in theirs, which they, in turn, derived from the Greeks.

On the Roman and Alban hillsides, where the patricians had their villas, the terrace, which was cut at first as a necessity to prevent wash-outs on the steep slopes, was soon cleverly utilised as a pictorial feature. A terraced hill, of course, necessitated steps and balustrades for convenience and safety, because the Romans, who lived much out of doors, entered their homes through their gardens. Pliny, in his letters, describes two of his villas, but so far no antiquarian has been able to identify them with the remains of any that are now known.[12] In the house of the Vettii at Pompeii we may see to-day a delightful little garden in the central court, faultlessly restored, where every room of the house opens upon it. The inmates of that home, whose bodies have been dust for nearly nineteen centuries, heard these very fountains splash their refreshing waters among the flowers. How near us does that little garden bring the everyday life of Pompeii!

With the delightful use of gardens as outdoor living-rooms, the utilitarian feature — vegetable patches, fruit trees, and vineyards — were banished either to a distant part of the Roman's estate or to an outlying farm, and the garden now came to be recognised as an adjunct to the house, partly architectural and wholly decorative. Accordingly, no pains were spared to make it so. The same principles of design which governed the house were extended to the grounds immediately surrounding it, and there they left off abruptly. Such weather-proof embellishments as the Roman patrician, connoisseur, and collector had inside his dwelling — beautiful statuary, sculptured seats and vases of marble — were taken to his open-air living-room for their greater enjoyment. Can we doubt that their chaste beauty was less appreciated when set on balustrades and terraces against the dark background of olive, ilex, and cypress?

But with the growth of luxury in the Empire decadence began; the topiary gardener did his worst, and innocent trees, frivolously clipped into the forms of impossible birds and beasts, with much else that was absurdly artificial, marked the decline of art in the Roman's once simple and dignified pleasure ground. After the fall of Rome, when the darkness of the Middle Ages settled down over Europe, gardening, with all her sister arts of peace, slumbered for centuries. The mediaeval garden, where it existed at all, we learn from old, illuminated missals, was merely a monastery's patch of "simples" or vegetables tended by a monk, or an enclosure within the castle's precincts, where herbs grew around the well and fruit trees were espaliered against the walls.

Inevitably, a great awakening would come to artistic Italy with the cessation of wars, holy and unholy, and the return of prosperity to the land. In those days of marvellous artistic activity which we call the Renaissance, when men delved among the archives of their Roman ancestors for inspiration in all the arts, the classic garden was rediscovered with acclaim. Restored in all its splendor throughout Italy, but given new breadth and freedom of treatment at the hands of some of the greatest artists of all time, Michelangelo and Raphael among them, the Italian garden of Lorenzo de Medici's day has become synonymous in the artistic world with garden craft carried to its highest degree.

Where lies the secret of its excellence? Doubtless in the discovery of the landscape. Heretofore the garden had been regarded merely as a circum-scribed architectural extension of the castle or villa, as rigidly formal as the walls of a room. But the master architect of the Renaissance, looking forth from the terraced hillside to the distant view, realised that his art might be fused with nature in the making of a picture where the imagination would enjoy a freedom of expression hitherto unknown. He knew, none better, the importance of adapting the garden to the lines of the house it joined — so did the Egyptian, the Greek, and the Roman. He realised the importance of adapting the garden in every case to the uses to which it would be put, providing accessible, shady paths, sheltered resting places in the most lovely spots, fountains to refresh the dweller in that hot, dry climate, and cascades down the terraced hillsides from the overflow of the aqueducts, bowling greens on the *tapis vert*, parterres, plantations of roses and fruit orchards for the enjoyment of his patron's family — in the union of beauty with the prac-tical he surpassed all his predecessors. But his genius lay first in discovering that the landscape lying beyond the house and garden should be the ultimate goal of his tributary art; and secondly, in seizing on the great and varied beauty of the Italian landscape, and fitting it into his design with an art which concealed itself. His scenic sense remains a marvel.

Whether one studies the Villa Lante gardens at Bagnaia, the incomparably beautiful Villa d'Este at Tivoli, the superb old estates at Frascati, the sumptu-ous pleasure grounds of the prelates in Rome itself or the charmingly simple Colonna garden of flowers on a hill-top in the very heart of the city, one sees masterpieces of composition in the large and in detail, calculated to inspire a nation of painters.

"I can't abide Italian gardens," a young architect once startled me by saying, for he had an uncommonly good eye.

"Did you ever see one — a real one in Italy?" I asked.

"No, I have never been there," he frankly admitted. "I have in mind only American 'Italian gardens,' I am afraid — geometric patterns patched on to the lawns of new estates, with little clipped trees set along the borders at exact intervals, and stiff, prim asters in rectangular beds, or a row of urns on a concrete balustrade with perhaps a few meaningless relics of Italian sculpture from some antique shop in New York, to make the garden convincing of its expense.

"Apropos, I must tell you a story," he went on. "Once I was dining in the house of some very rich people, where the lady on my right insisted upon talking about her imposing earthly possessions. Her Italian garden, of the type I have described, she dwelt upon in detail, telling me how much the marble work had cost, how expensive the topiary effects were to keep up, and every other painful particular. At last, unable to endure her prattle about a sarcophagus she had decided to use as a garden seat, I surprised her by saying: 'My wife, too, has an Italian garden.' 'Indeed?' she asked incredulously, knowing perfectly well that we live in a small suburban cottage. 'Yes,' I replied; 'it took two Italians three days to dig it.' Then she changed the subject."

In transplanting the Italian garden cult to America, via England, France and Holland, and after long subjugation there, the fundamental principles of the best formal garden making have been so far lost sight of in the great majority of cases that it has become well-nigh a travesty to call most of our meaningless imitations Italian gardens at all. It may be claimed that Italian ideals cannot be translated into our terms; that the garden magic of the Renaissance is dependent upon age, the peculiarity of the Italian climate and landscape, the wealth of deep-toned evergreens, the cheapness of labour, the social usages of an age of splendour, the Italian genius for artistic expression.

Age undoubtedly enhances the beauty of a garden planned on noble lines, but it can completely obliterate the poorly planned one that is dependent upon constant care; and after centuries the best Italian gardens have preserved their charm. Our summer skies are as blue as the Italian, and our spring and summer climate is not unlike that of Italy. We have our choice of a score of evergreens and a hundred flowers for every one that was known to the garden designers of the sixteenth century. Pyramidal junipers [*Juniperus*] and other columnar evergreens may be used in the Eastern United States, and the less hardy yews [*Taxus*] and cypresses [*Chamaecyparis*] in the South, as the tapering shafts of cypress were used in Italy; Lombardy poplars [*Populus nigra var. betulafolia*] thrive here as well as there; retinisporas [*Chamaecyparis*], magnolias, rhododendrons, laurel [*Prunus laurocerasus*], boxwood [*Buxus*], bay [*Laurus*], and a host of other possibilities are perfectly adapted to our needs. Certainly, there is no lack of wealth at the disposal of American home-makers, nor can it be spent in a better way to bring health and pleasure to a family than upon a garden. Many kinds of labour-saving devices, unknown in Europe three centuries ago, now help to lessen the expense of garden-making and maintenance. Fountains, sundials, garden seats, balustrades, steps, and other garden accessories are by no means essential to a lovely garden, but if one wants them, and cannot afford stone or marble, excellent reproductions in a special preparation of cement may be had at a small fraction of the cost of classic models. Thus a man of very moderate means may enjoy a duplicate of the fountain of lions at the Vatican; and the birds that come from the woods to his very door to bathe in the spray and drink from the basin, where goldfish play hide and seek under the lotus and lily leaves, show constant appreciation of his taste.

It is painfully true that we Americans, like the English, are too Teutonic to be an artistic people. Yet here and there among us arises an artist capable of making far more beautiful pictures on the landscape than he is the better content to paint on canvas; and so the limitation of art by the artists themselves continues to be a fruitful source of our artistic poverty. Very few excellent models inspire the garden makers in this new land. For nearly a hundred years garden making went out of fashion. The worthy formal gardens here can be counted on the fingers of one hand. But art out-of-doors shows encouraging signs of waking from its long sleep, and the few really competent designers are meeting with refreshing encouragement at last.

Perhaps it would be as futile as it is undesireable to servilely copy even the best Renaissance gardens, nevertheless we may, with the greatest profit, learn from them how a house and garden may become an integral part of the landscape, whether it be situated in Italy, New England, Illinois, or California, for happily the principles of their making are of universal application. What we chiefly need is the informing spirit; with it alone shall we learn how to meet our problems as successfully as the Italians met theirs. Even in Italy methods were necessarily adapted to various situations. The Roman's pleasaunce, overlooking the broad Campagna, was given a majestic breadth and simplicity of treatment in harmony with its environment, whereas, farther north, where the landscape is less imposing, compensations were offered in the wealth of garden details. The designer invariably took the cue for treatment of a place from the adjoining landscape. So must we learn of him.

A room that is not lived in never possesses the charm of one that is, however correctly furnished it may be. And so our gardens will never be what they might easily become until we make of them outdoor living-rooms after the good Old World custom. Piazzas, pleasant as they are, have doubtless retarded the adoption of the custom here; so has the tendency to do away with walls, tall hedges, and screen planting, so exposing to the gaze of every passer-by the intimate family life spent under the open sky.

The Renaissance garden maker planned the hedged-in, vine-clad, walled enclosures, sheltered from the winds and sun, for the family's comfort and convenience, as carefully as he did the rooms of the dwelling. Broad paths through pergolas, arbours or wooded alleys led from one subdivision of the garden to another, and so, by easy and almost imperceptible transition, the formal lines nearest the house flowed more freely and more informally into the naturalistic the farther one walked away from the house, until the stroll brought one out face to face with nature herself. Here was infinite variety in perfect unity. No "method" was despised by the artist designer to gain the end desired. The terraces, the stone work, the fountains, the sundial, the ilex walks, the parterres, the bowling green, the open sunny spaces, the shaded retreats, the rushing cascades down the hillsides, the mirror-like pools, the groups of trees, the converging lines of a straight-hedged path, the irresistible invitation of a disappearing curved one, the distant vista alluring the eye to the beauty of a distant panorama — all had a deeper harmony underlying them than the uninitiated observer could suspect. A glance at one of the old garden plans astonishes one. The design drawn on paper shows a rigid formality, perfect balance and intricacy of line comparable to Chinese fretwork. The finished garden seems to be a naturally perfect picture wherein the design is frequently lost to sight, and one is conscious only of harmony on every hand. Another matter for astonishment to the American is that the beauty of a Renaissance garden may be entirely independent of flowers. These were used lavishly in many gardens, it is true, while in others they were scarcely necessary at all, and were added, as Corot might have added a touch of colour to one of his landscapes, which, even without the pleasing detail, would form a well-nigh faultless composition.

Our simple democratic society has no need of imitating the great gardens of Italy, where Church and State vied with each other in the splendour of their open-air functions, or the excessively formal pleasure grounds of the French court to which Le Notre devoted his genius; but it is a mistake to assume that the formal garden may not serve our day and generation. What are the "old-fashioned" gardens around our Colonial homesteads, with their box-edged parterres and vine-covered arbours but an evidence of the Italian fashion in vogue in England, France, and Holland when our forefathers first came to these shores? We feel no prejudice against our grandmothers' formal gardens — quite the reverse — but that there is a decided modern prejudice against the formal treatment for anything but the large estates of the newly rich Americans one cannot deny. Our Teutonic blood prejudices us, as a people, toward a more general love for nature than for art; our training, derived from English text books, inclines us toward the naturalistic method; and our ignorance of the best examples of the formal school which may scarcely be found outside of Italy, might easily account for the scorn which Americans generally feel for formal gardens.

The refreshing truth is that nowhere so well as on a small place, where the house is the dominating object in the home picture, is the formal or architectural treatment of the grounds so well adapted. How much of the charm of the simple, dignified Colonial house, on the elm-lined village street in New England was due to the box-hedged path leading directly from the front gate to the front door, and the neat, trim parterres filled with flowers and herbs conveniently near, which preserved harmony in the yard of the perfectly balanced dwelling! In its modest way it was as satisfying an artistic composition as the Villa Medici, for our "Colonial" architecture, adapted after Palladio, and "Colonial" gardening were twin children of the Renaissance.

Country Life in America 14 (JULY 1908): 271–274.

ENDNOTES

1. Seaton's entry on Doubleday in *American Women Writers*, ed. Lina Mainiero (New York, 1979), 536–538. On Doubleday, also see *New York Times* (obituary), February 23, 1918, 13:5; *Dictionary of American Biography*, eds. Allen Johnson and Dumas Malone (New York, 1943), 392; *Notable American Women, 1607–1950*, 1, ed. Edward T. James (Cambridge, 1971), and Ernest Morrison, *J. Horace McFarland*, (Harrisburg, 1995) 63–64, 99–100.

2. For a late twentieth-century study of the Italian garden in America, see Keith N. Morgan, "The Rise and Fall of the Italian Garden in America," *Masters of American Garden Design IV: Influences on American Garden Design: 1895–1940* (New York, 1994), 7–16.

3. Anne-Robert-Jacques Turgot (1727–1781) was an economic reformer and advocate of free trade during the late years of the French monarchy. His most important book, written in 1770, was translated and published in New York in 1898 as *Reflections of the Formation and Distribution of Riches*.

4. Joseph Addison (1672–1719) advocated the natural rather than formal landscape garden in his essays for *Spectator*.

5. Poet and essayist Alexander Pope (1688–1744), created what he deemed a natural rather than formal garden at his home, Twickenham, and served to advance the cause of natural gardens in his writings.

6. Horace Walpole (1717–1797) wrote *On Modern Gardening* in 1770, campaigning on behalf of the eighteenth-century natural school of landscape design, as typified in his garden at Strawberry Hill.

7. Lancelot "Capability" Brown (1716–1783) was an eighteenth-century English landscape designer whose work exemplified the preference for landscape planning in broad, naturalistic sweeps. Humphry Repton (1752–1818) was an important follower of Brown.

8. On William Robinson (1838–1935), see above, xx.

9. Reginald Blomfield (1856–1942) was the author of *The Formal Garden in England* (1892) and chief spokesman for the architectural style of landscape design.

10. John Dando Sedding (1838–1891) was an architect whose views of garden design generally conformed to those of Blomfield. His book, *Gardencraft, Old and New*, was published shortly after his death.

11. Gaston Camille Charles Maspero (1846–1916) was a French Egyptologist whose three-volume *Histoire des peuples de l'Orient Classique* was translated into English; the first volume was *The Dawn of Civilization; Egypt and Chaldaea* (New York, 1894).

12. Robert Castell, in *The Villas of the Ancients Illustrated* (1728), made the earliest attempt to reconstruct the plans of the villas of the Roman statesman Pliny the Younger (c. 61–112).

FLETCHER STEELE
Tying Together House and Garden

FLETCHER STEELE (1885–1971) was born in Rochester, New York, and studied landscape architecture at Harvard.[13] His professional education was mainly derived, however, from his apprenticeship to landscape architect Warren Manning. His study of English and continental gardens during travels in Europe in 1913 served as an important source of inspiration during his subsequent career. When he returned from Europe he set up his own practice and wrote frequently for *Garden Magazine* and *Country Life in America* during the first seven years he was in business. After 1920 he mainly wrote for *House Beautiful* and the *Garden Club of America Bulletin*. He was also quite a popular public lecturer. Although most of his work was on millionaires' estates — he mixed easily with the high society of his day — he was interested in the design of smaller, suburban gardens; two of his books were *Design in the Little Garden* (1924) and *Gardens and People* (1963). He also had a strong interest in modernism and garden design. In March 1929 he wrote an article for *House Beautiful* in which he considered possible ways that landscape architecture might follow the modern trends of other art forms. His colleagues recognized him for his highly innovative, experimental approach to landscape design.

In this article Steele addresses the problem of unifying house and garden, a priority among proponents of the formal garden. He mentions that this integration existed in ancient Roman gardens but mainly stresses that our own colonial gardens had better interrelated grounds and architectural structures than those of his contemporaries. Like Doubleday, Steele believes that accessibility, shelter, and privacy were the foremost attributes that would make a garden an appealing, outdoor living room. An accompanying photograph shows a modest suburban home, making clear — perhaps clearer than Steele's text — the adaptability of the ideas in this article to the smaller homes and gardens of the middle class.

A STUDENT IN OLD POMPEII is puzzled to determine whether the houses are half garden or the gardens half house. Each one is intimately a part of the other. All is quite different to-day. Now a man builds a house, then walks, drives, service-yards, and a garden, each by itself, with little or no relation to the rest. We have outgrown the patchwork quilt and patchwork architecture, but as yet few have outgrown a patchwork arrangement of their estates.

This disunity of design is comparatively modern and altogether American. In our colonial days an orderly inter-relation of house, service buildings and grounds was always planned. As architects have turned back to study the buildings and decorators to the furniture, so designers of estates should study the colonial landscape architectural arrangement.

We might draw the lesson from old places in New Amsterdam, Pennsylvania, Virginia, or farther south. But nowhere were the conditions so like those of to-day as in New England, or was the arrangement so easily adaptable for the ordinary small homestead. Here we find two general types, the Dooryard Garden and what we may call the Straightaway Garden.

In early days the small frame houses were placed close to the highway. From the door in the middle of the front ran a straight walk to the street. A low paling followed the street line turning in at right angles to meet the corners of the house. The area thus enclosed became the little Dooryard Garden, sacred to the housewife. It was planted with flowers. But more important were the herbs for homemade remedies and for cooking. In other words, the garden was necessary. It was also easily accessible. But a step from the kitchen, and one could pick a bit of "sallat" at meal times or ladle the dishwater where most needed on "piny" of "fetherfew." The housewife was a busy woman and not a moment of the few that could be spared for tending the garden need be lost in going or coming.

The other type I call the Straightaway for the "straightaway path" which generally ran through it. These gardens belonged to the larger houses, inhabited by prosperous people whose womenfolk were helped by servants. I say helped advisedly, for though the mistress no longer scrubbed and swept she still spun and sewed, and her touch was recognized in every dish that left the kitchen. In those days there was little distinction between master and servant, service quarters, and drawing-room. But the life of the mistress was somewhat reserved and the needs of the household were large. The tiny Dooryard Garden was too public and small for her fancy, so she appropriated for her uses land on the side away from the street.

She rarely put her flower garden next to the house, however. That space was needed for bleaching and drying, and for sun-cooking the strawberry jam; for well, woodshed, and smoke-house, and divers out-buildings. So a small yard was set aside, irregular in shape, as controlled by conditions. It was fenced in on one or more sides to keep out prowling animals and to remind the farm hands, who passed this way from barns to house, that they were entering the precincts of the mistress. This yard was as much used in summer as the kitchen itself, for much the same purposes. It was a distinct, bounded unit of design. It was open. At one side a grape arbor was often built against the house, with two or three fruit trees near by. Around the edges were lilacs [*Syringa*] and ragged yellow day-lilies [*Hemerocallis lilio-asphodelus*]. Beyond the yard lay the garden. Opposite a door or principal window of the house an opening, sometimes arched, was made through the shrubs, and a long broad path led to a simple arbor at the end. Beds were laid out on either side. Flowers and herbs, vegetables and bush fruits, pears [*Pyrus*] and cherry [*Prunus*] trees were planted here and there (the apples [*Malus*] were gathered into an orchard at one side). But few feet away from the house, the garden was in effect merely the second extension of the useful apartments.

Landscaping in the modern suburban home in which the garden and house are success-fully tied together. Both the "dooryard" and "straightaway" principles are combined in this scheme.

Yard and garden were more than added comforts — they were necessary. Hence they were put close to the house, generally with regard for the architectural lines, and constantly used and tended.

Material conditions have changed since those times. Home use of medicinal herbs and smoke-house have passed with candledip and spinning wheel. Woodsheds and open fires are luxuries rather than necessities. A modern estate requires few of the old appointments. Their gradual displacement and the lack of imagination to replace the old with modern uses has resulted in our unhappy patchwork design and the divorce of house and grounds. But gardens have again come to their own, and soon we shall learn to find their uses along with the pleasures.

Accessibility plays quite as much a part in the good design of estates as it ever did. Gardens should be where they can be easily reached. It is a delight to be able to step from drawing-room directly into a flower garden. Where the house is occupied only during two or three seasons of the year one should by all means have a garden adjoining the house. It is always possible to keep a garden looking well for eight out of twelve months, but difficult and expensive to keep it at its best during the remaining four. Therefore the garden of an all the year round house should follow the second of the colonial types, having the garden near but not next to the dwelling, as none wishes to look out on to a shabby garden for four months. The yard separating the two should be designed as a unit with proper boundaries, planted simply with evergreens and shrubs having bright-colored twigs, flower and fruit which will be agreeable to look upon at all seasons.

Sometimes the intervening yard may be dispensed with in favor of some modern equivalent such as a broad terrace. Fitted up with comfortable chairs and awnings, with big pots for flowers, a terrace is a natural complement of the drawing-room which should open upon it. In winter the pots can be filled with greens and the awnings put away to let the sunshine pour into the house.

Another intermediate step is the typically American veranda. There is no need to explain the uses of such a place. But few seem to realize their wider possibilities. The best ones are large rooms without walls, not the timid, house-clinging things to which we are accustomed. Twenty feet square is none too much. Such a place may often be situated to advantage at a short distance from the house, connected by a passageway, so that the light will not be cut off from the windows. The floor should be down near or on the ground.

When I speak of gardens I mean any unit of the grounds which is designed to fit some special use. One that is growing in popularity is fitted up as a place to have meals served out-of-doors. "Any old place" will not do for a comfortable outdoor dining-room. It must be easily accessible from kitchen and china closet. A door should give on to it from the butler's pantry. The family should not have to enter by the deserted dining-room but by hall or terrace. Adequate protection from wind and sun are all-important. There is no pleasure in clutching tablecloth and candle-shades every moment or sitting under a glare of sun at mid-day. A sheltered corner of the house is best. Adjustable screens and thick planting will furnish the needed comfort. Some people will exclaim that bugs are always falling from a roof of foliage. But there should be no bugs in foliage that is properly looked after. Fly-screens, of course, are the only refuge from mosquitoes after every attempt has been made to eliminate them in other ways. Electric fans will help to keep insects away. It is necessary to have a fairly smooth hard floor to prevent wobbling of chairs and tables. There must be sufficient room for easy movement around the table. Lastly, there must be seclusion. The outdoor dining-room must be by itself, secure from the gaze and interruption of the public or unwelcome visitors.

There should be a special garden for reading and rest just as there is a special room — the library — in the house. If the house-lawn is a thing apart it will serve. But usually it is open to all sorts of intrusion. The best place of the sort that I know is in Cornish.[14] The designer enclosed a bit of sloping meadow and a few great oaks [*Quercus*] within stone walls and hedges. It is separated from the low windows of the drawing-room by a turf passageway and protected from sight on three sides. On the fourth and lower side stretches a broad view of valley and mountain. There is no trivial planting anywhere of flowering plants or bushes to disturb the restful simplicity of this garden. It is an ideal place for quiet reading or to lie on the sloping turf under high branches.

Italy has showed us tricks in gardens that we have been curiously slow to take advantage of, considering our climate. In the true Italian garden no matter how small, one finds a walk, sheltered from the winds, on which the sun pours down. On chill spring and autumn days — even in mild winter weather — one is grateful for such a cheery promenade out-of-doors. The reverse is also found, a walk through densest shades for use in torrid summer weather. Often the trickle of water down banks of ferns adds to the cool refreshment. Many and many a day out of the year would be made pleasanter here by such walks.

One end at least should be near the house. One does not like to traverse a long hot stretch to reach a shady path, or a blizzard-swept place to find a warm corner. Ordinarily there will be no difficulty in finding a place for such paths, as walks are needed everywhere to connect houses with outlying gardens or stables. A good use for them is to link house with game courts. Tennis is popular now and a court is wanted on most estates of any size. It is apt to be a noisy game and a dirt court is not a handsome object in itself. Consequently it should not be located near or in full sight of the house. They should be connected however. This may well be by a shady walk which will be agreeable for both players and onlookers.

Bowling, clock-golf and croquet are also more or less favored outdoor games requiring special greens or courts which may be made interesting features of design. Such features may well be put close to the house, tying it with flower gardens or other parts of the grounds.

When one considers the matter of cutting flowers for the house, the convenience of having a garden near at hand is obvious. A room of the house should be provided where possible in which to keep all shapes and sizes of flower vases. It should have running water from high faucets and stationary tubs. With the least possible delay after cutting, flowers should be brought to this room and floated until they can be finally arranged. This will noticeably prolong their lives. Less observed, though quite as important, are the good results of having kitchen near kitchen garden. This ensures the freshest of vegetables and economy of use.

No matter from what angle the question is studied, a recognized usefulness and easy accessibility will be the determining factors in tying house and grounds together. But there is one esthetic reason which should not be forgotten. If care is taken that every house window shall be a frame for a beautiful picture and that there be as much variety as possible in the views, the landscape will become a living picture gallery, tied up with the house in the best way.

The Garden Magazine 22 (AUGUST 1915): 12–13.

ENDNOTES

13. My information on Steele is from Robin S. Karson, *Fletcher Steele, Landscape Architect: An Account of a Gardenmaker's Life, 1885–1971* (New York, 1989).

14. Cornish, New Hampshire, was an important site for summer residences of artists in the late nineteenth and early twentieth centuries, and many of them had distinguished gardens. Architect Charles Platt had a country home in Cornish, as did sculptor Augustus Saint-Gaudens, artists Stephen and Maxwell Parrish, and other leading members of the arts community of the time. Perhaps Steele is here referring to a garden created in Cornish by Rose Standish Nichols, an important landscape designer, for her father.

Fitly Furnishing the Everyday Garden

"ITALY WAS THE PARENT of all garden furniture and all other countries borrowed from her": a statement from this article that the two preceding authors would probably have deemed accurate. Landscape architect Ruth Bramley Dean (1880–1932) designed magnificent gardens for wealthy patrons in the 1920s and early 1930s. She was born in Wilkes-Barre, Pennsylvania, and studied for two years at the University of Chicago before becoming associated with Jens Jensen's landscape practice.[15] While she was influenced by Jensen's zealous promotion of native plants and naturalistic gardens, she had a stronger predilection than he for formal, architectonic designs.[16] Her husband, Aymar Embury II, was a well-known architect. In addition to her work for wealthy clients she wrote practical pieces for the benefit of amateurs. Her book, *The Livable House, Its Garden*, was published in 1917 and she was awarded a gold medal in landscape architecture by the Architectural League of New York in 1929.[17] *Garden Magazine* was one of her most frequent journalistic forums, and this article on how to place ornament and furnishings in the garden is among her best short writings. Gardeners deciding where to put a bench, for example, would profit from her recommendation not to set it at the end of a straight path, but in a more secluded spot, and not next to the trunk of a tree but slightly off to the side. Her advice about situating arches is also excellent, and she offers her expert opinion on selecting appropriate furniture styles for the garden. The halftone illustrations — one is on the title page and another on the contents page of this chapter — show her own work and that of other landscape architects on a scale that would be adaptable to small properties.

"WHAT WOULD you do with Euripides and the rose arch and the circular white seat that Aunt Ellen gave us?" said my wistful new client who was having her first garden. A succession of gardens had taught Aunt Ellen many of the gardener's pitfalls but it had failed to overcome her native thriftiness and she had passed on to a bewildered niece the outgrown garden furniture she could not quite persuade herself to throw away. "Well," I hedged, "this plan doesn't provide any place for so large a seat, but I will try to find the right spot for it, and the rose arch could perhaps go in the vegetable garden, and Euripides at the end of the long path." Vanishing was the primness which was to have been the keynote of the garden, vanishing at the very threshold under the clumsy arch that threatened to displace the slender one designed to go with the house. Could I summon up the courage to tell her that Euripides must find a home in her neighbor's Italian garden down the road, that there was nothing at all to do with the "extra size" arch and ponderous seat but to burn them?

Not all garden furniture finds unsuitable surroundings by the gift method; deliberate purchase is responsible for just as many inappropriate combinations, partly because of the difficulty of obtaining good garden furniture ready made, and partly because the accessories of the garden have not been thought out, placed on a plan, designed and selected at the time the garden itself was being designed.

A seat that is put in because something must go at the end of a path, an arch because the president of the garden club has such a pretty arch in her garden, an arbor without regard to the fact that it leads to no place in particular, may be only jarring notes in a generally good garden, but the chances are they will be important enough to throw the whole garden out of key.

Seats for Comfort and for Pleasant Composition

The placing of a seat (to take the first example) is not to be thoughtlessly disposed of; a frequent and unfortunate position is on the central axis of the piazza where it is apt to be the most important feature of the garden, roofed over by an arbor, forming the semicircular head of the garden backed up by a wall, or otherwise elaborated. Now, of all the resting places under the sun, I can imagine none less interesting than this, where one has just come. A little ingenuity will devise a fitting terminus for the principal axis of the garden, and the seat can go off in a partially secluded place to one side, from which something more interesting is to be seen than the direct elevation of the piazza.

At the end of a straight path is another usual place for a seat, a location that is sometimes bad, particularly if, again, the path is not on direct axis with the house. There is something unpleasantly compelling about so obviously placed a seat, and the natural impulse is to turn away from it, to find a more secluded place to sit. A quiet spot under a shadowing tree, an opening in a tangle of shrubbery where the birds chatter and sing, a point whence there is a vista through garden flowers, to a piece of lawn beyond, or a vantage point for a view, are the most inviting places in which to come upon a garden seat.

In placing a bench under a tree a mistake to be avoided is centering the bench on the tree. The criss-cross formed by the horizontal line of the bench and the center vertical line of the tree makes a bad composition. The bench will be ever so much more pleasing placed to one side of the tree, where the tree frames and shades it and where the trunk of the tree is not unpleasantly cut off by the bench. Center a long path on a fine old tree if you wish but place the bench to one side — out of the vista.

The frequency with which a seat is placed at the end of a path, is due, I think, to a feeling that the vista formed by the path must be terminated. This is a tradition for which the Italian school is responsible. The skeleton of the Italian garden is formed by long, straight paths, and its keynote the terminated vista; but seldom is a seat the terminating object. The Italians used sculpture with a prodigal hand in their gardens; and fountains, temples, the

'A quiet spot under a shadowing tree.' The placing of a seat is not to be thoughtlessly disposed of. A little ingenuity will devise a fitting terminus for the principal axis of the garden and the seat can go off in a partially secluded place to one side. And incidently, this bench is particularly attractive in structure, conveying a sense both of lightness and of substantiality. Garden of Mrs. George M. Gales at Great Neck, New York, designed by Ruth Dean, Landscape Architect.

hermae or terminal figures, urns, pedestals surmounted by figures, all recur at frequent intervals to reward the gaze compelled along given lines by clipped avenues or tree-bordered paths.

Americans have an inherent dislike for sculpture in the garden, a dislike that is a heritage perhaps from the cast-iron reindeer period which is still near enough to haunt us. Or it may be the scarcity and expense of good sculpture that are accountable for our reluctance to use it, or our fear of that other bugaboo, "formality." Whatever the state of our minds regarding sculpture, we have got as far as granting that a vista must be terminated and, because a seat is one of the few objects we think permissible in a garden, we are forced to use it, regardless of its fitness for the purpose. It were better to design a place where the seat will be used and enjoyed and let the vista go unterminated.

Arbors in Their Logical Relation

Another accessory of the garden — the arbor — is, happily, more often treated as integral with the garden design than the seat. Once in a while one sees an arbor or a pergola that begins at no place in particular, and leads to no place at all, or an arbor that cuts down across a small parcel of property dividing it needlessly into badly proportioned pieces. It is an architectural feature and as such needs to have a logically related position in the garden scheme, related if possible to other buildings on the place rather than hanging loose in the landscape. If it cannot be hitched to any existing building its beginning and end are best lost in heavy planting which will tie it into the surrounding landscape; moreover the path that runs beneath it should connect easily with other paths, so that the arbor will appear to lead to some place. It has very definite direction of itself and should therefore be placed where its direction will be useful to emphasize length, or if the contrary effect is desirable, to produce a feeling of greater width by cutting off a too long prospect.

An arbor is seldom good over the center path of a garden by reason of the fact that it divides the garden into compartments — one on each side; and yet this rule must be amended to except an old garden I once saw, which had a low old-fashioned arbor spanning the central path with very close gardening in the area between the arbor and the high walls on each side. Tall trees above the walls shut off any view at the sides and one's entire attention was directed out under the arbor to the distant view framed at the end. Here the side walls, which, on account of the reinforcing trees, had the effect of being extraordinarily high, dwarfed the arbor so that the garden was still a unit, undivided by the arbor.

Do not go so far in an attempt to connect the arbor with the house as to bring its end up against a terrace; if the terrace is above the grade of the arbor path, one feels as if it would be impossible to descend into the arbor without bumping one's head. Even if the levels are the same the effort at a connection is too patent and the arbor would be better placed ten or twenty feet distant with a centering path that runs out from the terrace, and planting high enough to confine the view, and form a kind of tunnel to the arbor.

Very often an arbor can be used advantageously as the partial background for a garden (it will always look better in the landscape if in turn it has a background of trees rising above it), and so-used, it must be pierced by occasional openings to the garden itself. The path entering and leaving its ends should be a path which continues round the garden, returns to the house or takes one on some interesting excursion.

Where Arches Look Best

Another garden feature that one is sometimes at a loss to know for what purpose it was intended is the arch. An arch covered with blooming Roses is in itself a pretty thing, but not pretty enough to be dropped down in the middle of a lawn or for that matter to justify a purposeless existence at just any place in the garden.

The arch is a form of opening, and argues something in which to make an opening — a wall, a hedge, a shrub border, a row of fruit trees; it is an architectural form even if it is executed in plant materials, and as such it must be related to something. Tie your arches into the landscape and reinforce them at the sides by means of planting and place them where you want to lead from lawn to flower garden, from flower garden to vegetable garden or from one part of either to another part.

Of Pools and Sun-dials

An often disregarded axiom is to place the sun-dial in full sun; I have seen it set in the complete shade of trees or in the shelter of a wall, ideal locations for a fountain or a birdbath, but not the spot where an instrument for telling time by the sun could carry on its life work.

A pool on the other hand is pleasanter with some shadows on it, than in the open sun, and if in the design of the garden the pool seems to be finding itself out in an open glare of light, a casual bent tree planted near its edge as if it had happened to be there when the pool was built, will cast the welcome shadow. Often it is the chance thing about a carefully designed garden which gives it charm, and sets at naught all our calculated balancing.

൦

Expressly designed to fit the plan. Grape arbor and seats made to frame a formally arranged vegetable garden with dipping pool in the center of the path; at the home of Mrs. Charles G. Stamm, Westport, Connecticut: Marjorie Sewell, Landscape Architect.

Furniture to Fit the Plan

There is nothing to be left to chance, however, in the design and selection of the accessories themselves. The atmosphere of the house (providing the architecture is good) should be extended into the garden; if the house be Italian, the garden benches, flower-pots, sculpture should be Italian in feeling, and they should be chosen with similar care for English or any other given type of architecture.

Italy was the parent of all garden furniture and all other countries borrowed from her. The furniture underwent modifications in the borrowing, to be sure, so that England and France and Spain each set her own mark on the Italian type, and each produced variations. Moreover, each country has had certain pieces of furniture that characterize it particularly, as the wood benches of England, the iron seats and tables of France, and the Spanish use of tile in seats and fountains. American Colonial work had a very definite flavor, also in the white painted wood adaptations of English Georgian work — not to be confused with much of the heavy white painted stuff that is sold as "Colonial" to-day.

The importance of archeological correctness in the design of American gardens is a question for client and landscape architect to decide between them. A straightforward solution of a problem in design, one that is suited to the "lay of the land," the house and the client's wishes, with beautifully designed, or intelligently selected furniture, suitable in scale and character, is bound to produce a pleasing result, and one which has advanced a step in the evolution of garden architecture.

The Garden Magazine 39 (June 1924): 271–274.

ENDNOTES

15. On Dean, see the entry by Eve F. W. Linn in *Pioneers of American Landscape Design: An Annotated Bibliography*, ed. Charles A. Birnbaum and Julie K. Fix (Washington, D.C., 1995), 40–44. On Jensen: Robert E. Grese, *Jens Jensen: Maker of Natural Parks and Gardens* (Baltimore, 1992).

16. Linn, in *Pioneers of American Landscape Design* (1995), 41.

17. Deborah Nevins, "The Triumph of Flora: Women and Landscape Architecture," *Antiques* 27 (April 1985): 905 and 913.

How I Did It:
Clothesline or Cloister

THIS IS AN AMATEUR'S "how I did it" article, from a series of that title in *House Beautiful.* An editorial note introducing this article solicited such writings, offering to pay for essays and photographs that related personal gardening experiences. John Sheridan Zelie (1866–1942), was a clergyman who received his doctorate in divinity at Lake Forest College in 1930. During the First World War he served as a chaplain in France, and after the war he went to Russia on the staff of the American Relief Administration. He was pastor at the First Presbyterian Church in Troy, New York, the year that this article appeared in *House Beautiful;* the same year, a book that he had coauthored on Joseph Conrad was also published.[18] He occasionally wrote for *Atlantic.* At home this man of the cloth is vexed by the necessity of bowing to his neighbors all day as they walk past his front porch — "I do believe there is some connection between the front porch and nervous prostration." As in similar articles in which amateurs chronicle their garden experiences, the theme here concerns accomplishing a goal, despite a lack of cash, through creativity and determination. This author's intention is to screen his backyard and construct a pergola in order have a private place to occupy out-of-doors. The idea originates in his recollection of English backyard gardens, but the pergola was one of the defining features of the Italian garden.

I T WAS NOT until I dared to dissociate the whole matter from money that I ever came anywhere near having one of the things I had dreamed of all my life, a garden that could be lived in. There was our great yard at the rear of the house with plenty of sun and ample lawn and half a dozen splendid trees, yet no one ever dreamed of it as a place of retirement. Once a week the clotheslines and washlady ruled there supreme. The grocer and butcher crossed it on their errands and, with their business finished, the expanse seemed to have no other reason for existence. But I could not help thinking of the ease and universality of the little or large private garden in England and elsewhere and wondering vaguely how they came to pass.

Like all the neighbors around us, we sat on the front porch, seeing the same street and bowing again to the same people we had been bowing to all day. I do believe there is some connection between the front porch and nervous prostration.

At length I shook off the nightmare of taking it for granted that money and cost were the main items in such a matter. Those overseas people had no more of it than my neighbors and myself — mostly less. So I decided to try at least for a high wall of green all around that yard to shut it off from the street and the neighbors. It might be infinitely restful to them if they saw far less of our comings and goings. 'Love your neighbor and keep up your hedge,' says a Spanish proverb. I believed it could be done without great outlay and also without waiting years for it, but in order to keep my courage up I consulted nobody about it. And so within the week I had the whole back line of the yard closely planted with good strong well-grown privet plants [*Ligustrum*] at a cost of twenty-five cents each. I seem now to remember vaguely something about twenty-seven dollars in connection with that hedge, but that summer's growth yielded a thick screen higher than my head.

To the fences on the other sides of the lot I attached, at intervals of about seven feet, uprights reaching about eight feet from the ground, and, painting them green, they proved not unsightly. The great trusts had brought the price of chicken wire within reach of the most unworthy and I covered the spaces between the posts with that. For vines to turn it all into a solid wall of green I used nearly everything — honeysuckle [*Lonicera*], ivy [*Hedera*], Dutchmann's pipe [*Aristolochia durior*], clematis, woodbine [*Parthenocissus quinquefolia*] and grapevine [*Vitis*], and bittersweet [*Celastrus scandens*]. And though there were spots thinner than I could wish and it was always a bit difficult to get things to grow right down to the ground, yet the second summer had practically given us our enclosed garden.

All was going well and, growing bolder, I failed to see why pergolas should have much more to do with expense than green walls. One day with a carpenter and a load of cedar posts and no great outlay took care of that. The first pergola was up and the vines planted at every post. I had spent years thinking about it, but now the thing was done and that in a day or two. By fall the pleasant place was well shaded and the second summer we would often have all our meals out there and with no excess of labor.

At this juncture a lucky accident suggested what was best of all. Three very straight spruces near the house had to come down and just as they were to be cut up into firewood, I thought: 'Why not run a pergola the whole length of the opposite side of the garden with these trees cut into proper lengths for the thick posts thereof? If successful this would be going from

A view of the pergola from Main Street, just after it was started

clotheslines to cloisters with a vengeance. One Italian laborer and I put them into their places in a day. It was interesting to see the way everything helped just as soon as I got rid of that obsession about a lot of money being necessary and that other one which kept saying 'It isn't done.'

As I was wondering what I should do for poles with which to join these rough Italian-looking posts together, a gentleman farmer on the edge of Plainfield said his woods were full of chestnut poles which he had cut down and I was welcome to them. I confess the long pergola had seemed a bit too ambitious, but there were the great posts begging to be used and here were the poles with which to connect them. And even if the thick posts had not been at hand they could have been easily come by, as a telephone man told me that the telephone construction companies generally had on hand broken poles which would be just the thing for this purpose.

In the second year the front porch was little occupied. Everybody who went past did not have to bow to us any more. We had our afternoon tea out in our green-walled garden, the morning newspapers and coffee, too. Callers preferred it to the house when the weather was fine. Sometimes they were profuse in their appreciation and wondered how it was done, though they might all have had the same thing quite as well as ourselves, and, as a matter of fact, I was always trying to persuade them to imitate us.

What we wanted was greenness and privacy and things which did not entail much care. I found I could clip the hedges myself about as well as any-body and continued to do it. My main thesis had been that all this was feasible for nearly everybody, and so it proved. I cannot remember that I ever spent two hundred dollars on it. And after it was all over I found that Mr. Wells had put into words what I had always had vaguely in mind, in his description of Mr. Britling's garden: 'It didn't look as though it had been made or bought or cost anything, it looked as though it had happened rather luckily. . . .'[19] I can-not quite claim all that for it, but at any rate I am sure that my efforts were all headed in the right direction.

House Beautiful 58 (October 1925): 390.

ENDNOTES

18. *New York Times* (obituary), November 11, 1942, 25:4. *Who Was Who in America* 2 (Chicago, 1950), 599; *Who Was Who Among North American Authors* (Detroit, 1976), 1575.

19. Zelie refers here to Herbert George Wells, *Mr. Britling Sees Through It* (New York, 1916).

ᴄᴐ ROBERT S. LEMMON

The Flower in the Crannied Walk

THE LAYOUT OF PATHS was of crucial importance in formal gardens like the one shown in the first illustration of this article. British gardeners associated with the Arts and Crafts movement liked to place small plants among the stones of their paths, an idea they may have acquired by studying old formal gardens that were no longer scrupulously tended and had become fashionably overgrown. The technique of planting specimens among the stones was even more appropriate to the paths of informal gardens.

Robert Stell Lemmon, born in Englewood, New Jersey, in 1885, served as associate editor of *House and Garden* from 1915 to 1918, and as managing editor from 1918 to 1937. A rock garden enthusiast, he was treasurer of the American Rock Garden Society during the 1930s. He died in 1964. He was, most of all, a keen naturalist. Intrigued by the natural world since childhood, he traveled throughout the United States and to South America studying wildlife and plants. He was the author of many nature books, some written for children.[20] In this article his admiration for natural forms is unmistakable. He seems to have had a horror overly tidy paths, or at least of the overly tidy people who kept them that way. He begins the article with a childish story about a tiny blue flower growing in a brick path in old New Amsterdam, murderously dispatched by a fastidious Dutch housewife. Following this unfortunate start, the article provides an excellent argument for allowing plants to grow in the crevices between rocks in a path. Lemmon has studied the situation well and can inform the reader about exactly how to plant the walk, how to embellish it without going so far as to make it seem impassable. He tells how much space to leave between the rocks and which plants to use for sunny and for shady walks. This is another article in which the photographic illustrations lend great support to the thesis. When he asks the reader to imagine the sunny path without its plants, to see how unpleasant the effect would be, the reader has before him lovely pictures of planted paths that no one would want to see spoiled by careful weeding.

The garden walk that lies exposed to the full glare of the sun, without the softening effect of changing lights and shadows, most needs the relief of crannied flowers. Sometimes, as here, a pleasant mingling of formality and naturalness can be achieved. It is on the estate of L. H. Lapham, Esq., at New Canaan, Connecticut.

MORE YEARS AGO than the chronicles of any but our oldest families can record, a tiny plant clung to the soil between two of the bricks in a garden pathway of old Nieuw Amsterdam.

How it came there no one knew. A stray seed, perhaps, had blown in from the roadside or caught on one of the hausvrouw's great wooden shoes as she clumped home from her milking in the pasture meadow. At all events the plant flourished, and because it was so small and grew in so hidden a corner of the otherwise immaculate path, it escaped for six whole weeks the watchful eye of the good housewife. Low and creeping and tenacious of root, heedless of rain and wind and drought, it spread its modest mat of leaves and dull blue flowerets across the bricks, a pleasant contrast to their aching red.

It could not always go undetected, of course. In that spotless household all must be perfectly ordained, without doors as within. On a day there came a pause on the way to the well curb, a gasp of shocked surprise, a hurried pounce, and the small offender of neatness was no more. From that day to this, the flower in the crannied walk has been banned.

The Use of Pathway Plants

Why? Well, I suppose the reason lies partly in the fact that theoretically walks are made merely to walk on, to lead to flowers rather than to grow flowers themselves. Then, too, the plants which generally find roothold in the crevices of bricks or flagging belong to that despised company generically known as weeds, and consequently are the sworn enemies of all good gardeners and flower lovers.

But consider. Is not all flower growing based on an appeal to our artistic sense, a stimulation of the imagination through our appreciation of beauty? And does not delicate contrast, a slight tinge of the unusual, perhaps, enhance the power of this appeal? The real flower in the walk, the well chosen and

A fit subject for the planting of some of the more truly woodland flowers such as crane's bill and bluebells

Informality and intimacy should characterize a walk such as this. How much the flowers between the stones contribute to this desired result is suggested by a comparison with the photograph on the opposite page.

planted blossom that is no "weed," may add a touch that is no less desirable because seldom given.

Ideally, the pathway garden is a rare blending of flower color and form, a veritable landscaping achievement built upon careful thought and trial. Color harmony, contrast, succession of bloom, permanency — each deserves its share of attention, that a unified whole may result. Added to these considerations, or perhaps preceding them, is the fact that the walk itself must not cease to be a walk. Nothing within its borders should grow so tall as to be an inconvenience; nothing may spread so broad a carpet that it must perforce be trodden on. A mere meshwork of leaf and flower outlining some of the bricks or all of the larger stones is enough for the central part, with a few thicker masses at the less-used sides.

The walk that lies in the full glare of the sun is the one which most needs this relief of crannied plants. Here are no softening shadows, no changing lights to break the monotony. Such a walk is pictured at the beginning of this article. Visualize it shorn of its crevice planting — you see what the result would be, don't you?

But enough of generalizing. What matters most is just what to plant and how to plant it.

In almost every walk of flag or flattened fieldstone are interstices where rock plants may be sown. More satisfactory, perhaps, because special provision for certain effects can be made, is the walk which is laid with a definite thought for future planting. Here spaces of 1" to 8" or 10" can be left, especially at the sides, which will subsequently be filled with plants. In the case of the flowers here listed, no particular type of soil is needed if it is well drained and reasonably fertile.

For reasons too obvious to need mention here, the best plants are drawn from that large list which considerations of taste and adaptability have designated as suitable for the regular rock garden. The charmingly fragrant white rock cress (*Arabis albida*) [*A. caucasia*] is a good sort for the edges, as are also rock madwort (*Alyssum saxatile compactum*) [*Aurinia saxatilis* 'Compacta'] with its mass of little yellow blossoms in April and May, and saxifrage pink (*Tunica Saxifraga*) [*Petrorhagia saxifraga*], pinkish blossomed through the summer months. These three, with Baby's Breath (*Gypsophila repens*) and rose moss (*Portulaca*) will give enough variety to the dense mass effects. For contrast with them, I know of nothing more charming than our own ethereally dainty wild columbine (*Aquilegia*), rising here and there in clusters of but a few stems each, and crowned with fragile looking blossoms of coral and yellow.

Suitable also for the more used parts of the walk, because of their lower habit, are rock speedwell (*Veronica rupestris*) [*V. prostrata*] and snow-in-summer (*Cerastium tomentosum*). Moss pink (*Phlox subulata*) makes a splendid third, perhaps the best of all.

All of these do best in abundant sunshine, though most will succeed except where really shady conditions prevail. On the woodland walk where full sunlight is at a premium, such shade-loving species as blood-root (*Sanguinaria*), bluebell (*Campanula rotundifolia*) and wild crane's bill (*Geranium maculatum*) are valuable additions. If ferns are desired in addition, let them be of such comparatively low growing sorts as *Cystopteris bulbifera, C. fragilis, Phegopteris Dryopteris* [*Gymnocarpium dryopteris*], and *Ph. polypodioides* [*Polypodium polypodioides*].

There are others of course — there always are in any sort of gardening. You may vary my list at will so long as you remember the peculiar requirements of the case and hold always in mind that paraphrase which the successful flower experimenter is wont to apply to untried things:

"It's pretty, but will it grow?"

House and Garden 31 (MARCH 1917): 17, 72, 74.

ENDNOTES

20. *New York Times* (obituary), March 5, 1964, 30:4; *American Authors and Books 1640 to the Present Day*, ed. William J. Burke and Will D. Howe (New York, 1972),372; *Who Was Who in America, 1961–1968* 4 (Chicago, 1968), 567; *Authors of Books for Young People*, eds. Martha E. Ward, Dorothy A. Marquardt, Nancy Dolan, and Dawn Eaton (Metuchen, N.J., 1990), 427.

∽ RUTH DEAN

Practical Plans for the Home Grounds: Appropriate Planting for Formal Pools

POOLS WERE an important element of the formal garden — as well as the naturalistic garden. In this short piece, written for *Garden Magazine* as part of a series on landscape design, Dean informs the reader of the best ways to achieve beautiful and appropriate plantings for formal water gardens.[21] A month before, the magazine had carried an article she wrote about naturalistic water gardens. The advice, once again, is as useful today as it was more than eighty years ago. The photographs of two formal water gardens, the James Parmalee garden in Washington, D.C., and the Samuel Knopf garden in Cedarhurst, Long Island, are stunning and definitely fortify her message. [22]

AN OLD GARDENER used to explain to me his aversion for Ferns and Lilies around the foundation of a house, by saying — "Oh, but you cannot plant such damp tings dere. Dey make you tink always of vet feed." And when you stop to consider it, they do make you think of wet feet. Around a pool, however, or along a stream it is just exactly these reminders of marshy places that we want, especially if the pool be naturalistic. With a formal pool or fountain, one may take more liberties in the way of planting than with a pool which is trying to simulate Nature. The former is usually in the midst of a garden, and because the garden is the first consideration, Phlox, Petunias and Hollyhocks [*Alcea rosea*] near the water, are not the incongruities they would be in a woodsy garden.

In planting even the architectural pool, however, it is best to try to recall something of the feeling which belongs to watersides. Iris and grasses will contribute to this atmosphere, so will the little Forget-me-not [*Myosotis*] of streams and the brilliant Cardinal Flower [*Lobelia cardinalis*], with tall Marshmallows [*Althea officinalis* or *Hibiscus moscheutos*], purple Ironweed [*Vernonia*], and rosy Joe-Pye-Weed [*Eupatorium purpurea*] as background

Around even a formal pool one should plant such reminders of marshy places as Iris and Grasses. (James Parmelee, Washington, D. C.)

flowers. It is surprising how at home these plants are in the garden proper, among their more cultivated companions, and how much of real charm, a charm which is due to their appropriateness, they lend to the water near which they grow.

If the pool is to have a friendly, intimate feeling, the planting should extend in places to the water's edge. Nothing is colder and less inviting than the stone-rimmed pool set in the midst of gravel. It has a harsh ungracious look, that just a few leaves bending over the edge would mitigate, or a stray vine soften. On the other hand it is bad to surround a pool entirely with flowers and shrubs so as to make it inaccessible. Places for planting near the border should be incorporated in the design in some such way as that shown on the accompanying plan which provides walks to the water's edge and intervals two feet wide between for Iris or Ferns or Grasses.

Planting for the surface of the water has its difficulties as well, not the least of which is scale. More often than not pools too small to warrant such huge leaves are planted with Lotus, or tall Cat-tails [*Typha latifolia*], or both, when their size really demands the smallest of the Nymphaeas and the fine

Good border planting for a pool with just enough lily pads on the water's surface. The columns at back materially help the picture. (Samuel Knopf, Cedarhurst, L. I.)

leaves of Spike Rush [*Eleocharis*] or Scirpus Tabernæ [*Schœnoplectus lacustris*]. Most aquatics grow rapidly and unless they are constantly thinned out they cover the entire water surface and leave no mirror to reflect bending purple Flags [*Iris versicolor*], and white clouds. With a little taste and care in thinning — the groups of Lily pads [*Nymphaea*] and Grasses remaining, may be made into compositions interesting in themselves.

The aquatics in the average pool, should consist of hardy varieties which may be bedded in the pool bottom itself, rather than the tender sorts which are usually for convenience sake, planted in pots. The pots are too apt to show through the water, and introduce an artificial quality which detracts from the grace of the pool.

Fitness, which is only a synonym for appropriateness depends, in pool planting as in all other kinds, upon attention to details which will contribute to the effect we wish to produce. In a rock garden we plant alpines, plants which naturally make their homes in the scant pockets of earth between rocks, and if the stones are not large, we use the smaller flowering and smaller foliaged plants, reserving those with coarse leaves and large flowers for the

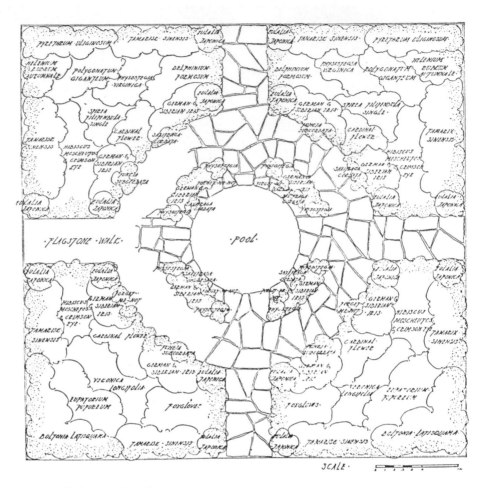

Suggested planting for a formal pool in which walks at intervals approach clear to the water's edge.

garden which can boast boulders. Similarly, about a pool, however formal its character, those things should grow which emphasize the feeling of water, and if the pool is a large one, the flowers and shrubs may be big, whereas, if it is small, they must not reduce its size still more, by too great contrast.

The Garden Magazine 23 (JULY 1916): 331–332.

ENDNOTES

21. On Dean, see above 223.

22. On the Parmalee garden: Keith N. Morgan, *Charles Platt: The Artist as Architect* (New York, 1985, 249; Mac Griswold and Eleanor Weller, *The Golden Age of American Gardens: Proud Owners, Proud Estates, 1890–1940* (New York, 1991), 154.

✍ BEATRICE STEVENS
Letter to the Editor

BEATRICE STEVENS (1876–1947) was a landscape painter and illustrator. The magazines in which her work appeared included *Country Life in America, Century, Scribner's, Woman's Home Companion,* and *House Beautiful*. This letter, written to the editor of *Country Life* in hopes of convincing him to publish drawings of her garden, and perhaps a short text, was printed in a column that appeared from time to time in the magazine, Our Contributors Off Guard. In it the editor printed letters that he had received from prospective contributors and that he thought might be of interest to readers. He confessed that "occasionally the letters make better reading" than the finished articles. Stevens complains in her letter that wild birds have taken over the walled garden at her home in Pomfret, Connecticut.[23] Judging from her drawing, the garden seems to have been quite a pleasant place with a formal plan, enclosed by walls, and organized around a rectangular pool and vine-covered arbor. Only one drawing was published with the letter. Constructing a small pool is in fact one of the best ways to attract wildlife to one's garden, for better or worse.

Brisk-to-High,

Pomfret, Conn.

My Dear Mr. Saylor:

I am sending you some drawings (in pen and ink and color) of our walled garden — inside and out — which I think might be of interest to you as an example of gardening with a small outlay of money. Of course, in any garden, the outlay of time is always incalculable, and of labor, nothing short of herculean.

This walled garden opens out of my studio, and I intended to use it for a summer workroom. But the first year the vines did not cover the arbor

where I meant to keep my table, and it was too sunny. Consequently, just at first I did not use it, and so you see, the birds took it; and now they won't let me have it. They only permit me to set my foot in there for the necessary garden work and care of the pool, and even then there are always one or two around to shriek in my ear every few minutes. It is the headquarters for the Birds' Public Baths; the Wyndham County Birds' Lunch Club; the Junior Recreation Grounds; the Northern Connecticut Birds' Winter Sports; the Pomfret and Woodstock Mothers' Aid and Day Nursery for Young Birds, and the Homemakers' and Nesters' Union. Consequently it is difficult to see where I come in, but it is not hard to see where I get off. I have had to spend hours sitting by the door where I could rescue idiotic young robins from drowning themselves in the pool, and when I fished them out and dried them I got only blame from their parents for letting them fall in at all. I have been literally assaulted and battered by tree swallows for just walking past their houses. At Brisk-to-High we call tree swallows Blue Tin Devils. And with reason.

To go back to the garden — which is a nice garden, and I would like to be in it more — would you care to use a set of drawings with a small working plan of the gardens, and a little explanatory text of the planting to go with each picture, or possibly a short story of it? We have no really good photographs — the garden is too small to photograph excepting in detail. We tried several times last summer, but with very unsatisfactory results.

I trust that you will use some of the drawings, for these birds have to be fed in the winter, and they do not care a whoop for Mr. Hoover[24] or any one else. Of course *we* expect to live on a peanut now and then, ourselves.

Yours sincerely,
BEATRICE STEVENS.

Country Life in America 33 (MARCH 1918): 60.

ENDNOTES

23. Mary G. Page of the Pomfret Historical Society provided information on Stevens. Stevens exhibited four paintings at the 1934 American Salon at Rockefeller Center and some of her art is preserved today at the Pomfret School in Pomfret, Connecticut. She lived at Brisk-to-High with her companion, Ella M. Boult. Boult was a photographer who also wrote garden articles (for example, "The Garden of Mistress Mary," *Country Life in America* [August 1907], 423–425, illustrated with her photographs). Original copies of Boult's photographs, which appeared in leading magazines (they illustrated the two articles by Walter Prichard Eaton in this anthology: "The Garden in Spring" and "The Garden Beside the Highway") have apparently not survived.

24. Herbert Clark Hoover, who later became President of the United States, was named chairman of the American Relief Commission at the outbreak of World War I in 1914. For the duration of the war he organized the collection of food and clothing in the United States to send to Belgium and Northern France.

Chapter Seven

THE PHILOSOPHICAL GARDENER: *Collegiality, Class Warfare, Feminism, and Intangible Rewards in the Garden*

THIS CHAPTER GATHERS together the diverse thoughts, opinions, and observations that garden writers expressed about themselves, their fellow gardeners, and the impact of gardening on their lives. The first two articles recount garden visits that were spiritually and aesthetically fulfilling, but the next two tell how frustrating some visits can be for the gardener and how irksome for the visitor. Politics and social reform come into play as the next articles address the essentially democratic nature of gardening and its connection to the women's suffrage movement, as well as the importance of asserting one's individuality in the garden. While the following two authors consider how gardening teaches us to live wiser, more contented lives, the next drolly refutes this idea, and the last describes communion with his garden as a kind of sacrament of natural religion.

On My Friend's Porch

Hazel Wood Waterman began writing articles for *The House Beautiful* in 1902, after Irving Gill, the Arts and Crafts architect who had designed her granite cottage in San Diego, encouraged her to pursue her interest in architectural design.[1] Her articles typically concerned the aesthetic relationships among architecture, interior design, and landscaping, and proposed that the mental and physical health and happiness of a family could be enhanced by functional and visually pleasing surroundings. Widowed in 1903, Waterman began a formal program of studies in architecture and started working as a draftsman for Gill. In 1906 she began designing homes, exhibiting an outstanding ability to combine modern with vernacular, historical styles.[2] The archetypal Arts and Crafts integration of nature and architecture, and the capability of such inspired design to elevate the human spirit, is the theme of this article in which Waterman recounts an afternoon visit on her friend's porch, entering the garden by the side gate. The porch is an integral part of the garden, which her friend keeps in perfect order with wise and loving care. The reading material displayed on the table proves that the friend's taste in literature is highly suitable for a member of the educated middle class around the turn of the century. This essay exemplifies one type of garden-visit article: a responsive and appreciative visitor is welcomed to, enchanted with, and uplifted by the garden described.

I⸛ has been my privilege to spend pleasant hours with a dear friend. I am in the habit of coming in at the side gate, where trailing vines and nestling plants partially conceal the simple fence of wire netting. Nearest the gate is a chorizema with little flame-like blossoms and long, feathery twigs. On one side of the curving path, irregularly bordered by unobtrusive greenery and low-growing shrubs, is a group of choice roses. A trellis background, covered with a profusion of blossoms, is quite a part of their seemingly unstudied arrangement.

On the porch and now at the step is my friend, her face speaking of pleasure. The bright coreopsis beside the step smile up her greeting, their rich yellow more sunny, their brown center deeper, when she says, with her charming sincerity: "It is beautiful that you have come! You are going to spend the afternoon with me."

We do not go in. It is almost an ever-abiding joy of our Southern California life that we may be out of doors. Here one is most content on the deep-covered porch. It forms the southeast corner of the house. A large bow of plate-glass, with broad window-seat beneath it, incloses the southern side, and affords protection from the cool sea breezes without obstructing the view. On this side is pictured the near canon slopes with their characteristic California covering, here relieved of monotony by ever-varying effects of light and shade, by gradual changes from brown to green and then to brown. There is a picturesque brick cottage with a grouping of trees, the herbarium of a well-known scientist; a boat going down to the bay; craft of commerce and pleasure on the blue water; and quite in the distance, brighter colors mark the gay cottages, hotel, and tented city of Coronado Beach. The bay is bordered by slopes of wonderful color — green, orange, or violet, merging into serious bluffs of darker and deeper tone. Beyond it all is the Pacific Ocean, reaching out toward the world of other peoples. On this porch one feels most a sense of the great enlarging influences of the beautiful world in which it is set.

Yet here is secluded, restful home quiet. A hammock in the most protected corner, substantial wicker or bamboo furniture, are suggestive of leisurely tastes and habits, and give a most satisfying living-room quality. Fashion, though not ignored, is no dictator here; nor is artistic arrangement distinct from all essential comfort and a degree of elegance. A potted plant or two, appropriate to its setting on the broad rail, a Japanese vase with delightfully characteristic arrangement of flowers or branches, are among the little things that make this porch attractive. They leave room for children's playthings, and offer enough of freedom to tempt loungers — not the chance passer-by, but the circle of friends who make this an objective point and love to come and linger here.

I have been made cozy in the bamboo reclining chair, the one with the extension foot-piece. My friend has a trick of setting the adjustable back at the most restful angle, and of using about me in the most comfortable way pillows whose desire to be used is proclaimed in material and design. Near there is a table with books and magazines — *The Other Wise Man* by Van Dyke, Maeterlinck's *Wisdom and Destiny*, a volume of Phillips Brook's sermons, *The Outlook*, or other favorites, and some new work of present interest.[9] Sometimes she reads aloud to me, or we "take turns," as the children say.

I am offered tea — tea in a Japanese cup of blue and white. To be served where there has been artistic perception in the selection of inexpensive and dainty china is peculiarly gratifying. It is even a satisfaction to note the exquisite laundering of the doily, whose simple pattern but heightens the

The southeast corner.

effect of the teak-wood tray with its unique carving. In addition to this, the charm of a gracious hospitality pervades my friend's tea-table.

I hear her say, "You have brought your mending. How you inspire me to do mine!" Still half absorbed in the blue of my teacup, and dreamily quoting, "Blue as the skies after rain," I take up my work; boys' stockings whose holes in the knee suggest severe reproof, but usually obtain loving leniency toward marbles and tops. We accomplish very little. Both being mothers of small children, we feel that we have no time "to waste." "Mending" is a salve to my conscience when I mean to spend several hours chatting or dreaming. Of course we talk about the children, then perhaps drift into domestic economies. But there is a certain subtle something here, which makes remote the striving workaday life, and elevates commonplace thoughts and things.

The porch is but a part of the surrounding shrubbery. The bougainvillea, whose luxuriant foliage, beautiful at all seasons, screens one side, gives of its terra-cotta bloom with a joyous generosity. Though controlled and wisely trained, it vigorously strives to cover walls and roof. Climbing roses with trailing twigs are allowed to stray in the most natural way. The vines frame the view, the refreshing bit of bay with its varied life and color, the great expanse of sky. On the eastern side there is an irregular boundary of shrubbery, whose tops, differing in height, open to a background of rolling mesa and purple hills. A clump of acacias, some of them unusual specimens, give a pleasing effect in harmonious shades of green. The seasons through they seem to aim at a perfection worthy of an environment where standards are high. The wild one which sprung up on the outer edge has as tender care as any, although it is my friend's special thought for it that it shall be untrimmed and untrained, and allowed to grow in its own natural way.

In this corner of the garden there is no lawn, but the soil has a quality such as only frequent hoeing, pulverizing, and raking can impart. The very shadows seem to have a feeling of affection for it; though changing from hour to hour, they express appreciation of its generous giving by decorations of contrasting and ever-deeper tones of color.

Little flowering plants, a few among the shrubs, have their place — asters, daffodils, carnations, eschscholtzias, some beauty for each season. Other low-growing, creeping things cover the whole plots with an ecstasy of spontaneous expression. Nasturtiums [*Tropaeolum majus*], marigolds [*Tagetes*], and wild strawberries [*Fragaria*] are seemingly allowed to run riot; here they, too, have consideration and courtesy, never taking possession where they are not welcome, as they are apt to do in other Southern California gardens.

It is not a large garden, but there is no sense of crowding. In the partially hidden recesses there is calm, in the grouping of the shrubs there is symmetry of outline. One feels that this corner is in harmony with the great whole of which it is part. Unconsciously one responds to the spell of the environment, and the "spirit of God's out-of-doors."

The House Beautiful 12 (September 1902): 220–222.

ENDNOTES

1. Most of my information on Waterman derives from Sally Bullard Thornton, *Daring to Dream: The Life of Hazel Wood Waterman* (San Diego, 1987). On Gill and Waterman, also see Karen J. Weitze, "Utopian Place Making: The Built Environment in Arts and Crafts California," in *The Arts and Crafts Movement in California: Living the Good Life*, ed. Kenneth R. Trapp (New York, 1993–4), 73–77.

2. Weitze, 77.

3. Henry Van Dyke (1852–1933) was a celebrated American clergyman and popular author whose writings combined a religious fervor, a reformist attitude typical of the Progressive era, and a love of nature in the tradition of Thoreau. *The Other Wise Man* (1896) was his best-known book. Maurice Maeterlinck (1862–1949) was a Belgian Symbolist author whose writings were immensely popular in the United States until about 1930. *Wisdom and Destiny* was one of his most highly mystical works. Phillips Brooks (1835–1893) was another American clergyman renowned for his social liberalism and the deep spirituality of his writings. On *Outlook*, see above, xxv and xxvi.

RUTH R. BLODGETT
A Studio in a Garden

RUTH ROBINSON BLODGETT was born in Boston in 1883. She performed social work for the Red Cross and during World War I worked overseas for Y.M.C.A.[4] She was also a novelist who occasionally contributed fiction to magazines. Like many of her contemporaries, she believed that gardening might provide a cure for the social malaise that afflicted humanity, and she wished it were a more popular pastime among writers and artists. This story tells of a chance visit to a garden the narrator discovers while out for a walk "in a sleepy country town." Like Waterman's article, this is about the kind of visit every gardener longs for: one in which the caller is clearly smitten by the garden's "lovable, livable" design and its delightful, flourishing plants. The gardener in this story is an artist, and her studio in the garden has about it a distinct aura of wholesomeness and simplicity — those cardinal virtues of the era. Also as in Waterman's article, the domestic environment provides the aesthetic enrichment necessary to improve the human condition.

WHEN "the April wind wakes the call for the soil," Dallas Lore Sharp says, "I hold the plough as my only hold upon the earth, and, as I follow through the fresh and fragrant furrow, I am planted with every foot-step, growing, budding, blooming into a spirit of spring."[5] A great many of us, who did not know this contact-with-the-soil creed before, have learned it since the war began. We have learned that more of the "earth-earthiness" would solve our social problems, remove many isms from our vocabulary, and purify our art. And so we often wish that those who interpret life for us by pen or brush would buy a trowel and a paper of seeds. They don't all do it. However, last summer I went on a delightful voyage of discovery in a sleepy country town, and received a rich reward: I found a studio in a garden!

It was not April, but late July. I was wandering aimlessly along a broad, elm-shaded street. There was little to see and not much to do; and there was plenty of time in which to do it. A tall, austere house of lugubrious complexion sat primly by the board walk. The tall lilac [*Syringa*] hedge behind intensified its lugubriousness. Then I noticed a little board walk that

A muslin curtain fluttering in the open casement window seemed a beckoning finger, and a black knocker is no more to be resisted than a hole in a hedge.

ran up through an arched opening in the hedge. The ability to resist openings in hedges is not within my powers of self-control. And why should I not take up this challenge to explore a mysterious Beyond, even if it meant only a clothesline or a woodpile? Thankful for an elastic conscience and for the absence of horrid signs to discourage trespassers, I marched straight up the walk and through the dusky thickness of the hedge. And there I found the studio in the garden.

It was down at the other end of a grapevine [*Vitis*], woodbine [*Parthenocissus quinquefolia*] covered pergola — a wee bit of a house in a pink ruffled petticoat of sweet William [*Dianthus barbatus*]. A big iron knocker on the half-open door urged me cordially to rap, and a comfortable hammock on the little porch invited me to rest and meditate. The gingerbread house of Hansel and Gretel! Perhaps a witch inside! So I did not take the broad highway of the pergola path, which might lead to a witch's oven, heated for a dainty human morsel. Instead, I lingered in the garden.

For on both sides of the pergola there was a garden that brought forth an unconscious "Oh" of delight — a lovable, livable garden. The smooth lawns, the carefully tended flowerbeds which fringed them, the dainty informal garden furnishings, all spoke of loving hands; and the whole effect spoke of a feminine personality — a woman's hands without a doubt. Lilac hedges and a neighbor's orchard gave the place a sweet seclusion and restfulness. Although the dimensions of the whole garden were small, it being built on a Petit Trianon scale to suit the miniature house, nevertheless there was a sense of the dignity of space.

In the middle of the lawn at the right of the pergola was the rose garden. "Roses ranged in a valiant row," — rows of them in fact. "She loves you, noble roses, I know," I added aloud, as I breathed the fragrant air. Courtly delphiniums ran along at a right angle to the roses — ladies-in-waiting, making stately courtesies in the summer breeze. And, beyond the roses by the house, snowbanks of spiraea shut in a bird bath on three sides. Lilac hedges everywhere, shutting out — what? At last my curiosity was at rest, enclosed by the lilac hedge. No glory of the There could transcend the roses of the Here.

The garden at the left was in reality a green expanse of fresh-mown lawn with a sun-dial for a center-piece, and, all along the further side, a glorious, wide flower border, embroidered in riotous shades. Leaves told of flowers gone and flowers to come, iris, poppies [*Papaver*] and forget-me-nots [*Myosotis*] earlier, phlox and monkshood [*Aconitum*] not yet in bloom. At present, hollyhocks [*Alcea rosea*], Canterbury bells [*Campanula medium*], anchusa, English primroses [*Primula vulgaris*] and foxgloves [*Digitalis*] were all "tossing their heads in sprightly dance."

Their joy was intoxicating. I would have danced with them on the fairy green, if Pan had piped a tune. Instead, I sat down on the garden-seat and

envied "her" for whom these flowers bloomed. For even on the faces of the flowers there was an easily imagined pleasure, a pleasure because they could so richly reward some one's devoted care.

And now for the witch's oven! A muslin curtain fluttering in the open casement window seemed a beckoning finger, and a black knocker is no more to be resisted than a hole in a hedge. I picked a daisy from the border. "Shall I? Shall I not? Shall I? Shall I not? I shall." And I did. A little uncertain about my form of introduction, and somewhat surprised at my boldness, I walked across the lawn, stepped up on the little porch and rapped. No answer? I crossed the threshold. It was a studio!

Pictures, paints, pots, palettes — all the P's of a painter. And inspiration pouring in with the happy sunshine through open windows and doors; vistas on all sides of vine-shaded walks, restful lawns, dazzling flowers and lilac hedges. No wonder the pictures on the walls and easel spoke of happy and joyous things; no wonder that there was no affectation and a simplicity, refreshing in this day when we are all trying to be "individual."

There was the same simplicity about the studio itself — a feeling of plenty of space filled with plenty of air from the wholesome outdoors.

The bareness was relieved by the muslin curtains and rag rugs, by cretonne covered window-seats and a few pieces of old furniture, by the high shelves holding old demijohns and jugs, fascinating studies for still-life.

Some one was singing outside. I stepped out on the porch. She was coming down the pergola-path. I felt sure it was the "she" of the garden. Strange to say there was no embarrassment in our meeting. She did not seem surprised to see me.

"This is your garden," I stated, rather than inquired.

"Yes, do you like it? I have made it all myself."

"I love it!" I exclaimed.

"So do I," she answered simply.

The House Beautiful 43 (MARCH 1918): 216–217.

ENDNOTES_____

4. On Blodgett, see *Who Was Who Among North American Authors* 1 (Detroit, 1976), 169.

5. Dallas Lore Sharp (1870–1929) was the author of popular nature books and articles.

ꕔ [BARBARA CHENEY]

The Contributors' Club: Garden Blights

> NOT ALL GARDEN VISITORS are as obliging as those portrayed in the two preceding articles. Barbara Cheney describes three types of visitors no one wants in their garden but who are probably the most likely to appear.

GARDENING, I TOLD MYSELF, is the most sociable of hobbies. The very nature of one's field of activities demands an audience. No one wants flowers to blush unseen or waste their sweetness. This was what I thought until last week.

Last week I worked hard, weeding, setting out new plants, dividing old ones. When at last I arose from my muddy knees, I felt elated, though weary, and eager to display the fruits of my labors. My first hope was an old friend who dropped in for tea. I restrained my impatience until she had been properly fed. Then I led her forth.

'Oh yes,' she cried, 'I'd love to see your garden. I'm so fond of flowers.'

As we neared the scene of my triumphs, and I was slowing down to begin my introductory speech, she tucked her arm in mine and said, 'I'm so glad to have a chance to chat with you alone. We have so many, many weeks to catch up.'

'Yes indeed,' I said vaguely. 'Now here is the entrance, you see. I'm very proud of my iris. I planned these clumps so that I have three months of continuous bloom.'

'How nice,' she said. 'Have you heard from Ann lately?'

'No,' I said, thinking to block that detour. It was the wrong answer.

'Well, I have,' said my guest, firmly planting her foot on my favorite sedum. 'She's been to a psychiatrist and has a new ego — not a very nice one, if you ask me.' Nothing would have induced me to ask her, but that made no difference. I learned all about Ann's ego.

'We'll stay here by these clumps of iris until she looks at them,' I thought, but I finally took pity on the sedum and led her on. Ann's ego absorbed her until we had passed the peonies, about which I was bursting to talk. At last she paused for breath.

'You must notice my Scotch broom [*Cytisus scoparius*],' I said hastily. 'It's very rare in this country.'

'Did you know the Scotts were getting a divorce?' she asked. This time I knew better than to say no.

"Yes," I said, concealing my surprise, 'I heard all about it.' But that didn't work, either.

'Oh, did you?' she said, 'I doubt if you know the whole truth. Few people do.' The whole truth carried us past my violas, my prize lupines [*Lupinus*], my rare old pinks [*Dianthus*]. The only interruption was when she fell over the watering pot.

'I didn't see it,' she explained.

'No,' I said coldly, 'you weren't looking.'

It was several days before I recovered from this interview. I chose my next visitor more carefully. She was a real gardener, deeply interested in gardens, and she approached mine as eagerly as I did.

'The hedge,' I explained, 'has not recovered from the terrible winter of 1934. It died right down to the ground.'

'Don't talk to me about the winter of '34,' she cried. 'Do you know that I lost two box [*Buxus*] bushes that were a hundred years old, and that lovely Dr. Van Fleet rose that I planted myself in 1920?'

I expressed genuine sympathy and then began again. 'I'm very proud of my iris,' I said.

'Have you any Ambassadeurs?' she asked. 'You must get some. Mine are beautiful. They actually stand almost three feet high. I have another new variety, too — Moonlight. It's perfectly beautiful.'

I hurried her on to the peonies [*Paeonia*]. 'These I divided and set out myself,' I said proudly, knowing that a real gardener would appreciate what a feat this was.

'You have no single ones, have you?' she asked. 'I have the prettiest ones, pale pink, the Japanese variety. You must come over and look at them before they go by.'

I was speechless after this, but she was not. My lovely blue lupines reminded her of her lovelier pink ones, my violas of the apricot ones she had at last achieved.

'Haven't you any dahlias?' she asked.

'No,' I said firmly, 'I hate them.'

'Oh, but my dear, you wouldn't hate mine if you once saw them. The flowers are five inches across, they really are, and such lovely colors. I have some extra roots. I'll send them over.'

'What I really want,' I said to myself plaintively, 'is someone who will look at my garden for just a few minutes. It doesn't seem too much to ask.' It wasn't. I found her. She was the worst of all.

I'm very proud of my iris,' I began.

'My dear,' she cried, 'how beautiful they are! I never saw a prettier combination of colors. Those pale lavender ones next to the deep purple are perfect, and that touch of yellow adds just the right contrast.' My soul began to expand.

'They are so perfect,' she went on, 'I think they ought to be where they would show off more. Couldn't you put them over there with the stone wall for a background?'

'The peonies are there now,' I protested. 'I set those all out myself. You have no idea what a job it was digging up the old roots and dividing them.'

'Well, if I were you,' she said, 'I'd put the peonies over here,'

'Yes,' I said doubtfully, 'but these lupines took five years to grow, and they don't move well once they're established.'

'Oh, my dear,' she said, 'that's what the books tell you, but don't you believe it. You can move anything if you do it carefully. Speaking of moving,' she went on, 'I'm not sure I wouldn't move that hedge. It seems to me it would be more effective if you set it back about three feet.'

'Next year,' I said, 'I'm going to have a new hedge, a very tall one, made entirely of thorns.'

Atlantic Monthly 157 (June 1936): 767–768.

The Point of View:
Other People's Gardens

THIS ARTICLE FROM SCRIBNER'S The Point of View tells the other side of the garden visiting story. It is written by an anonymous author who has been grievously oppressed by friends who have recently taken up gardening.

THIS IS THE SEASON when your friends once again talk about their gardens. This is no attack on flowers. Even the geranium in a sooty window draws the attention of every passer-by; how much more the color and perfume of a well-ordered garden. But I for my part was better pleased in those almost forgotten days when gardeners did the gardening. They were stern, autocratic men, jealous tyrants who forbade as far as possible the picking of any fruit or flowers; they did not, certainly, create color-schemes as beautiful as those evolved nowadays by our gifted amateurs. But they did let you enjoy the general results of their handiwork in peace and quiet. The most you were ever expected to say was: "Ah, MacFarlane, how well the fuchsias are doing!"

But things are changed nowadays. The gardens of our friends! How half an acre of land can destroy conversation, friendship, and indeed all the finer relations of life. The garden-lover has no conscience. Neither has the man who is building a house, but he commits his atrocity only once in a lifetime. The garden, on the other hand, is like a spoiled beauty. There is no limit to its demands for admiration. It is new not only each spring, but each month, almost each day of the year. You may be required to find something fresh to say about it at least twenty-five times in one season, something which usually turns out to be grossly ignorant and unsatisfactory.

You arrive weary and dusty at the country house of a friend, and have hardly swallowed your tea, when — "Wouldn't you like to see my garden?" says your hostess. Ten to one you have been sitting for twenty minutes in some pergola or piazza from which the garden was designed to be viewed; but in your hostess's question the verb "to see" takes on new and sinister meaning. It signifies counting buds, chasing small insects, listening to long, confusing names, and allowing opinions to dragged from you on matters about which you have neither information nor intuitive judgment. For hours afterward sentences like this ring through your head: "Do tell me, should I do better with a group of golden-throated asterisks against that wall, or do you like the azure-eyed Armerias better?" "Give me your opinion about this twelfth-century well-head that we picked up at Ampelopsis last summer. Doctor Bones thinks it's a genuine Marie Corelli."

Not only the suffering of the moment is to be considered, but the fact that painful associations are gradually being set up in connection with all growing things. Your heart sinks at the mention of a crocus. The smell of damp, freshly turned earth — once so full of a pleasant promise — now suggests nothing but wet feet, a backache, and hours of interminable waiting beside a digging friend, who knows just as well as you that luncheon is getting cold.

"God Almighty," said Lord Bacon, himself a gardener, "first planted a garden." Very true, but that garden was Paradise — that is to say, Adam and Eve were spared a personally conducted tour of inspection.

Scribner's Magazine 58 (JULY 1915): 123–124.

[PAULINE G. WIGGIN LEONARD]
The Contributors' Club: Democracy and Gardening

PAULINE GERTRUDE WIGGIN LEONARD's humorous article attests to the indignation and sense of moral superiority that some middle-class gardeners felt toward the rich at the turn of the century, as well as the increasing awareness in American culture of women's quest for equal rights. Leonard was born in 1869, earned a master of arts degree at Radcliffe in 1895 and a degree in library science at New York State Library School in 1902. She was an instructor of English first at Vassar and then at Wellesley from 1895 to 1899. By 1907 she was a librarian at West Virginia University. Editor of two early twentieth-century publications of Shakespeare's plays, she wrote a book on the authorship of the Middleton-Rowley plays and also "numerous articles on nature study and social questions."[6] For this anonymously published piece Leonard writes in the guise of a man recounting a conversation with his wife. They are a middle-class, gardening couple who have hoed their patch on the hottest day of summer and squished the worms on their tomato plants. They discuss a book by Countess Elizabeth von Arnim (Mary Annett Beauchamp), *Elizabeth and Her German Garden*.[7] The couple, particularly the wife, is disgusted that Elizabeth was too afflicted with a Sense of Propriety to engage in manual labor, even though she claimed that she really wanted to do her own weeding. The wife concludes that Elizabeth is not only a snob but hopelessly obtuse for failing to see that gardens are intrinsically democratic. The couple congratulate themselves for not being too aristocratic to enjoy working in their garden. The article culminates with the suggestion that someone write a more up-to-date book on women and gardening next year with a title like *The Effect of the Emancipation of Women upon Gardening*.

Now that the calendars and the catalogues of the seedsmen have announced the spring, I have begun looking over last year's crop of gardening books, and wondering sadly whether this year's must not, like most second crops from gardens, be rather small potatoes.

How good they were! The other day I was reading over again *Elizabeth and her German Garden* (or was it *A Solitary Summer*? It does not matter), and it almost persuaded me that the possession of a garden was the only reasonable aim of civilized woman. If you had that, with a few babies and visitors enough to quarrel with, just to keep you from stagnation, it was clear that you might snap your fingers at the world. To be sure, there was a serpent, as there always is in gardens. Mine, I notice, appears in the form of a perennial striped snake, who eats up an equally perennial nest of young song sparrows under a peavine, and who is miraculously renewed every season, in spite of the fact that he seemed to die the year before, under the stones I threw at him. Elizabeth's took the form of a gardener. He was, of course, the real owner of her garden, and only of his kindness allowed her to walk there; and I suppose it is her misfortune that she is high-born and a German, and therefore so afflicted with that painful disease known as a Sense of Propriety that not even a garden can cure her. She says she should love to hoe, but she does not dare; for "with what lightning rapidity would the news spread that I had been seen stalking down the garden path with a hoe over my shoulder, and a basket in my hand, and weeding written large in every feature! Yet I should love to weed." Poor Elizabeth!

I read this to Theodora, who was sitting by the other window, pencil in hand, trying to decide whether she should put sweet peas [*Lathyrus odoratus*] or stocks [*Matthiola*] in the bed next to the pink and white hollyhocks [*Alcea rosea*].

"I suppose there must be something disgraceful about weeding," I mused. "But how often, Theodora, we have weeded! Do you remember the sweet peas and the melons we hoed, the hottest day last summer? And the tomato worms we killed? The green stuff squirted out of them and made us very sick, but we should not have enjoyed those tomatoes half so much if we had a gardener to kill the worms. On the whole, I am glad I am so mildly inoculated with the virus of propriety that I can still hoe. I am glad I am not aristocratic."

Theodora tore herself away from her seed catalogues, drawn by the irresistible attraction of a pet aversion. (If this sounds paradoxical, I cannot help it. So is truth.) "I have no patience with Elizabeth!" she cried. "She is a snob. And as you would naturally expect of a snob who has the privilege of living in a garden, she is obtuse. Do you remember how she goes through the village on chilly days, when her temper is bad, dispensing jelly and criticism in equal quantities, and she thinks the people are beasts because they prefer the jelly? Then she says if she were poor, she 'would sit, quite frankly poor, with a piece of bread and a pot of geraniums and a book.' I wonder how she thinks she would get the time. And she fairly hugs herself with conceit because she would rather lie on the grass all day than talk to her neighbors. Now I put it to you: is that a thing to get vain about? It is ridiculous! It is even immoral!"

I mildly pointed out the fact that it was not unknown for us ourselves to go up into the woods of a summer morning, and lie for hours on a certain bearberry [*Arctostaphylos*] bank, looking up at the sky, without so much as speaking to each other. But Theodora properly remarked that this was quite beside the point, since the question was not what one did but the spirit in which one did it; and I was compelled to admit that aristocratic sensibilities were out of place in a garden.

"Perhaps they are grafts of that Tree of Knowledge whose fruit cast Adam and Eve out of Eden," I suggested.

"When you think of it, is there anything so democratic as a vegetable?" went on Theodora. "A stump speaker, a small boy, even a cat has his own awe; but where will you find a weed with any scruples about thrusting itself into the most select circles of vegetable society? And last year, for all I could see, our roses grew as comfortably among the potatoes as anywhere else; and the honeysuckle [*Lonicera*] deserted that elegant trellis we built for it, to go and twine itself around a sunflower [*Helianthus*]. It did not seem to care in the least that the ultimate destiny of its beloved object was the henyard. No, a garden, properly interpreted, is a school of republicanism."

These curious and interesting experiments in the innate democracy of vegetables to which Theodora referred were conducted last season in our garden, under the auspices of an aged Portuguese farmer whom we hired to do our planting in our absence. It was his evident belief that the palate should not be pampered at the expense of the nobler senses even in a vegetable garden; so all summer long, bunches of marigolds [*Tagetes*] and cinnamon pinks [*Dianthus*] blossomed in among our cabbages, and a bed which we had fondly designed for late lettuce offered instead an aesthetic display of pale pink poppies [*Papaver*]. Yet the little girl who lives with us assures me that none of the flower fairies have turned-up noses. She ought to know, for she ate fern seed every night before she went to bed; and if that won't make a person see fairies, I should like to know what will.

"Yes," repeated Theodora, "a snobbish person who lives in a garden must certainly be obtuse. It shows a lack of sensitiveness to one's surroundings."

And now that she spoke of it, I began to believe that it might really be true that Elizabeth and her compeers were a trifle behind the times. Since they have called the world's attention to gardening as a popular subject for literature, — in fact, shouted it from the housetops, — there may be hopes of something even better in that line this year, after all; something more original, more significant of the present age. For instance, The Effect of the Emancipation of Women upon Gardening ought to prove an inspiring theme. Or, since long titles have come into fashion, why not have a book called The Confessions of a Free American Woman who Dared to Hoe?

There is no copyright on these titles. They are quite at the service of any serious-minded person of a literary turn who properly appreciates the charms of weeding.

Atlantic Monthly 85 (MAY 1900): 714–716.

ENDNOTES

6. *Bibliography of West Virginia University: Its Faculty and Graduates*, (Morgantown, West Virginia, 1907), 41–42.

7. Editions of this book, first published in 1898, were brought out in 1900 by Macmillan (London and New York), and by Laird and Lee (Chicago). Further editions were printed during the next two decades. It was issued once again in 1994 and given a laudatory review in *Horticulture: The Magazine of American Gardening* 73 (March 1995): 67 and 69. Apparently not everyone viewed *Elizabeth and Her German Garden* in the same way that the couple in this article did. In fact, it has been cited as a feminist work that helped initiate women's move into the garden as independent writers and gardeners (Virginia Lopez Begg, "Frances Duncan: The 'New Woman' in the Garden," in *Pioneers of American Landscape Design: An Annotated Bibliography*, ed. Charles Birnbaum and Lisa E. Crowder [Washington, DC, 1993], 29).

❧ ANNE HIGGINSON SPICER
The Gardening Women in Our Town

ANNE HIGGINSON SPICER belonged to a highly democratic group of women gardeners: all possessed gardens of equal size and the same basic conditions; each was endowed with individual strengths and beset by her own special garden pests. From the vantage point of this collegial society, Spicer sees women progressing first from control of their own gardens to the beautification of roadsides, next to civic planning, and finally to demanding the right to vote: "Most of us do not realize as we wield trowel and rake that we are doing a deed of national significance."[8] Like some other contemporary women garden writers, she enjoys voicing her contempt for men, whom she considers worthless in the garden. Children, on the other hand, she finds can prove quite useful as weeders. Spicer was born around 1874 to a prominent Chicago family and in 1893 married an engineer who invented railroad devices. She was active in North Shore, Chicago, society. She studied and later exhibited woodcarving, ceramics, and metalwork at the Art Institute of Chicago, and was also a poet of some note; one of her poems was set to music by John Philip Sousa. Her garden in Kenilworth, Illinois, was well known and widely admired. In 1905 she wrote an article for *House Beautiful* about her experiences making the garden, providing both photographs and plans of the space.[9] She lived until 1935.

FIFTEEN YEARS AGO there were only two hardy gardens in our little town, one belonged to a man, the other to a woman. The woman was considered a trifle odd! Today I doubt if you will find more than two homes in the village that do not boast a garden of sorts, where hardy perennials flourish or languish, according to the zeal of the gardener. With few exceptions these gardens are all managed and worked by the feminine contingent of the household, usually the wife, but sometimes sister, daughter, or mother.

This phenomenon may be in part, attributable to the flood of gardening literature which has swept over the land in the last ten years or so, but I believe it to be significant of a deep rooted and vital movement; the utilizing of some of the leisure time of the modern woman, that important economic factor which William Hard tells us has been set free by modern industrial conditions.[10] What more natural, wholesome method of utilization could be found? Gardening is a further manifestation of the mothering instinct in woman, shown in the fostering and nursing of seedlings and slips. It is also a widening of the housekeeping arts, for we are no longer content that the house shall be as immaculate, sanitary and pretty as paterfamilias' purse will allow. We want the grounds about that house, be they but a few square feet or many acres, to be an integral part of the house, and show the same thoughtful planning and meticulous care. From our own grounds the next logical step is to the attention to parkways and streets and from these again to membership on park boards and civic improvement leagues, until the final step leads to the vote which shall determine the final "say-so" in these matters. It is a perfectly logical sequence. The woman who steps from her door step to plant a few handy "yarbs" at its foot, has quite unwittingly taken her first unconscious step towards the suffrage. (So too has the permeating word wormed its way into these pages!) Most of us do not realize as we wield trowel and rake that we are doing a deed of national significance!

In our little village there are no large estates. We all have approximately the same amount of ground to play with, and we have the same problems to face in soil, drainage, and general outlook. It is these very facts which, to my mind, make all our woman-run gardens interesting. If we had large grounds with hill and dale, rivulet or pond, heath and forest, what intricacies of land-scape-gardening, what settings for our borders we might conceive! As it is, we are rather like children who have been given a certain number of letters with which to spell out if possible, each a different word. Or we are even more like the past generation of ourselves in the church-fair and cake-baking era, when, given the same ingredients to bake the cake, it would always turn out that Mrs. A's cake would be substantial, but a trifle heavy; Mrs. B's cake light but tasting like fluff; Mrs. C's always soggy in the middle; To Mrs. D. alone would be given the medal for making the cake that was "just right!"

So it is with us. Although none of us achieves perfection, for gardens, like souls, are always in process of improvement. Perfection is never to be expected, yet each of us has her little triumphs. Mrs. Green can always "point with pride" to the first crocus, while envious neighbors gnash their teeth and wonder how she manages to lure it forth while the frost is still quite hard. Mrs. Grey's garden we look on with commiseration until early in July when her Madonna lilies [*Lilium candidum*] bloom. There they stand like a row of immaculate white angels! The mysterious "boarder" which troubles Lilium Candidum in other gardens passes hers by, as though she had murmured some secret spell to protect them.

Mrs. Brown's garden we tolerate at all times. It is a pretty garden, there's no denying it; but when her tall row of Delphiniums [*Delphinium elatum*] raise their majestic spires, from six to ten feet high, ranging through all shades of blue, from celestial, with black bee centers, to an iridescent purple, we make excuses to saunter up her street and engage her in conversation, while we surreptitiously abstract the ripened seeds from their pods and secrete them in our pocket-handkerchiefs. Your true garden woman will generally be found to have a few seeds of some hardy plant hidden in her pocket-handkerchief!

Mrs. Black has no luck with bulbs; spring flowering things piddle away and die mysterious and lamented deaths in her yard. Later on she has compensation, for the separate florets in the blossom clusters of her hardy phloxes [*Phlox paniculata*] are twice the size of those in any other garden, and we are always glad to bring pieces of the roots of our early primroses [*Primula*] and clumps of forget-me-nots [*Myosotis*], to exchange for offshoots of those wonderful phloxes.

Then, too, although a border is a border, and certain things are sure to be planted in it, still personal preferences count for a great deal, and this makes for variety. Also there are grades in gardening, as distinctly discernible as those in schools. The kindergarten grade for example is that when one "is

One of the gardens is old-fashioned in 'atmosphere' suggesting another century.

Mere man is permitted as a useful accessory and only at long intervals.

glad of anything." This means that one accepts gifts of Golden Glow [*Rudbeckia laciniata*], and plants it in a prominent position. Later on we change all this, and Golden Glow became the acknowledged medium for screening garbage cans and other unsightly spots in the yard.

We discuss fertilizers with the same absorbing interest that we used to devote to servants and clothes! Some of us pin our faith to "blood and bone," others to bonemeal, or sheep fertilizer, but many still prefer to use barn-yard manure, in spite of the attendant weeds which must be fought so heroically.

Certain gardens seem to produce certain weeds, too, and each gardening woman considers her own particular weed problem the most difficult of solution. Purslane [*Portulaca oleracea*] is the bane of one garden, chickweed [*Stellaria*] of another, and some un-named, mysterious visitant, of a third. Some of us burn weeds, some bury them, others offer them to our own or our neighbors' chickens (although there are not very many chickens kept in our little town. Those round-eyed feathered idiots can produce as much devastation in a garden as a city visitor with a hoe!)

We all have our preferences in garden tools, some using light hoes, and some heavy ones, some preferring to loosen the earth around each plant with a trowel, while some give a perfunctory scratching with a rake and hope for good results, but seldom get them. When we discuss weeds, or the depredations of the cabbage worms or dahlia-beetle, the newest problem novel becomes of faint interest, and we never gossip. We can say as awful things as we like about bugs and worms, and no one's feelings are hurt. That striped tiger-beetle, for example, or my own pet abomination "Cosmopeplis

We believe that it is wise to begin with the children. They are often our most enthusiastic gardeners.

Carnifex," a little beast with 'orid 'abits, as he will eat the heart out of all the finest columbine [*Aquilegia*] seeds that one is saving most lovingly. As for the cut-worm, he is the best thing on which to wreak a passing ill-humor that I know of. Cutting him in two with a spade and tossing the fragments where the watching birds can find him eases one's mind quite a bit when one has found a whole row of dear little seedlings mown prostrate.

Sometimes we make little discoveries and confidences concerning the men appendages to our gardens. Men as a class, we find, seem to be devoted to grass and red geraniums [*Pelargonium x hortorum*]. They are sure to evidence lack of variety in their taste. Do I not remember my first gardener? He was a German, and to every suggestion as to the planting of seeds in the beds, he would look at me with a fishy gleam in his eye, and ejaculate, "Budunias iss nize" and lapse into silence again. Not only that, but I verily believe that he exuded Petunias, for they seemed to appear spontaneously in every bed he touched, thus teaching me very early the valuable gardening lesson that if you want a thing planted, plant it yourself!

The man who may be trusted with gardening tools is a rare article. Didn't a man hoe up one hundred newly transplanted foxgloves [*Digitalis*] in my garden? A whole morning's back-breaking job was gone for nothing. I hasten to explain that it was no member of the family, but a well-meaning guest who thought to make himself useful in my absence. My glad welcome was put to a severe strain as with joyful mien he pointed to the remains of his hoeing orgy, saying, "You had an awful lot of plantain in your beds, but I got them all out."

Sometimes the children can be made very useful. When we get in fine frenzies of weeding, a spry small person with a basket will not come amiss, to collect the wreckage we toss out upon the grass. Sometimes, too, those little feet can be trained to step into small spaces where bigger ones would be disastrous. It is while eyes are young that they can be most easily taught to recognize the first pushing spires in spring.

Yes, truly, for all ages and conditions of women, the garden is a great resource. A gardening woman is a contented woman, and the price of a contented woman is beyond rubies!

The House Beautiful 33 (MARCH 1913): 103–104.

ENDNOTES

8. It would, however, be another seven years until women were given the right to vote.

9. Anne Higginson Spicer, "A Suburban Garden," *The House Beautiful* 17 (May 1905): 7–9. On

Spicer, see *Chicago Daily Tribune* (obituary), September 10, 1935, 16:1; *Who Was Who in America* 1 (Chicago, 1943), 1163.

10. William Hard, *Women of Tomorrow* (New York, 1911).

REBECCA J. LOSE
Everybody's Garden

REBECCA JUSTINA LOSE was born in 1857, lived in Williamsport, Pennsylvania, and was active in the women's suffrage movement, both writing and lecturing for the cause.[11] Her "Platform for Women," which presented the essential doctrine of the crusade, was published in *The Forum* magazine in January 1911.[12] She also wrote short stories, sports articles, and essays on a variety of topics for magazines and newspapers. In this article she champions gardeners blessed with independent spirits, chronicling an outbreak of garden anarchy in her neighborhood. The insurrection starts when one woman gardener defiantly resolves to rip everything out of her garden and replant it entirely with sweet williams, hundreds upon hundreds of them, in deliberate disregard of the dictates of taste and in the face of her family's ridicule. The effect is magnificent, if short lived. Her triumph inspires similarly liberated behavior on the part of another young woman who loves just sweet peas, and the trend gains momentum. Although Lose applauds her neighbors for striking a blow for horticultural freedom of expression, she cannot bring herself to commit such wholesale heresy. Nonetheless it does give her courage to finally and completely satisfy her longing for a surfeit of blue dolphiniums and corn flowers, scattering them more abundantly throughout the garden than she has ever before dared. And maybe, in recognition of her neighbor's victory, she will even plant all three hundred of her own sweet williams in one glorious bed.

IT IS AN AXIOM that variety of interest is a necessity for the successful pursuit of health, wealth and happiness. One of my neighbors, when overtaken by grief or perplexity, shuts herself up in the laundry and washes things — towels, napkins, sheets, tablecloths — anything she can find. A young fellow down street took his fishing rod and tackle and started for the creek the minute he returned from burying his bit of a wife. I do not presume to say that digging in the ground can rival the blue sky, the running water, the wind among the trees in healing and comforting, yet I protest that anxiety and foreboding can be better endured, that one sleeps better and eats better and is easier to be lived with if one grows some sort of a garden.

Further — this garden I should have everyone grow exactly to suit themselves. Last summer a year, my next-door neighbor-but-one announced that she had never had enough Sweet William [*Dianthus barbatus*] in her life, and that once before she died she intended to have all she wanted. Her family laughed derisively. Spurred, no doubt, partly by this derision, she deliberately proceeded to have everything dug out of every flower bed on the place — every single thing. In their places she planted Sweet William, and nothing else.

I did not sympathize with this proceeding at all. I approved of her growing what she wanted to grow, of course. But now, really, her choice of flowers was almost absurd. Sweet William I like. I want it in my garden. I want, even, a good many patches of it here and there. But all Sweet William? Oh, no! Yet I assure you, when those hundreds and hundreds of young plants came at once into masses of gorgeous bloom, I was almost a convert.

Nor was I the only convert, for while they were in the height of their glory, a high-school girl who lives just back of me consulted me over the fence, confessing that sweetpeas [*Lathyrus odoratus*] were the joy of her life, and saying that if my lady uptown could revel at will in Sweet William, why not sweet peas alone for her? And I encouraged her. Of course, I did. It was the first sign of individuality or initiative she has ever shown, and may change her whole life.

At any rate, she stuck to it, and this summer she has devoted herself to sweet peas. Rows and rows of them she has grown, of every variety she could hear of. Up and down each path she had them, around every tree, across every fence, and every other place where there was room. Such sweet peas I have never seen. The town turned out to see them, and I look for further developments next year.

Now, I do not share this feeling of my neighbors. I could not be satisfied with just one brand of flowers. I must have variety. I want the early and the late. I want flowers blooming in my garden the minute spring comes, and all the summer long, and all the fall until the earth itself freezes, and the snow comes and provides a new heaven and a new earth to look at.

But I know something of how they feel, these others. I even know what I should plant, were I following in their footsteps, and it would not be Sweet William, nor yet sweet peas. It would be delphiniums that I should plant — the hardy larkspurs of all proper English country novels. They are more or less strangers to me, yet I know that ever since I first saw them, not so many years ago, there has been a spot somewhere within me that has longed for a whole garden full of the heavenly blue of this most heavenly of flowers.

But I should not plant them entirely alone, either. If I had those flowerbeds of my lady up street, and were free-foot to do as I pleased with them, I'd fill them all moderately full this fall of thrifty young delphiniums. I could furnish her with the plants, myself, if she would but have them. Then, in the spring, early, I'd sow the beds full of corn flower — ragged robin [*Centaurea cyanus*], we call it — in two shades, the light blue and the dark blue. Then I'd sit down and wait for results. I do not have to wait for results, myself. I can shut my eyes, this minute, and see it — the mass on mass of shaded blue below, the great waving plumes of marvelous blue above.

But my Sweet William lady will have none of my advice, and I, as I said, I cannot do without the others. How could I, for instance, turn out the long border that from year to year has been growing fuller of the flowers my grandmother loved in her day — columbine [*Aquilegia*], hollyhock [*Alcea rosea*], foxglove [*Digitalis*], Canterbury bells [*Campanula medium*], phlox and a dozen others, many, it is true, so changed by time that my blessed grandmother would scarce recognize them, but all grown, as were hers, from the seed to maturity right under my own eyes.

No, my grandmother's flowers are safe from me, and so are the tulips and daffodils, the snowdrops [*Galanthus nivalis*] and crocuses, whose early blossoming is the only thing that each year can quiet my ever recurring doubt as to the veracity of the almanac, and assure my soul that the long winter is really past.

Even for the flowers that have to be replanted each year I must save some place. There is salvia — "splendid sage," [*Salvia splendens*] my mother called it; my garden would not be the same to me, lacking its brilliance. Each year I plant a box of it in my window on the afternoon of Washington's Birthday, having discovered that salvias so fathered present a far more gorgeous array in the last days of October than any sown on any other day of the year. No — I do not know why. I only know it is true.

Then, cosmos! I should miss that too. True, one grows cosmos on a sporting chance, the chance that it will not bloom. None the less there is something about it that always fires my imagination. It grows so straight, and never hurries, though it must know that unless it does hurry the frost will get it. Sometimes I feel like shaking it, to bring it to its senses. Then, if Nature is kind, and the frost holds off, and it does come into bloom it is so ethereally beautiful that I am always sure it more than repays itself for its steadfastness and patience.

All these and more, oh, many more, I must keep where they have always grown. Yet I shall find a place for my new blue loves. Indeed, I shall find so many places for them that it is already fairly evident to me that my whole garden next year will present a bluish cast — that will however represent neither erudition nor pessimism.

First, I shall plant a great many of the strangers in the bed of white lilies [*Lilium candidum*], under my dining-room window. They certainly will become each other, those two. Whether the stately delphiniums will mitigate the feeling stately lilies have given me, ever since they began looking in my dining-room, remains to be seen. For those lilies always make me a trifle uncomfortable, especially when I am very hungry. They seem to expect me to live up to them, learn the minuet, say, or be led to the festal board by cavaliers in wigs and ruffles.

Then, I shall surely take my own advice to my lady up street, since she will have none of it, and plant me a large bed, moderately full now, of the delphiniums, and in the spring sow all about their feet the corn flower aforementioned. Also I'll scatter the new favorite here and there through the old flower bed, and quite fill a large bed, that is already growing with roses and white phlox — and perhaps in various other places, if the plants hold out.

And as for Sweet Williams — there are three hundred of the bonny little plants growing in my garden. I was out and counted them but now. They tempt me sorely. I know Sweet Williams are stiff, that their remains are brown and unbeautiful, and that I have said many things against them. Yet those flowers up street were gorgeous. There is a large empty bed by the little porch. Perhaps, after all, I'll give in, and plant the whole three hundred right there.

The Craftsman 30 (MAY 1916): 152–159.

ENDNOTES

11. *Woman's Who's Who of America*, 1914–1915, ed. John William Leonard (Detroit, 1976), 501.

12. *The Forum* 45 (January 1911): 91–93.

A Tussie-Mussie for These Times

IN THE AUTUMN of 1931, Americans were beginning to recognize that they were indeed in the grip of a profound economic depression. However, not yet realizing just how long or devastating it would be, they might still make what we may now unfairly deem fatuous statements regarding the silver lining in that incomparably black economic cloud. Richardson Wright (1886–1961), distinguished editor of *House and Garden* since 1914 and author of numerous garden books, often made gardens the subject of his monthly editorials, or at least mentioned gardening in passing while ruminating on other topics.[13] In this essay gardening is the vehicle expressing his thoughts about the "pressing thumb of depression" and its effects on the country. He reflects that there are some advantages in slowing the hectic pace that characterized the previous era of material prosperity. He predicts that during the current hard times Americans will gain in wisdom as gardeners and as people; they will be more content with what they have, demand quality in what they acquire, and learn to be more patient.

JOHN PARKINSON, who in his day was a godfather of English gardening, once wrote (the year was 1629) a delightful book that met the public eye under the name of *A Garden of All Sorts of Pleasant Flowers*. In it he uttered, among other aphorisms, the words, "There be some flowers make a delicious Tussie-Mussie or Nosegay both for sight and smell."

That word "Tussie-Mussie" has long since entered into the parlance of gardeners. Though nosegays seem little worn these days, and flower shows almost never suggest them as competitive subjects, there is scarcely a gardener but finds his experiences becoming a Tussie-Mussie — and both for sight and smell. We are constantly gathering these nosegays, we gardeners, and from them our lives are measurably enriched.

There was that old climbing Rose which has spilled its prodigality of bloom each June over the top garden wall. This spring it appeared to be ailing. The combination of old age, profuse flowering and a touch of canker had written its doom. I routed it out and put a newly-created climber in its place and that night went indoors to write the ending and beginning of these Roses. The search for the date of the planting of this Rose sent me chasing back into the yellowing pages of my garden notes. Finally I found it — for thirteen Junes it had spilled that scarlet wave over the wall. In that search I also gathered a poignant Tussie-Mussie, one that all gardeners eventually collect — I realized how many Roses and dozens of other kinds of plants in those thirteen years I had set out and never saw again.

Nature is prodigal — and so are most gardeners. We plant far more than we ever bring to successful blooming. In these days of careful spending, perhaps it might be well for us to question the wisdom of this prodigality. Were it not better to have few plants and grow them well, than an unending variety and bring only a few to successful fruition?

Another Tussie-Mussie I have been gathering in these days of economy is the enjoyment of the plants I have. We all suffer the temptation to buy more and more plants, to bite deeper and deeper into the frontiers of our gardens. More gardens and more plants exact more work and more care. The end of the day finds us so exhausted that we are too tired to enjoy the beauty surrounding us.

Lest I should miss this enjoyment, I have made a practice each week of going around the garden and collecting a Tussie-Mussie of everything in bloom. These make a jumbled bouquet that is set on my desk to study as I write. First come the Crocus and the other harbingers of spring, then the varieties of fruit trees and early flowering shrubs — the gamut that runs from Forsythia ovata in March, to the full orchestra of the fruit trees, the flowering Crabs [*Malus*] and Plums [*Prunus*] and Japanese Cherries [*Prunus serrulata*] and Bush Honeysuckles [*Diervilla*] of May, commingled with an abundance of Narcissus. So on, week by week, these beauties are revealed to me, and as I study their infinite variety I am determined not only to grow better the plants I already possess, but to enjoy them more.

Through this survey I find myself not only becoming better acquainted with these flowers, but growing more critical of what constitutes a good flower. My Tussie-Mussie is a nosegay of discernment, of higher standards. I am determined that whatever new flower shall henceforth enter this garden shall be possessed of superior merit.

Still another nosegay of experience that I would collect is the practice of growing more of these treasures from seed. Doubtless the majority of them could be bought somewhere, but I am determined to follow that slower course which growth from seed requires. Perhaps some of the seed will fail to germinate, perhaps some of the maturing plants will find their environment uncongenial. From each of these I hope to gather a rich Tussie-Mussie of experience.

Having gathered these three nosegays, may I have the good sense to sit still a while in my garden and extract from them the nectar of their wisdom. From the first: satisfaction with what I have. From the second: a finer discernment. From the third: the practice of patience.

During the past few years, these three excellent habits have been throw very much into the discard. The rush of material prosperity caused many people to become discontented with what they already had. In the hectic acquiring of new and more possessions, they forgot their standards. They grew very impatient with anything that failed to prove instantly successful. The tendency of the last few months, since we felt the pressing thumb of depression, has been to slow up the tempo of living. Whereas heretofore we sped past many a thing of beauty and merit, we are now moving more slowly, we have time to enjoy the sights and smells and delicacies of our impressions and are gradually acquiring a whole new set of standards by which to judge them. Not alone are men and women now demanding real quality in goods they buy, they are requiring also that life repays them for the solicitude with which they live it.

Only the dumb and obdurate will fail to realize that the old order has changed, and that the new offers far more than the old ever did in the enjoyment of life. For the same discernment that a gardener will turn on a new flower can be turned on every other kind of pleasure — on new books, new furniture, new music, new architecture, new contacts of man with man. From our lives we shall be gathering an entirely new kind of Tussie-Mussie, gathering it with more exacting taste, with more patience. And perhaps we shall be gathering them more frequently.

House and Garden 60 (October 1931): 60.
Courtesy *House and Garden*. Copyright © 1931
(renewed 1959) by the Condé Nast Publications, Inc.

ENDNOTES

13. In another editorial, "We Buy Ourselves a Birthday Cake," *House and Garden* 40 (July 1921): 24, Wright noticed the growth of cultural nationalism in the United States, contending that World War I had made Americans more appreciative of many aspects of their country, including its native plants, and that "we must evolve an individuality [in gardens] as distinct and complete as any of the styles on the Continent." On Wright, see Virginia Lopez Begg, "Richardson Wright," *Pioneers of American Landscape Design: An Annotatated Bibliography*, ed. Charles A. Birnbaum and Lisa E. Crowder (Washington, D.C., 1993), 133–135.

Garden, Inc., In Account with Me

GRACE EARHART CHAFFEE, born in 1891, was assistant professor of sociology at the State University of Iowa. During the 1930s she occasionally wrote essays on gardening for magazines, as well as articles on social work for professional journals, and in 1940 contributed two chapters to a book, *Modern Marriage*, edited by Moses Jung. In this article for *House Beautiful* she gives prudent consideration to whether there was a net value in the hard work and expense required by gardening. One by one she examines the overwhelming number of problems demanding resolution in her garden, until she becomes so discouraged that she is ready to give it all up. Then the sight of a patch of crocus she had forgotten planting the past fall lifts her spirits with their joyful announcement of spring. Such autobiographical affirmations of the indefinable but incalculable benefit of gardening to one's well-being — despite all its difficulties and disappointments — were an important and recurrent theme in the garden articles of early twentieth-century magazines.

To-DAY AS I stepped into my garden, I did a sum in my head. I sat down by the sundial and totaled up the profits and losses of last season — garden accounting, as it were. Did the results of last year show a net return on labor and management and capital expenditure, or would it be better to trundle the wheelbarrow into the cellar, hang up the hoe and the dibble, and take up golf? Now was the time to take stock and decide.

I began with the house at the back, where it met the stone terrace under the pergola, the back wall of my outdoor living-room. A winter's dirt had left a thick deposit on the white shingles. I sighed. A white house, like any other ideal in this grimy world, is all very well as a goal, but rather difficult to attain. The green blinds had faded so that they failed to match the cedars by the rock wall. The blinds, at least, must be painted. The rock steps had settled out of line. A new frost crack accounted for the teetering in the second one as I came down. And the brick of the cellarway needed pointing up. How could mortar melt away from between cracks? The Geraniums [*Pelargonium x hortorum*] on the coping, in my imagination a beautiful red, had bloomed into a sickly pink, ghastly against the chrome-yellow pots. And the pots themselves had been too porous to hold moisture. Even the pergola looked tipsy. There was too much to be done. Why start at all?

But other departments needed to be invoiced. I must go on. The hardy border came next, that border so well balanced between shrubs, peonies [*Paeonia*], lilies [*Lilium*], and iris, with plenty of room between for the first aid of annuals. Forsythia was too loose-jointed, after all, to use as a background. I must move it against the house. But that would mean uprooting the lilac [*Syringa*], Ludwig-Spaeth, just getting set into its corner, sturdy Teuton that it was. Besides, the drippings from the porch might kill the forsythia just as they had the Rugosa rose, whose dead stalks reproached me. *Spiraea thunbergii* would have to come back. After all, history is written by survivors. Next to the forsythia, *Philadelphus virginalis* had crowded against the Russian-olive [*Elaeagnus angustifolia*] in a most unmaidenly manner. And the Japanese quince [*Chaenomeles*] had shoved the flowering almond [*Prunus*] out of sight. Nothing would do here but a general pulling out and replanting. I groaned in spirit. That would mean the front of the border as well.

I gave it my attention for a moment. The iris, for instance, planted with such hope that hot July day, how had it fared? Princess Beatrice had bestowed her royal favors with a lavish hand, but Lord of June had rotted in the ground, and Lent A. Williamson had stubbornly refused to bloom. The pink peony, Therese, had been planted by mistake next to red Longfellow. It must be moved, and that would be another season without bloom. And the Canterbury-bell [*Campanula medium*] next to the Delphinium hybrid did not give either one a chance to show its lovely color. Color schemes were all very well before the fire on a winter evening, but they did not always work out. *Lilium regale* had been eaten by the mice and *candidum* had not come up either. Planted too deeply, probably. How did one ever know?

Moving down the log steps, I went into the lower garden. Here gravel paths terraced the slope, the ferns and ladyslippers [*Cypripedium*] filled the ravine. At least, it was planned that they should. But the gravel had washed away in the spring thaw, and late in the fall a deep root of poison ivy [*Toxicodendron radicans*] had thrust up its red leaves among the ferns and Japanese spurge [*Pachysandra terminalis*]. I walked along the path it had pleased my fancy to plant to primroses. *Primulis veris* and *vulgaris* alike have disappointed me. Only three out of two dozen had come up last year. Probably there would be none this year. Middle-aged females should have done with primrose paths, anyway. I would plant pansies [*Viola x wittrockiana*] and accept the inevitable.

I glanced at the pool on the other side. If there is anything more depressing than the bare rocks of a pool before the shrubs and lilies have leafed out, I have not seen it. I remembered that the lemon lily [*Lilium parryi*] and the Siberian iris [*Iris sibirica*] had made a bright splotch of yellow on the upper side, but the bog planting on the lower side had been a total loss. It had seemed very appropriate, — wild iris [*Iris versicolor*] and arrowhead [*Sagittaria*] and cattails [*Typha latifolia*] around the rim of the pool, — but the only net result had been the family joke, 'Why go on a picnic? We raise our own mosquitoes.' Families cramp one's style. They should be banished, along with gardens.

A wooden bridge spans the ravine beyond the pool. That, at least, had come through the winter. Not even the bark had peeled from the rough slab floor. The bittersweet vine [*Celastrus scandens*] on the handrail showed a faint flush of green. I leaned my elbows on it and poked a meditative stick into the drifted oak leaves. A bit of purple color shone down there. What could it be? I threw away my stick and stepped down. Just showing above the soggy black soil it was, that little purple nodule. And just beyond, another, and another. On the edge of the bank the leaf mulch had shifted a little in the winter wind, and from under its dull cloak came a gleam of brightest yellow. Of course. I remembered now. At the end of a long day's planting, just to have done, I had stuck a handful of crocus culls into the loam down by the bridge. And here they were, shining through my discouragement on this late March day. With the snow hardly gone, they had gathered themselves together, joined hands, as it were, to throw aside the winter's darkness and announce the spring.

House Beautiful 73–74 (March 1933): 92, 119.

Reprinted by permission from *House Beautiful*, copyright © March 1933. The Hearst Corporation. All Rights Reserved.

[WINIFRED MARGARETTA KIRKLAND]

The Contributors' Club: Discontent in a Garden

In 1900 *Atlantic Monthly* published Candace Wheeler's three-part article, "Content in a Garden."[14] In 1901 Wheeler produced a small book from this text, which convincingly set forth a winning thesis: that gardening is a source of great joy and contentment in life. So successful was Wheeler in conveying her message that, as Winifred Kirkland observes, the phrase "content in a garden" entered into the common vocabulary of garden writing in the decades following the publication of Wheeler's article and book. The phrase seems to have expressed what gardeners then most aspired to achieve: not just a beautiful landscape but an improved, healthier state of mind. Gardening was therapeutic; it would help the gardener survive the challenges of modern life.[15] It is precisely this idea that Winifred Kirkland wittily disputes. According to her observation, gardeners actually suffer increased anxiety and furthermore jeopardize the mental health of others. She writes to warn people of the perils of gardening. Kirkland, a novelist and author of religious books, was born in Columbia, Pennsylvania, in 1872, received her A.B. degree from Vassar in 1897, and attended graduate classes at Bryn Mawr from 1898 to 1900. She taught English at several schools before devoting her full time to writing after 1902. She died in Sewanee, Tennessee, in 1943.[16]

Our literature has recently been enriched by a fragrant phrase, 'Content in a Garden.' The words breathe of boxwood and of roses, but observation leads me to the opinion that the phrase is as fallacious as it is fragrant.

I write as one who has for unnumbered years lived with gardeners without becoming one. I have never planted or transplanted anything, or weeded anything, but I have been torn from many a book, wrenched away from performing many a charitable deed, caught back to earth when I was walking the sky on many a country ramble, by people who demanded that I stop, and listen to the doings of the dirt. Gardeners among my kinsfolk and acquaintance have grasped me by the inoffensive nape of my neck and incontinently thrust my nose into the mud in order that I might see therein an indiscernible green line of lettuce.

Now, unlike other germs, the horticultural bacillus is increasing in virulence. More people garden to-day than ever before in history. Against the spread of the epidemic I have exerted my personal influence and private eloquence, but so far with small effect. I have therefore resolved to appeal to a larger public and to raise in print my warning voice, pointing out the perils to poise and to peace inherent in any intimacy with the soil.

Theoretically, I should expect as much disquietude among gardeners as I have practically observed. They voluntarily expose themselves to disillusion. Much may be said in favor of hitching your hopes to a star, but what about burying your hopes in sixty square feet of spring mud? The wise ancients always represented the devious ways of deviltry as taking place in the hidden bowels of the earth, yet the modern horticulturist is always expecting archangelic behavior from the blackest bit of mould into which he dares to delve. In the fifth act of *The Bluebird,*[17] where the little unborn mortals are exhibiting their transcendent inventions, portentous with future disappointment, the preponderance of disillusion is given to the gardeners. The gardeners who are going to be born and the gardeners who have been born long enough to know better are alike in expecting their daisies to be big as cartwheels, their peas to be larger than grapes, their apples to rival melons, their melons to outstrip the pumpkin. Should an intelligent investor of his life's happiness bank all on the uncertain behavior of the weather and the weevil?

Intelligence, however, is not a quality to be looked for *a priori* in a gardener. What clearness of view could you expect from people who are continually curled into a ball tending sordid seedlings? Does one not shudder to mention the mental and moral disintegration risked by association with vegetables, — instance the gross irregularities of cucumbers and cantaloupes when they neighbor each other! Is there anything in the nature of the case that should make intimacy with cabbage-heads and beet-tops contribute to spiritual uplift? Yet such is the popular fallacy.

Passing from theory to experience, one finds the gardener of all men most dissatisfied. Live with a gardener, and then prove him-her (in a discussion of horticulture, I may be excused for Burbanking my pronouns) contented if you can![18] Often have I welcomed a roomful of visitors and launched them into spirit-warming talk, only to have them, at some unguarded allusion, make for the open, demanding the titles of the lady-roses at the windows, and pressing on into the private life of the spinach and the cucumber — conversation that leaves me out in the cold, for not even appendicitis can produce the clacking congeniality of comparing flower-beds. After the guests are gone, I am called upon to comfort my household horticulturists for envy implanted by boastful visitors; I am told that our peas and our pansies are not so large as we supposed — and yet they tell me they are contented folk, these gardeners!

To me the gardening mania is but one more example of the modern unrest, so extensively advertised. True, there might be content in gardens if owners were ever satisfied with them as they are; but they are haunted by new combinations, new experiments. They are always wanting to paw their parterres to pieces and set them out anew. You no sooner get used to a garden than it isn't there. You try to follow a primrose path and you become entangled in blackberry bushes. You put forth your hand to pluck a violet and you prod up a radish.

Another form of restlessness exhibited by gardeners is their fret after fertilizer. They can never get enough, and they can never get the right kind. If only they could, their dreams might come true. Fertilizer becomes an obsession from which they never escape. If you take a gardener with you on a country ramble, he-she will be wanting to dig up the woodland loam to enrich the back yard. He-she will never see the white-dotting loveliness of old farms, without wanting to scoop whole barnyards into the picnic lunch-basket. If you are caught up to the sky on the wings of the sunset, you will be hauled down with the Whitmanesque appeal for your sympathy,

'Behold this compost! behold it well!'

I have noted with pain the subtle disintegration of mind and character which awaits those addicted to horticulture. The utter uncertainty of the material with which they deal causes the sanest people to become superstitious, so that you will have them solemnly declaring that certain seeds must be planted at the waning of the moon. Sweet peas have some mysterious association with St. Patrick's Day. I am not sure whether some of my friends would not go the length of an incantation, or of a pact with Satan, to achieve a perfect cantaloupe.

You might expect the winter solstice, by its absence of stimulus, to repair the moral ravages of the summer, with its demoralizing sowing and reaping. On the contrary, when the winds of January whip the windows, out come the flower catalogues, those glowing monuments of false promise. Forgetful of last season's failures, the gardener's eyes, feasting on pictured roses, grow bright with delirium. In hectic rhapsody he whispers enchanted names — Fiery Cross, Phantom Blue, Sunnybrook Earliana, Arabis Alpina, Beauty of Hebron (this last a potato). By means of the flower catalogue is the gardener rendered perpetually credulous, only to be perpetually disillusioned — a hardy perennial of discontent. These same ornate annuals corrupt honest minds, so that you will discover gardeners practicing deception, concealing their bright flower-books in laps that appear to be reading the war news, and you are constantly intercepting clandestine trips to the mail-box and the dropping therein of surreptitious mail-orders.

A love of gardening is the root of still another evil: misanthropy.

Gardeners become suspicious of even their nearest and dearest; they bring monstrous accusations, charging them with rolling upon the asparagus bed, with blighting the strawberry blossoms, with devouring a ten-foot row of young onions. Cynicism extends even to the birds of the blue, so that for all their singing throats they are looked upon as marauders only, and cheery redbreast is despised for his delinquencies in regard to ripe cherries. Thus does the gardener, his soul buried fast in furrow and flower-bed, look askance at both man and nature. I ask, do any of the qualities he exhibits justify his pride in that gentle phrase, 'Content in a Garden'?

Atlantic Monthly 117 (JUNE 1916): 852–854.

ENDNOTES

14. See introduction, xxiv.

15. See introduction, xxiii.

16. *New York Times* (obituary), May 15, 1943, 15:3; *Who Was Who in America*, vol. 2 (Chicago, 1950), 301–302.

17. A play by Maurice Maeterlinck (1862–1949); on Maeterlinck, see above 251 n.3.

18. Luther Burbank (1849–1926) created many new varieties of ornamental and agricultural plants at his California nursery, primarily through hybridization. It is apparently to this practice of hybridization that Kirkland is referring when she says she is "Burbanking" her pronouns.

ꙮ WALTER A. DYER
The Humble Annals of a Back Yard: Morning Chapel

THIS ARTICLE BY DYER demonstrates that a kind of domesticated nature worship had infiltrated popular American culture by
the early twentieth century. Here the garden rather than the wilderness serves as a "natural church," but the author uses the same language that Emerson and Thoreau, and more recently Muir and
Burroughs, had employed to express their rapturous communion
with nature.[19] Dyer cheerfully attests to finding all the religion he
needs by foregathering with his tomatoes and beans, poppies and
roses, and cannot understand people who are blind and deaf to such
God-given joys. Partaking in the sacrament of nature joins him spiritually with a community of fellow believers, "brother backyardsmen" who venerate God in their gardens' beauty. This article, like
the one by Dyer in Chapter One, was later included in his book, *The
Humble Annals of a Back Yard* (1916).[20]

I AM NOT ONE of those garden enthusiasts who arise at beauty-sleep time
and go out to work feverishly with trowel and hoe for an hour or two before
breakfast. For one thing, waking up is a long and solemn rite with me, not to
be hurried through thoughtlessly. If I get down by the time the coffee percolator is bubbling I feel sufficiently virtuous. And though I pride myself on being
a conscientious gardener, I take my garden pleasures calmly and at such times
as circumstances grant me leisure. I do not hotly pursue joy in my garden; I
jog along comfortably with it.

But if by some lucky chance I beat the coffee percolator by five or ten
minutes, I do enjoy a tour of the backyard while the dew is on the grass — a
brief but unhurried tour of critical observation not unmixed with a sort of
morning adoration. It seems to start the day.

In college days we were most of us opposed to compulsory worship on
general principles, and yet I know that if a poll had been taken of the

undergraduates, there would have been an overwhelming majority in favor of morning chapel. It was a traditional exercise that we would not have wanted to abolish if we could. Not that we felt the need so much of a daily religious service; morning chapel was rather a social observance. It got us together as a college; the ties were knit closer; the day was started as it should be in such a community.

And so now I like to foregather with my tomatoes and my beans, my Shirley poppies [*Papaver rhoeas*] and my roses, before they and I actually buckle down to the day's work that is appointed to us.

Already the shadows are shortening and the sun is pouring his vitalizing beams upon all the growing things. The robins that seem to have a nest high up in our ridiculous old pear [*Pyrus*] tree are singing joyfully because the weather is what it is, and a kindly mortal has spread before them a feast of worms.

There are prayers said in this morning chapel. Here is a row of seedlings praying for water; there is a groaning dahlia praying for a stake. But for the most part there is a hymn or two of praise and then a gay commingling in social intercourse; and if there is a mild undercurrent of worshipful intent, that is all the religion I and the garden seem to require.

Our backyard is small; the garden is Lilliputian. And yet within its modest boundaries I can always find more joyful surprises in my short perambulation than a day in the whirling city can offer me. Never a morning, between frost and frost, that does not present some new attraction unsuspected or only hoped for the day before. The buds have broken on the grapevine; or a yellow crocus is in bloom; or the tender green of the lettuce shows in a delicate line on the brown soil; or our first rose has appeared; or there are tiny pods on the pea vines; or the corn is in tassel; or a tomato glows rich red; or — but the list is endless.

Oh, it is worth while to plant and tend and garner! I cannot understand the man or woman with a backyard who is blind to these morning surprises, and deaf to the call of his bit of the soil. I cannot understand the heart that will deliberately close its doors to these free and God-given joys.

I am one of those fortunate ones who can go to work afoot, and after breakfast I can prolong my morning chapel, in a manner, by glimpses into other yards along the pleasant way to the shop. I like to fancy that Dr. Ludlow is rejoicing over the full-blown beauty of his symmetrical cherry tree, or that Mrs. Saunders has gazed with astonished delight that morning upon her first pink peonies. I wave a mental salutation as I pass, and feel that we understand each other.

And then in June there is the square white house with the supergorgeous array of blue cornflowers [*Centaurea cyanus*] and pink roses behind it. I mean to get acquainted and enter that backyard some day. I feel that it would be worth while. I know that it would put our humble rose-bed to shame, though

I am still haunted by the conviction that our Killarneys are just a shade the finest roses ever grown in the open.

God bless you, brother backyardsmen. May your lettuce never fail to head nor your hollyhocks to bloom. And at your morning worship know that I am with you in spirit, and that our common text is "Consider the lilies."

The Craftsman 26 (June 1914): 270–271.

ENDNOTES

81. See above, xxxiv–xxxv n.36.

82. On Dyer and *The Humble Annals*, see above, 22.

BIBLIOGRAPHY

I. Additional Articles Suggested for Further Reading

Adams, H. S. "The Beauty of Plants That Are Left Alone." *Country Life in America* 21 (January 15, 1912): 15–16.

――――. "Simple Rock Garden Effects." *The Garden Maqazine* 23 (April 1916): 156.

Allen, James J. "An Experience with the Soil: Wild Gardening in Little — The Trials of a Suburbanite and the Rewards." *Country Life in America* 1 (February 1902): 131–133.

"Among My Weeds." *Lippincott's Monthly Magazine* 41 (May 1888): 671–675.

Aust, Franz A. "American Hedges for America." *Better Homes and Gardens* 3 (March 1925): 10, 70–71.

Author of 'The Garden in the Wilderness' [Hanna Rion]. "The Garden of the Many Little Paths." *The Craftsman* 17 (March 1910): 619–628.

Bartlett, Rose. "How One Man Made His Town Bloom." *The Ladies' Home Journal* 27 (March 1910): 36, 80, 82.

Barron, Leonard. "An Outdoor Winter Garden." *The Garden Magazine* (December 1906): 240–242.

Blanchan, Neltje [Nellie Doubleday]. "Naturalistic Gardens." *Country Life in America* 14 (September 1908): 443–445.

――――. "The Garden Any One May Have." *The Ladies' Home Journal* 25 (April 1908): 44.

――――. "The Joy of Gardening." *Country Life in America* 17 (March 1910): 541–544.

Boult, Ella M. "The Garden of Mistress Mary." *Country Life in America* 12 (August 1907): 423–425.

Brinkle, William Draper. "The Genesis of an Inexpensive Garden." *The House Beautiful* 24 (August 1908): 53–54.

Burnett, Vivian. "Craftsman Gardens for Craftsman Homes." *The Craftsman* 18 (April 1910): 46–58.

Cable, George W. "The American Garden." *Scribner's Magazine* 35 (May 1904): 621–629.

――――. "The Midwinter Gardens of New Orleans." *Scribner's Magazine* 47 (January 1910): 58–70.

Chandler, Warren J. "Planting Retaining Walls." *The Garden Magazine* 15 (May 1912): 240–242.

Chesley, Charles H. "Native Plants for Rock Gardens." *Gardeners' Chronicle of America* 41 (November 1937): 305–306.

Childs, Hortense Ferguson. "A Little Garden on the Lewis and Clark Trail." *Country Life in America* 17 (March 1910): 527–530, 586–587.

Clark, Bertha A. "The Society of Little Gardens." *The House Beautiful* 41 (January 1917): 72–75, 102.

————. "Little War Gardens." *The House Beautiful* 43 (March 1918): 208–210, 250.

Clark, Elizabeth Bootes. "Berries and Evergreens for Winter." *The House Beautiful* 19 (December 1910): 12–13.

————. "The Joys of Naturalizing, I." *The House Beautiful* 31 (April 1912): 156–157.

————. "The Joys of Naturalizing, II." *The House Beautiful* 31 (May 1912): 190–191.

————. "Covered Ways." *The House Beautiful* 32 (July 1912): 57–58.

————. "Water Gardens." *The House Beautiful* 34 (July 1913): 60.

————. "Plants Suitable for Water Effects in the Garden." *The House Beautiful* 34 (August 1913): 75–76.

Coe, Sarah Leyburn. "Making the Most of the Porch." *House and Garden* 21 (June 1912): 30–32, 51–53.

Clark, Mrs. Jay. "When a Man Gardens: A Woman's Summing up of the Male Point of View." *House Beautiful* 75 (January 1934): 30–31.

Cooper, May Louise. "Friendly Beetles." *The House Beautiful* 34 (March 1916): 134–135.

Cowgill, Kathleen. "Rock Plants for the South." *Gardeners' Chronicle of America* 42 (January 1938): 7–8, 16.

Cowles, Henry Chandler. "The Ecological Relations of the Vegetation on the Sand Dunes of Lake Michigan." *Botanical Gazette* 27 (1899): 97–117, 167–202, 281–308, 361–391.

Day, Frank Miles. "An Architect's Garden." *House and Garden* 2 (April 1902): 126–139.

Dean, Ruth. "Foundation Planting for the Suburban Lot." *The Garden Magazine* 23 (April 1906): 167.

————. "On Informal or Naturalistic Pools." *The Garden Magazine* 23 (June 1916): 286–287.

————. "Garden Shelters." *Country Life in America* 24 (June 1918): 44–47.

————. "The New Swimming Hole." *House and Garden* 41 (April 1922): 44–45, 112, 114, 116.

Duffy, Sherman. "Planting for Winter Effect." *Country Life in America* 19 (December 1910): 147–148.

————. "Native Asters for Fall Gardens." *The Garden Magazine* 16 (September 1912): 45–48.

————. "Philosophizing with Anchusas." *The Garden Magazine* 19 (July 1914): 341.

————. "Planting for 'After June' Bloom in the Flower Border." *The Garden Magazine* 39 (April 1924): 121–124.

Duncan, Frances. "The Use and Abuse of the Pergola." *Country Life in America* 21 (February 15, 1912): 28–30.

————. "Planting Your Own Vine and Fig Tree." *The Garden Magazine* 15 (April 1912): 158–160.

_____. "How to Teach Gardening to Children." *The Ladies' Home Journal* 39 (April 1912): 46, 88.

_____. "The Old Back–Yard Fence: What You Can Do with It This Spring." *The Ladies' Home Journal* 31 (March 1914): 44.

Dyer, Walter A. "School Gardens: In Helping the Children the Nation Profits." *The Craftsman* 26 (June 1914): 286–291.

Earle, Alice Morse. "Old-Time Flower Gardens." *Scribner's Magazine* 20 (August 1896): 162–178.

Eaton, Florence Taft. "Picturesque Garden Accessories." *The House Beautiful* 49 (January 1921): 40–41, 58.

_____. "Bringing Up My Garden Family." *The American Home* 1 (January 1929): 317, 358.

_____. "The Embroidery of the Garden Path." *Better Homes and Gardens* 9 (April 1931): 31, 80.

Egan, W. C. "Why and How I Made My Country Home." *Country Life in America* 3 (March 1903): 211–213.

Elliott, Bernice. "The Garden Experience of a Business Woman." *The House Beautiful* 49 (June 1921): 496–497, 522.

Farrington, Edward I. "'Common' Plants in a Lovely Garden, Designed and Managed by One Woman." *The Craftsman* 30 (September 1916): 475–482.

Fellows, Katherine Fording. "Hedges and Edgings." *Gardeners' Chronicle of America* 41 (June 1937): 167–169.

"Flowering Shrubs for the Highways and Byways: Suggestions for Beautifying our Rural Roads." *The Craftsman* 28 (May 1915): 163–171.

Frye, Else M. "The Season Passes in a Western Rock Garden." *Gardeners' Chronicle of America* 41, (January–December 1937): 24, 55, 88, 122, 154, 187–188, 212, 240, 270, 302, 327, 354.

"Gardens Imagined: An Actual Garden." *Scribner's Magazine* 57 (June 1915): 775–778.

Garrison, Lydia. "An Honest-to-Goodness Garden." *The House Beautiful* 49 (March 1921): 181–183, 224.

Goldsmith, Margaret. "Friday to Monday Garden." *House Beautiful* (February 1934): 18–19, 74–75.

"Growing Individuality of the American Garden." *The Craftsman* (April 1911): 54–62.

Hansen, Albert A. "Taming Native Wild Shrubs." *Nature* 12 (November 1928): 316–319.

Hillweg, E. C. "'The City of Lakes and Gardens': Civic Progress in Minneapolis." *The Craftsman* 28 (April 1915): 48–57.

Horsford, F. H. "The Best Native Asters for Cultivation." *The Country Calendar* 1 (September 1905): 465.

Howell, E. N. "A Wild-Flower Bed in a City Yard." *The Garden Magazine* 7 (June 1908) 272–274.

"Intermittent Gardener: A Hillside Garden in the Middle-West Made by One Woman Out of Office Hours." *The Touchstone* 1 (July 1917): 262–268.

Jocelyn, Susan E. W. "A Back-Yard Study." *The House Beautiful* 16 (July 1904): 12.

Jones, Helen Lukens. "How to Make a Garden for Birds." *Country Life in America* 3 (April 1903): 249–250.

Joor, Harriet. "My Garden in the Snow." *Country Life in America* 21 (December 15, 1911): 17–20.

King, Mrs. Francis [Louisa Yeomans King]. "Succession Crops in the Flower Garden." *The Garden Magazine* 12 (September 1910): 58–59.

———. "Color Harmonies in the Spring Garden." *The Garden Magazine* 15 (May 1912): 236–238.

———. "Summer Thoughts in Winter." *House and Garden* 34 (November 1918): 14, 58, 60.

———. "My Garden in May and June." *House and Garden* 39 (April 1921): 50, 86, 90.

———. "A Chronicle of My Own Garden." *House Beautiful* 56 (October 1924): 354–355.

———. "Short and Simple: Annuals of the Poor." *House and Garden* 69 (March 1936): 69, 94.

Klingle, George. "A Weedy Garden." *House and Garden* 22 (July 1913): 6–7, 57.

"Landscape Architecture in America and Its Possibilities for the Future." *The Craftsman* 26 (June 1914): 279–285.

Lawrence, Elizabeth. "These Are Chrysanthemums." *House Beautiful* 78 (July 1936): 18–19, 64.

———. "Biennials — An Uncertain Quantity." *Gardeners' Chronicle of America* 43 (May 1939): 147, 150.

Le Gallienne, Richard. "The Soul of a Garden." *House and Garden* 33 (March 1918): 19–20.

Lockwood, Sarah M. "Somehow Gardens." *Country Life in America* 49 (May 1924): 59–60.

Lounsberry, Alice. "From Woods to Garden: Common Wild Flowers that Respond to Cultivation." *The Delineator* 73 (May 1909): 701.

Loveland, Lillian S. "My Wild Corner." *House and Garden* 25 (January 1914): 74–77.

Manning, Warren. "The Two Kinds of Bog Garden." *Country Life in America* 12 (August 1908): 379–380.

———. "Unique Little Gardens." *Country Life in America* 19 (April 15, 1911): 443–445.

McAdam, Thomas. "How We Can Beat the World at Wild Gardening." *The Garden Magazine* 8 (November 1908): 172–174.

———. "Join the Roadside Gardening Club Now." *The Garden Magazine* 7 (July 1908): 322–324.

McColm, Viola. "A Garden of Prairie Wild Flowers." *Country Life in America* 7 (March 1905): 504–505.

McFarland, J. Horace. "Dolobran — A Wild-Gardening Estate." *Country Life in America* 4 (September 1903): 338–365.

———. "The Surroundings of a Country Home." *The Country Calendar* 1 (September 1905): 467.

———. "Among the New Natural Roses." *House and Garden* 39 (April 1921): 40–41, 66, 70.

McIlvaine, Charles. "The Dodder." *Lippincott's Monthly Magazine* 48 (July 1891): 121–123.

Miller, Julia. "Some Notes on Paths in the Flower Garden." *House Beautiful* 43 (March 1918): 202–204.

Miller, Wilhelm. "Wild Gardening Beside a Wooded Lake." *Country Life in America* 9 (March 1906): 548–552.

Morrison, Ben Y. "A Three-Tier Herbaceous Border." *The Garden Magazine* 21 (February 1915): 15–17.

Mowbray, J. P. "A Snift at Old Gardens." *Country Life in America* (November 1901): 7–12.

"Nature Is Head–Gardener on the Estate of Mr. T. A. Havemeyer." *The Touchstone* 2 (October 1917): 44–52.

Nichols, Rose Standish. "How to Make a Small Garden." *The House Beautiful* 32 (August 1912): 88 90.

Ortloff, H. Stuart. "Native Shrubs for American Gardens." *House and Garden* 39 (June 1921): 52–70.

"Ounce of Prevention." *House Beautiful* 53 (May 1923): 503–504.

Parry, Edward H. "Inviting the Birds." *The Garden Magazine* 34 (October 1921): 74–76.

Patterson, J. M. "Flowering Shrubs for the Middle South." *The Garden Magazine* 24 (November 1916): 137–139.

Pease, Cora A. "My Garden." *The House Beautiful* 30 (November 1911): 190–191.

"Pergolas in American Gardens." *The Craftsman* 20 (April 1911): 33–40.

Perry, Isabel. "Delphiniums in the South." *House Beautiful* 63 (March 1928): 289, 341–342.

Phillips, Gertrude W. "Misty Effects in the Garden." *Gardener's Chronicle of America* 41 (February 1937): 37–38.

Powell, E. P. "Laying Out a Country Home." *House and Garden* 8 (November 1905): 193–196.

Rathbone, Alice M. "A Plea for Gay Little Gardens." *Country Life in America* 1 (December 1901): 52.

Rehmann, Elsa. "In a Southern Garden." *House and Garden* 35 (February 1919): 25.

————. "Geometric Garden Plans." *House Beautiful* 6 (March 1925): 242–243, 286.

————. "How to Make a Simple Flower Border." *Better Homes and Gardens* 4 (May 1926): 21, 55.

Rexford, Eben E. "A Garden of Native Plants" *Lippincott's Monthly Magazine* 69 (April 1902): 483–488.

Richardson, Don. "My Rock Garden: A Pocket Edition." *Gardeners' Chronicle of America* 43 (May 1939): 148–149.

Roberts, Mary Fanton. "The Soul of the Garden." *The Craftsman* 28 (April 1915): 20–25, 124.

Roosevelt, Eleanor. "Mrs. Roosevelt's Page: Gardens." *The Ladies' Home Journal* 62 (March 1935): 4.

Rothe, Richard. "American Rock Gardens." *Gardeners' Chronicle of America* 25 (March 1921): 497–499.

Rowlee, W. W. "Goldenrod, Queen of the American Autumn." *Country Life in America* 1 (October 1901): 33–34.

Rowntree, Lester. "Plants for Pavements and Steps." *Gardeners' Chronicle of America* 41 (June 1937): 177–179.

"Rustic Furniture Especially Appropriate for the Informal Garden." *The Craftsman* 24 (June 1912): 349–352.

"Rustic Seats and Shelters, Formal and Fantastic." *The Craftsman* 24 (August 1915): 515–517.

Saunders, Charles Francis. "Home Gardening in Southern California." *The Garden Magazine* 8 (December 1908): 225–228.

————. "Awakening Self–Consciousness in the California Garden." *The Garden Magazine* 36 (December 1922): 191–194.

Saylor, Henry H. "Garden Entrances." *Country Life in America* 11 (March 1907): 501–506.

Shore, Grace R. "How We Can Make Our Gardens Attractive to the Birds." *The Craftsman* 21 (February 1912): 575–576.

_____. "Birds as Under–Gardeners." *The Craftsman* 26 (June 1914): 335–336.

Spicer, Anne Higginson. "A Suburban Garden." *The House Beautiful* 17 (May 1905): 7–9.

"Spectator, The." *The Outlook* 82 (January 6, 1906): 16–18.

Stapley, Mildred. "Suitable Garden Shelters." *House and Garden* 21 (June 1912): 35–37, 48–49.

Strang, Elizabeth Leonard. "The Green and White Garden." *House and Garden* 29 (February 1916): 24–25, 64.

_____. "Developing a City Garden." *House and Garden* 29 (May 1916): 42–43, 62, 66.

_____. "Planting a Pink Garden." *House and Garden* 31 (March 1917): 20–21, 76.

_____. "Planting the Deciduous Trees and Shrubs." *House and Garden* 34 (November 1918): 38–39, 54.

_____. "Effective Combinations in the Flower Garden." *The House Beautiful* 57 (March 1925): 250–251.

Tabor, Grace. "Utilizing Natural Features in Garden Making." *House and Garden* 16 (October 1909): 124–126.

_____. "Insect Helpers." *House and Garden* 17 (June 1910): 242.

_____. "Wild Flowers in the Garden." *House and Garden* 24 (July 1913): 29–31, 52–54.

_____. "The Right Use of Evergreens." *House and Garden* 24 (August 1913): 96–99, 111–112.

_____. "Phlox: An American Plant." *House and Garden* 26 (October 1914): 218–220, 249–251.

_____. "The Best White Flowers." *House and Garden* 31 (June 1917): 32–33, 64, 66, 68.

_____. "Community and Civic Garden–Making." *Woman's Home Companion* 54 (April 1927): 38, 40.

_____. "Arbors, Summer–Houses and Trellises." *House and Garden* 33 (May 1918): 46, 62, 64, 66.

_____. "Our Gardens Are Growing Up." *Woman's Home Companion* 62 (January 1935): 42.

Warthin, Aldred Scott. "A Garden of Little Labor and Much Delight." *The Garden Magazine* 14 (September 1911): 58–60.

Watts, Harvey Maitland. "A Plea for the Juniper." *House and Garden* 6 (September 1904): 124–128.

Webster, Rose Glen. "Our Garden in the Far North." *Better Homes and Gardens* 9 (December 1931): 21, 36.

Wheeler, Candace. "Content in a Garden." *Atlantic Monthly* 85 (June 1900): 779–784; 86 (July 1900): 99–105; 86 (August 1900): 232–238.

Wilder, Louise B. "The Care of the June Garden." *Good Housekeeping* 64 (June 1917): 33, 145–146.

_____. "Shrubs for the Rock Garden." *House and Garden* 48 (September 1925): 92–93, 156, 158.

_____. "Fragrance of a Rose of Today and Long Ago." *House and Garden* 59 (June 1931): 46–47, 108, 110.

_____. "Spring Scillas." *House and Garden* 70 (September 1936): 72, 95, 97.

Wright, Mabel Osgood. "A Poor Man's Paradise: The Spell of the Wild." *The Country Calendar* 1 (September 1905): 431–434.

_____. "A Poor Man's Paradise: The Flower Corner." *The Country Calendar* 1 (October 1905): 557–561.

Yeomans, Harry Martin. "Sanctifying the Backyard." *The House Beautiful* 31 (March 1912): 109–111.

II. BIBLIOGRAPHY

Albanese, Catherine L. *Nature Religion in America: From the Algonkian Indians to the New Age.* Chicago History of American Religion, series edited by Martin E. Marty. Chicago: University of Chicago Press, 1990.

Albee, Helen Rickey. *Mountain Playmates.* Boston: Houghton Mifflin, 1990.

_____. *Hardy Plants for Cottage Gardens.* New York: H. Holt, 1910.

_____. *A Kingdom of Two: A True Romance of Country.* New York: Macmillan, 1913.

Alexander, Charles C. *Here the Country Lies: Nationalism and the Arts in Twentieth-Century America.* Bloomington: Indiana University Press, 1980.

Anderson, Dorothy May. *Women, Design, and the Cambridge School.* West Lafayette, Indiana: PDA Publishers, 1980.

Arnim, Elizabeth von [Mary Annette Beauchamp]. *Elizabeth and Her German Garden.* New York: Macmillan, 1900.

Balmori, Diana. "The Arts and Crafts Garden." *Tiller* 1 (July–August 1983): 18–28.

Barrier, Robert G. "*Scribner's Magazine.*" In *American Literary Magazines*, edited by Edward E. Chielens, 308–314. Westport, Connecticut: Greenwood Press, 1992.

Begg, Virginia Lopez. "Frances Duncan: The 'New Woman' in the Garden." *Journal of the New England Garden History Society* (fall 1992): 28–35.

_____. "Frances Duncan." In *Pioneers of American Landscape Design: An Annotated Bibliography*, edited by Charles A. Birnbaum and Lisa E. Crowder, 45–46. Washington, D. C.: U. S. Department of the Interior, National Park Service, Cultural Resources, 1993.

_____. "Louisa Yeomans King." In *Pioneers of American Landscape Design: An Annotated Bibliography*, edited by Charles A. Birnbaum and Lisa E. Crowder, 74–76. Washington, D. C.: U. S. Department of the Interior, National Park Service, Cultural Resources, 1993.

_____. "Louise Beebe Wilder." In *Pioneers of American Landscape Design: An Annotated Bibliography*, edited by Charles A. Birnbaum and Lisa E. Crowder, 132–133. Washington, D. C.: U. S. Department of the Interior, National Park Service, Cultural Resources, 1993.

_____. "Richardson Wright." In *Pioneers of American Landscape Design: An Annotated Bibliography*, edited by Charles A. Birnbaum and Lisa E. Crowder, 133–135. Washington, D. C.: U. S. Department of the Interior, National Park Service, Cultural Resources, 1993

Bell, Leonie. Introduction to *Old Roses*, by Ethelyn E. Keays, 1935. Reprint, New York: Earl M. Coleman, 1978.

Betsky, Celia. "Inside the Past: The Interior and the Colonial Revival in American Art and Literature." In *The Colonial Revival in America*, edited by Alan Axelrod, 241–277. New York: W. W. Norton, 1985.

Bogart, Michele H. *Artists, Advertising, and the Borders of Art.* Chicago: University of Chicago Press, 1995.

Bok, Edward. *The Americanization of Edward Bok: The Autobiography of a Dutch Boy Fifty Years After.* New York: C. Scribner's Sons, 1921.

Boris, Eileen. *Art and Labor: Ruskin, Morris, and The Craftsman Ideal in America.* Philadelphia: Temple University Press, 1986.

Boutell, Sara Holmes. *Julia Morgan, Architect.* New York: Abbeville Press, 1988.

Bowers, William L. *The Country Life Movement in America, 1900–1920.* Port Washington, New York: Kennikat Press, 1974.

Bowman, Leslie Greene. *American Arts and Crafts: Virtue in Design.* Los Angeles: Los Angeles County Museum of Art; distributed by Bulfinch Press, 1990.

Boyle, Eleanor Vere. *Days and Hours in a Garden.* Boston: Roberts Brothers, 1884.

Brinkley, M. Kent, and Gordon W. Chappell. *The Gardens of Colonial Williamsburg.* Williamsburg: Colonial Williamsburg Foundation, 1996.

Brown, Catherine R. "Women and the Land: A Biographical Survey of Women Who have Contributed to the Development of Landscape Architecture in the United States." Built Environment Studies, Morgan State University, Baltimore, 1979. Photocopy.

Burke, Doreen Bolger, et al. *In Pursuit of Beauty: Americans and the Aesthetic Movement.* Metropolitan Museum of Art, New York; New York: Rizzoli International, 1986.

Callen, Anthea. *Women Artists of the Arts and Crafts Movement, 1870–1914.* New York: Pantheon Books, 1979.

Clark, Robert Judson, ed. *The Arts and Crafts Movement in America, 1876–1916.* Princeton University Art Museum; Art Institute of Chicago; Renwick Gallery, National Collection of Fine Arts, Smithsonian Institution, 1972–1973. Princeton: Princeton University Press, 1972.

Clayton, Virginia Tuttle. *Gardens on Paper.* Washington, D. C.: National Gallery of Art; distributed by University of Pennsylvania Press, 1990.

————. "Reminiscence and Revival: The Old-Fashioned Garden, 1890–1910." *Antiques* 137 (April 1990): 894–905.

————. "Wild Gardening and the Popular American Magazine, 1890–1918," *Nature and Ideology: Natural Garden Design in the Twentieth Century,* edited by Joachim Wolschke-Bulmahn, 131–154. Washington, D. C.: Dumbarton Oaks, 1997.

Close, Leslie Rose. *Portrait of an Era in Landscape Architecture: The Photographs of Mattie Edwards Hewitt.* Bronx, New York: Wave Hill, 1983.

Corn, Wanda. *The Color of Mood: American Tonalism, 1880–1910.* San Francisco: M. H. DeYoung Memorial Museum, 1972.

Cornforth, John. *The Search for a Style: Country Life and Architecture, 1895–1935.* New York: W. W. Norton, 1988.

Dean, Ruth. *The Livable House, Its Garden.* New York: Moffat, Yard, 1917.

Desmond, Ray. "Nineteenth-Century Horticultural Journalism." In *John Claudius Loudon and the Early Nineteenth Century in Great Britain,* edited by Elisabeth Blair MacDougal, 79–97. Washington, D.C.: Dumbarton Oaks, 1980.

Doell, M. Christine. *Gardens of the Gilded Age: Nineteenth-Century Gardens and Homegrounds of New York State.* Syracuse: Syracuse University Press, 1986.

Doubleday, Nellie [Neltje Blanchan]. *The American Flower Garden.* New York: Doubleday, Page and Company 1909.

Dyer, Walter A. *The Humble Annals of a Back Yard.* New York: Pilgrim Press, 1916.

Earle, Alice Morse. *Old Time Gardens.* New York: New York: Macmillan, 1901.

———. *Sun Dials and Roses of Yesterday.* Macmillan, 1902.

Earle, Edward W. *Halftone Effects: A Cultural Study of Photographs in Reproduction, 1895–1905 Bulletin of the California Museum of Photography* 8, no. 1, 1–24. Riverside: University of California, 1989.

Eaton, Walter Prichard. *Everybody's Garden.* New York: Alfred A. Knopf, 1932.

———. *Wild Gardens of New England.* Boston: W. A. Wilde, 1936.

Elliott, Brent. *The Country House Garden: From the Archives of Country Life, 1897–1939.* London: Reed Consumer Books, 1995.

Eppard, Philip B., and George Monteiro. Introduction to *A Guide to the Atlantic Monthly Contributors' Club.* Boston: G. K. Hall, 1983.

Fleming, Nancy. *Money, Manure, and Maintenance.* Weston, Massachusetts: Country Place Books, 1995.

Gamble, William. *The Beginning of the Half-Tone: A History of the Process.* New York: Edward Epstean, 1927.

Grese, Robert E. *Jens Jensen: Maker of Natural Parks and Gardens.* Baltimore: Johns Hopkins University Press, 1992.

Griswold, Mac, and Eleanor Weller. *The Golden Age of American Gardens: Proud Owners, Proud Estates, 1890–1940.* New York: Abrams, in association with the Garden Club of America, 1991.

Harris, Neil. *The Artist in American Society.* Chicago: Chicago University Press, 1982. Originally published, New York: G. Braziller, 1966

Hill, May Brawley. "Grandmother's Garden." *Antiques* 142 (November 1992): 727–735.

———. *Grandmother's Garden: The Old-Fashioned Garden, 1865–1915.* New York: Abrams, 1995.

Hitchmough, Wendy. *Arts and Crafts Gardens.* New York: Rizzoli International, 1997.

Hosmer, Charles B., Jr. "The Colonial Revival in the Public Eye: Williamsburg and Early Garden Restoration." In *The Colonial Revival in America,* edited by Alan Axelrod, 52–70. New York: W. W. Norton, 1985.

Hunt, John Dixon. *The Figure in the Landscape: Poetry, Painting, and Gardening during the Eighteenth Century.* Baltimore: Johns Hopkins University Press, 1976.

Kaplan, Wendy, ed. *"The Art That Is Life": The Arts and Crafts Movement in America, 1875–1920.* With essays by Wendy Kaplan, Eileen Boris, Richard Guy Wilson, Robert Judson Clark, Robert Edwards, Cheryl Robertson, and Sally Buchanan Dinsey. Boston, Museum of Fine Arts; distributed by Little, Brown, New York, 1987.

Karson, Robin S. *Fletcher Steele, Landscape Architect: An Account of a Gardenmaker's Life, 1885–1971.* New York: Abrams, 1989.

Keays, Ethelyn E. *Old Roses.* New York: Macmillan, 1935.

King, Caroline Blanche Campion. *Rosemary Makes a Garden.* Philadelphia: Penn Publishing, 1930

———. *This Was Ever in My Dream.* Caldwell, Idaho: Caxton, 1947.

King, Louisa Yeomans [Mrs. Francis King]. *The Well-Considered Garden,* with a preface by Gertrude Jekyll. New York: C. Scribner's Sons, 1915.

Lears, T. J. Jackson. *No Place of Grace: Antimodernism and the Transformation of American Culture, 1880–1920.* New York: Pantheon Books, 1981.

Lee, P. R. "Twenty-Five Years of It: The Social Service of Frederic Almy." *The Survey* 42 (May 24, 1919): 309–310.

Lewis, Pierce. "The Making of Vernacular Taste: The Case of *Sunset* and *Southern Living.*" In *The Vernacular Garden*, edited by John Dixon Hunt and Joachim Wolschke–Bulmahn, 107–136. Washington, D.C.: Dumbarton Oaks, 1993.

Link, Arthur S., and Richard L. McCormick. *Progressivism*. Arlington Heights, Illinois: Harlan Davidson, 1983.

Linn, Eve F. W. "Ruth Dean." In *Pioneers of American Landscape Design II: An Annotated Bibliography*, edited by Charles A. Birnbaum and Julie K. Fix, 40–44. Washington, D. C.: U. S. Department of the Interior, National Park Service, Cultural Resources, 1995.

Lockwook, Alice, ed. *Gardens of Colony and State: Gardens and Gardeners of the American Colonies and of the Republic Before 1840*. New York: C. Scribner's Sons, 1931–1934.

Lowell, Guy. *American Gardens*. Boston: Bates and Guild, 1902.

Marx, Leo. *The Machine in the Garden: Technology and the Pastoral Ideal in America*. New York: Oxford University Press, 1964.

McFarland, J. Horace. *Memoirs of a Rose Man*. Emmaus, Pennsylvania: Rodale Press, 1949.

McKenny, Margaret. *The Wild Garden*. Garden City, New York: Doubleday, Page, 1936.

McKenny, Margaret, and Edward Loomis Davenport Seymour, *Your City Garden*. New York: D. Appleton, 1937.

Miller, Perry. *Errand into the Wilderness*. Cambridge: Belknap Press of Harvard University Press, 1956.

Miller, Wilhelm. *What England Can Teach Us About Gardening*. Garden City, New York: Doubleday, Page, 1911.

Moore, James R. *The Post-Darwinian Controversies: A Study of the Protestant Struggle to Come to Terms with Darwin in Great Britain and America, 1870–1900*. New York: Cambridge University Press, 1979.

Morgan, Keith N. *Charles Platt: The Artist as Architect*. New York: Architectural History Foundation; Cambridge: MIT Press, 1985.

————. "The Rise and Fall of the Italian Garden in America." In *Influences on American Garden Design: 1895–1940*, edited by Robin Karson. Masters of American Garden IV. New York: Garden Conservancy, 1994.

Morris, Elisabeth Woodbridge. *The Jonathan Papers*. Boston: Houghton Mifflin, 1912.

Morrison, Darrel G. Foreword to *American Plants for American Gardens*, by Edith A. Roberts and Elsa Rehmann, 1929. Reprint, Athens: University of Georgia Press, 1996.

Morrison, Ernest. *H. Horace McFarland: A Thorn for Beauty*. Harrisburg: Pennsylvania Historical and Museum Commission, 1995.

Mott, Frank Luther. *A History of American Magazines*. 5 vols. Cambridge: Harvard University Press, 1938–1968.

Nash, Roderick. *Wilderness and the American Mind*. New Haven: Yale University Press, 1967.

Nevins, Deborah. Introduction to *The English Flower Garden*, by William Robinson. 15th edition, 1933. Reprint, New York: Amaryllis Press, 1984.

————. "The Triumph of Flora: Women and the American Landscape, 1890–1935." *Antiques* 27 (April 1985): 904–921.

Ottewill, David. *The Edwardian Garden*. New Haven: Yale University Press, 1989.

Parker, Gail Thain. *Mind Cure in New England*. Hanover, New Hampshire: University Press of New England, 1973.

Peters, Lisa N., and Peter M. Lukehart, eds. *Visions of Home: American Impressionist Images of Suburban Leisure and Country Comfort.* With essays by May Brawley Hill, Lisa N. Peters, and David Schuyler. Trout Gallery, Carlisle, Pennsylvania; Florence Griswold Museum, Old Lyme, Connecticut; distributed by University Press of New England, Hanover, New Hampshire, 1997.

Powell, Edward Payson. *The Country Home.* New York: McClure, Phillips, 1904.

Pyne, Kathleen A. "John Twachtman and the Therapeutic Landscape." In *John Twachtman: Connecticut Landscapes.* Washington, D. C.: National Gallery of Art; distributed by Abrams, New York, 1989.

————. *Art and the Higher Life: Painting and Evolutionary Thought in Late Nineteenth-Century America.* Austin: University of Texas Press, 1996.

Ray, Gordon N. *The Illustrator and the Book in England from 1790–1976.* New York: Pierpont Morgan Library, 1976.

Rehmann, Elsa, and Antoinette Perrett. *Garden-Making.* [n.p.], 1926.

Rehmann, Elsa. *The Small Place: Its Landscape Architecture.* York: G. P. Putnam, 1918.

Rion, Hanna. *The Garden in the Wilderness.* New York: Baker and Taylor, 1909.

————. *Let's Make a Flower Garden.* New York: McBride, Nast, 1912.

Roberts, Edith A., and Elsa Rehmann. *American Plants for American Gardens.* 1929. Reprint, with a foreword by Darrel G. Morrison, Athens: University of Georgia Press, 1996.

Schmitt, Peter J. *Back to Nature: The Arcadian Myth in Urban America.* New York: Oxford University Press, 1969.

Schneirov, Matthew. *The Dream of a New Social Order: Popular Magazines in America, 1893–1914.* New York: Columbia University Press, 1994.

Schuyler, David. *Apostle of Taste: Andrew Jackson Downing, 1815–1852.* Baltimore: Johns Hopkins University Press, 1996.

Seaton, Beverly. "The Garden Autobiography." *Garden History: The Journal of the Garden History Society* 7 (spring 1979): 101–120.

Sedgwick, Ellery. *Atlantic Harvest: Memoirs of the Atlantic.* Boston: Little, Brown, 1947.

Shapiro, Laura. *Perfection Salad: Women and Cooking at the Turn of the Century.* New York: Farrar, Straus and Giroux, 1986.

Shelton, Louise. *Beautiful Gardens in America.* New York: Charles Scribner's Sons, 1915.

Shi, David E. *The Simple Life: Plain Living and High Thinking in American Culture.* New York: Oxford University Press, 1985.

Spielmann, M. H., and G. S. Layard. *Kate Greenaway.* New York: G. P. Putnam's Sons, 1905.

Steele, Fletcher. *Design in the Little Garden.* Boston: The Atlantic Monthly Press, 1924.

————. *Gardens and People.* Boston: Houghton Mifflin, 1964.

Stein, Roger B. *John Ruskin and Aesthetic Thought in America, 1840–1900.* Cambridge: Harvard University Press, 1967.

Szarkowski, John. *Photography Until Now.* New York, Museum of Modern Art; distributed by Bulfinch Press, Boston, 1989.

Tabor, Grace. *Old-Fashioned Gardening: A History and a Reconstruction.* New York: McBride, Nast, 1913.

Tankard, Judith. "Women Pioneers in Landscape Design." *Radcliffe Quarterly* 79 (March 1993): 8–11.

————. "Gardening with *Country Life.*" *Hortus* 30 (summer 1994): 72–86.

_____. "The Influence of British Garden Literature on American Garden Design." In *Influences on American Garden Design: 1895–1940*, edited by Robin Karson. Masters of Garden Design IV. New York: Garden Conservancy, 1994.

Tatum, George B. "The Downing Decade (1841–1852)." In *Prophet with Honor: The Career of Andrew Jackson Downing, 1815–1852*, edited by George B. Tatum and Elisabeth Blair MacDougal, 1–42. Washington, D.C.: Dumbarton Oaks, 1989.

Thaxter, Celia. *An Island Garden*. 1894. Reprint, with an introduction by Allen Lacy, Boston: Houghton Mifflin, 1988.

Thornton, Sally Bullard. *Daring to Dream: The Life of Hazel Wood Waterman*. San Diego: San Diego Historical Society, 1987.

Trapp, Kenneth R., ed. *The Arts and Crafts Movement in California: Living the Good Life*. With essays by Richard Guy Wilson, David C. Streatfield, Karen J. Weitze, Cheryl Robertson, Joseph A. Taylor, Kenneth R. Trapp, Leslie Green Bowman, and Bruce Kamerling. Oakland Museum, Oakland, California; Renwick Gallery of the National Museum of American Art, Smithsonian Institution, Washington, D.C.; Cincinnati Art Museum, Cincinnati, Ohio; distributed by Abbeville Press, New York, 1993–1994.

Vernon, Christopher. "Wilhelm (William) Tyler Miller." In *Pioneers in American Landscape Design: An Annotated Bibliography*, edited by Charles A. Birnbaum and Lisa E. Crowder, 86–88. Washington, D. C.: U. S. Department of the Interior, National Park Service, Cultural Resources, 1993.

_____. "Wilhelm Miller and *The Prairie Spirit in Landscape Gardening*." In *Regional Garden Design in the United States*, edited by Therese O'Malley and Marc Treib, 271–275. Washington, D. C.: Dumbarton Oaks, 1995.

Waugh, Frank. *The Natural Style in Landscape Gardening*. Boston: Richard G. Badger, 1917.

Wilder, Louise Beebe. *Colour in My Garden*. Garden City, New York: Doubleday, Page, 1918.

Wolschke–Bulmahn, Joachim, and Gert Groening. "The Ideology of the Nature Garden. Nationalistic Trends in Garden Design in Germany During the Early Twentieth Century." *Journal of Garden History* 12 (January–March 1992): 73–80.

Wolschke–Bulmahn, Joachim. "The 'Wild Garden' and the 'Nature Garden' — Aspects of the Garden Ideology of William Robinson and Willy Lange." *Journal of Garden History* 14 (July–September 1992): 183–206.

CREDITS

COLOR ILLUSTRATION CREDITS

Front cover: *House and Garden,* October 1917. Illustration by Charles Livingston Bull. Copy photograph: Dean Beasom. Courtesy of Horticulture Branch Library, Smithsonian Institution Libraries, Washington, D.C.

Plate 1. Copy photograph: *House and Garden*

Plate 2. Copy photograph: Lee B. Ewing. Courtesy of Horticulture Branch Library, Smithsonian Institution Libraries, Washington, D.C.

Plate 3. Copy photograph: Hartford Public Library

Plate 4. Copy photograph: Dean Beasom. Courtesy of Horticulture Branch Library, Smithsonian Institution Libraries, Washington, D.C.

Plate 5. Copy photograph: Dean Beasom. Courtesy of Horticulture Branch Library, Smithsonian Institution Libraries, Washington, D.C.

Plate 6. Copy photograph: Library of Congress, Washington, D.C.

Plate 7. Copy photograph: Dean Beasom. Courtesy of Horticulture Branch Library, Smithsonian Institution Libraries, Washington, D.C.

Plate 8. Copy photograph: *House and Garden*

Plate 9. Copy photograph: Boston Athenaeum

Plate 10. Copy photograph: Boston Athenaeum

Plate 11. Copy photograph: Lee B. Ewing. Courtesy of Horticulture Branch Library, Smithsonian Institution Libraries, Washington, D.C.

Plate 12. Copy photograph: *House and Garden*

Plate 13. Copy photograph: Dean Beasom. Courtesy of Horticulture Branch Library, Smithsonian Institution Libraries, Washington, D.C.

Plate 14. Copy photograph: Dean Beasom. Courtesy of Horticulture Branch Library, Smithsonian Institution Libraries, Washington, D.C.

Plate 15. Copy photograph: Dean Beasom. Courtesy of Horticulture Branch Library, Smithsonian Institution Libraries, Washington, D.C.

Plate 16. Copy photograph: *House and Garden*

Plate 17. Copy photograph: Lee B. Ewing. Courtesy of Horticulture Branch Library, Smithsonian Institution Libraries, Washington, D.C.

Plate 18. Copy photograph: Library of Congress, Washington, D.C.

Plate 19. Copy photograph: Lee B. Ewing. Courtesy of USDA, National Agricultural Library, Beltsville, Maryland

Plate 20. Copy photograph: Lee B. Ewing. Courtesy of Horticulture Branch Library, Smithsonian Institution Libraries, Washington, D.C.

Plate 21. Copy photograph: Lee B. Ewing. Courtesy of Horticulture Branch Library, Smithsonian Institution Libraries, Washington, D.C.

CREDITS FOR BLACK AND WHITE ILLUSTRATIONS

TITLE PAGE "Behind the scenes of every well-kept garden." From *House and Garden* 67 (March 1935): 35. Photograph by Harold Haliday Costain. Copy photography courtesy of Horticulture Branch Library, Smithsonian Institution Libraries, Washington, D.C. Printing: Lee B. Ewing.

COPYRIGHT PAGE Photograph by Antoinette Perrett. Copy photography courtesy of Horticulture Library, Smithsonian Institution Libraries, Washington, D.C. Printing: James Locke, Visual Prose

x "It's July in My Garden and Steel-Blue Are the Globe Thistles." From Sherman Duffy, "Planting for 'After June' Bloom in the Flower Border," *Garden Magazine* 39 (April 1924): 121. Photograph anonymous. Printing: James Locke, Visual Prose.

2 From Walter Prichard Eaton, "Spring in the Garden," *House and Garden* 23 (April 1913): 267. Photograph by Ella M. Boult. Copy photography courtesy of Horticulture Branch Library, Smithsonian Institution Libraries, Washington, D.C. Printing: James Locke, Visual Prose.

3 *Above:* "At the end of a short brick walk hedged with clipped Van Houtte's spirea is a dull green wooden arch over which climb pink rambler roses. At the left, as you look through the gateway from the space of turf and dwarf pine without, is Lady Gay, and at the right Paradise." From Mrs. Francis King, "My Garden in Midsummer," *House and Garden* 39 (May 1921): 67. Photograph anonymous. Copy photography and printing: Lee B. Ewing. *Below:* "The Oriental poppy (Papaver Orientalis) is the most splendid of the red flowers of June. The young seedlings are often winter-killed and so should be protected the first year." From Helen R. Albee, "A Garden of Bright Red Flowers," *Garden*

Magazine 5 (February 1907): 16. Photograph by Henry Troth, N. R. Graves, or anonymous. Printing: Lee B. Ewing.

5 Photograph by Ella M. Boult. Copy photography courtesy of Horticulture Branch Library, Smithsonian Institution Libraries, Washington, D.C. Printing: James Locke, Visual Prose.

6 Photograph by Ella M. Boult. Copy photography courtesy of Horticulture Branch Library, Smithsonian Institution Libraries, Washington, D.C. Printing: James Locke, Visual Prose.

14 Photograph anonymous. Copy photography and printing: Lee B. Ewing.

30 Photograph anonymous. Copy photography: Library of Congress, Washington, D. C. Printing: James Locke, Visual Prose.

36 "The Rose Garden should be suitably framed because of its color display and to shelter the plants from winds." From Harold J. Staples, "Outdoor Roses for Northern Gardens," *Garden Magazine* 23 (April 1916): 160. Photograph by N. R. Graves, Henry Troth, or anonymous. Copy photography and printing: Lee B. Ewing.

37 *Above:* "Ramblers on a rustic arbor at Auburn, N.Y." From W. S. Rogers, "The Autumn Planting of Roses," *Garden Magazine* 14 (October 1911): 118. Photograph by Emil J. Kraemer or anonymous. Copy photography and printing: Lee B. Ewing.
Below: "The golden-green laburnum in blossom." From Jessie Vaughn Harrier, "Boisfleury," *House Beautiful* 67 (May 1930): 621. Reprinted by permission from *House Beautiful,* copyright © May 1930. The Hearst Corporation. All Rights Reserved. Photograph by Ernest S. Higgins. Copy photography courtesy of USDA, National Agricultural Library, Beltsville, Maryland. Printing: James Locke, Visual Prose.

40 Photograph by George H. Van Anda or anonymous. Copy photography courtesy of USDA, National Agricultural Library, Beltsville, Maryland. Printing: James Locke, Visual Prose.

42 Photograph by George H. Van Anda. Copy photography courtesy of USDA, National Agricultural Library, Beltsville, Maryland. Printing: James Locke, Visual Prose.

49 Photograph by E. J. Wallis. Copy photography: James Locke, Visual Prose.

53 Photograph by E. J. Wallis. Copy photography: James Locke, Visual Prose.

61 Photograph anonymous. Copy photography: Library of Congress, Washington, D. C. Printing: James Locke, Visual Prose.

62 Photograph by N. R. Graves. Copy photography: Library of Congress, Washington, D. C. Printing: James Locke, Visual Prose.

65 Photograph by Ernest S. Higgins. Copy photography courtesy of USDA, National Agricultural Library, Beltsville, Maryland. Printing: James Locke, Visual Prose.

71 Photograph by Mattie Edwards Hewitt. Copy photography: Library of Congress, Washington, D. C. Printing: James Locke, Visual Prose.

84 "Olmsted Brothers, Landscape Architects. Plants of refined and delicate form can be scattered lightly through the borders in a way that is sometimes called dribbling in the plants." From Elsa Rehmann, "The Distribution of Flowers in the Garden," *House Beautiful* 58 (October 1925): 349. Reprinted by permission from *House Beautiful,* copyright © October 1925. The Hearst Corporation. All Rights Reserved. Photograph by Antoinette Perrett. Copy photography courtesy of Horticulture Library, Smithsonian Institution Libraries, Washington, D.C. Printing: James Locke, Visual Prose.

85 *Above:* "Mott Schmidt, Architect, and Ellen Shipman, Landscape Gardener. A delightful corner in the tulip garden of Ormsby Mitchell, Mamaroneck, Connecticut." From Antoinette Perrett, "Modern Color in Tulip Gardens," *The House Beautiful* 52 (October 1922): 325. Photograph

by Antoinette Perrett. Copy photography: Library of Congress, Washington, D. C. Printing: James Locke, Visual Prose.
Below: Detail of photograph on page 114.

89 Photograph by Antoinette Perrett. Copy photography courtesy of Horticulture Library, Smithsonian Institution Libraries, Washington, D.C. Printing: James Locke, Visual Prose.

96 Two photographs by Mattie Edwards Hewitt. Copy photography courtesy of USDA, National Agricultural Library, Beltsville, Maryland. Printing: James Locke, Visual Prose.

104 Photograph by Antoinette Perrett. Copy photography: Library of Congress, Washington, D. C. Printing: James Locke, Visual Prose.

109 Photograph anonymous. Printing: James Locke, Visual Prose.

112 Photograph anonymous. Copy photography: Library of Congress, Washington, D. C. Printing: James Locke, Visual Prose.

114 Photograph anonymous. Copy photography: Library of Congress, Washington, D. C. Printing: James Locke, Visual Prose.

117 Three photographs by Walter Beebe Wilder. Copy photography courtesy of USDA, National Agricultural Library, Beltsville, Maryland. Printing: James Locke, Visual Prose.

122 Photograph by Nathan R. Graves or Charles Jones. Copy photography courtesy of USDA, National Agricultural Library, Beltsville, Maryland. Printing: James Locke, Visual Prose.

132 "Wall gardening and rock gardening are closely allied. Copy nature's methods in planting." From Fletcher Steele, "Wall Gardens for America," *Garden Magazine* 20 (September 1914): 40. Photograph by Mary H. Northend. Printing: James Locke, Visual Prose.

133 *Above:* "The delicately tinted blossoms of the hepatica take kindly to woodsy soil and partial

shade and will reappear from season to season." From E. O. Calvene, "The Wild Garden," *House and Garden* 22 (July 1912): 22. Photograph by Ella M. Boult. Copy photograpy courtesy of USDA, National Agricultural Library, Beltsville, Maryland. Printing: James Locke, Visual Prose.
Below: "Violets like sunny banks, and, as they are of social habit, they should be permitted to grow in clumps and allowed to spread freely over the ground." From E. O. Calvene, "The Wild Garden," *House and Garden* 22 (July 1912): 22. Photograph by Ella M. Boult. Copy photography courtesy of USDA, National Agricultural Library, Beltsville, Maryland. Printing: James Locke, Visual Prose.

137 Photograph by Ella M. Boult. Copy photography courtesy of USDA, National Agricultural Library, Beltsville, Maryland. Printing: James Locke, Visual Prose.

140 Photograph by Ella M. Boult or Henry Hodgman Saylor. Copy photography courtesy of USDA, National Agricultural Library, Beltsville, Maryland. Printing: James Locke, Visual Prose.

145 Photograph by Ella M. Boult or Henry Hodgman Saylor. Copy photography courtesy of USDA, National Agricultural Library, Beltsville, Maryland. Printing: James Locke, Visual Prose.

149 Photograph by Charles Darling. Copy photography courtesy of Horticulture Library, Smithsonian Institution Libraries, Washington, D.C. Printing: James Locke, Visual Prose.

151 Photograph by Charles Darling. Copy photography courtesy of Horticulture Library, Smithsonian Institution Libraries, Washington, D.C. Printing: James Locke, Visual Prose.

165 Photograph by John Kabel. Copy photography: Library of Congress, Washington, D. C. Printing: James Locke, Visual Prose.

172 "Where grandmother's favorites still hold pleasing sway. Larkspur (Delphinium) and Canterbury bells (Campanula Medium) continue to fill our gardens with the color and charm that delighted our forbears and the trellised Rose still gaily climbs." From Louise Beebe Wilder, "Old-Fashioned Gardens that Continue to Charm," *Garden Magazine* 34 (November 1921): 132. Photograph by Frances Benjamin Johnston. Copy photography: Library of Congress, Washington, D. C. Printing: James Locke, Visual Prose.

173 "This Philadelphia dooryard garden is a delight both from house to garden and garden to house. The white gate and arch of Roses are pleasant features." From Aymar Embury, "Doorways to the Garden," *Garden Magazine* 23 (April 1916): 176. Photograph by Aymar Embury or anonymous. Copy photography and printing: Lee B. Ewing.

177 Photograph by Mattie Edwards Hewitt. Copy photography: Library of Congress, Washington, D. C. Printing: James Locke, Visual Prose.

195 Photograph anonymous. Copy photography courtesy of Horticulture Library, Washington, D.C. Printing: James Locke, Visual Prose.

196 Photograph anonymous. Copy photography courtesy of Horticulture Library, Smithsonian Institution Libraries, Washington, D.C. Printing: James Locke, Visual Prose.

199 Photograph anonymous. Copy photography courtesy of Horticulture Library, Smithsonian Institution Libraries, Washington, D.C. Printing: James Locke, Visual Prose.

206 "Giving the dial a chance. 'Place the sun-dial in full sun, not in the shade of trees or shelter of a wall, ideal locations for a fountain or bird-bath, but not the spot where an instrument for telling time by the sun can carry on its life work.' In a Minnesota garden designed by Holm and Olson, Landscape Architects." From Ruth Dean, "Fitly Furnishing the Everyday Garden," *Garden Magazine* 39 (June 1924): 274.

Photograph by Harry G. Healy, John Wallace Gillies, or the Juul Studios. Copy photography courtesy of Horticulture Library, Smithsonian Institution Libraries, Washington, D.C. Printing: James Locke, Visual Prose.

207 "Bird-bath as the terminus of a vista. 'Whatever the state of our minds regarding sculpture, we have got as far as granting that a vista must be terminated.' Garden of Mrs. Daniel E. Pomeroy at Englewood, New Jersey; Ruth Dean, Landscape Architect." From Ruth Dean, "Fitly Furnishing the Everyday Garden," *Garden Magazine* 39 (June 1924): 272. Photograph by Nathan R. Graves or Charles Jones. Copy photography courtesy of USDA, National Agricultural Library, Beltsville, Maryland. Printing: James Locke, Visual Prose.

219 Photograph by C. H. Miller, H. E. Angell, or anonymous. Copy photography and printing: Lee B. Ewing.

225 Photograph by Harry G. Healy, John Wallace Gillies, or the Juul Studios. Copy photography courtesy of Horticulture Library, Smithsonian Institution Libraries, Washington, D.C. Printing: James Locke, Visual Prose.

228 Photograph by Harry G. Healy, John Wallace Gillies, or the Juul Studios. Copy photography courtesy of Horticulture Library, Smithsonian Institution Libraries, Washington, D.C. Printing: James Locke, Visual Prose.

232 Photograph by John Sheridan Zelie. Copy photography courtesy of Horticulture Library, Smithsonian Institution Libraries, Washington, D.C. Printing: James Locke, Visual Prose.

235 Photograph by Wurts Brothers. Copy photography courtesy of USDA, National Agricultural Library, Beltsville, Maryland. Printing: James Locke, Visual Prose.

236 Photograph by John Wallace Gillies. Copy photography courtesy of USDA, National Agricultural Library, Beltsville, Maryland. Printing by James Locke, Visual Prose.

237 Photograph by Wurts Brothers. Copy photography courtesy of USDA, National Agricultural Library, Beltsville, Maryland. Printing: James Locke, Visual Prose.

240 Photograph anonymous. Copy photography and printing: James Locke, Visual Prose.

241 Photograph anonymous. Copy photography and printing: James Locke, Visual Prose.

242 Plan by Ruth Dean. Copy photography and printing: James Locke, Visual Prose.

244 Drawing by Beatrice Stevens. Copy photography courtesy of Horticulture Library, Smithsonian Institution Libraries, Washington, D.C. Printing: James Locke, Visual Prose.

246–247 "A wee bit of a house down at the end of a grapevine, woodbine covered pergola." From Ruth R. Blodgett, "A Studio in a Garden," *The House Beautiful* 43 (March 1918): 217. Photograph anonymous. Copy photography courtesy of Horticulture Library,

Smithsonian Institution Libraries, Washington, D.C. Printing: James Locke, Visual Prose.

247 "Looking east." From Hazel Wood Waterman, "On My Friend's Porch," *The House Beautiful* 12 (September 1902): 220. Photograph anonymous. Copy photography: Library of Congress, Washington, D. C. Printing: James Locke, Visual Prose.

250 Photograph anonymous. Copy photography: Library of Congress, Washington, D. C. Printing: James Locke, Visual Prose.

253 Photograph anonymous. Copy photography courtesy of Horticulture Library, Smithsonian Institution Libraries, Washington, D.C. Printing: James Locke, Visual Prose.

254 Photograph anonymous. Copy photography courtesy of Horticulture Library, Smithsonian Institution Libraries, Washington, D. C. Printing: James Locke, Visual Prose.

267 Photograph anonymous.

Copy photography courtesy of Horticulture Library, Smithsonian Institution Libraries, Washington, D.C. Printing: James Locke, Visual Prose.

268 Photograph anonymous. Copy photography courtesy of National Horticulture Library, Smithsonian Institution Libraries, Washington, D.C. Printing: James Locke, Visual Prose.

269 Photograph anonymous. Copy photography courtesy of National Horticulture Library, Smithsonian Institution Libraries, Washington, D.C. Printing: James Locke, Visual Prose.

287 "An Iris Border." From Elizabeth Bootes Clark, "The Iris Garden," *The House Beautiful* 28 (July 1910): 41. Photograph anonymous. Copy photography: Library of Congress, Washington, D.C.

BACK COVER: same as 287.

Index

This index is divided into two parts, the first for names and subjects and the second for plants. In both parts page numbers in italics refer to illustrations. The plant index provides only genus names if the entry cites more than one species or if the text does not designate the species.

I. INDEX OF NAMES AND SUBJECTS

Albee, Helen Rickey, 16–21
Almy, Frederic, 168–171
"American" garden style, xxv, 47, 277n. 13; from native land-scape and plants, xxii, 48, 132, 150
American plants. *See* native plants
arbors and pergolas, *228, 232, 245, 254*; in colonial gardens, 197–198, 219; inexpensive construction of, 230–233; in Italian gardens, 206, 209, 214; placement of, 226–227
Arnold Arboretum, 29, 51, *149, 151*, 152,
Arts and Crafts movement, xxiv, 206, 234; and American gardens, xix–xxiii; authors associated with, 16, 86, 101, 248
Atlantic Monthly, ix, xxiv–xxv; articles from, 161–163, 188–191, 256–258, 261–264, 281–284

Bailey, Liberty Hyde, xxvii, 47
Barron, Leonard, 48, 55n. 8
benches and seats, 34, 176, 181; in colonial gardens, 229; in Italian gardens, 206, 209, 211, 213; placement of, 224–226, *225*
Blodgett, Ruth R., 252–255
Blomfield, Reginald, 174, 176, 206, 210
Bok, Edward, xxvi, 44
Browne, Matilda, xvii
Burlingame, Edward Livermore, xxv
Burroughs, John, xxiv, xxix, xxxv n. 36, 285

Cable, George Washington, xxv
Cahoon, E. P., 60–63
Calvene, E. O., 134–138
Chaffee, Grace E., 278–280
Cheney, Barbara, 256–258
Clark, Mrs. Jay, Jr., 24–28, 29
Clinton, A., 192–193
Coffin, Marian Cruger, 38
colonial gardens: arbors and pergolas in, 197, 219; benches and seats in, 229; charm, dignity, and simplicity of, 180, 181, 194, 197, 201; design of, 197–198, 218–220; and formal or Italian gardens, 197, 209, 215; interrelation of houses with, 217, 218; outdoor living in, 194, 195; paths and walks in, 197, 215, 218; plants in,

197–201. *See also* "old-fashioned" gardens
colonial revival, xxi, 194; gardens, 172, 202–205
cottage gardens, xxii, 59n. 11, 180, 181
Country Life in America, xvii, xxii, xxvii–xxviii, 4, 22, 47; articles from, 44–46, 148–153, 194–201, 209–216, 243–245
Country Life movement, xxii, xxvii–xxviii
Craftsman, xxiii, xxix; articles from, 22–23, 32–35, 74–79, 119–120, 192–193, 271–274, 285–287
Cunningham, Mary P., 55n. 6, 148–155

Dean, Ruth, 223–229, 239–242
Depression, the Great, xii, 275–277
Doubleday, Frank Nelson, xxxvi n. 61, 68, 208
Doubleday, Nellie, xxii, xxvii, xxviii, 68, 206, 208–216
Doubleday, Page and Company, xxvii–xxviii, 68, 208
Downing, Andrew Jackson, xv
Duffy, Sherman R., 106–110
Duncan, Frances, xxxii n. 3, 44–46
Dyer, Walter A., xxix, 22–23, 285–287

Eaton, Walter Prichard, 4–11, 16, 139–147

ecology and plant communities, 132, 135, 154–160
Emerson, Ralph Waldo, xxxv n. 36, 285
English gardens: and American gardens, xxii, 132, 148, 174, 210, 217

formal gardens, xix, 64, 65, 174, 176; and small properties, 206, 215–216; promotion of, 208–216; history of, 209–212; interrelation of houses with, 206, 208, 211, 217; disapproval of, 142, 144, 146, 206, 212–213; paths and walks in, 176. *See also* Italian gardens
furniture, garden, 223–229. *See also* arbors and pergolas; benches and seats

Garden, xxviii
Garden Magazine, xxviii–xxix, 47–48; articles from, 48–55, 68–73, 106–110, 174–179, 217–222, 223–229, 239–242
Gardener's Chronicle of America, xxvi; article from, 80–83
Gardener's Magazine, xv
Gordon, Elizabeth, xxxix
"grandmother's gardens." *See* "old-fashioned" gardens
Greenaway, Kate, xxxiii n. 26, xxxiv n. 34, 56, 59n. 11

Harrier, Jessie Vaughn, 64–67
Harvey, Henry Blodgett, xxix
Hay, Arthur, 119–120
hedges, 51, 56–59; in colonial gardens, 197, 198
Hersey, Jean, 116–118
Hewitt, Mattie Edwards, 92
Horticulturist, xv–xvi
House and Garden, xix, xxix, xxx–xxxi; articles from, 4–11, 12–15, 38–43, 60–63, 92–97, 111–115, 134–138, 139–147, 234–238, 275–277
House Beautiful, xix, xxix–xxx; articles from, 24–28, 56–59, 64–67, 86–91, 98–100, 101–105, 116–118, 130–131, 154–160, 180–183, 192–193, 202–205, 230–233, 248–251, 252–255, 265–270, 278–280

Howells, William Dean, xxiv
Howland, William, 68

Independent, xxv–xxvi; article from, 184–186
indigenous plants. *See* native plants
Italian gardens, 212–215, 221, 225–228; arbors and pergolas in, 206, 209, 214; relation of architecture to, 208, 214; benches and seats in, 206, 209, 211, 213; disapproval or misunderstanding of, xxii, 142, 144, 208, 212–213; outdoor living in, 214; paths and walks in, 209, 214, 215, 221. *See also* formal gardens

Japanese gardens, 139, 141–142, 163
Jekyll, Gertrude: authors influenced by, xx, 84, 86, 110; and Mrs. Francis King, 12, 15n. 7
Jensen, Jens, 48, 147n. 4, 223

Keays, Ethelyn E., 80–83
King, Caroline Blanche, 111–115
King, Mrs. Francis, 12–15, 106
Kirkland, Winifred Margaretta, 281–284
Klapp, Eugene, xxix–xxx, 56–59

Ladies' Home Journal, xvii, xxvi–xxvii, xxix, 44; article from, 16–21
Lane, Gertrude, xxvii
lawns, 29, 31, 162, 164, 166
Lawrence, Elizabeth, 120n. 13
Lemmon, Robert S., 234–238
Leonard, Pauline G. Wiggin, 261–264
Lose, Rebecca J., 271–274
Loudon, John Claudius, xv

McClure's Magazine, xxiv
McFarland, J. Horace, 68–73, 80
McKenny, Margaret, 202–205
Manning, Warren, xxxii n. 3, 68, 217
Miller, Wilhelm, xxviii–xxix, 47–55, 56
Mitchell, Henry, 80
Morgan, Julia, 64, 65

Morris, Elisabeth Woodbridge, 188–191
Morris, William, xix, xx

nationalism, cultural, xxi, 4, 47, 139, 277n. 13
native plants, xxiii; and the Arts and Crafts movement, xix, xxi, xxix; for "American" gardens, 55n. 6, 148–153, 277n. 13; popularity of, 148, 150; for "wild" gardens, 132, 134–138
natural gardens. *See* wild gardens
Nichols, Rose Standish, 222n. 14

"old-fashioned" flowers, xx, 31, 66, 172; listings of, 175, 178, 182–183, 184–186, 273.
"old-fashioned" gardens, xx–xxi, xxii–xxiii, 29, 148, 172, *177*, *195,196, 199, 264*; descriptions of, 174–179, 184–187, 192–193, 194–201; atmosphere of, 172, 177; British inspiration of, 174, 176; charm and simplicity of, 179, 180, 184; to escape modern life, 188–191; to be lived in, 172, 174, 176–177, 184, 186, 194. *See also* colonial gardens
Olmsted, Frederick Law, 161, 162
Ortloff, Henry Stuart, 194–201
Outlook, xxv–xxvi; article from, 168–171

paths and walks: plants for, 190, 198, 219, 234–238
Peck, Anna, xvii
pergolas. *See* arbors and pergolas
Perrett, Antoinette, 86, 101–105
photography and gardens: amateurs gifted in, xi, xxxii n. 2; in magazines, xvi–xvii, 68, 92, 101, 116
Platt, Charles, 222n. 14, 239
pools, *195*, 227, 241, 242–245; *245*, plants for, 239–242
porches, 230–231, 233, *247*, 248–251, *250*
Powell, Edward Payson, 184–187

Rehmann, Elsa, 86–91, 101, 148–153, 180–183, 188

II. INDEX OF PLANTS

spike rush (*Eleocharis*), 241
Spiraea, 60, 107, 138, 182
Spiraea x vanhouttei, 13, 55, 203
spotted wintergreen (*Chimaphila
   maculata*), 158
spruce (*Picea*), 13, 151,
squill (*Scilla*), 91, 99, 100, 104; in
   "old-fashioned" gardens, 204;
   in "wild" gardens, 167
Stachys byzantina (lamb's ear),
   26
Stachys officinalis (betony), 96
star-of-Bethlehem (*Ornithogalum
   umbellatum*), 178
Sternbergia (autumn daffodils), 28
stock (*Matthiola*), 113–114, 182,
   201
Stokesia, 109
sumac (*Rhus*), 62, 63, 153, 198,
summer sweet (*Clethra alnifolia*),
   152, 198
sunflowers (*Helianthus*): for autumn bloom, 26, 108; in garden design, 97, 110; in
   "old-fashioned" gardens, 185
swamp milkweed (*Asclepias incarnata*), 169
sweet alyssum (*Lobularia maritima*), 113
sweetpeas (*Lathyrus odoratus*),
   115, 184
sweet pepper (*Clethra alnifolia*),
   152, 198
sweet rockets (*Hesperis
   matronalis*), 96, 178, 200
sweet williams (*Dianthus
   barbatus*), 14, 19, 110, 182

sycamore (*Platanus x acerfolia*),
   43, 159
Syringa. See lilacs (*Syringa*)

Tagetes (marigolds), 87, 90, 118,
   175, 201
tamarisk (*Tamarix*), 41
Taxus (yew), 13, 67, 151, 158,
   213
Thalictrum (meadow rue), 88,
   138, 183
thornapple (*Crataegus*), 41, 60,
   183, 204
Thuja. See arborvitae (*Thuja*)
thyme (*Thymus*), 28, 198, 204
Trillium, 137, 169
Trollius (globe flowers), 79
Tropaeolum (nasturtiums),
   130–131, 185, 201
tuberoses (*Tuberosa*), 88, 114
tulips (*Tulipa*), 118, 130; in garden
   design, 88, 89, 91, 101–105,
   104; in "old-fashioned" gardens,
   185, 201; wild, 169
tulip poplar (*Liriodendron
   tulipfera*), 43
tunic flowers (*Petrorhagia saxifraga*), 238
Typha latifolia (cattails), 240

Ulmus americana (elm), 43, 159

Vaccinium corymbosum (high-bush
   blueberry), 170
Valeriana, 178, 182, 200
Verbena tenuisecta (moss verbena),
   88

Vernonia (ironweed), 239
Veronica (speedwell), 18; in garden design, 88, 96, 99, 100; in
   "old-fashioned" gardens, 200;
   in paths, 238; wild, 138
Viburnum, 52, 62, 155, 182, 198
Viola pedunculatum; V. tricolor
   (johnny-jump-ups), 185, 200
Viola x wittrockiana (pansies),
   115, 130, 185
violets (*Viola*): in garden design,
   88, 99; for night gardens, 115;
   as "old-fashioned" flower, 183;
   wild, 100, 108, 135, 137, 169
Virginia creeper (*Parthenocissus
   quinquefolia*), 27, 63, 138

wallflowers (*Erysimum cheiri*),
   200
waterlilies (*Nymphaea*), 169, 240,
   241, 155, 156
white ash (*Fraxinus americana*),
   63
wild indigo (*Baptisia tinctoria*), 88
willow (*Salix*), 43, 46
wintergreen (*Pyrola*), 158
woodbine (*Parthenocissus quinquefolia*) 27, 63, 138

yarrows (*Achillea*), 96, 110, 138,
   166
yellow star grass (*Xyris*), 108
yew (*Taxus*), 13, 67, 151, 158,
   213
Yucca, 87, 94, 95, 114, 115

Zinnia, 87, 88, 90, 95